Beyond Semantics and Pragmatics

Beyond Semantics and Pragmatics

EDITED BY
Gerhard Preyer

OXFORD
UNIVERSITY PRESS

OXFORD
UNIVERSITY PRESS

Great Clarendon Street, Oxford, OX2 6DP,
United Kingdom

Oxford University Press is a department of the University of Oxford.
It furthers the University's objective of excellence in research, scholarship,
and education by publishing worldwide. Oxford is a registered trade mark of
Oxford University Press in the UK and in certain other countries

© the several contributors 2018

The moral rights of the authors have been asserted

First Edition published in 2018

Impression: 1

Published in the United States of America by Oxford University Press
198 Madison Avenue, New York, NY 10016, United States of America

British Library Cataloguing in Publication Data
Data available

Library of Congress Control Number: 2018933074

ISBN 978-0-19-879149-2

Printed and bound by
CPI Group (UK) Ltd, Croydon, CR0 4YY

Contents

Part IV. New Frontiers in Semantics

List of Contributors

MADELEINE ARSENEAULT, Philosophy, Suny—The State University of New York at New Paltz, New York

KENT BACH, Philosophy, San Francisco State University

CLAUDIA BIANCHI, Philosophy, Università Vita-Salute San Raffaele, Milano

JONATHAN COHEN, Philosophy, University of California San Diego

WAYNE A. DAVIS, Philosophy, Georgetown University

ROBERTO G. DE ALMEIDA, Psychology, Concordia University, Montreal

MICHAEL GLANZBERG, Philosophy, Northwestern University, Illinois

MITCHELL GREEN, Philosophy, University of Connecticut

ANDREW KEHLER, Linguistics, University of California, San Diego

JESSICA KEISER, Philosophy, Yale University

ERNIE LEPORE, Philosophy and Cognitive Science, Rutgers University, New Jersey

GERHARD PREYER, Sociology, Goethe-Universität, Frankfurt am Main

ADAM SENNET, Philosophy, University of California, Davis

MANDY SIMONS, Linguistics and Philosophy, Carnegie Mellon University

ROBERT J. STAINTON, Philosophy, Western University, Ontario

WILLIAM B. STARR, Philosophy, Cornell Philosophy, New York

UNA STOJNIĆ, Philosophy, Columbia University, New York

MATTHEW STONE, Computer Science, Rutgers University, New Jersey

CHRISTOPHER VIGER, Philosophy, Western University, Ontario

Introduction
Linguistic Structure and Meaning

Gerhard Preyer

The study of meaning in language embraces a diverse range of problems and methods. Philosophers think through the relationship between language and the world; linguists document speakers' knowledge of meaning; psychologists investigate the mechanisms of understanding and production. Up through the early 2000s, these investigations were generally compartmentalized: indeed, researchers often regarded both the subject matter and the methods of other disciplines with skepticism. Since then, however, there has been a sea change in the field, enabling researchers increasingly to synthesize the perspectives of philosophy, linguistics, and psychology and to energize all the fields with rich new intellectual perspectives that facilitate meaningful interchange. One illustration of the trend is the publication of Lepore and Stone's *Imagination and Convention*, an integrative interdisciplinary survey—though perhaps an opinionated and idiosyncratic one—of research on meaning, inference, and communication. The time is right for a broader exploration and reflection on the status and problems of semantics as an interdisciplinary enterprise, in light of a decade of challenging and successful research in this area. This book aims to reconcile different methodological perspectives while refocusing semanticists on the new problems where integrative work will find the broadest and most receptive audience.

The following themes figure prominently in the volume:

- Making sense of the fundamental concepts of meaning. We have in mind such notions as grammar, context, reference and speech acts, which require the precision of philosophical analysis but must accommodate linguistic data and comport with psychological models of language acquisition and processing.
- Delimiting the scope of semantics. New philosophical arguments, emerging cross-linguistic fieldwork, and new probabilistic models of language processing challenge researchers to rethink how much of the interpretation of language is due to linguistic knowledge and how much is due to indirection, strategizing, and mind reading.

- Characterizing interpretive inference. Our contributors put a special emphasis on "local coherence", a kind of pragmatic inference that has been insufficiently investigated in the science of meaning but in fact offers telling probes of differing views in philosophy, linguistics, and psychology—and so far fits no theory of interpretation.

One of the traditions represented here engages with formal semantics; and, while this research once focused exclusively on truth-conditional meanings delivered by sentence-level grammar (e.g., Montague 1974), recent work is much broader in its scope, including a variety of formal theories of presupposition (e.g., van der Sandt 1992; Beaver 2001), expressive meaning (e.g., Potts 2005), projective and not-at-issue meaning (e.g., Tonhauser et al. 2013), and the interpretive links that connect multi-sentence discourse (e.g., Asher and Lascarides 2001, 2003). Several essays in this volume include discussion of whether these developments require philosophers of language to come up with new conceptual tools in order to clarify the relationship between grammar, meaning, interpretation, and communication; or whether a truth and reference tradition still dominates. And, indeed, a major thread of discovery in some of the discussions that follow is whether H. P. Grice's notion of 'what is said' can capture all of what language encodes, or all of how grammar shapes interpretation.

Another tradition some of the essays engage with is psychological in nature, one that aims to explain how language users can make sense of utterances and their speakers. One relatively recent common suggestion concerns whether interpretations can be constructed creatively (Atlas 1989, 2005), for example, by taking words to signal new 'ad hoc' concepts (Carston 2002), by understanding phrases to be implicitly 'enriched' to more specific interpretations (Recanati 2004), and by loosening and transferring literal interpretations in light of inferences that matter in context (Sperber and Wilson 1986, 2008). Not all researchers agree, as will become clear in the essays that follow. For example, some researchers attribute interpretive effects to our empirical understanding of others' choices (e.g., Pinker, Nowak, and Lee 2008), or to open-ended processes of imaginative engagement (e.g., Camp 2008). These diverse models are discussed in what follows, as requiring us to refine various philosophers' received constructs for characterizing pragmatic inference, notably, of course, Grice's entrenched notion of a 'conversational implicature'. Both sides of the debate over the utility or efficacy of Grice's fundamental pragmatic notion of a conversational implicature are represented and both are fiercely defended in this volume.

Any attempt at bringing together these various perspectives of current research in semantics and pragmatics, not surprisingly, of course, elicits challenges. These essays offer an array of different takes on this new intellectual landscape. Collectively, however, they provide the reader with a broad overview of the philosophical positions currently available, as well highlighting some of the research directions these different views afford. In the process, various disputes about which, if any, lessons should be learned about the linguistic rules that guide interpretation are well represented. For example, several of the essays take up, and either challenge or defend the contention that context-sensitivity is much more closely governed by linguistic rules than has been generally appreciated. How much more diverse these rules and principles need to be than what already figures in traditional conceptions of semantics is hotly debated. And, perhaps, more importantly, included are several discussions about whether the rules that are alleged to be required for interpretation should be sensitive to principles of *discourse coherence* or not; in particular, whether the rules that link context-sensitive expressions to their semantic values must be stated in terms of the overall organization of coherent discourse.

Broad characterizations of linguistic structure and meaning are crucial for philosophers to be able to correctly diagnose the interplay between semantics and pragmatics. A particularly fruitful, but oddly neglected, case is intonation, which linguists model as a level of grammar that helps to signal the *information structure* of sentences in context, via the abstract meanings it encodes. Such structures can be implemented in a variety of ways both within and across languages; some of these ways are illustrated in essays below, particularly in semantic models of discourse coherence and context-dependent meaning.

Another topic amply discussed in these essays is whether there are lessons to be learned about whatever interpretive mechanisms are involved in appreciating the *points* that speakers have, and are trying to get across, in using utterances. For some contributors, whatever insights we gain from an utterance often come from thinking about it in specific, creative ways. As will become clear, there is considerable disagreement over whether a correct account of metaphor (as well as other instances of figurative (non-literal) speech) must resort to imaginative engagement in order to explain its contribution to discourse. Several of the contributors see metaphor as a distinctive way of thinking of one thing as another—one whose effects can differ from person to person and from occasion to occasion, and cannot be fully characterized just in terms of propositional content. This broadly Davidsonian view (elaborated in Lepore and Stone (2010)), is the impetus for a broadly critical (by some) take on conversational implicatures (and on pragmatics, in general). Interpreting a metaphorical utterance, on this view, requires the hearer to engage in this process of metaphorical thinking, and to appreciate the insights this thinking engenders. In some cases, on this account, listeners can perhaps gain a deeper understanding into a speaker's intentions in using a metaphor, as a side effect of their own metaphorical thinking. This, of course, flips the direction of explanation taken by many of the contributors, following pragmatic accounts of metaphor, such as Searle's (1979) Gricean account, or Sperber and Wilson's (2008), in terms of relevance theory, which attempt to show how general reasoning about a speaker might prompt a listener to pursue associated or enriched interpretations which theorists might characterize retrospectively as metaphorical.

One last comment on the limits of knowledge of language: a major dispute in these essays is over how much conventional information does knowledge of language demand: some authors push a healthy attribution of knowledge of conventional information that includes not only the truth conditional content that is at issue in the use of a sentence, but also content that is encoded yet *not* at issue, for example, because it is marked as a presupposed background, or because it is attached to a form as a matter of conventional implicature. Others defend a much narrower conventional reach. A related dispute concerns whether the insights the imagination prompts have the status of content—whether this be conventionally or pragmatically determined. Some contributors explore the idea that such insights are an integral part of speakers' ear for the tonality of language—following up the influential suggestion of Frege that words can carry tone that does not contribute to the thoughts of that sentence; others insist for meaning account of their contributions.

In short, this collection offers an extended discussion of the cognitive architecture of collaborative language use. This introduction has emphasized the polemical side of this collection and its implications. But it also includes a survey of important theories, data, and arguments that are relevant to ultimate mapping of the relationships between semantics and pragmatics. Even though the contributors may not agree on all the particulars, it is still possible to come away from this collection with a feeling for how broad the phenomena are that bear on the interface of semantics and pragmatics, a deeper appreciation for the kinds of facts that seem to distinguish most strongly among the theoretical alternatives, and a road map to the open problems where future work is likely to bring challenges to which all current theories must respond.

References

Asher, Nicholas, and Alex Lascarides. 2001. Indirect Speech Acts. *Synthese*, 128(1–2): 183–228.

Asher, Nicholas, and Alex Lascarides. 2003. *Logics of Conversation*. Cambridge: Cambridge University Press.

Atlas, Jay D. 1989. *Philosophy Without Ambiguity*. Oxford: Clarendon Press.

Atlas, Jay D. 2005. *Logic, Meaning, and Conversation: Semantical Underdeterminacy, Implicature, and Their Interface*. Oxford: Oxford University Press.

Beaver, David. 2001. *Presupposition and Assertion in Dynamic Semantics*. Stanford, CA: CSLI Publications.

Camp, Elisabeth. 2008. Showing, Telling and Seeing: Metaphor and "Poetic" Language. In Elisabeth Camp (ed.), *The Baltic International Yearbook of Cognition, Logic and Communication*, III. A Figure of Speech, pp. 1–24. Riga: University of Latvia.

Carston, Robyn. 2002. *Thoughts and Utterances: The Pragmatics of Explicit Communication*. Oxford: Blackwell.

Lepore, Ernie, and Matthew Stone. 2010. Against Metaphorical Meaning. *Topoi*, 29(2): 165–80.

Montague, Richard. 1974. *Formal Philosophy. Selected Papers of Richard Montague*, Thomason, Richmond H. (ed.). New Haven, CT: Yale University Press.

Pinker, Steven, Martin A. Nowak, and James J. Lee. 2008. The Logic of Indirect Speech. *Proceedings of the National Academy of Sciences of the United States of America*, 105(3): 833–8.

Potts, Christopher. 2005. *The Logic of Conventional Implicatures*. Oxford Studies in Theoretical Linguistics. Oxford: Oxford University Press.

Recanati, François. 2004. *Literal Meaning*. Cambridge: Cambridge University Press.

Searle, John R. 1979. Metaphor. In Andrew Ortony (ed.), *Metaphor and Thought*, pp. 265–77. Cambridge: Cambridge University Press.

Sperber, Dan, and Deirdre Wilson. 1986. *Relevance: Communication and Cognition*. Cambridge, MA: Harvard University Press.

Sperber, Dan, and Deirdre Wilson. 2008. A Deflationary Account of Metaphor. In Ray W. Gibbs (ed.), *The Cambridge Handbook of Metaphor and Thought*, pp. 84–105. Cambridge: Cambridge University Press.

Tonhauser, Judit, et al. 2013. Toward a Taxonomy of Projective Content. *Language*, 89(1, March): 66–109.

van der Sandt, Rob A. 1992. Presupposition Projection as Anaphora Resolution. *Journal of Semantics*, 9(4): 333–77.

PART I

Explaining Pragmatic Phenomena

1

Two Questions about Interpretive Effects

Robert J. Stainton and Christopher Viger

1. Introduction

Our discussion of *Imagination and Convention* by Ernie Lepore and Matthew Stone (2015) will center around two questions that all semanticists and pragmaticians seemingly face:

Qe: What interpretive effects can linguistic utterances have?

Qc: What causes give rise to interpretive effects?

The first question pertains to *what gets done content-wise* when we speak: for example, we draw attention to objects, ask questions, tell jokes, and encourage reflection. The second pertains to *how all of this gets done*: for example, phonology, lexical semantics and syntax all play a role in fixing in-context content; so, frequently, do the attitudes/ intentions of interlocutors. There are two facets to each question. There's the general question of what overarching kinds of effects and causes there are, that is, what taxonomic *categories* of meaning-involving effects and causes are appropriate. Then there is the specific question of which particular linguistic phenomena fall where, given such a taxonomy.

We need to stress that taking Qe and Qc as the expository core is not something Lepore and Stone do. Indeed, so phrased, these questions don't appear anywhere in their book. But we think this restructuring affords an illuminating take on *Imagination and Convention*, and on Lepore and Stone's stances therein. The essay will proceed as follows. We will spend significant time explaining our twin questions, and what we reconstruct as Lepore and Stone's views on them. We dedicate so much space to exposition because theirs is a complex and philosophically deep work: despite their claim that "there is no hiding our agenda in this book" (p. v), and despite the helpful summaries and "look-aheads" included throughout, we repeatedly found ourselves lost on our initial readings. In particular, the work's innovative use of terminology (especially what they mean by 'contribution', 'convention', 'disambiguation', 'imagination', 'interpretive effect', 'pragmatics', and 'semantics') can cause confusion. The section's length notwithstanding, we necessarily abstract away from many subtle and ingenious details.

After the expository discussion, we evaluate what we take to be the book's answers to Qe and Qc, mostly focusing (as is usual in philosophical reviews) on points of disagreement. We argue that, even taking onboard their taxonomic categories, they are mistaken about where certain specific linguistic phenomena fit. More importantly, we go on to take issue with the overarching kinds of interpretive effects, and causes of them, which they posit. We end by recalling another long-standing take on the semantics–pragmatics boundary, namely Relevance Theory's—suggesting that one can accommodate many of the important empirical insights of *Imagination and Convention* while resisting its very radical theoretical outlook.

Part One: Explaining Lepore and Stone's View

2. Four Key Notions from David Lewis and Donald Davidson

To explain Qe and Qc, and what we reconstruct as Lepore and Stone's answers to them, we need some key notions, which they adapt from David Lewis and Donald Davidson, specifically 'contribution', 'convention', and 'imagination'. We'll provide a brief sketch here, fleshing out details as our essay progresses.

Contributions are changes to the "conversational scoreboard", a notion Lewis (1979) introduced, and which can be thought of as the total "state of play" of a conversation. Lepore and Stone think of such changes as involving inquiry-type meaning—content pertaining to public coordination on a precise answer. As a conversation progresses, the objective state of play changes, and the scoreboard is updated to reflect these new contributions.[1] Sub-varieties of contributions include: the truth-conditions of assertions, as in all standard accounts of semantics; other informational updates to the common ground, for example, via the accommodation of presuppositions, conventional implicatures or indirect speech acts; the speech act kind to which the utterance belongs (e.g., whether a request, question, command, or statement); and information structure.

Non-contributions (our term, not theirs) are interpretive effects of other sorts: we characterize them negatively as those interpretive effects that are not contributions. Lepore and Stone hold that this class is far from empty, because the interpretive effect of an utterance need not always be a public contribution. To characterize the notion positively, consider a very familiar example: metaphor. Drawing on Davidson's (1978) account, Lepore and Stone urge that a metaphor does not contribute a non-literal

---

[1] To clarify a point that can easily be missed, and can lead to confusion when reading their text: As we understand it, Lepore and Stone take the "scoreboard"/"conversational record" to be a state of the world. It is not a representation thereof—whether by the conversational participants or by some imagined third party. That is, unlike a baseball scoreboard, the conversational record does not attempt to *display* the score; it *is* the score. Thus our phrase 'state of play' may capture the idea better than Lewis' own terminology does.

meaning, in the sense of a potential answer to a question. Sentences used metaphorically merely express their literal meaning—though they have the additional effect of nudging the hearer (in a direction influenced by the utterance, though not determined by it). Crucially, Lepore and Stone generalize Davidson's account, arguing that it is not just metaphors that have this kind of invitation-to-explore interpretive effect. Other sub-varieties of non-contributions, according to them, include hints and non-serious speech (such as humor, irony, and sarcasm). Very controversially, Lepore and Stone deny that any of the above involve an indirect propositional meaning of the sort associated with Gricean conversational implicatures (197).

Following Lewis (1969), Lepore and Stone construe a *convention* as a regularity that a population adopts as a solution to a coordination problem, such that a genuine alternative regularity exists. For example, we can drive on the left side of the road or the right. It does not matter which, as long as (nearly) everyone does the same thing. To overcome familiar empirical objections to Lewis (1969) from generative grammarians, Lepore and Stone extend his notion to include innate universals (where there likely isn't a nomologically possible alternative), and to allow for unconscious linguistic conventions.

Finally, *imagination* encompasses a set of open-ended cognitive processes with no determinate target. While these may incline the hearer to organize her thinking in a particular way, the point of imagination-oriented utterances is only to set the hearer on that path, with no specific destination intended.

We find chess-playing to be a helpful analogy for explicating these four key notions. Linguistic contributions are analogous to moves in a chess game properly so-called, such as taking the opponent's queen or moving a pawn forward one space. By contrast, linguistic non-contributions are analogous to gamesmanship-type non-moves, such as a player intentionally letting time run off her own clock to create a tense atmosphere, which might force an opponent into an error. Linguistic conventions are analogous to the official rules for playing chess, as codified by FIDE (i.e., la Fédération Internationale des Echecs); imagination is analogous to psychological processes in an opponent that a chess player might encourage.[2]

3. Lepore and Stone's Answers to Qe and Qc

With these ideas in place, we can now present the taxonomic categories of meaning-involving effects and causes with which Lepore and Stone answer our twin questions. There are two overarching kinds of interpretive effects of a linguistic utterance: those that impact upon the contributions to the conversational scoreboard (e.g., an ordinary assertion of a proposition) and those which do not (e.g., a metaphor). As for kinds of

---

[2] An important point about nomenclature which will prove essential in section 6(A) below: Lepore and Stone equate convention with *grammar*, and imagination with *inference*. Hence their subtitle *Distinguishing Grammar and Inference in Language.*

causes, there are linguistic conventions on the one hand and imagination on the other. To summarize things in terms of a chart of our own devising:

INTERPRETIVE EFFECTS	Caused by Convention	Caused by Imagination
Contributions (Impact the Scoreboard)		
Non-Contributions (Don't Impact the Scoreboard)		

Chart 1.1

As Chart 1.1 makes clear, four options arise from possible pairings of the two effects with each of the two causes: it is logically possible to have some contributions that are caused by convention while others could be caused by imagination, and similarly for non-contributions. Lepore and Stone do not think that all of these possibilities obtain, however. They hold that contributions are caused (almost) entirely by convention (top left quadrant of Chart 1.1), while non-contributions are caused by imagination (bottom right):

The interpretive effects of utterances arise through the contributions speakers signal with utterances – through convention – and through the further explorations speakers invite – through imagination.   (193)

It's important to stress that we read this most fundamental of their claims—we'll call it their 'bold conjecture'—as an empirical hypothesis. We understand them to be saying: as a matter of fact, the intensionally distinct notions of 'due to convention' and 'contribution' turn out to (pretty much) share the same extension; as do the intensionally distinct notions of 'due to imagination' and 'non-contribution'. For reasons that will emerge below, we do not read the above as an implicit definition of '(non-)contribution' in terms of 'imagination'/'convention'.

To flesh out this bold conjecture regarding Qe and Qc, we need to say more about contributions, conventions, and imagination. Beginning with the first, an essential background idea is the Lewisian one that the aim of conversation is to coordinate on beliefs and actions; and that moves relevant to doing so become part of the score. Numerous elements of Lewis' scoreboard will be very familiar: the salient domain of discourse, what is mutually believed, what question is being addressed, etc. What requires more comment is an important addition that Lepore and Stone make to that familiar list, namely, information structure.

Broadly speaking, information structure pertains to how the contributions connect, and is roughly what is encoded in English by intonation. More specifically, "The grammar of information structure foregrounds what's important about each new utterance, contrasts it with other relevant possibilities, and marks its place in the dynamics of the interaction" (128). Information structure has several dimensions. One dimension is the contrastive one, which differentiates an utterance from its possible alternatives—in English, by placing prosodic accents for emphasis (132). Information structure also has a relational dimension: linking some parts of an utterance to what has gone before, and marking other parts as moving the conversation forward. Specifically, what Lepore and Stone have in mind here is the difference between the theme of an utterance (roughly, which question the utterance is addressing) and the rheme (roughly, which answer is being given). The final dimension of information structure is interaction: whose turn it is to speak, whether the speaker needs acknowledgment before continuing, whether the contribution is complete, etc.

Turning to conventions and imagination, as Lepore and Stone repeatedly stress, there exist quite diverse sub-varieties of each. Neither is monolithic: "The rules of language are much more diverse than has been generally acknowledged, but the mechanisms through which we engage with utterance interpretation are also more varied than is often supposed" (197). Within the kind "linguistic convention", for instance, there are those that apply at the sentence level, but there are also discourse-level conventions such as those mentioned immediately above. As one might say, traditional syntactic trees and compositional semantic rules do not exhaust linguistic conventions. Regarding sub-varieties of imagination, according to Lepore and Stone interpreting metaphor, non-serious speech and hints all require different cognitive mechanisms within the overarching kind "imagination", which lead to distinctive creative interpretive engagement. *Very* briefly, metaphor is a kind of perspective taking that attunes us to certain distinctions in the world (170–1); sarcasm is an invitation to explore the contrast between the apparent contributions of an utterance and how things actually are; irony invites engagement with an imagined speaker; humor invites a hearer to imagine surprising and contrasting perspectives (173); and finally, hinting shifts the initiative of a conversation, leaving it to the audience to carry on in a particular direction (189).

The foregoing reconstruction of Lepore and Stone's answers to Qe and Qc needs to be tweaked, because our strict dichotomy between convention and imagination is actually an idealization. Lepore and Stone allow the two to work in conjunction. In particular, ambiguities are often resolved by convention plus a soupçon of imagination. We call this "third kind of cause", which straddles our top quadrants, 'convention$^+$'. Utterances can be ambiguous, in Lepore and Stone's sense, in at least two ways: "about what form a speaker has used and what she has in mind" (131). More specifically, sources of ambiguity include how phrases combine, the co-indexing of bound variables, reference for context-sensitive terms, and linking of words to a sense with an appropriate extension (216). Crucially, convention$^+$ does not "propose" any new content for the scoreboard, that is, it does not introduce new meanings. It is a much thinner category than traditionally imagined: "…understanding involves choosing the reading that makes the most sense from the candidates delivered by the grammar. Understanding does not involve enriching those readings to transform them from ones that do not make sense to ones that do" (119).

With this threefold contrast in hand, we can more accurately summarize their bold conjecture about which causes give rise to which interpretive effects:

Linguistic Conventions: Provide potential contributions;
Imagination: Provides non-contributions;
Convention⁺, convention with a soupçon of imagination: Disambiguates, selecting among the potential contributions.

And, recalling the specific question of which particular linguistic phenomena fall where in the taxonomy, their answer is captured by a filled-in version of our chart:

INTERPRETIVE EFFECTS	Caused by Convention	Caused by Imagination

Contributions	*Truth-Conditional Contributions*:
	- truth conditions of assertions
	- other informational updates to the common ground (i.e., public coordination on answers)
	  - presupposition
	  - conventional implicatures
	  - indirect speech acts
	
	Non-TC Contributions:
	- other ways of adding to the public coordination-type content, such as marking which linguistic action is taking place
	- various ways of structuring contributions, including how parts of the discourse connect
	
	Part of Disambiguation:
	- certain aspects of disambiguation among potential contributions, whether done by sentence-level grammar or discourse-level grammar
		- The other, intention recognition, aspects of disambiguation

Non-Contributions		- Open-ended, non-propositional prompts involved in directing the other person's thought; i) metaphor and other tropes; ii) non-serious speech such as humor, irony, and sarcasm; iii) hints

Chart 1.2

4. Qe, Qc and the Semantics–Pragmatics Boundary: Qs/p

Lepore and Stone's answers to our twin questions, along with their innovative understanding of terms like 'contribution', 'convention', and 'imagination', reshape the landscape of the semantics–pragmatics debate. It will thus be helpful, as a final step in exposition, to introduce a third question:

Qs/p: Which causes/effects are semantic and which are pragmatic?

To appreciate how radical Lepore and Stone's reconception of the semantics–pragmatics boundary is, recall that, since Grice (1975), it has often been supposed that semantic effects equate to "what is said", while pragmatic effects equate to what is implicated. As for causes, the old-fashioned Gricean is said to recognize exactly two of those as well: the conventional meaning of the expression used, which mostly fixes both "what is said" and conventional implicatures; and general-purpose reasoning about rational cooperation, whose main role is to fix conversational implicatures. ('Mostly' and 'main' are required because of disambiguation and assignment of reference to context-sensitive items.)

Lepore and Stone roundly reject this Grice-inspired take on things. First, it is too monolithic. There are, for them, a rich variety of conventions, which yield an equally rich variety of contribution-type interpretive effects, as we saw above. Similarly, there are a variety of cognitive mechanisms beyond detecting and repairing violations to rational cooperation, and they underwrite a sundry range of non-contributions. Second, and related, the whole category of conversational implicature is ill-conceived:

Put most starkly: we have no use for a category of conversational implicatures, as traditionally and currently understood.   (6)

Given the broader space of meaning and interpretation, we are quite skeptical that any useful work can be done specifically by the category of conversational implicature; and so, to the extent that the traditional division between semantics and pragmatics relies on the category of [conversational implicature], we are deeply skeptical about this division.   (150)

Their reason should be clear by now: such an alleged effect, a genuine conversational implicature as understood by traditional Griceans, would be a *contribution* to the scoreboard caused by *imagination* (i.e., belonging in the top-right quadrant of our chart). The bulk of the text argues that this is an empty category—save for disambiguation.

In place of the Grice-inspired take on the boundary, Lepore and Stone propose a three-way classification, which maps onto their answers as to which causes produce which interpretive effects. There are potential contributions to the scoreboard, afforded entirely by convention. That is semantics. There is a role for convention+ in selecting among the potential contributions. This is pragmatics. Non-contributions, finally, are caused by imagination. That is, in terms of Chart 1.1, Lepore and Stone replace the Gricean semantics–pragmatics boundary with a tripartite division: semantics sits at the top left; pragmatics straddles the top two quadrants; and the bottom right quadrant is "neither". (The bottom left quadrant remains empty: for Lepore and Stone, any interpretive effect caused by convention makes a contribution.)

In rejecting Grice, Lepore and Stone consider a number of utterance types traditionally classified as conversational implicatures and argue that none of them belongs in the top right quadrant. Some alleged examples are really done by convention according to them, for example, both indirect speech acts and additional utterance content attaching to logical connectives (see Part 2 of *Imagination and Convention*). As we hinted above, they make the case by advocating for an enriched range of linguistic rules: "This goes beyond syntax and semantics as usually conceived, but, we will argue, it is part of speakers' linguistic grammar nonetheless" (92). The remaining alleged examples of conversational implicatures, such as non-serious speech and hinting, do not belong on the conversational scoreboard at all, because they are not genuinely propositional (see Part 3 of *Imagination and Convention*).

In brief, Lepore and Stone deploy Lewisian ideas to move some alleged conversational implicatures to the left in Chart 1.1 and Davidsonian ones to move the remainder down. Chart 1.3 captures this final element of exposition:

INTERPRETIVE EFFECTS	Caused by Convention	Caused by Imagination
Contributions	- Semantics - The conventional part of pragmatics (i.e. of disambiguation) [Some alleged conversational implicatures go here: e.g., indirect speech acts, enriched meanings for logical connectives, and scalar implicatures (*See Part 2 of the book*)]	- The inferential part of pragmatics (i.e., of disambiguation) - This quadrant is otherwise empty ◀— [Alleged Conversational Implicatures] ↓
Non-Contributions		- Neither semantics nor pragmatics [Some alleged conversational implicatures go here: e.g., hints, irony, and sarcasm (*See Part 3 of the book*)]

Chart 1.3

A very brief recap is in order before we turn to the critical portion of the essay. At the outset we introduced two general questions, which seem to confront all of us: Qe, concerning the interpretive effects of linguistic utterances, and Qc, concerning the causes of those effects. As we read their book, Lepore and Stone present novel answers on both fronts, drawing insightfully on Lewis (1969, 1979) and Davidson (1978).

Specifically, contributions, which come in a number of sub-varieties, derive almost entirely from various Lewis-style conventions; all other interpretive effects, which equally come in a number of sub-varieties, derive from variations on Davidson-style imagination. These answers, we saw, contrast sharply with the traditional Gricean take on things. Indeed, Lepore and Stone reject the standard semantics–pragmatics divide as inherited from Grice. For them, semantics pertains to contributions and conventions, the top left quadrant of our chart. Pragmatics is disambiguation, which involves conventions and a soupçon of imagination, thereby straddling the top two quadrants of our chart. They also introduce a third domain into the landscape—which is neither semantics nor pragmatics—namely, the domain of non-contributions achieved by the imagination. This third domain in the lower right of our chart is not even countenanced by traditional views (with the notable exception of Davidson).

Part Two: Evaluating Their View

As we said at the outset, our evaluative focus will be on concerns about Lepore and Stone's view. In passing, however, let us consider several ways in which their position might well be philosophically superior.

Because they apply convention much more broadly than Grice does, their view may render more of conversational interaction tractable using familiar rule-based tools. In particular, it may explain in empirical detail how we convey clear and precise messages in cases that have been traditionally treated as based on general-purpose inference. Three test cases seemingly illustrate the promise of their approach. According to Lepore and Stone, their convention-heavy view can explain with greater detail and finesse why 'Can I have French toast?' is used to place an order; why 'Oil prices have doubled and demand for consumer goods plunged' conveys more than a truth-functional conjunction; and why 'Well, it looked red', said with the right intonation, can express doubt about whether the object in question actually was red. The suggestion, as we understand it, is not that there are ambiguities produced by traditional sentence-level syntax and sentence-level compositional semantics. As they suggest, the word 'and' is not lexically ambiguous between & and &+*then* (126). Instead, there are previously underappreciated linguistic conventions (e.g., discourse-level linguistic conventions) that yield richer potential readings *of the sentence in this discourse context*—with pragmatics then merely choosing among these.

Their view also seemingly explains certain cases of confusion, ignorance, and deceit where an intention-based view of speech act content gets the wrong results. Returning to our chess analogy, a novice is able to make an unintended move because the conventional rules of the game entail that the physical changes she makes to the board have that effect. Similarly, Lepore and Stone hold that conventions explain how people can actually commit themselves to quite specific things, even if they lack the right Grice-style intentions (e.g., inadvertently committing to plant an elm, by saying 'I promise to plant an elm', even while having beeches in mind). And they explain why liars, who are not cooperating, and who are masking their intentions rather than revealing them, nonetheless communicate quite specific things: their overarching aim notwithstanding, the conventions fix what they have said.

Also very promising is their view that in linguistic utterances, neither the causes nor the effects are monolithic. The interpretive effects are not just truth evaluable messages that the speaker means and the hearer must recover. The causes are more than just compositional truth-conditional semantic rules operating on sentence-level trees, plus "general cognition". (If anything, as will emerge immediately below, we think that Lepore and Stone understate the variety of things we do with language, and the variety of special-purpose tools that natural languages provide.)

5. Empirical Objections

A. Linguistic Conventions Without Contributions

To be clear, in both this sub-section and the next, we are posing empirical critiques which take on board, for the sake of argument, Lepore and Stone's general taxonomic categories. That is, for the time being, we are granting that the right way to construe Qe and Qc really is in terms of how Chart 1.1 should be filled in. Our plaint immediately below will be that, even framing the issues in this way, there are cases which look like counterexamples to what we have called their 'bold conjecture'. That all of this is *pro tem* is important because, in the next section, we will ultimately urge that theirs are not the right classificatory categories in any case.

Consider first terms like 'alas', 'amen', 'bravo', 'bye', 'cheers', 'congrats', 'damn', 'gesundheit', 'hello', 'hurray', 'mazel tov', 'our condolences', 'yeah', and 'thanks'. We take it to be obvious that the performative roles of such *phatic expressions* (as we label them) are conventionally fixed: other languages use other sounds to perform the corresponding acts. Yet these don't seem to be "inquiry-type meanings", whose point is to arrive at a public solution to a coordination problem. The meaning of 'gesundheit' is something like: *Used as a response when someone sneezes*. (This would be how one would explain its meaning to a foreigner learning English.)

In a similar vein, there is a clear conventionalized difference in meaning among 'barf', 'vomit', and 'emesis'—a difference in register, specifically *level of formality*. A second language learner who thought them perfect synonyms, and used them interchangeably, would not have mastered English. Similarly, in French there are subtle differences in the conventional uses of 'vous' and 'tu'. 'Vous' is normally the more formal and polite expression, so that in contexts where friendship and familiarity are assumed, its use over 'tu' can be a slight. Still, the differences in both cases do not pertain to information—whether stated, presupposed, or conventionally implied. The way the world must be for 'tu fumes', said to Alex, to obtain is exactly as it must be for 'Vous fumez' to obtain.

Nor do the differences seem to impact upon speech act kind or information structure as elaborated in the text.[3]

Another very intriguing candidate for the bottom left quadrant are *evaluative statements*, for example, aesthetic ones, which trace to discourse-level linguistic conventions.[4] To make the point, we first need to introduce an entertaining, if unkind, example. *The WB's Superstar USA* was a 2004 reality TV program in which, unbeknownst to the performers, the judges were looking for America's worst singer. The benighted contestants, who massively overestimated their singing abilities, supposed that it was the usual kind of contest. Not to give away the true objective, the performances therefore had to be characterized in a purposely misleading way. So as not to lie, the panelists systematically uttered sentences that were strictly speaking true, but subject to a double entendre in terms of evaluation. They would say, for example, things whose strict truth-conditions pertained to a mental effect in them: 'Your singing was utterly astonishing', 'I will remember your performance for the rest of my life', 'That was truly intense, and deeply affected me'. They would accurately describe the rarity of the performances, uttering sentences like: 'No one else comes close to performing that tune the way that you do' and 'Your rendition was truly exceptional and extraordinary'. Or they would comment on how the singing might be reported: 'Anyone seeing that would be left speechless', 'Your interpretation of that song will be the talk of the town'. A key point here is that, as the television audience well understood, all of these utterances in fact exhibited some kind of negative-valence meaning. That was part of the intended and actual interpretive effect—one which the unfortunate singers failed to grasp.

This connects to Lepore and Stone's taxonomy as follows. In the usual circumstances, the sentences produced really do carry a positive valence. We don't wish to take a stand on what exactly the nature of this special positive- versus negative-valence meaning in evaluations amounts to. That is a very difficult question indeed. Happily, it doesn't matter for present purposes, as long as it wouldn't be a contribution by Lepore and Stone's lights—and, reflecting on the negative case, it certainly seems that this "evaluative content" belongs in the same class as metaphor, non-propositional hints, etc. Now consider *why* it is so heard in the usual case: it's seemingly because there is a discourse-level linguistic convention, specific to this genre. In reviews of movies,

---

[3] For additional discussion, see Stainton (2014). The tendency to disregard phatic expressions and the like traces, we suspect, to the implicit presumption that the paradigm of language use is proto-scientific debate: "To engage in conversation is, essentially, to distinguish among alternative possible ways that things may be" (Stalnaker 1978: 184). Putting it polemically, it's as if all linguistic interaction fundamentally pertained to either theoretical philosophy (regarding what we should believe) or to practical philosophy (regarding how we should act). In a related vein, this disregard traces historically to the implicit presumption that our spoken tongues are just more complex and unruly versions of artificial logical languages. Both presumptions, we would urge, should be rejected by empirically minded philosophers of language as yet another monolith.

[4] The following owes a debt to Isidora Stojanovic's paper "Mutual Beliefs in the Interpretation of Evaluative Statements", and to discussion with her.

musicals, concerts, etc., and in the more usual sort of reality TV competition, it is a convention that utterances of 'That was truly intense, and deeply affected me' et al. will constitute high praise. As a matter of convention, that is, in those contexts, such sentences are not used wholly descriptively. That is precisely why the contestants, believing that the conventional circumstances obtained, naturally heard the judges' observations as laudatory, while the television audience, who knew that the usual conventions were not in play, (correctly) heard them otherwise. What this shows is that valence-type content—that is, the positive evaluative valence of the usual case as opposed to the joking negative one—can derive, in large part, from the rules governing this discourse situation. It seems, then, that we have yet another interpretive effect which is not a contribution, and yet which traces to linguistic convention.

To summarize, we have identified three linguistic phenomena which, seeming to fit Lepore and Stone's criteria both for non-contributions and for interpretive effects which trace to convention, defy their classification. Having drawn attention to these three, we expect readers will be able to identify numerous others (for example, phrases used for sheer emoting: 'Fucking jerk' yelled at a driver, or looking at the Grand Canyon and saying 'Wow'). All afford theory-internal challenges to what we have dubbed their 'bold conjecture'.

B. Contributions Owing Heavily to Imagination

It seems to us that there are many, many cases where a precise proposition can be meant, and can be recognized as "updating the public state of play", without convention doing the heavy lifting. That is, the upper right quadrant is also heavily populated. Previous critics, including Carston (2016) and Szabó (2016), have stressed this very point. Carston, drawing on examples from Hirschberg (1991) and Simons (2014, 2017), points to scalar-type implicatures but without a requisite convention, as in (1); and she notes lexical enrichment not owing to convention but rather to real-world knowledge, as in (2):

1.   A: Have you mailed that letter?
     B: I'm typing it right now
     (Conveys that B has not mailed the letter)

2.   A: What's making all that noise in the attic?
     B: Either there's a nest up there or some squirrels have moved in
     (Pragmatically enriches to include only inhabited non-squirrel nests)

Another class of examples involves sophisticated mind reading, in which speaker meaning is determinate, though linguistic conventions are insufficient to fix that meaning. Here is an example that we owe to Sperber and Wilson (1986). During the cold war, Americans Alice and Bonnie both reject allegations that the USSR is repressive, has food shortages, etc., as mere US propaganda. They both hold that it is really a workers' paradise. Alice decides to move there, and to write back to her friend about the actual conditions. Just to be sure that her message isn't censored, they agree on a code: *if it isn't a workers' paradise, but censorship prohibits her from saying so, Alice will write in purple ink*. Six months letter, Bonnie receives a letter written in blue ink. It says:

3.   Comrade, we were right. Conditions in the USSR are wonderful and there is complete freedom of expression. It is utter propaganda that there are widespread shortages. Oddly, there is one thing one cannot purchase here, and that is purple ink.

The crucial lesson of this example is that Alice conveys their entirely precise, agreed-upon, message with (3). Yet the interlocutors have not established a convention that the phrase 'Oddly, there is one thing one cannot purchase here, and that is purple ink' shall have that meaning.

A third set of examples in which there seems to be a precise truth-conditional meaning (hence a contribution, according to Lepore and Stone), yet not fixed by linguistic conventions, involves non-conventional uses of expressions. We'll mention three types. Consider first (successful) malaprops. Marga Reimer (2004) provides a lovely example. A mother and son want to buy a painting for the father's birthday. The dad is a fan of surrealist art. The son points to a copy of Munch's *The Scream* and says:

4.   That painting is sure realistic

The key data point is this. On the one hand, the son means a quite specific and determinate proposition, namely that the salient painting is surrealistic; indeed, he means something true in this instance; so, it would seem, this ought to count as a genuine contribution. On the other hand, the linguistic conventions of English do not determine any such meaning for (4). We get the same result in cases of other speech errors, such as:

5.   My wife does not drink alcohol these days because she is embarrassed [said by a Spanish speaker, not realizing that 'embarazada' translates to 'pregnant' in English]

6.   That's irrevalent

7.   Smith looks very tired [said of Jones, seen at a distance]

8.   Great Britain has voted to leave the UN

Neologisms such as (9) and (10) also express determinate meanings not solely determined by conventions:

9.   The boy porched the newspaper (Clark and Clark 1979)
10.   Gamesmanship-type non-moves (Stainton and Viger, section 2, above)[5]

---

[5] See Stainton (2016b) for additional discussion of such non-conventional uses. We cannot resist noting, by the way, that precise speaker meanings frequently occur, without being wholly fixed by conventions or convention+, in cases of sub-sentential speech. For example, a speaker indicates the location of a table leg with the Prepositional Phrase 'On the stoop'. The speaker means the *de re* proposition, about the table leg, that it is on the stoop; this is a perfectly precise inquiry-type public meaning that, again, surely ought to count as the speaker's contribution by Lepore and Stone's lights. Nonetheless, Stainton (2006) has argued (at *exhausting* length) that this is not because the expression produced, itself, means that proposition, not even relative to the set of contextual parameters. The conventions of English do not fix this meaning— barring some kind of semantic or syntactic ellipsis account, which remains empirically implausible. For the most recent volleys on the latter topic, see Martí (2015) and Botterell and Stainton (2017).

We end with some counterexamples where Lepore and Stone themselves *must* concede that there aren't conventions at work, namely in hints. Lepore and Stone rightly hold that hints are a paradigm case of the non-conventional; but they are mistaken to add that hints are individuated in terms of a kind of content, specifically non-propositional content. Rather, as Stainton (2016a) urges, hints are individuated in terms of *how* the message is conveyed (namely, indirectly), and *why* the speaker opted for an indirect method (e.g., to avoid breaking a rule, or to avoid taking full responsibility for the message). A couple of examples will adequately illustrate. Suppose that a person has promised Alex not to tell the police where he is. Even consonant with that, the promise-maker can phone a tip line and say:

11.   I'm calling about the $5000 reward for Alex. I saw him two minutes ago. I swore not to *tell* anyone where he is, but, um…his car is parked in Betty's garage

On the one hand, the speaker means something quite precise by this—something about Alex's location, and something that seemingly merits Lepore and Stone's label 'contribution'. On the other hand, there isn't a linguistic convention to the effect that (11) can be used to mean that Alex is at Betty's house. (That's why this is a hint, and doesn't strictly break the promise.) A second example along the same lines: A teacher could utter:

12.   The rules say I cannot tell you your final grade, but have you heard that all apples almost always appear around April?'

What is hinted is clear: the final grade was an A. But, again, the whole point of using this roundabout manner of speaking is that this is not a conventional way of communicating that. It is not a telling, but only a hinting.

The foregoing—scalar-type implicatures and lexical enrichments which rely on real-world knowledge; sophisticated mind reading under censorship in the purple ink case; various kinds of perfectly interpretable speech errors; and determinate, precise, and propositional hints—are all potential counterexamples to the bold conjecture that contributions derive from convention (save for a smidge of disambiguation). Like numerous other commentators on *Imagination and Convention*, we thus think that, even granting their classificatory scheme, there are plenty of linguistic phenomena which belong in the upper right quadrant of Chart 1.1

The most obvious rejoinder for Lepore and Stone to make is to insist that all of our alleged counterexamples are simply additional grist for their mill. Where there are contributions, there are also, they may insist, unnoticed linguistic conventions at work. And where there are conventional meanings they didn't discuss—for example, phatic expressions, levels of formality, and evaluative valence—there are unnoticed sub-varieties of contributions. Indeed, this is essentially the stance they take in their most recent publication on these topics (Lepore and Stone 2016: 204 *ff.*) The most glaring problem with this rejoinder, of course, is that positing conventions and contributions whenever required to save the hypothesis will strike their opponents as ad hoc. But there is a less obvious and deeper problem: such an appeal highlights the fact that Lepore and Stone offer up too little in the way of independently-motivated grounding for their key notions of 'contribution' and 'linguistic convention'. This leads us to our final evaluative sections: methodological objections, and a critique of their overarching framework.

6. Methodological Objections

The first set of objections were theory-internal. From here forward, we will take issue with the taxonomic categories with which Lepore and Stone approach interpretive effects and their causes.

A. Changing the Topic on the Linguist

On first reading *Imagination and Convention*, one understands 'linguistic convention' as another term for 'grammar' or 'knowledge of language'. Lepore and Stone's own usage very much encourages this:

On the other hand we have our view: that the specific interpretations we find in these cases[6] are always a matter of linguistic knowledge that associates forms with interpretive constraints which completely determine the content of interpretation. Pragmatics merely disambiguates.

(94; see also pp. 89, 143–4, and 148)

That, in turn, seemingly connects the book to what mainstream linguists paradigmatically inquire about, something along the lines of the nature of a certain autonomous system: of naturally occurring phonological, morphosyntactic and semantic rules; operating over special hierarchical structures (such as phonemes, morphemes, phrases, sentences, etc.); likely stored in a separate and special-purpose module of the mind; exemplified by such tongues as East Cree, English, Swahili, and Urdu. (A subject matter, in short, which is very *unlike* the game of chess.)

Reading the book as addressing such topics, 'linguistic convention' obviously would not encompass cultural practices which have nothing especially to do with communicative signaling. Conventions like:

13.
  i.   In Australia and England, they drive on the left
  ii. One usually tips the bell hop at a hotel, but not the manager
  iii. Sandals are not formal footwear
  iv. Westerners wear black to a funeral
  v.   Taxi passengers sit in the backseat
  vi. The smaller fork is used for salad

---

[6] That is, their three parade cases: 'Can I have French toast?' to place an order; 'Oil prices doubled and demand for consumer goods plunged' encoding that oil prices doubled first; 'Well it looked red' meaning that possibly it wasn't really red.

Nor would 'linguistic convention' have in its extension symbols that do not belong to natural languages. Among the many signaling systems excluded would be:

14.
  i.   Semaphore
  ii. Military hand signals or gang-sign
  iii. Morse code
  iv. Figures such as a circle with a line through it, or a stylized male and female side-by-side
  v.   Turn signals and stop lights
  vi. Blue meaning cold, red meaning hot
  vii. That moving the light switch to the "up" position turns the light on
  viii. That the big hand being at 12 and the little hand at 1 means one o'clock

Finally, understanding 'linguistic convention' to pertain to grammar and knowledge of language, it presumably wouldn't even include cultural knowledge specifically about language use, such as:

15.
  i.   In French, a silent 'e' is pronounced when singing (as in the bedtime lullaby *Frère Jacques*).
  ii. In English, one says 'cheese' when photos are taken (as opposed to 'whiskey' in Spanish and 'eggplant' in Chinese).
  iii. Scandinavians answer the phone with their first name, rather than with 'Hello'.
  iv. In English, formal letters begin with 'Dear', rather than 'Esteemed'; 'Hey' or other slang is not used.
  v.   '@#$%' stands for foul language.
  vi. In the US the date is written as MM/DD/YY, whereas in Canada it is DD/MM/YY.
  vii. Christians read aloud the 23rd Psalm at funerals and First Corinthians 13 at weddings.
  viii. One whispers in church and in libraries, and at the symphony, but one shouts at rock concerts.
  ix. In the US, someone named Shaniqua Washington is likely African American, while someone named Jesus Gonzalez is likely Latino.
  x.   In Canada, human height is given using 'foot' and 'inch', but driving distances are given using 'kilometer'; gas and milk prices are given using 'liter', but beer prices are given using 'ounce'.
  xi. People say grace before the meal, not after.
  xii. In London, Ontario fans yell, 'Let's go Majors' at baseball games but 'Go Knights go' at hockey games.

Having clarified what 'grammar', 'knowledge of language', and 'linguistic convention' are customarily understood to mean (by highlighting what they would ordinarily *not* encompass), we can now raise our first methodological objection. If, as they seem wont to do, Lepore and Stone address the counterexamples in (1)–(12) by massively expanding 'linguistic convention', then their book loses much of its bite for linguists. This holds doubly if they re-construe 'contribution' and 'disambiguation' to accommodate our other problem cases. Doing so, what they will have shown is:

> *On Qe and Qc*:   Linguistic conventions (in an unfamiliar and very broad sense) together with disambiguation (in an unfamiliar and very broad sense) are necessary and sufficient for linguistic contributions (in a peculiar technical sense).

> *On Qs/p*:   Semantics pertains to linguistic convention (in an unfamiliar and very broad sense) and linguistic contributions (in a peculiar technical sense), while pragmatics is merely disambiguation (in an unfamiliar and very broad sense).

B. No Answer to Qe and Qc?

Recall Lepore and Stone's bold conjecture: disambiguation aside, there are contributions where and only where the interpretive effect derives from convention; all other interpretive effects are open-ended invitations to explore, and they involve imagination. (Related to this, they hold that semantics pertains to contributions; that pragmatics is merely disambiguation; and that imagination-driven interpretive effects are neither.) In terms of our chart, Lepore and Stone predict that the bottom left and top right quadrants are essentially empty. This hypothesis, we suggested, faced two kinds of (seeming) counterexamples: conventions without contributions, and contributions without conventions. There is, of course, a very natural response. Diversify still further the range and variety of conventions and contributions—thereby not only defanging our alleged counterexamples, but reinforcing their central point that neither the causes nor the effects in linguistic utterances are monolithic. In the last section, we presented a first methodological objection to this gambit. If 'linguistic convention' is read in an unfamiliar and promiscuous way—for instance, such that it might include (15 i–xii), (14 i–viii) or maybe even (13 i–vi)—then the book cannot have the radical import for linguistics that they want it to: it will simply cease to engage the long-standing question of the roles of grammar and knowledge of language, because Lepore and Stone will have covertly changed the topic. We turn now to a second methodological concern.

It is consistent with what we wrote in the previous section that Lepore and Stone do provide perfectly fine answers; it's just that they have re-construed seemingly shared questions in (for some) a disappointing way.[7] We now want to press a much stronger complaint, namely that *Imagination and Convention* may not provide satisfactory answers to our twin questions at all, even when re-construed.

---

[7] For instance, and in line with their claim to "offer an account of language as a specifically social competence for making our ideas public" (198), one might read them as addressing interesting and important questions about interpretive effects in social semiotics generally, rather than in natural language (*cf.* Gregory 2009 and Halliday 1985).

Start with Qe. Granting that phatic expressions, level of formality and evaluative valence are all conventional, it's easy enough for Lepore and Stone to maintain that they are simply novel sub-varieties of non-truth-conditional contributions. That it's easy enough is, however, precisely the problem. Making such a move, their category of contributions ceases progressively to look like a genuine kind. One is left, instead, with a rag-bag. At best, a sympathetic reader may share the nebulous intuition that there is a "family resemblance" at play; but even such an intuition would, we fear, be too heavily driven by antecedent commitment to Lepore and Stone's framework. What's more, appealing to such theory-laden intuitions would fit ill with their admirable call for a more empirical approach. At worst, what genuinely unites all of the "sub-varieties of contributions" into a non-arbitrary class is that they all arise from convention—which would mean that the *if it's a convention, it's a contribution* half of their bold conjecture is not an empirical hypothesis after all, but a definitional truism.[8] Either way, we are left without a satisfying take on Qe.

Turning to Qc, Lepore and Stone can indeed grant that our cases—scalar implicatures and lexical enrichment based on real-world knowledge (as in (1)–(2) above); terrifically clever redeployment of codes, relying on lots of sophisticated mind reading (as in (3)); malaprops and other speech errors (as in (4)–(8)); on-the-fly coinages (as in (9)–(10)); and determinate propositional "hints" (as in (11)–(12))—are all contributions. They can do so by insisting that there are unnoticed linguistic conventions at work. Again, however, that they can deal with purported counterexamples so readily is not a virtue of the view. To the contrary, whereas genuine explanation requires severe constraints on causal posits, they can introduce their conventions *ad libitum*.

An emerging theme is that admission to one of Lepore and Stone's classificatory categories comes "too cheap". Their categories are insufficiently robust. An even deeper aspect of this complaint is that genuine explanation requires causes. (By definition, an answer to Qc does so.) What they offer instead are regularities. And regularities, *per se*— even ones that solve coordination problems, whose point is signaling, and where there are logically possible alternatives—are *so* cheap that they aren't proper causes at all. True, Lepore and Stone make reference to mechanisms, but they say too little about how to characterize one. What's more, the burgeoning literature in philosophy of neuroscience, which appeals to mechanisms as explanations of cognitive phenomena, requires a multi-level account in which a phenomenon at any given level is a result of components and their activities at another level (see, e.g., Bechtel 2008 and Craver 2007). Neither convention nor imagination, broadly construed, seem analyzable in such terms.[9]

---

[8] A related point: Lepore and Stone seem to be fellow travelers with King and Stanley (2005), Martí (2015), Merchant (2010), Stanley (2000), and Stanley and Szabó (2000) in striving to render more of linguistic interaction tractable using just the linguist's familiar formal tools. If the book is to achieve this goal, however, their bold conjecture cannot be a matter of implicit definition—for example, "something is a properly linguistic interaction if and only if it can be handled using the familiar techniques of linguistics"— but must instead be an empirically supported discovery.

[9] To come at this methodological complaint in terms of pedigree, *Imagination and Convention* could well have carried the sub-title, "Displacing Grice with Davidson/Lewis". Now Grice, correctly in our view, took the mental very seriously in his philosophy of language. In contrast, both Davidson and Lewis are

In brief, to overcome worries about giving empirically false ones, Lepore and Stone risk giving no satisfying answers to Qe and Qc at all.

7. A Relevance Theoretic Response

We end our discussion of *Imagination and Convention* with some brief remarks on an alternative approach to Qe and Qc, one which does not change the topic away from grammar/knowledge of language, and which (we think) invokes genuine kinds.

To properly address Qc, we propose seeking out genuine cognitive mechanisms instead of mere behavioral patterns. Specifically, we propose following Relevance Theorists in the search for psychological kinds as the relevant objectively-individuated causes. One such cause will be the language faculty—which, importantly, tracks what is usually meant by 'grammar' and 'knowledge of language' (for related ideas, see Collins 2016). The others will be various mental modules—long-term memory, mind reading, perception of one's present environment, etc.—that, in conversational exchanges, operate on the outputs from the language-specific part of the human mind. Given this picture, the investigator discovers which causes are properly linguistic. Yes, we have pre-theoretical intuitions about this: for example, it certainly seems that knowing when to say grace, and how to pronounce silent letters when singing in French, do not trace causally to the language faculty. Ultimately, however, such intuitions get confirmed or disconfirmed by evidence from a host of areas, including previously unexpected ones: for example, acquisition studies, language deficits, eye-tracking experiments, comparative linguistics, brain scans, etc.

Coming at Qc this way allows one to address troubles about the taxonomy of effects as well. That latter classification should not be artificial either, nor adjudicated by vague and theory-internal intuitions. We propose a straightforward solution: don't attempt to independently taxonomize interpretive effects (e.g., in terms of the scoreboard), thereafter asking what cause achieves which effects. Instead, deal with the threat of *covertly* classifying effects in terms of causes—thereby turning a seeming empirical discovery into a definitional truism—by *overtly* so classifying. We propose, that is, wholeheartedly embracing the sorting of effects in terms of their psychological causes.[10] (This is not, of course, a novel idea. It's an application of the Chomskyan program: find the nature of the linguistic competence, and then hive off as performance-effects

students of Quine; and Quinean leanings don't jibe with generative grammar in particular, or realist cognitive science in general. What's on offer, to the contrary, is a behaviorist ersatz: knowledge of language as simply "an abstract way of characterizing what a language user is able to do" (Lepore and Stone 2016: 208).

[10] To forestall a charge of inconsistency, and a potential misunderstanding: our point is not that effects *cannot* be taxonomized except in terms of their causes. To the contrary, as Stainton (2016a) stresses, one can and should classify utterances in terms of what impacts they have on normative states of affairs. (For instance, an utterance should be classified as a full-on statement only if it makes its speaker lie-prone.) Crucially, however, that kind of taxonomizing is not a precursor to empirically identifying the causes of effects so classified. To the contrary, a main point of Stainton (2016a) is that one should not even attempt to pair up effects classified normatively (e.g., as a full-on statement vs. something merely conveyed) with causes characterized in linguistic, physical, and psychological terms (e.g., as a sincere production of a declarative sentence).

the ones that do not trace causally to it.) Putting this in terms of semantics versus pragmatics, and closely echoing Relevance Theory, "semantic effects" are simply those that derive exclusively from knowledge of language; "pragmatic effects" are content-aspects of utterances deriving from other parts of the mind. The latter then sub-divide into content-effects which arise from enriching items within the decoded representation (that is, "developing the logical form"), and those which arise from conjoining wholly new representations to that logical form. As above, it then turns out to be an empirical issue both whether an effect is linguistic at all, and if so, what sub-kind it belongs to. Are truth-conditions in general, and what is strictly speaking asserted, "semantic effects"? What about the speech act kind? Phatic exchanges? Are any of (15 i–xii) properly linguistic? One finds out by considering whether these do or do not derive from the language faculty.

We close our evaluative discussion by briefly echoing important observations by Bezuidenhout (2016: 182–4). We have urged that Relevance Theory is attractive methodologically and philosophically: it promises to afford genuine kinds as causes; and, on the basis of those, one can hope to taxonomize interpretive effects in a more empirically grounded and revealing fashion. But it also has important advantages in terms of capturing data—ones which may surprise those readers of *Imagination and Convention* who aren't steeped in Relevance Theory's recent evolution.

Among the very promising empirical insights of Lepore and Stone's book, we said, was its recognition of a diversity of linguistic rules and of inferential processes, along with the insistence that interpretive effects go beyond the recovery of determinate propositional contents. That is, there is more at work than bare-bones syntax-semantics on the one hand, and general rationality on the other, yielding specific messages which the sender has in mind (and which the interlocutor needs to recover). Now, Lepore and Stone suppose that embracing this diversity of causes and effects differentiates them from all Grice-influenced pragmaticians. Yet, coming to the aforementioned advantages of Relevance Theory, Lepore and Stone have allies therein. Open-endedness of interpretive effects has been an important part of the theory since the 1986 edition of *Relevance*. Regarding grammar, Relevance Theorists are wholly open to the rules of grammar being diverse and more sophisticated than mainstream generative syntax supposes. And it is a core tenet nowadays that there isn't just one monolithic "inference engine", but instead numerous discrete modules at work in pragmatic processing. One could profitably read the empirical parts of *Imagination and Convention*, then, as drawing attention to novel and important linguistic phenomena, all the while thinking that the best way to address them is with the underappreciated tools of present-day Relevance Theory (Bezuidenhout presents numerous detailed examples). What's more, it seems to us that Relevance Theory has the empirical upper hand in one crucial respect. Positing as it currently does both input modules and central system modules, it becomes eminently possible that, rather than having a mechanism specific to each of metaphor, irony, humor, etc., there is, instead, the same set of modular mechanisms, but interacting in divergent ways.

8. Summary

It truly has been a long and winding road. So, at the risk of belaboring the point, one last summary may prove helpful. We framed our discussion around twin questions:

Qe: What interpretive effects can linguistic utterances have?
Qc: What causes give rise to interpretive effects?

Drawing on key concepts from Lewis and Davidson, we read Lepore and Stone as recasting these questions in a specific form:

- Which interpretive effects are contributions to the conversational record, and which are merely invitations for open-ended exploration?
- What role does convention play in causing these interpretive effects, and what role does imagination play?

The answer, which we termed their 'bold conjecture', is that contributions are fixed by convention (augmented by a soupçon of imagination when required for disambiguation), whereas imagination simply nudges the hearer to organize her thoughts in various creative ways. Lepore and Stone also insist that there is enormous diversity with respect to sub-varieties of contributions, open-ended explorations, conventions, and imaginative processing. The result, then, is not so much a disagreement about where to place various interpretive effects of utterances within the familiar semantic–pragmatic terrain, but rather about the very landscape itself in which the debate should be conducted: semantics becomes potential contributions provided by linguistic convention; pragmatics merely amounts to selecting among the potential contributions using only linguistic convention and convention[+]; and non-contributions deriving from imagination belong to neither category.

Having spent considerable space on exposition, we next presented objections. They were of two types. First, granting to them the terms of the debate, we urged that there are examples that defy the bold conjecture. Specifically, we presented cases which, seemingly by their own lights, are caused by conventions, but are not contributions to the scoreboard—phatic expressions, level of formality, and evaluative valence. We also presented cases of interpretive effects, which should presumably count as contributions, in their sense of the term, but are not the result of convention-plus-disambiguation. Our second type of objection was methodological. Lepore and Stone face a dilemma: either their view is empirically inadequate, or it requires re-construing 'convention' and 'disambiguation' so broadly, and 'contribution' so theory-internally, that it loses much of its initial bite vis-à-vis linguistics. The latter horn, which seems to be what tempts them, invited a second methodological objection as well, namely, that because their classificatory categories—which we had granted them for the sake of argument— turn out, in the end, not to be sufficiently robust, Lepore and Stone do not offer a satisfactory answer to our questions at all. We suggest that the methodological solution is to follow Relevance Theory: address Qc in terms of psycholinguistic causes; give priority to Qc over Qe; and couch the semantics/pragmatics boundary in terms of those human-specific cognitive kinds which turn out to be at work in our conversational interactions.[11,12]

References

Armstrong, Josh and Eliot Michaelson (2016). "Introduction for *Inquiry* Symposium on *Imagination and Convention*". *Inquiry* 59(1–2): 139–45.

Bechtel, William (2008). *Mental Mechanisms: Philosophical Perspectives on Cognitive Neuroscience*. New York: Psychology Press.

Bezuidenhout, Anne (2016). "What Properly Belongs to Grammar?" *Inquiry* 59(1–2): 180–202.

Botterell, Andrew and Robert J. Stainton (2017). "Logical Form and the Vernacular Revisited". *Mind and Language* 32(4): 495–522.

Carston, Robyn (2016). "Linguistic Conventions and the Role of Pragmatics". *Mind and Language* 31(5): 612–24.

Clark, Eve and Herbert Clark (1979). "When Nouns Surface as Verbs". *Language* 55: 767–811.

Collins, John (2016). "Putting Syntax First". *Mind and Language* 31(5): 635–45.

Craver, Carl (2007). *Explaining the Brain: Mechanisms and the Mosaic Unity of Neuroscience*. Oxford: Oxford University Press.

Davidson, Donald (1978). "What Metaphors Mean". *Critical Inquiry* 5: 31–47.

Gregory, Michael (2009). "Notes on Communication Linguistics". In J. de Villiers and R. Stainton (eds.) *Communication in Linguistics, Vol. 2: Michael Gregory's Proposals for a Communication Linguistics*. Toronto: Éditions du GREF, pp. 145–266.

---

[11] Here is another important (and clearly unintended) lesson one can take away from *Imagination and Convention*. As Armstrong and Michaelson (2016: 139) note, the book falls within a broad class of semantic theories—a class which is quickly becoming a new orthodoxy. Said approaches treat context-change potential, dynamic updating, etc., as the standing meaning of expressions: for example, to know what a sentence S means is to know a function from every potential initial scoreboard to the post-utterance scoreboard that would result from tokening S. Ironically, one can read *Imagination and Convention* as reinforcing a worry about this approach. Lepore and Stone's examples show something very important, namely, just how much needs to be on the scoreboard, and just how rich the update rules need to be, for this program of research to succeed. All of their conventions—both the ones they mention, and those they would need to add to account for the potential counterexamples—would have to be incorporated into the presumed updating function. But, runs the worry, the result is implausibly massive and motley. To come at it from the point of view of a cognitivist, Lepore and Stone's examples underscore the astonishing variety and richness of information that would need to be stored in the human language faculty, if update semantics is to describe our semantic competence. In light of this, the cognitivist concludes that it's better to treat patterns of updating (if such there be) as interaction effects: such patterns reflect both what the expression means in the language, but also the many non-linguistic factors which are the mainstay of pragmatics (as classically understood). And it's better to treat the scoreboard not as a notion central to linguistic theory, but as a hodgepodge of performance effects.

[12] We would like to thank Ash Asudeh, Axel Barceló, Anne Bezuidenhout, David Bourget, Robyn Carston, Ernie Lepore, Angela Mendelovici, and Matthew Stone for feedback on earlier drafts. We also appreciate the input of members of Western Ontario's Language and Cognition Reading Group, particularly Danny Booth, David Conter, Grace Gomashie, Leila Habibi, Jiangtian Li, Vivian Milliken, and Jody Tomchishen. A draft of the chapter was delivered at the Faculty of Foreign Languages, Shan'xi University, on August 22, 2016. We are grateful to the audience members, including especially Sandy Goldberg, Mitch Green and Isidora Stojanovic, for very helpful feedback. Funding for this project was provided by the Social Sciences and Humanities Research Council of Canada. We dedicate this chapter to our fathers, R. Keith Stainton and Chopin L. Viger.

Grice, H. Paul (1975). "Logic and Conversation". In his (1989) *Studies in the Way of Words*. Cambridge, MA: Harvard University Press, pp. 22–40.

Halliday, M.A.K. (1985). *Introduction to Functional Grammar*. London: Arnold.

Hirschberg, Julia B. (1991). *A Theory of Scalar Implicature*. New York: Garland.

King, Jeffrey C. and Jason Stanley (2005). "Semantics, Pragmatics, and the Role of Semantic Content". In Z. Szabó (ed.) *Semantics versus Pragmatics*. Oxford: Oxford University Press, pp. 111–64.

Lepore, Ernie and Matthew Stone (2015). *Imagination and Convention: Distinguishing Grammar and Inference in Language*. Oxford: Oxford University Press.

Lepore, Ernie and Matthew Stone (2016). "The Breadth of Semantics: Reply to Critics". *Inquiry* 59(1–2): 203–16.

Lewis, David (1969). *Convention*. Cambridge, MA: Harvard University Press.

Lewis, David (1979). "Scorekeeping in a Language Game". *Journal of Philosophical Logic* 8(3): 339–59.

Martí, Luisa (2015). "Grammar vs. Pragmatics". *Mind and Language* 30(4): 437–73.

Merchant, Jason (2010). "Three Kinds of Ellipsis". In F. Recanati, I. Stojanovic, and N. Villanueva (eds.) *Context-Dependence, Perspective and Relativity*. Mouton: De Gruyter, pp. 141–86.

Reimer, Marga (2004). "What Malaprops Mean". *Erkenntnis* 60: 317–34.

Simons, Mandy (2014). "Local Pragmatics and Structured Contents". *Philosophical Studies* 168(1): 21–33.

Simons, Mandy (2017). "Local Pragmatics in a Gricean Framework". *Inquiry* 60(5): 466–92.

Sperber, Dan and Deirdre Wilson (1986). *Relevance*. Cambridge, MA: Harvard University Press.

Stainton, Robert J. (2006). *Words and Thoughts*. Oxford: Oxford University Press.

Stainton, Robert J. (2014). "Philosophy of Linguistics". In S. Goldberg (ed.) *Oxford Handbooks Online*. DOI: 10.1093/oxfordhb/9780199935314.013.002

Stainton, Robert J. (2016a). "Full-On Stating". *Mind and Language* 31(4): 395–413.

Stainton, Robert J. (2016b). "A Deranged Argument Against Public Languages". *Inquiry* 59(1–2): 6–32.

Stalnaker, Robert C. (1978). "Assertion". In P. Cole (ed.) *Syntax and Semantics, Vol. 9: Pragmatics*. NY: Academic Press, pp. 315–32. Reprinted in M. Ezcurdia and R.J. Stainton (eds.) (2013) *The Semantics-Pragmatics Boundary in Philosophy*. Peterborough, ON: Broadview, pp. 179–93.

Stanley, Jason (2000). "Context and Logical Form". *Linguistics and Philosophy* 23(4): 391–434.

Stanley, Jason and Zoltán Gendler Szabó (2000). "On Quantifier Domain Restriction". *Mind and Language* 15(2–3): 219–61.

Stojanovic, Isidora (2016). "Mutual Beliefs in the Interpretation of Evaluative Statements". Paper delivered at the Faculty of Foreign Languages, Shan'xi University, August 21, 2016.

Szabó, Zoltán (2016). "In Defense of Indirect Communication". *Inquiry* 59(1–2): 167–79.

2

Exaggeration and Invention

Kent Bach

> *"The reports of my death are greatly exaggerated."*
> —Mark Twain (as commonly misquoted)

The same could be said for the semantics/pragmatics distinction. Its premature obituary is presented early in *Imagination and Convention*, and its would-be autopsy fills the rest of that book. Letting their imaginations run in defiance of philosophical convention, Ernie Lepore and Matthew Stone (2015) deploy a rich variety of examples in an extended effort to undermine Gricean tradition. They dismiss Gricean accounts of "the kind of meaning that figures in linguistic communication" (202), and they deny that this kind of meaning, speaker meaning, comes into play with figurative utterances, since these invite "imaginative engagement," not recognition of the speaker's communicative intention. Lepore and Stone (hereafter L&S) allege that "pragmatics can be at most a theory of disambiguation," hence that "the category of conversational implicature does no theoretical work" (83). What could have led them to such extreme conclusions?

L&S arrive at those conclusions from two different directions. On the one hand, and in opposition to what they deem orthodoxy in semantics, they develop a highly expansive conception of linguistic meaning according to which many expressions have considerably more meanings than is commonly supposed. On the other hand, and in opposition to orthodoxy in pragmatics, L&S contend that when a speaker is not using a sentence in any of its conventionally determined ways, there is no unique content for the hearer to get right. The speaker intends the hearer to construe her utterance in some nonliteral way, but she has no specific communicative intention for him to get right (or wrong).[1]

So, according to L&S, what a speaker can mean is limited to something that is conventionally determined by the semantics of the uttered sentence. Anything else is not a

---

[1] For convenience I will use 'she' for *speaker* and 'he' for *hearer* (addressee). Also, I will limit the discussion to utterances of single sentences as opposed to mere phrases and sequences of sentences. Obviously, this common stipulation oversimplifies.

matter of "meaning-making." Evidently, try as you may to convey something that isn't encoded in the words you utter, you won't succeed. Indeed, it seems to be L&S's view that you can't even try.

Why should we believe this? Why should we find it even remotely plausible? Let's grant that L&S are right to maintain both that the extent of conventionally determined meaning is much greater than commonly supposed and that what is elicited by "evocative and figurative speech" is often open-ended. But that hardly shows, or even begins to suggest, that a speaker never means anything not conventionally determined by some meaning of what she utters, and that in no instance can the addressee figure out what this is. L&S's view is, in effect, that there is no speaker meaning beyond disambiguated linguistic meaning. This would seem to entail that any failure of communication, at least of the sort that requires the addressee's recognition of the speaker's intention, is due only to either linguistic error or mistaken disambiguation.

The most straightforward way to rebut L&S's two main claims is to produce convincing counterexamples. Since this has already been done (see Clapp (2015), Szabo (2016), and Carston (2016) for a nice variety), and since serving up counterexamples doesn't by itself get to the heart of the problem, I will (in §1) but briefly add to this effort. A more effective way to rebut these two claims is (in §2) to draw out their implausible implications. And the most illuminating route to rebuttal is (in §3) to identify certain misconceptions underlying these two claims. L&S overlook the key ingredient in the notion of speaker meaning, misinterpret Grice's theory of conversation and notion of conversational implicature, fail to single out the kind of coordination specific to communication from further aspects of conversational cooperation, and disregard various important distinctions in pragmatics and speech act theory.

1. Counterexamples

Are there plausible examples of acts of implicating and of other indirect speech acts, each made with a recognizable communicative intention, whose force and content are not determined by semantic rules linking form to meaning? If so, this would refute L&S's first claim, that for communicative success all putative instances of this require disambiguation. Here are a few sentences each of which can be used to implicate or convey something not determined by linguistic meaning, at least in certain conversational situations. For example, uttering "That book is over 600 pages long" can, under suitable circumstances, be a successful way of implicating that it can't be read at one sitting, uttering "The door's unlocked" can be a successful way of inviting someone to come in, and uttering "This bean dip needs a little salt" can be a successful way of making a suggestion to add some salt, in each case without the benefit of any meaning convention. And, as is easy to see, each of these sentences, without any change in linguistic meaning, can be used to do other things in other conversational situations.

L&S's second claim, that figurative utterances fail to be communicative, is based on specific examples where that seems plausible because no one interpretation stands out as what the speaker (or writer) intended and could have reasonably expected the hearer (reader) to identify. Many poems provide excellent examples of this. Indeed, the French poet Stéphane Mallarmé would have agreed. He reportedly "expressed a desire to write a poem that, if read on five consecutive days, would yield five new meanings."[2] And Bob Dylan is reputed to have said that he doesn't know what his songs are about (of course, he may have been kidding when he said that). At any rate, one can unearth all the plausible examples one wants of non-literal utterances made without communicative intentions, but that would not show that others are not made *with* communicative intentions, indeed readily recognizable ones. So, for example, it seems that a speaker who utters "Hiring a good agent will open the curtain to success" can successfully convey her assurance to the addressee that hiring a good agent will lead to his success, and a speaker who utters "Solving this puzzle is like getting to the other side of a Möbius strip" can successfully convey the opinion that the puzzle has no solution. The sensible view about figurative utterances, it seems to me, is that some are made with communicative intentions and some are not.[3]

Concentrating on implicatures (including indirect speech acts) and figurative utterances (non-literal speech acts), L&S neglect utterances whose contents are enrichments of the semantic contents of what is uttered. Not taken up by Grice, these are known in the literature as *explicatures* (Sperber and Wilson 1986) or *implicitures* (Bach 1994). If I said to you, "I prefer Scotch" or "Scotch is better," not specifying what I'm comparing Scotch to (maybe bourbon, maybe brandy, maybe something else), presumably I'd intend and expect you to be in a position, based on what we've been talking about, to figure it out (if not, I'd make it explicit, including it in what I said). This is a matter of rational intention, not semantic convention. Similarly, if I said, "San Francisco is larger than Seattle" without specifying in what respect (population or land area), presumably I'd intend and expect you to be in a position to figure it out. And if I said, "John and Martha will be attending," I wouldn't do so without having reason to expect you to know which event I mean, and, if we mutually believed that John and Martha are a couple, that I mean they will be attending together. Finally, if I said, "My lizard lost its tail, but it didn't care," presumably I'd mean that the lizard, not its tail, didn't care that it lost its tail, whereas if I said, "My lizard lost its tail, but it grew back," presumably I'd mean that the lizard's tail, not the lizard, grew back. This is a matter of rational intention, not convention.

As L&S make clear, the relevant notion of convention here, the one specific to semantics, applies to "rules that link form to meaning in language" (25). This is distinct from the looser notion that applies to broad regularities in linguistic (and other social)

---

[2] Mallarmé's wish was reported by Gary Bolick in a letter to *The New Yorker*, June 6 and 13, 2016.

[3] This issue reminds me of the debate in aesthetics about the so-called intentional fallacy. The sensible view is that recognizing the author's or artist's intent sometimes is relevant to understanding and appreciating a work of literature or a work of art, and sometimes is irrelevant. Or, it might be relevant to some features of a given work and not to others.

behavior, such as those which Grice's theory of conversation tries to capture.[4] At any rate, L&S do claim that "in all the cases we consider, where alternative approaches have postulated pragmatic processes of enrichment, what's really going on is disambiguation: finding the right reading of the utterance, understood as a grammatically specified pairing of form and meaning" (88). They claim this all right, but the range of cases they consider is rather narrow. Indeed, L&S acknowledge that they "have no general arguments that we apply to the category of CIs [conversational implicatures] as a whole" (88). This raises the question of whether they are entitled to generalize from the particular examples they discuss (assuming they're right about them). Are these really representative of what occurs when a speaker means something she doesn't say?

It seems that L&S have overstated their case. Even so, and although I would challenge their contention that the "bare-bones" conception of semantics they bemoan is as "traditional" or "received" as they suggest, I certainly agree that there is no reason to confine the reach of semantics to contributions to truth-conditional content.[5] L&S discuss such topics as presupposition, information structure, and discourse coherence.[6] To those we could add grammatical mood, register, expressives, speech-act indicators, discourse markers, and utterance modifiers.[7] And I don't dispute the claim that many figurative uses of language are intended to elicit flights of imagination rather than communicate some specific message.

2. Problematic Implications

Serving up counterexamples to L&S's two sweeping claims doesn't really get at what's problematic about them. To get at that, we need to identify their implausible implications. In the next section we will try to diagnose what could have led L&S to make such claims.

2.1 One Obvious Implication

If L&S are right, then no one ever utters anything with a communicative intention whose content is not semantically expressed by what she utters (on one of its readings,

---

[4] It seems to me that when L&S discuss coherence (in chapter 6) and coordination on the conversational record (in chapter 14), they operate with a looser notion of convention, applying to practices of doing certain things in certain situations. For a comparison of different sorts of social regularities, see the appendix of Bach and Harnish (1979).

[5] While comparing different formulations of the semantics/pragmatics distinction, I pointed out that, far from clarifying this distinction, invoking the difference between truth-conditional and non-truth-conditional meaning actually obscures it. That's because, just as L&S insist, there are various sorts of expressions and constructions whose meanings make non-truth-conditional contributions (see Bach 1999a: 70–1). Philosophers focused on truth-conditional semantics may not recognize this, but linguists generally do.

[6] L&S's discussion of information structure in chapter 8 takes up stress and intonation but not it-clefts, wh-clefts, and fronting. For a classic study of information structure, see Lambrecht (1994).

[7] Harnish (1994) presents an in-depth study of moods and their role as speech-act indicators. As for utterance modifiers, locutions like 'for example', 'frankly', 'be that as it may', 'in a nutshell', and 'figuratively speaking', they function as second-order speech-act indicators. A taxonomy of them is presented in Bach (1999b: 456–60).

if it's ambiguous). That is, if you're not speaking literally, you have no communicative intention, and there is nothing for the hearer to recognize as what you meant. Or, if you can have such an intention, it has no hope of being fulfilled. That is because, assuming with L&S that pragmatics can be at most a theory of disambiguation, the hearer can only identify such an intention by disambiguating an utterance. So if, on any of its readings, it does not semantically express a plausible candidate for what the speaker is intending to communicate, the hearer should not bother trying to identify some other candidate. Instead he should just let his imagination go to work and find some way of taking the utterance whether or not the speaker intended it to be taken in that way. But surely this can't be right. After all, what's to stop a speaker, having formed a certain communicative intention, from trying to make this intention evident even by uttering a sentence none of whose readings comprises the content of that intention? And what's to stop the hearer from thinking that this is what the speaker is doing? To be sure, not every figurative utterance has an identifiable communicative intention behind it, but that doesn't begin to suggest that none does, such that the hearer, in Gricean fashion, can manage to identify it.

2.2 Another Obvious Implication

Consider also L&S's contention that different sorts of imaginative engagement are invited by different sorts of figurative utterances, depending on whether the speaker intends irony, metonymy, simile, metaphor, or some other figure of speech. How does the hearer determine how to imaginatively engage with the utterance if not by trying to identify the speaker's communicative intention? L&S can insist that there are "distinctive mechanisms at work in the different cases" (191), but that leaves open which interpretive "mechanism" is put to work in any given case. In their zeal to establish that "there is no unique and general mechanism behind all of these practices" (191), L&S do not address this question.

L&S recognize that semantic conventions are not confined to expressions' contributions to truth-conditional content and that there are also speech act conventions and other conventions of use. But it hardly follows that what speech act is performed is always, or even generally, determined by some convention exploited by the speaker. For there could never be enough conventions to govern all the things one could do with words. Indeed, if L&S were right, a speaker could never do anything unless there were already some conventionally encoded way of doing it for her to exploit.

2.3 A Neologistic Thought Experiment

L&S seem to recognize that before a certain form of words can become a conventional means for doing something, at least one speaker must use it to do that. For instance, you might make up the word 'overshow' and have the bright idea to use the phrase 'to overshow' as an utterance modifier indicating that you are about to give one more example than you need to support a claim you've been making. Even though its use would be unprecedented, you would probably succeed in communicating what you're using it to do. To grasp your use of it, the hearer would not need to disambiguate anything but, rather, would have to figure out that you're using 'to overshow' to characterize the rest of your utterance. If you kept on using this made-up phrase in that way and others started doing so as well, it and this use of it would gradually become familiar to more and more people and might eventually become conventionalized. Leaving aside the complication that, as L&S mention, "conventions are established gradually" (241), hence that conventionalization is a matter of degree, we can see from this example that a speaker can use a novel phrase in a novel way with a certain recognizable communicative intention before it comes conventionalized as well as after. Yet L&S's doctrine of no communication without convention arbitrarily precludes such cases.

Two classic examples of conventionalized phrases are 'spill the beans' and 'kick the bucket'. Unlike 'dead metaphor', these metaphors are so dead that most speakers use them without the slightest idea how they ever came to mean what they mean (there is, in fact, no consensus on either one). Yet in the earliest non-literal use of, for example, 'spill the beans', some speaker must have intended some audience to recognize her intention in using it to mean *divulge a secret*. Like 'kick the bucket' (meaning *die*), it has long since become an idiom, with its own conventional meaning, so that no creative intention or inference is needed any longer (or is even feasible any more). Even so, it is hard to imagine how such a phrase could have become an idiom without having previously been used metaphorically to mean what it now conventionally means.

To overshow, consider the exclamation 'OK', often paraphrased as 'all right'. It is used to express agreement, acknowledgment, acceptance, approval, concession, or willingness.[8] There is no consensus, though many hypotheses, about its origin, but before there was any semantic convention for 'OK', at least one person must have started using it in at least one of these ways. Moreover, although these uses are closely related, each indicating some way of going along with one's interlocutor, there do not seem to be distinct conventions for each way of using it. Which way a speaker is using 'OK' in any particular case is a matter of the speaker's communicative intention, not convention. Of course, which way of using it is appropriate, hence how a given use can plausibly be taken, will depend on what the speaker is responding to.[9] For example, you can't express your willingness to comply with a request if no request has been made. But there is no specific convention, and no need for a convention, to use 'OK' as an expression of willingness to do something the speaker has requested only if a request to do it has just been made.

So it seems that L&S's two main claims have implausibly extreme implications. They are unwarranted extensions of reasonable observations about the range and diversity of linguistic conventions and the role of imagination in interpreting figurative utterances (ones whose contents go beyond linguistic conventions). By overgeneralizing

[8] Notice that both 'OK' and 'all right' also occur as an adjective and an adverb but only 'OK' is also used as a verb (meaning to approve or to authorize) or as a noun (meaning an approval or an authorization).

[9] Interestingly, 'OK' also has a use that is not a response to an interlocutor's utterance, as when a yoga instructor says, "OK, now let's practice Triangle."

from special cases, these two claims implausibly imply that no speaker can or ever does intend to convey anything that is not linguistically encoded in what she utters, much less succeed in communicating it. What could have led L&S to make these overgeneralizations?

3. Diagnoses

To me the most striking feature of *Imagination and Convention* is its emphasis on things hearers engage in, such as what L&S call "interpretive reasoning" and "utterance interpretation," and its very limited attention, at least until late in the book, to the actions and intentions of speakers. L&S seem to assume that if an utterance is literal there is always some right, readily available interpretation, namely the one determined by the "mechanism" of disambiguation that selects a "specific grammatical analysis" intended by the speaker, which "determines a specific contribution to the conversation" (206). In contrast, interpretations of utterances that are not literal "seem intrinsically open-ended" (150), as if the speaker could not possibly have a determinate, never mind recognizable communicative intention. Evidently this is why L&S think that if pragmatics is concerned with recovering meanings of utterances, disambiguation is its only legitimate business.

With their almost exclusive emphasis on the hearer's task of utterance interpretation, L&S neglect the process whereby the speaker comes up with an utterance in the first place.[10] Even when they touch on the speaker's role, they misdescribe it as "a speaker's choices in contributing content to conversation....For Grice, speakers appeal to the norms of rationality to add layers of meaning to what they say" (60). Speakers do indeed make choices about what they contribute to conversation, but what Grice's theory primarily concerns is how they implement their communicative intentions by choosing what to utter. To be sure, speakers rarely communicate without having further intentions, but normally one chooses what to utter at least in order to implement one's communicative intention. To implement it is to make it evident to one's addressee. The naive idea about this is that it is simply a matter of the speaker putting a thought into words and of the addressee reversing the process, by decoding those words and thereby identifying the thought that was linguistically expressed. This simplistic view might seem to apply to the simplest case, where the content of what the speaker utters is identical to what the speaker intends to convey, but there is no requirement, certainly not by semantic convention, that any sentence be used literally.

Because they downplay the primacy of the speaker's communicative intention, L&S misleadingly say things like this: "Grice's theory of CIs frees the content a speaker

---

[10]   Assume for simplicity that it's an utterance of a sentence, rather than a mere phrase or a sequence of sentences. Phrases can, of course, be used to perform speech acts (see Stainton (2006) for an in-depth study of phrasal utterances), and multi-sentence utterances can be performances of such speech acts as illustrating, explaining, rebutting, and recounting.

contributes to conversation from the conventional rules that link form to meaning in language" (25). But it's not this (or any) theory that does this; it's the speaker's communicative intention. That intention precedes and is independent of the conventional content of the sentence she uses to make this intention evident. It's up to the speaker, given what she intends to communicate, how she intends to communicate it. Also misleading is L&S's suggestion that "the Gricean idea is that pragmatics starts from literal meaning" (67).[11] It starts from speaker meaning. Of course, to succeed in communicating a speaker can't utter just any old thing. She must utter something such that what she utters, the fact that she utters it (and often also the fact that she utters *it* rather than something else), and the circumstances under which she utters it, combine to make what she means evident to her audience. But this leaves open whether, in any given case, what she means is identical to the semantic content of what she utters or is distinct from it, whether because she means something else as well or something else instead.

Grice is best known for two big ideas, his account of speaker meaning in terms of reflexive intention and his theory of conversation, with its account of conversational implicature.[12] By downplaying the centrality of communicative intentions and by neglecting subsequent improvements on Grice's original formulations, L&S do not do justice to either one. As we will see, although they profess to "believe in drawing useful and principled distinctions" (v), they neglect or at least downplay a number of tried and true ones, drawn by philosophers from Austin and Grice on.

3.1 Understanding Speaker Meaning

For a speaker to mean something by uttering a sentence is, intuitively, for her to intend to communicate it.[13] Noting that Grice's aim is "to distinguish the kind of meaning that figures in linguistic communication" (203), L&S focus on Grice's original account of what it is for a speaker to mean something: "to produce some effect in an audience by means of the recognition of this intention" (202).[14] Having announced early on that

[11] Note that the literal/non-literal distinction applies not to meanings of linguistic expressions but to uses or utterances of them. Expressions can be used literally or non-literally, but they do not have both literal and non-literal meanings.

[12] A third big idea, of no less importance, is Grice's program of intention-based semantics, that is, of reducing facts about linguistic meaning to facts about speaker meaning and other psychological states. At times, L&S seem to confuse this third idea with the first, as when they write, "Grice saw intention recognition as constitutive of communication—for Grice, this was a way to naturalize linguistic knowledge" (6). Later, however, when L&S say they "reject Grice's particular way of grounding meaning in speakers' intentions" (197), evidently they are not alluding to intention-based semantics, since they never take it up. His first and third big ideas were presented initially in "Meaning" and refined in, respectively, "Utterer's meaning and intentions" and "Utterer's meaning, sentence meaning, and word meaning." His second big idea appeared, of course, in "Logic and conversation." All these papers were reprinted in Grice (1989).

[13] The phrase 'speaker meaning' can also be construed as the intended semantic content of the uttered sentence. Grice called the first 'occasion-meaning' and the second 'applied timeless meaning': "We must be careful to distinguish the applied timeless meaning of X (type) with respect to a particular token x (belonging to X) from the occasion-meaning of U's utterance of x" (1989: 119).

[14] This is quoted from "Meaning" (Grice 1989: 219), immediately after which Grice comments without elaboration, "this seems to involve a reflexive paradox, but it does not really do so."

"nothing in this book hinges on any analysis of speaker meaning, so we abstract away here from the various details of Grice's view" (13), L&S later assert not only that "Grice's original idea was on the wrong track" but also that "subsequent proposals inherit all the same problems. The key difficulty… is the prospective nature of communicative intentions on Grice's view" (204). That is, as they read Grice, "a communicative intention… commits the speaker to effects that go beyond what she can control or orchestrate. It commits the speaker to a whole network of expectations about the consequences of her action, informed by her background beliefs and desires" (204). As an alternative what they deplore as Grice's misguided "*prospective* intentionalism," according to which "the meaning of an utterance derives from the changes that the speaker plans for the utterance to bring about in the conversation" (200), L&S propose what they call "*direct* intentionalism," according to which we "attribute to the speaker… a basic intention of contributing the grammatically specified meaning of what she says" (208), along with further "intentions in action" and a "future-oriented intention" including the speaker's plan whose implementation begins with her utterance. As L&S explain with the help of examples involving different sorts of collaboration, not only conversation, "agents can further their collaborations by recognizing their collaborators' future-oriented intentions, their basic intentions and any aspect of their intentions in action" (227).

L&S are right to insist that meaning intentions are not future-oriented, but wrong to assume that a Gricean view must suppose that they are. By summarily dismissing subsequent efforts to improve upon Grice's original account of speaker meaning, L&S fail to appreciate that a Gricean approach need not, and should not, be prospective. The key move is, to use the jargon of speech act theory, to distinguish the illocutionary effect of achieving uptake from further, perlocutionary effects whose achievement depends on achieving uptake. L&S recognize that "intentions and intention recognition contribute to interlocutors' collaborations" (215), but when they insist that intention recognition is nothing special, on the grounds that it facilitates collaboration and joint activity in general, they overlook the special relationship between speaker meaning and intention recognition when it comes to communication. Even when they mention uptake, L&S misconstrue what it is, as when they complain that

prospective intentionalism ties meaning closely to particular mechanisms for audience uptake. In the Gricean tradition, the mechanism is a kind of collaboration. It's uncontroversial that people collaborate, and the inference involved in collaboration—recognizing intentions, taking them up, and furthering them—is just what Grice calls for.   (205)

Unfortunately, this characterization just doesn't get at what hearer uptake is and what's special about it as the complement to speaker meaning.

Even if they had bothered with nothing else, L&S at least should have considered, especially given its title, Strawson's "Intention and convention in speech acts" (1964), the first and perhaps still most important effort to improve upon Grice's original account.[15] As Strawson observed, "in the case of an illocutionary act of a kind not essentially conventional, the act of communication is performed if uptake is secured, if the utterance is taken to be issued with the complex overt intention with which it is issued" (1964: 458).[16] The idea is that, regardless of what further intentions the speaker may have in uttering something, the speaker's communicative intention is one that requires (for its fulfillment) being recognized by the audience. Indeed, the audience is to recognize it partly on the supposition that the speaker intends him to recognize it.[17]

Searle, citing Strawson, makes a similar point: "In the case of illocutionary acts we succeed in doing what we are trying to do by getting our audience to recognize what we are trying to do. But the 'effect' on the hearer is not a belief or response, it consists simply in the hearer understanding the utterance" (Searle 1969: 47). In contrast, "the Gricean reflexive intention does not work for perlocutionary effects." The intention to achieve a further effect, such as being believed or being complied with, is not fulfilled just by being recognized. The hearer has to go along with the speaker, not just understand her.

I have just resorted to using jargon from speech act theory, a subject that L&S almost totally ignore.[18] Austin introduced the terms 'locutionary', 'illocutionary', and 'perlocutionary' for the three main aspects of the total speech act, and even though they have been widely used ever since, L&S never use or mention any of them.[19] If they had,

---

[15] L&S do take up several "reinterpretation[s] of Grice" (43) in their early chapters, but these concern implicature and his theory of conversation, not speaker meaning and uptake.

[16] Strawson acknowledges borrowing the term 'uptake' from Austin, who wrote: "The performance of an illocutionary act involves the securing of uptake" (1962: 116). Strawson excludes "essentially conventional" illocutionary acts, such as adjourning, christening, and voting, the conditions for whose successful performance is determined by institutional conventions. For them, uptake is not their point but merely their verification (1964: 456). Strawson criticizes Austin for using conventional illocutionary acts as a model for illocutionary acts in general. Of course he is not denying that performing an illocutionary act of any kind involves the use of conventional *means*, namely linguistic expressions. But that is just to say that all speech acts (utterances) are conventional at the locutionary level.

[17] It was more than two decades before Grice, in his "Retrospective Epilogue," addressed Strawson's complaint that he, Grice, had "misidentified the intended…effect in communication [as] some form of acceptance (for example, belief or desire) [rather than as] understanding [or] uptake" (1989: 351). Grice dismisses Strawson's refinement on account of "attributing to speakers an intention which is specified in terms of the very notion of meaning which is being analyzed (or in terms of a dangerously close relative of that notion" (1989: 352), but he does not spell out what this "circularity" consists in, and why it isn't as free of "reflexive paradox" (see note 14 above) as his own account. For further discussion, see Bach (2012: §2).

[18] L&S do take up the special case of indirect speech acts in chapter 6, but theirs is really a special case of this special case. They say there that they "explore speech acts, particularly the indirect speech acts epitomized by…'Can I have the French Toast?'," but this and the other cases they consider all involve the use of standardized forms of words. L&S correctly liken these to generalized implicatures, as opposed to particularized ones (Grice 1989: 37–8), but they do not really extend their defense of conventionalism to particularized implicatures. Indeed, the term 'particularized' appears in but a single paragraph (59). Bach and Harnish review the 1970s debate about regularized forms of indirect speech acts in their chapter 9. They reject both the ambiguity thesis, which L&S endorse, and the conventions-of-use thesis, in favor of the view that, as with generalized implicatures, these forms enable hearers to make "streamlined inferences," compressed by precedent, thanks to the fact that they are standardized for the performance of indirect speech acts.

[19] Note that Austin subdivided the locutionary act into three aspects: "phonic," "phatic," and "rhetic" (1962: 92–3). When one utters a sentence, one intends to produce a series of sounds, which combine to form a piece of language with a certain syntactic and semantic structure.

they might have been clearer on the difference between understanding a sentence, recognizing a speaker's communicative intention in uttering it (that's uptake), and responding in further ways to the utterance. The last might involve cooperation, but many communicatively successful utterances elicit indifference or even resistance.

Inspired by Strawson and Searle, as well as by Grice, Bach and Harnish explain the notion of a communicative intention in terms of expressing an attitude (a belief, desire, appreciation, regret, or whatever). Expressing an attitude does not entail actually possessing that attitude. Rather, on our definition, "to express an attitude is reflexively to intend the hearer to take one's utterance as reason to think one has that attitude" (Bach and Harnish 1979: 15).[20] Correlatively, communicative success consists simply in the hearer recognizing what attitude (including its content) one is expressing. The fulfillment of other intentions one may have, such as hearer belief or compliance, requires the hearer to respond in some further way, but "the fulfillment of a communicative intention consists simply in its recognition" (ibid.). By isolating the purely communicative effect of an act of utterance, this formulation makes sense of Grice's idea that speaker meaning essentially involves a reflexive intention.

L&S's discussion of intention recognition and their complaint that Gricean approaches are inherently "prospective" completely overlooks the special status of intention recognition as the mark of communicative success. Their chapter 13, entitled "Interpretation and Intention Recognition," addresses the general role of intention recognition in collaboration and joint activity. Obviously it is often important to know what one's collaborators are doing, as when you're playing basketball or moving a piano, but intention recognition, though necessary for successful action in such cases, is generally not what successful action consists in. But with communication it is. That is why it is irrelevant for L&S to point out that "intention recognition turns out to be ubiquitous and heterogeneous" and to insist that "it is not a useful construct for getting clear on specific kinds of knowledge, reasoning, or effects in conversation [or] to characterize meaning" (201).

Similarly, when in their last chapter L&S play up the notion of "coordination on the conversational record" (256), they do not single out the specific sort of coordination that constitutes successful communication, namely coordination on the speaker's communicative intention. And when they invoke game theory (236ff), they do not mention the type of coordination game involved in linguistic communication. The best game analogy I can think of is Charades, in which one player uses gestures, facial expressions, and other bodily movements to help the other guess what she has in mind. Something like the reflexive intention involved in communication operates here, for part of what the first player intends the second player to take into account is the very fact that she intends her bodily movements to enable him to guess what she has in mind.

---

[20] Bach and Harnish develop a taxonomy of illocutionary acts classified in part by type of attitude expressed (1979: chapter 3). We distinguish the communicative (illocutionary) intention involved in expressing an attitude from further perlocutionary intentions to produce responses beyond uptake (understanding). For an overview of communication and speech acts, see Bach (2012: 148–55).

3.2 Conversation, Implicature, and Communication vs. Cooperation

Grice is best known for his theory of conversation, with its account of conversational implicature, but L&S misinterpret it, partly with the help of Grice himself. They often refer to implicatures as inferences (presumably things inferred, not processes of inferring them), e.g. when they describe "particularized CIs [as] creative nonce inferences" (59).[21] L&S generally seem not to appreciate that, just as implicating is something speakers do, implicatures are things speakers mean. If they did appreciate this, they would not repeatedly refer to Grice's Cooperative Principle and attendant maxims of conversation as "interpretive principles," especially considering that the maxims all pertain not to the hearer but to the speaker (in brief, be truthful, be informative, be relevant, and be perspicuous). L&S confuse the issue further by also describing them as "maxims of practical collaboration" (20) and as "principles of rationality," even though they pertain to communication in particular, not to whatever further aims interlocutors may pursue, whether or not collaborative (or even cooperative), that presuppose communicative success. L&S downplay the difference.

It is important to stress that interlocutors are often not cooperative, even when they communicate successfully. People can insult, accuse, deceive, manipulate, harass, and bully one another, and these are not exactly cooperative things to do. Unfortunately, Grice himself uses the language of cooperation, as in the phrase 'Cooperative Principle', but his theory really makes no sense unless interpreted to pertain specifically to communication. L&S do not appreciate this, instead emphasizing such things as the conversational record and "the principles of rational cooperation that govern conversation" (15).

Also, L&S mistakenly assume that the CP and the maxims come into play only when what the speaker means is distinct from the semantic content of what she utters. Grice's theory of conversation is better understood as a framework for making sense of communication in general rather than just a theory of conversational implicature. The CP and the maxims are meant to supplement the analysis of speaker meaning as communicative intention, that is, to identify possible considerations that the speaker intends the hearer to take into account, partly on the basis of taking her to intend him to take into account, in identifying what she means. Contrary to L&S's contention that the "CP and the four maxims provide standards for *purposeful* communication" (19), these are better understood as providing considerations relevant to achieving *successful* communication, purposeful or not.[22] They constrain what the speaker can utter in order to reasonably expect to make her communicative intention evident to the hearer and, complementarily, what the hearer can reasonably take the speaker's communicative

---

[21] The somewhat popular idea that implicatures are inferences is but one of many common misconceptions about conversational implicature. I identify what I take to be nine others in Bach (2005).

[22] For this reason I think they are better thought of as presumptions, and should be reformulated accordingly (Bach and Harnish 1979: 62–4). For example, the Cooperative Principle becomes the Communicative Presumption, to the effect that whenever a speaker says something, she does so with a communicative intention. This is only a presumption, of course, because she could be joking, reciting, rehearsing, or the like.

intention to be, given that, under the circumstances, she uttered what she did. Grice did not intend his theory as a psychological model of how people understand one another. So it is unfair to complain that his "overarching framework... can't be the whole story" (83). It was never intended to be.[23]

Finally, L&S seem to think that according to Grice, when speakers mean something distinct from what they say, by exploiting the CP and its attendant maxims, they "add additional layers of meaning to their utterances" (20), as if there is some one thing, an utterance, which has both an encoded conventional meaning and an additional meaning.[24] Otherwise, they would not speak of an utterance whose content allegedly goes beyond linguistically encoded meaning as "a pragmatically derived meaning that enriches and transforms whatever semantics is specified by grammar" (62). And they would not suggest that Grice's "interpretive principles" are supposed to "enrich or reinterpret the linguistically determined meaning" (148). Grice never suggests that an expression acquires an additional meaning when used to implicate something. Expression meaning is one thing, speaker meaning is another (of course, speakers don't *have* meanings). This is true even when, because the speaker is being literal and fully explicit, they happen to coincide. One is a fact about language, the other a fact about the speaker.

3.3 Red Herrings: Misinterpreting the Semantics/Pragmatics Distinction

Combining these points about meaning and implicature leads to a straightforward conclusion regarding what L&S describe as the "distinction between conventional semantics and inferential pragmatics" (40). By failing to appreciate what is distinctive about speaker meaning, the fact that conversational implicatures are things speakers mean, and that Grice's theory of conversation is not confined to implicatures, L&S construe the received version of the semantics/pragmatics distinction in a way that makes it easy to dismiss. As they construe it, it corresponds to two aspects of one thing, meaning. There is the linguistically determined aspect and the speaker-determined aspect, between which there is something sometimes referred to as the "semantics–pragmatics inter-face." But linguistic meaning is one thing and speaker meaning another. Like spelling, pronunciation, and syntax, linguistic meaning is a property of linguistic expressions. Speaker meanings are things speakers intend to communicate. This suggests that semantics and pragmatics have different subject matters. However, L&S apparently think that on the received view of the semantics/pragmatics distinction, semantics and pragmatics concern some one thing, utterance interpretation. This is suggested by

---

[23] For more on this interpretation of Grice's theory, including commentary on the widely cited passages (1989: 30–1) in which he spells out when a speaker "may be said to have implicated" something and why (and how) "the presence of a conversational implicature must be capable of being worked out," even if it is merely "intuitively grasped," see Bach (2012).

[24] This is illustrated by L&S's occasional equivocation on the word 'meaning', as when they complain that a Gricean approach "invites us to give parallel accounts of meaning whether it's conventionally encoded or improvised. In a conventional use, the hearer is getting some uptake of the literal meaning, but with an indirect use, the hearer is also getting uptake of some calculated meaning" (205).

their persistent use of the phrase 'utterance interpretation' (or 'interpretation' by itself). In fact, this phrase is semantically ambiguous. There is utterance interpretation in the sense of identifying the intended semantic content of what a speaker utters, and there is utterance interpretation in the sense of identifying what the speaker means (communicatively intends) in uttering it.

Once we appreciate that semantics and pragmatics have different subject matters, we can readily accept L&S's perfectly reasonable contention that the reach of semantics is not confined to expressions' contributions to truth-conditional contents. We can agree that many expressions (and constructions) introduce presuppositions, mark information structure, indicate illocutionary force, or specify how an utterance fits into a conversation. But this is not news to linguists or philosophers interested in language use. What L&S call "bare-bones" semantics is a red herring. Even when fully fleshed out, semantics still pertains to linguistic expressions, and not, or at least not directly, to the actions people perform in using them. That's the business of pragmatics. With their different subject matters, there's no problem of how to draw the line between them.

A second red herring is Grice's Modified Occam's Razor, "Senses are not to be multiplied beyond necessity" (1989: 47). This leaves open, as Grice himself makes clear, just what necessity requires. Suppose that L&S have made a plausible case (contra Szabó 2016) for the ambiguity of words like 'and', 'can', and 'looks', hence that the stronger uses of such words are not pragmatically derived but comprise distinct semantic senses. And suppose that L&S are right to claim that semantic ambiguity is even more rampant than most lexical semanticists already suppose. Even then, they would have no basis for maintaining that "pragmatics merely disambiguates" (94). They have offered no reason for supposing that speakers never attempt to communicate, much less succeed in communicating, anything distinct from (either in addition to or instead of) the semantic content of what they utter.

A further red herring arises from the supposition that successful communication requires what L&S call "public" or "shared" content between the interlocutors. This supposition is perfectly reasonable, but there is no basis for L&S's apparent assumption that content can be shared only if literally and explicitly expressed. As mentioned earlier, there is no requirement on any sentence that it be used literally. So, even if interlocutors share linguistic knowledge of a sentence's meaning, there is no guarantee that this determines what the speaker means in using it. Indeed, sometimes it is less than evident that a speaker means what she says even when she does; and sometimes it is perfectly obvious that a speaker means something she doesn't say. In short, content can be shared even if not semantically expressed and can fail to be shared even if it is semantically expressed.

Yet another red herring is the issue of indeterminacy in what speakers mean.[25] L&S stick Griceans with the assumption that what a speaker means, whether directly or by

---

[25] This is not to be confused with the hearer's uncertainty about what the speaker means or, for that matter, the speaker's uncertainty about what the hearer will think the speaker means.

implication, must be some determinate proposition. L&S mention that Grice allows for this possibility, as when he mentions the "indeterminacy that many actual implicata do in fact seem to possess" (1989: 40), but they suggest, without elaboration, that "this move comes with substantial costs" (22n). Later they suggest that when it is uncertain what a speaker is implicating, "this uncertainty gives implicatures an indefinite, open-ended character" (77). However, this may be compatible with a Gricean view. Indeed, as Buchanan (2010) has argued, it is often indeterminate, not merely uncertain, what a speaker means (at least if this must be a proposition) even when speaking directly and literally (though not fully explicitly).

The final enrollee in this school of red herrings is the issue of whether linguistic communication is governed by general interpretive principles (4) or by many differ-ent "mechanisms." L&S attribute to Grice and his followers (and even to some of his critics) the view that linguistic communication is governed by "general interpretive principles," aka "principles of rationality" (5), and involve "general pragmatic processes" (100). However, as we saw earlier, any sensible Gricean can agree with L&S that once we move from an overarching philosophical theory of conversation to psychological explanation, we should seek out "genuinely heterogeneous interpretive reasoning principles" (83) that explain how hearers manage to identify various kinds of conver-sational implicature. This does not suggest any reasons to abandon the semantics/pragmatics distinction.

To sum up, once we recognize that semantics has one subject matter, the meanings of linguistic expressions, and pragmatics has another, the actions and reactions of language users, we can grant that the scope of semantics is extensive and diverse and that the means by which utterances are interpreted are varied without having to abandon the semantics/pragmatic distinction.

4. Bottom Line

Lepore and Stone's two main claims are that linguistic communication, at least of the sort that requires intention recognition, can only be of what is conventionally encoded, and that when speakers use language in non-conventional, improvised ways, their intention is not to convey some specific identifiable thing but rather to invite the hearer into a bit of imaginative engagement. If these two complementary claims were correct, it would follow that no one ever attempts to communicate anything that isn't semantically encoded in what they utter, hence that in order to recognize a speaker's communicative intention (present only in fully literal speech), the addressee never has to do more than disambiguate the utterance, and that when imaginative interpretation is required, there is no communicative intention needing to be recognized. In other words, all speaker meanings are linguistic meanings, and all utterance interpretations that go beyond linguistic meanings, as opposed to those that merely select among linguistic meanings, aren't communicated or even intended to be. All this is wildly implausible.

L&S's effort to undermine the semantics/pragmatics distinction depends on neglecting or at least downplaying a number of other distinctions, including these:

- linguistic meaning vs. speaker meaning
- generalized vs. particularized implicature
- locutionary vs. illocutionary vs. perlocutionary acts (and intentions)
- communicative vs. perlocutionary success (uptake vs. impact)
- coordination vs. cooperation

It would have been undramatic for Lepore and Stone, as "exponents of the richness of human experience and the creativity of language" (v), merely to take an eclectic approach to linguistic meaning and to celebrate the diversity of language uses. It would not challenge the distinction between semantics and pragmatics to contend that linguistic conventions are more extensive and diverse than commonly supposed and that many non-literal utterances (and even literal ones) are made with no specific communicative intent behind them. That much would not have challenged the conventional wisdom that speakers can and often do intend to communicate things other than what they say. This less dramatic contention would still encourage further research into both the variety of linguistic phenomena that are governed or otherwise constrained by semantic conventions and the diverse kinds of utterances that people make even without fully communicative intentions. These would be empirical investigations conducted on a case-by-case basis. They would be motivated not by anti-Gricean doctrine that overgeneralizes from an assortment of special cases but instead by the intrinsic interest of the subject matter. Such investigations would clarify rather than mystify the role of intention and convention in speech acts.

References

Austin, J. L. (1962), *How to Do Things with Words*, J. O. Urmson and G. J. Warnock (eds.), Oxford: Oxford University Press.

Bach, Kent (1994), "Conversational impliciture," *Mind & Language* 9: 124–62.

Bach, Kent (1999a), "The semantics-pragmatics distinction: What it is and why it matters," in Ken Turner (ed.), *The Semantics-Pragmatics Interface from Different Points of View*, Oxford: Elsevier, pp. 65–84.

Bach, Kent (1999b), "The myth of conventional implicature," *Linguistics and Philosophy* 22: 327–66.

Bach, Kent (2005), "The top ten misconceptions about implicature," in Betty J. Birner and Gregory Ward (eds.), *Drawing the Boundaries of Meaning: Neo-Gricean Studies in Pragmatics and Semantics in Honor of Laurence R. Horn*, Amsterdam: John Benjamins, pp. 21–30.

Bach, Kent (2012), "Saying, meaning, and implicating," in Keith Allan and Kasia M. Jaszczolt (eds.), *The Cambridge Handbook of Pragmatics*, Cambridge: Cambridge University Press, pp. 47–68.

Bach, Kent and Robert M. Harnish (1979), *Linguistic Communication and Speech Acts*, Cambridge, MA: MIT Press.

Buchanan, Ray (2010), "A puzzle about meaning and communication," *Noûs* 44: 340–71.

Carston, Robyn (2016), "Linguistic conventions and the role of pragmatics," *Mind & Language* 31: 612–24.

Clapp, Lenny (2015), Review of *Imagination and Convention* by Ernie Lepore and Matthew Stone, *Notre Dame Philosophical Reviews*, 2015.8.21. http://ndpr.nd.edu/news/59984-imagination-and-convention-distinguishing-grammar-and-inference-in-language/

Grice, Paul (1989), *Studies in the Way of Words*, Cambridge, MA: Harvard University Press.

Harnish, Robert M. (1994), "Mood, meaning, and speech acts," in Savas L. Tshohadzis (ed.), *Foundations of Speech Act Theory*, London: Routledge, pp. 407–59.

Lambrecht, Knud (1994), *Information Structure and Sentence Form*, Cambridge: Cambridge University Press.

Lepore, Ernie and Matthew Stone (2015), *Imagination and Convention: Distinguishing Grammar and Inference in Language*, Oxford: Oxford University Press.

Searle, John R. (1969), *Speech Acts: An Essay in the Philosophy of Language*, Cambridge: Cambridge University Press.

Sperber, Dan and Deirdre Wilson (1986), *Relevance: Communication and Cognition*, Cambridge, MA: Harvard University Press.

Stainton, Robert J. (2006), *Words and Thoughts: Subsentences, Ellipsis, and the Philosophy of Language*, Oxford: Oxford University Press.

Strawson, P. F. (1964), "Intention and convention in speech acts," *Philosophical Review* 73: 439–60.

Szabó, Zoltán Gendler (2016), "In defense of indirect communication," *Inquiry* 59: 163–74.

3

Calculability, Convention, and Conversational Implicature

Wayne A. Davis

Imagination and Convention seeks to show that the traditional approach to meaning and interpretation inspired by Grice is fundamentally mistaken, and to provide a more fruitful alternative. In particular, Lepore and Stone argue that the Gricean way of distinguishing between semantics and pragmatics is misguided. They have no use for the notion of conversational implicature because meanings are not calculable. They draw these conclusions from the role of convention, imagination, and intention in meaning. Lepore and Stone differ from Grice on the intentions involved in meaning, and offer a Lewisian approach to conventions.

I believe that Lepore and Stone convincingly show that much meaning beyond what is said is not derived from general pragmatic principles, and that much more of it is conventional and imaginative than is acknowledged by Gricean, Neo-Gricean, and Relevance theories. Some of the conclusions Lepore and Stone draw, however, appear to throw the baby out with the bath water. I will argue that despite being non-calculable, a wide variety of implicatures are dependent on the speech context and not part of sentence meaning. Many, but not all of these are linguistic conventions. Conventions provide solutions to coordination problems, but are constituted not by mutual expectations, but by practices that perpetuate themselves in certain ways.

1. Are Any Implicatures Calculable?

Here are two familiar examples, adapted from Grice (1989: 32) and Horn (1984: 14).

(1)　Ann:　I'm out of gas.
　　　Bob:　There's a gas station around the corner.
　　　　　　B'_1:　Ann can get gas at the station around the corner.
(2)　Cal:　Who ate all the cookies?
　　　Dan:　Mickey ate some.
　　　　　　D'_1:　Mickey did not eat all of the cookies.

By saying what they did, it would be typical for Bob to have meant that Ann can get gas at the station around the corner, and Dan to have meant that Mickey did not eat all of the cookies. According to Grice, the fact that they meant what they did is calculable from what they said together with conversational principles and background assumptions. Grice used the Cooperative Principle: "Make your conversational contribution such as is required...by the accepted purpose or direction of the talk exchange in which you are engaged," which he took to be a particular instance of a general principle of rational action. The crucial premise in a Gricean derivation is that the speaker could not have been obeying the Cooperative Principle unless he believed and meant something other than what he said.

Griceans take the Cooperative Principle to entail "maxims," including Relation ("Be relevant"), Quantity ("Make your contribution as informative as required"), and Quality ("Make your contribution true"). They take B_1' to be derivable from Relation. The idea is that Bob's response would not be relevant to the purpose of the conversation unless Bob meant and believed that Ann can get gas at the station. Griceans take (2) to be derivable from Quantity. A typical derivation goes as follows:

Dan has said that Mickey ate some of the cookies. If Dan was in a position to make the stronger statement that Mickey ate all of the cookies, Cal's question required him to do so. Otherwise Dan would have violated the maxim of Quantity. Dan therefore must have believed and meant that Mickey did not eat all the cookies.

Neo-Griceans like Horn (1989) and Levinson (2000), and Relevance theorists like Sperber & Wilson (1986), also subscribe to calculability, while differing over the applicable conversational principles. Horn, for example, replaces Quantity and Relation with Q ("Say as much as you can") and R ("Say no more than you must").

I argued at some length in Davis (1998) that what speakers mean in cases like this is not derivable from conversational principles in the way Grice and others believe, and many of my arguments had well-known antecedents in the literature (e.g., Harnish 1976; Wilson & Sperber 1981). It is gratifying that others are now taking the baton and running with it.

1.1 The Symmetry Problem

If Quantity is applied to Bob's response the way it was applied to Dan's, we get the opposite of what Grice derived from Relation.

Bob has said that there is a gas station around the corner. If Bob was in a position to make the stronger statement that Ann could get gas at the station around the corner, Ann's statement required him to do so. Otherwise Bob would have violated the maxim of Quantity. Bob therefore must have believed and meant that Ann could *not* get gas at the station.

Similarly, it would be just as legitimate to reason that Dan must have meant that he *did* eat all the cookies, for otherwise his response would not be relevant. Grice's derivations "overgenerate." Since they lead to contradictory conclusions, they cannot be sound.

Lepore and Stone (2015: 143ff) call this the "symmetry" problem because the conflicting derivations have the same form.

The Gricean explanation of (2) is based on the fact that *Mickey ate all the cookies* is stronger and more informative than *Mickey ate some of the cookies*. This gives rise to another symmetry problem. There are countless other stronger statements, including *Mickey ate only some of the cookies* and *Mickey ate some but not all of the cookies*. But then the derivation from Quantity given above can be reapplied to give the opposite conclusion:

Dan has said that Mickey ate some of the cookies. If Dan was in a position to make the stronger statement that Mickey ate only some of the cookies, Cal's question required him to do so. Otherwise Dan would have violated the maxim of Quantity. Dan therefore must have believed and meant that Mickey did not eat only some the cookies. If Dan said that Mickey ate some and meant that Mickey did not eat only some, then he must have meant and believed that Mickey ate all of the cookies.

Another stronger statement is *Mickey ate a few cookies*. But *Mickey ate some cookies* is not related to *Mickey did not eat a few cookies* the way it is related to *Mickey did not eat all the cookies*. ⟨*Some, all*⟩ is what Horn (1989: §4.4) calls a quantitative "scale" in English, while ⟨*some, only some*⟩ and ⟨*some, few*⟩ are not. Given that these differences are not derivable from principles of conversation or rationality, Lepore and Stone correctly conclude that they reflect arbitrary conventions of English usage.

1.2 Conflicting Principles

Lepore and Stone (2015: §3.1) note that as formulated above—the way they are normally used to derive the implicatures in (1) and (2)—Horn's principles are directly opposed, making it impossible to actually calculate anything. But Lepore and Stone go on to say the following:

Horn's proposal is that general principles like Q and R CONSTRAIN pragmatic interpretation, but leave certain details open that must be specified on a case-by-case basis. The key is the mutual reference of Horn's principles. The Q principle isn't just "Say as much as you can"—it's say as much as you can GIVEN R. The R principle isn't just "Say no more than you must"—it's say no more than you must GIVEN Q. We have, in effect, a set of simultaneous equations that narrow the CIs [conversational implicatures] that might arise, but do not determine them fully. The balance between Q and R, the exact set of solutions that a language chooses to satisfy the two constraints, depends on further linguistic rules.   (Lepore & Stone 2015: 44)

This understates the problem. In saying that the "simultaneous equations" constrain the conversational implicatures, Lepore and Stone are assuming that the equations have a solution. Not all simultaneous equations do. Consider:

(3) $x = y + 1$.
(4) $y = x + 1$.

Given that Horn's Q and R without the mutual reference clauses make opposed predictions, they cannot have a solution any more than (3) and (4) do. With the mutual reference clauses, Q and R are like:

(5) $x = y + 1$ given (6).
(6) $y = x + 1$ given (5).

There is still no solution. It is hard to see how the symbol sequences comprising (5) and (6) could even express propositions: given their mutual references, we cannot know what (5) says without knowing what (6) says, and vice versa. On pain of contradiction they cannot both express true propositions.

The suggestion that general conversational principles constrain interpretations without determining a unique interpretation better fits Grice's principles. Here are two other possibilities for example (2):

D'_2:   Mickey ate all the cookies.
D'_3:   Mickey may not have eaten all the cookies.

All three contributions could provide additional relevant information. We cannot know which contribution is truthful without knowing what Dan believes. The goal was to calculate what Dan had to believe given what he said, but the conversational principles do not tell us what Dan had to believe. The point Lepore and Stone stress is that D'_1 and D'_3 would be conventional interpretations, but D'_2 would not be. This is a fact about the use of English. Since there is no non-linguistic reason why "NP V not all N" and "NP may not V all N" but not "NP V all N" are commonly meant by saying "NP V some N," the practice is to some extent arbitrary, not dictated by rationality.

Lepore and Stone (43–4) note that propositions stronger than what was said are meant in other cases. Consider another example from Horn (1984: 15):

(7)   Eve: John was able to solve the problem.
         E'_1:   John did not solve the problem.
         E'_2:   John did solve the problem.
         E'_3:   John may not have solved the problem.

Given what Eve said in (7), it would be natural for Eve to have meant that John *did* solve the problem (E'_2), rather than E'_1 or E'_3. It is hard to see how those results could be obtained from any principles that yield the opposite results for (2). The pairing of meanings with forms again appears to be arbitrary and conventional.

Grice's principles do conflict with other norms of conversation, such as the principle of Politeness ("Be Polite") stressed by Leech (1983). Suppose Mary asks John how she looks. Quantity and Quality may require him to say "Terrible." The desire to be polite might nonetheless lead him to say "Wonderful!"

1.3 The Possibility of Figurative Speech

After describing a tall and boxy building in New York that stands out in its neighborhood and that galvanized the neighborhood to change its zoning restrictions, Lepore and Stone (192) note that Fay's utterance could be interpreted literally, sarcastically, metaphorically, or ironically:

(8)   Fay: That building is a landmark.
         F: That building is a prominent object that serves as a navigation guide.
         F'_1:   That building is an eyesore.
         F'_2:   That building marked a turning point in neighborhood history.
         F'_3:   That building is totally nondescript.

These are all things Fay could have meant in a typical conversation. But none of the interpretations is required by the purposes of the conversation because the other interpretations are also consistent with those purposes. They are all things the speaker could have cooperatively contributed. In the same vein, Dan could mean D'_2 by engaging in understatement, or D'_4 by engaging in irony.

   D'_4:   Mickey ate none of the cookies.

Grice thought figures of speech illustrated the "flouting" of conversational principles, wherein some maxim is violated at the level of what is said, but observed at the level of what is implicated. He provided the following examples, with illustrative "glosses."

> *Irony.*   X, with whom A has been on close terms until now, has betrayed a secret of A's to a business rival. A and his audience both know this. A says *X is a fine friend.* (Gloss: It is perfectly obvious to A and his audience that what A has said or made as if to say is something he does not believe, and the audience knows that A knows that this is obvious to the audience. So, unless A's utterance is entirely pointless, A must be trying to get across some other proposition than the one he purports to be putting forward. This must be some obviously related proposition; the most obviously related proposition is the contradictory of the one he purports to be putting forward. (Grice 1989: 34)

> *Metaphor.*   Examples like *You are the cream in my coffee* characteristically involve categorical falsity, so the contradictory of what the speaker has made as if to say will, strictly speaking, be a truism; so it cannot be *that* that such a speaker is trying to get across. The most likely supposition is that the speaker is attributing to his audience some feature or features in respect of which the audience resembles (more or less fancifully) the mentioned substance. (Grice 1989: 34)

Lepore and Stone (38–9) observe that while the obvious falsity of what these speakers said may be a signal *that* they mean something else, it does not tell us *what* they meant. It should be obvious on reflection that what Grice thought they meant was not *required* by the purpose of the conversation. To see that there are many alternatives, note that the symmetry problem arises again. If the second speaker is attributing to his audience some feature in which he resembles the cream in his coffee, why couldn't the first speaker be attributing to X some feature in which he resembles a fine friend? Grice thinks the fact that the contradictory of what the speaker said in the second case is a truism blocks that interpretation, but why is the ironic interpretation of the first example not similarly blocked by its obvious truth? Moreover, other cases of metaphor do not involve categorical falsity. I might say *You are a maestro* to a chef to convey that his cooking skills are like those of a great conductor. Why, given Gricean principles, should this be more likely than that I intended to convey "the most obviously related proposition," that you are not a great conductor? Finally, there is also the possibility that the speaker in Grice's cream example is engaging in *ironic metaphor*, meaning that his audience does *not* resemble the cream in his coffee in certain respects.

Here is another point to ponder. If being a cooperative speaker is compatible with saying something false and thereby violating Quality, why is it incompatible with not thereby *implicating* what is required to be cooperative? Why would it not suffice for the speaker to go on to *say* what is required? Indeed, this is often what happens when people are joking around. They might say something false that startles or shocks their audience, and after savoring that experience add "Just kidding." From the fact that their joke violates Quality, we cannot infer that they must have meant something true by saying what they did.

1.4 Other Possible Implicatures

Despite the arguments we have been presenting, Lepore and Stone say at one point that, in some cases, the alleged implicature *is* something the speaker is required to believe and mean if he is to be cooperative. Their case is like example (2) except that Cal asks a yes–no question: *Did Mickey eat all the cookies*?

Unless we recognize 'Mickey ate some' as contributing that Mickey ate some but not all of the cookies, we can't take it as answering Cal's question, even partially. The utterance wouldn't make sense in context.   (Adapted from Lepore & Stone 2015: 142)

Lepore and Stone believe this is required, not by conversational principles, but by "grammar." For they believe *some* must be marked intonationally for contrast, the contrast being with *all* (145). But this is still too much like the Gricean explanation. Contrastive stress would not be required if Cal were engaging in understatement or irony. Indeed, stress on *some* blocks the understatement or irony implicatures D'_2 and D'_4. But it does not block the epistemic implicature D'_3. Dan could perfectly well have answered *Did Mickey eat all the cookies?* by saying *Mickey ate some of the cookies, but he may not have eaten all of them*. He could just as well have answered by saying *Mickey ate some of the cookies* and implicating *Mickey may not have eaten all of them*. One can also answer a question by saying or implicating "I don't know." It should be noted too that *some* can be used to implicate *not all* even when the speaker is not answering a question. That is another case in which contrastive stress is not required.

1.5 Detachability

Grice said that if implicatures are calculable, they must be "non-detachable." But he then added an exception contradicting that claim:

Insofar as the calculation that a particular conversational implicature is present requires, besides contextual and background information, only a knowledge of what has been said..., and insofar as the manner of expression plays no role in the calculation, it will not be possible to find another way of saying the same thing, which simply lacks the implicature in question, except where some special feature of the substituted version is itself relevant to the determination of an implicature (in virtue of one of the maxims of Manner).   (Grice 1989: 39)

Grice's exception is motivated by the fact that the temporal and causal implicatures of (9)(a) and (b) are reversed.

(9)   (a)   Oil prices doubled and demand for consumer goods plunged.
       (b)   Demand for consumer goods plunged and oil prices doubled.
       (c)   Oil prices have doubled and demand for consumer goods has plunged.

(9)(a) implicates that the doubling of oil prices preceded and caused[1] the plunge of demand; (9)(b) implicates that the plunge of demand preceded and caused the doubling of oil prices. The two sentences clearly differ in syntax, but they do not seem to differ in meaning. So the causal and temporal implicatures appear to be detachable. Grice claims that the implicatures are derived from the maxim of Manner ("Be orderly"), which he takes to imply that conjuncts must be presented in order from earliest to latest. However, forward narrative order is not the only way to be orderly. Moreover, if calculability means deriving an implicature from what is said, the order of the words in the sentence uttered should not matter unless it affects the meaning of the sentence. So Grice's exception seems unwarranted, and his derivations in this case are invalid.

Lepore and Stone (96–7, 117) bypass the order question by using (9)(c), in which the conjuncts are in the same order as in (9)(a). They claim that the aspect difference between (9)(a) and (c) "seems not to carry any truth-conditional contrast." Yet (9)(c) also lacks the temporal and causal implicatures of (9)(a). There is a problem with this argument. While (9)(a) and (c) are very close in meaning, they are not completely equivalent. For one thing, only (9)(a) is compatible with *but the levels have returned to where they were*. Lepore and Stone's (§§7.2–7.3) insightful observation, that the aspect differences impose different constraints on the temporal interpretations of the verbs in (9)(a) and (c), also shows that they are not synonymous. So this pair does not clearly show detachability. I believe it is further evidence of non-calculability, though, for the difference in meaning and truth conditions between (9)(a) and (c) is irrelevant to the causal and temporal implicature. The difference in implicature cannot be derived from the difference in meaning.

There are clearer examples of detachability.

(10)   (a)   John fell and broke his collarbone.
        (b)   John both fell and broke his collarbone.

---

[1] Lepore and Stone do not discuss the causal implicature. It cannot be accounted for by their discussion of anaphora and tense in §7.2.

(10) (a) and (b) clearly have the same truth conditions and seem completely synonymous. Nevertheless, (10)(a) has the temporal and causal implicature, but (10)(b) does not. Similarly, *John was able to solve the problem* in (7) seems synonymous with *John was capable of solving the problem* and *John could have solved the problem*, but only the first implicates that John did solve the problem. We can thus sustain Lepore and Stone's conclusion that in some cases a sentence has an implicature because of an arbitrary convention connecting it to the particular sentence form.

The facts presented in this section do not exhaust the case against calculability, as we shall see. While highly attractive to social scientists, the idea that implicatures can be explained and predicted using conversational principles must be abandoned.

2. Are There Any Conversational Implicatures?

From their arguments against calculability, Lepore and Stone appear to conclude that there are few, if any, conversational implicatures. They say that "the empirical considerations of Part II seem to substantially diminish the scope of CI" (148). And referring to all the "interpretive effects" discussed in Part II, they say "If we are right, these effects are not CIs" (154). In other places, they only conclude that "the category of conversational implicature does no theoretical work" (83).

> Put most starkly: we have no use for a category of conversational implicatures, as traditionally and currently understood.   (6)

We thus have two questions. Does the conclusion that calculability claims fail entail that there are no conversational implicatures? If not, does it entail that conversational implicatures are not theoretically important?

The answer depends on how the technical term 'conversational implicature' is defined. Lepore and Stone begin with the following:

> (11)   In brief, a conversational implicature (CI) is a contribution associated with an utterance that the speaker does not explicitly say but that can be CALCULATED from what the speaker does say on the assumption that her utterance is a reasonable way for her to advance the purposes of the conversation. (Lepore & Stone 2015: 2)

This definition is adapted from the characterization of conversational implicature offered by Grice (1989: 30–1), which is widely accepted in the literature.[2] If (11) is the definition of 'conversational implicature', then it follows from the arguments of section 1 that 'There are no conversational implicatures' is true. Nothing a speaker contributes to a conversation is such that making that contribution is required by conversational principles. There are too many other ways to advance the purposes of a conversation.

---

[2] See Harnish (1976: 333); Bach & Harnish (1979: xvii, 6); Wilson & Sperber (1981: 160); Levinson (1983: 113; 2000: 15); Neale (1992: 527); Green (1995: 98); Saul (2010: 170).

It is not clear, though, that (11) is best regarded as a stipulative definition of 'conversational implicature' rather than a theoretical characterization of a category of implicature identified independently of calculability. Grice first introduces the general term 'implicature,' and then divides its extension into at least two species. 'Implicature' is introduced as follows:

Suppose that A and B are talking about a mutual friend, C, who is now working in a bank. A asks B how C is getting on in his job, and B replied, *Oh quite well, I think; he likes his colleagues, and he hasn't been to prison yet.* At this point, A might well inquire what B was implying, what he was suggesting, or even what he meant by saying that C had not yet been to prison. The answer might be any one of such things as that C is the sort of person likely to yield to the temptation provided by his occupation...It is clear that whatever B implied, suggested, meant in this example, is distinct from what B said, which was simply that C had not been to prison yet. I wish to introduce, as terms of art, the verb *"implicate"* and the related nouns "implicature" (cf. implying) and "implicatum" (cf. what is implied). The point of this maneuver is to avoid having, on each occasion, to choose between this or that member of the family of words for which "implicate" is to do general duty.   (Grice 1989: 24)

Grice is clearly stipulating that 'implicature' is to denote cases in which what is meant, implied, or suggested is distinct from what is said. This definition, or something close to it, has been adopted widely.[3] I make some changes to simplify the definition and make it better accord with how Grice and others actually use the term. First, Grice only applied the term 'implicature' to cases in which the speaker expressed the belief that something is the case. Saying "Given his fancy new car, perhaps C stole some of the money" counts as suggesting that he did, but not as implicating that he did. Second, 'mean that p' can mean either expressing the belief that p or directly expressing the belief that p. 'Imply that p' means indirectly expressing the belief that p: expressing the belief that one thing is the case by expressing the belief that another is. So we can cover all the cases with *mean* in the inclusive sense. Third, the meaning and the saying are not independent: an implicature is something meant *by* saying something else. If B meant that C is the sort of person likely to yield to the temptation provided by working in a bank, he did so by saying that C hasn't been to prison yet, not by saying that C likes his colleagues. Yogi Berra famously meant that Texas had a lot of electoral votes when he said that Texas had a lot of electrical votes. This is not a case of implicature because what he meant was not a result of what he said. He meant that Texas had a lot of elect-oral votes by uttering the sentence 'Texas has a lot of electrical votes' *despite* the fact that he thereby said that Texas has a lot of electrical votes. This gives us:

(12)   Speaker S implicates that p iff S means (expresses the belief) that p by saying that something else is the case.

---

[3] See, for example, Harnish (1976: 325); Sadock (1978: 365); Gazdar (1979: 38); Levinson (1983: 97; 2000: 13ff); Leech (1983: 9); Horn (1989: 145ff); Neale (1992: 519, 528); Bach (1994a: 144); Horn (2004: 4); Davis (2007: §I; 2014: 1–2).

Thus defined, implicature is a type of indirect speech act, one that is extremely common. (1), (2), (7), (8), and (9) are all typical examples. In (1), for example, Bob did not say that Ann can get gas at the station around the corner. He meant that by saying that there is a gas station around the corner. So Bob implicated that Ann can get gas at the station around the corner. The speech acts of saying that p and implicating that p have the same content; they differ in the way that content is expressed.

Grice's next move is to distinguish two types of implicature.

> In some cases the conventional meaning of the words used will determine what is implicated, besides helping to determine what is said. If I say (smugly), *He is an Englishman; he is, therefore, brave*, I have certainly committed myself, by virtue of the meaning of my words, to its being the case that his being brave is a consequence of (follows from) his being an Englishman. But while I have said that he is an Englishman, and said that he is brave, I do not want to say that I have *said* (in the favored sense) that it follows from his being an Englishman that he is brave, though I have certainly indicated, and so implicated, that this is so...So *some* implicatures are conventional, unlike the one with which I introduced this discussion of implicature.
>
> (Grice 1989: 25–6)

Grice (1989: 32–7) later presents many other examples of implicature that are like the one with which he opened the discussion, including a British variant of example (1), an ignorance implicature, and various figures of speech including irony and metaphor. These examples are all non-conventional in Grice's sense: the implicatures are not determined by the meaning of the sentence used, and are dependent on features of the speech context. Hence the implicatures are cancelable either explicitly or implicitly. In example (1), the speaker could have canceled the implicature by adding "But it is not open." The usual *not-all* implicature of 'Some of the fish are dead' would be canceled implicitly if the speaker and hearer were both staring at a tankful of clearly dead fish. Grice could not have canceled his consequence implicature by saying "But being brave does not follow from being English"; that would have been incoherent. And nothing could implicitly cancel it. This yields what I believe to be the definition of 'conversational implicature' that reflects the actual use of most linguists and philosophers:

(13) A conversational implicature is an implicature that depends on features of the speech context and is not part of the meaning of the sentence used.

Speech acts satisfying this definition are ubiquitous, as illustrated by (1), (2), (7), (8), and (9).

Grice, however, proceeds in a different way:

> I wish to represent a certain subclass of nonconventional implicatures, which I shall call *conversational* implicatures, as being essentially connected with certain general features of discourse... (Grice 1989: 26)

As the next five pages make clear, by 'essentially connected with certain general features of discourse,' Grice means "calculable from general conversational principles."

I am now in a position to characterize the notion of conversational implicature. A man who, by (in, when) saying…that p has implicated that q, may be said to have conversationally implicated that q, provided that (1) he is to be presumed to be observing the conversational maxims, or at least the Cooperative Principle; (2) the supposition that he is aware that, or thinks that, q is required in order to make his saying…p (or doing so in *those* terms) consistent with this presumption… (Grice 1989: 30–1)

This, of course, is the characterization Lepore and Stone adapted in (11). What is doubtful, to me at least, is that Grice intended this to be a merely stipulative definition, rather than a bold empirical hypothesis about what examples like (1), (2), (7), (8), and (9) have in common, which the implicatures he called "conventional" lack.

The evidence that leads me to say that linguists and philosophers actually use (13) is illustrated by Horn in his candid moments. Horn readily acknowledges how difficult it is to show how conversational implicatures can be calculated. When he does so, however, he does not even entertain the possibility that his examples of non-conventional implicatures are not conversational implicatures after all. Consider what Horn says when he confronts the clash of his Q and R principles:

[W]e must produce an algorithm for computing which of the two opposed principles and inference strategies prevails in a given discourse context; this issue has been addressed…but not definitively solved. Maxim clash, for example, arises notoriously readily in indefinite contexts.

(Horn 1989: 196)

One of Horn's examples is from Grice (1989: 32):

(14) Gil: Where does C live?
      Hal: Somewhere in the south of France.
          H'_1: I do not know where in the south of France C lives.
          H'_2: C lives somewhere in the south of France that I shouldn't mention.
          H'_3: C does not live in Nice.

(14) Horn says that H'_1 is a possible Q implicature while H'_2 is a possible R implicature. H'_3 is a different Q implicature. Despite acknowledging his inability to say how we could derive any of these, given that Q and R clash, Horn does not even consider reclassifying these as non-conversational implicatures.

3. Are Generalized Implicatures Conversational?

Grice (1989: 37–8) noted an important difference between the implicatures illustrated by (1) and (2). B'_1 is a *particularized* implicature, whereas D'_1 is *generalized*. Bob's use of 'There's a station around the corner' to implicate that Ann can get gas there depended on special features of their context, including the fact that Bob is speaking to Ann, and that Ann said she is out of gas. Such an implicature is not common when saying that there is a station around the corner. Nothing in the sentence itself signals this implicature. In contrast, 'Mickey ate some of the cookies' would typically be used to implicate that Mickey did not eat all of them. Sentences containing *some* are commonly used with a *not all* implicature in a wide variety of contexts. Sentences containing 'some' *can* be used with other implicatures. For example, 'Mickey ate some of the cookies' could be used to mean that he ate none (irony) or even all (understatement), or that Jeannie did not eat some (natural in a context in which Cal suspected that either Mickey or Jeannie ate the cookies). But those implicatures are not associated with a specific feature of the sentence, and are not commonly conveyed when the form is used.[4] They are "particularized."

I have argued that a generalized conversational implicature is conventional in the same sense that lexical and driving conventions are.[5] It is a "practice established by general consent or usage; custom" (*Webster's Encyclopedic Unabridged Dictionary*). In more detail, conventions are common practices that perpetuate themselves by precedent, social acceptance, habit and association, traditional transmission from one generation to another, and their success in serving common purposes such as communication and avoiding collisions. And as Lepore and Stone stress, generalized implicatures are arbitrary; recall the symmetry and detachability problems noted in section 1 above. They are not as arbitrary as lexical or syntactic conventions, but there are alternative practices that would have served the purposes of communication and could have perpetuated themselves in the same way. Knowledge of generalized implicatures is essential to complete mastery of a natural language. It is picked up from other speakers in the process of learning a language the way lexical and syntactic knowledge is. Without knowledge of generalized implicatures, hearers will not fully understand speakers, and speakers are liable to be misunderstood. Consequently, a complete description of a language must catalog its generalized implicatures. A complete description of English, for example, must record that *some* is related to *many* and *most*, but not *a few* or *half*, the way it is related to *all*. Horn scales are useful for this purpose.

The temporal and causal implicatures of (9) are also generalized implicatures. Lepore and Stone (39) say that "speakers normally would succeed in contributing implicated content with such utterances" because "They are delivered by conventional rules."

Perhaps the conclusion should be that the devices for conventional implicatures are more pervasive and flexible than has hitherto been recognized.   (Lepore & Stone 2015: 149)

Given that Grice distinguished conversational implicatures from conventional implicatures, it might seem to follow that generalized implicatures are not conversational, despite what Grice and his followers have said. I have taken great pains to show that this inference would be a fallacy of equivocation. As discussed in section 2 above, Grice called an implicature "conventional" provided the implicature is part of the

---

[4] Lepore and Stone (145) observe that focal stress is often used to signal one implicature rather than another. For example, focal stress on *Mickey* rules out the *not all* implicature. But it does not rule in the *not Jeannie* implicature; Dan might have had someone else in mind. Moreover, focal stress is not necessary, as written sentences make clear. And it often has other functions.

[5] See Davis 1998: chs. 5–6; 2003: ch. 9; 2014: §2; 2016: §4.

conventional meaning of the sentence used and does not depend on features of the conversational context. *Conventional implicatures in Grice's sense are determined by the conventions that give sentences their linguistic meanings.* This is not true of the *not all* implicature of *some* or the *and consequently* implicature of *and*. Speakers can use 'Mickey ate some of the cookies' with its conventional meaning but without implicating that Mickey did not eat all of the cookies. Generalized implicatures like this are cancelable, unlike implicatures that are conventional in Grice's sense. Nonetheless, it is conventional (customary) to use an affirmative sentence 'Σ(some)' containing *some* with its usual meaning to implicate the proposition expressed by 'Σ(not all),' the sentence obtained from 'Σ(some)' by replacing *some* with *not all*. And the use of 'Mickey ate some of the cookies' to implicate that Mickey did not eat all of the cookies is an instance of that practice. So this implicature is, in an ordinary but non-Gricean sense, a conventional conversational implicature. Dan's conversational implicature in the gas example is conventional in neither sense.

The conventions that give sentences their meanings are not the only linguistic conventions. Conversational implicature conventions are secondary conventions in that they depend on the primary semantic conventions. 'Mickey ate some of the cookies' implicates that Mickey did not eat all of them because it is conventional to use a sentence of the form 'Σ(some)' to *say* that Σ(some) and thereby *mean* that Σ(not all). This convention depends on the meaning of *some* and the fact that 'Mickey ate some of the cookies' means that Mickey ate some of the cookies. In my view, *some* means "some" because speakers conventionally use *some* to mean (or directly express the idea or mental representation) "some" (and hearers conventionally interpret speakers as meaning "some" by 'some'). Sentences have implicatures because they have certain meanings, and because sentences with a particular form are conventionally used to perform an indirect speech act: meaning something else by meaning and saying what the sentence means. The implicatures Grice called conventional are a part of the meaning of the sentence. The primary semantic conventions attach them to words like *but* and *therefore* and the sentences containing them.

Linguistic conventions can thus do more than attach meanings to sentences. They can also attach conversational implicatures to sentences. As Lepore and Stone put it,

The rules of language are NOT exhausted by a bare-bones semantics.   (5)

Lepore and Stone go on to conclude that "linguistic meaning is broader in scope than Grice imagined" (6). This conclusion does not follow if 'linguistic meaning' denotes word meaning. Sentences do not mean what they conversationally implicate. *Mickey ate some of the cookies* does not have "Mickey did not eat all of the cookies" as one of its meanings, and does not mean that even when speakers mean it by uttering the sentence. But instead of concluding that there are rules of language other than semantic rules, Lepore and Stone broaden the definition of semantics.

Semantics, on our view, can be taken to include all the linguistic information that we use to recover the content that speakers contribute to a conversation through their utterances.   (265)

Hearers use their knowledge that it is conventional for speakers uttering sentences of the form 'Σ(some)' to mean "Σ(not all)" to figure out what speakers like Dan mean. But there is no reason to conclude that this is semantic information: that rule tells us nothing about what sentences containing *some* mean.

4. Is All Meaning Determined by Convention?

In several places, Lepore and Stone appear to maintain that meaning is determined by convention. That premise may seem to lead directly to the conclusion that there are no conversational implicatures. One reason such an argument is problematic was noted in section 3: by definition, conversational implicatures cannot be conventional implicatures in Grice's sense (implicatures determined by sentence meaning), but they can be conventional in the sense of customary, as generalized conversational implicatures show. We will see in this section that the premise is problematic too.

Here are some of the passages suggesting that Lepore and Stone would answer "Yes" to the question heading this section.

Language settles the contributions we make to conversation, much more than Grice imagined... There are no special meanings, over and above the meanings of our utterances, that interlocutors infer by calculation from a Cooperative Principle... (199)

[O]n our view, meaning is a matter of conventions, and listeners normally recover the meanings of utterances by recognizing the conventions involved, not by reasoning about the speaker in any deeper sense. For example, interpreting the use of the word *I*, we know from the rules of language that the word picks out the speaker—regardless of whatever intentions its user might have. (199)

Grice's theory is that the speaker intentions determine the meanings of utterances, in a very particular way...By contrast,...we will recommend [that] the speaker's intentions determine the meaning of an utterance by linking it up with the relevant conventions. We call our view DIRECT INTENTIONALISM. (200)

These claims are problematic, however, because of a distinction Lepore and Stone generally seem to accept: the distinction between word meaning and speaker meaning. All word and sentence meaning is conventional, but not all speaker meaning is conventional. Moreover, what words and sentences mean or implicate on particular occasions is not determined by any conventions.

4.1 Particularized Implicatures

In (1), the distinction between word and speaker meaning is clear:

(15)　(a)　By uttering 'There's a gas station around the corner,' Bob meant that Ann can get gasoline at the station around the corner. (True)

　　　(b)　The sentence Bob uttered does not mean that Ann can get gasoline at the station around the corner. (True)

Given the conventions of English, *There's a gas station around the corner* does not express a proposition about Ann, and does not entail that anything is open. Nonetheless, (15)(a) is true: Bob, the speaker, expressed the belief that Ann can get gas at the station around the corner. Lepore and Stone are correct in concluding that what the speaker meant in this case cannot be calculated from what the sentence means and any conversational principles, and rightly reject Grice's account of the intentions that constitute speaker meaning. But it is also true that there is no linguistic convention connecting what Bob meant with what the sentence Bob uttered means. So this is a case of meaning (speaker meaning) that is not conventional meaning. It is a clear case of conversational implicature as defined by (13).

Lepore and Stone's account of how a speaker decides how to express a particular thought is overly simple given the alternative ways there are of expressing it.

Finally, there is no mystery on this view about how a speaker chooses what to say . . . she arrives at a commitment to contribute some content P to the conversation. She works through her grammar and her background knowledge about meaning, and infers that a particular sentence S means P and will do the work that she wants to contribute P to the conversation . . . moreover, she can derive a grammatical analysis of a particular sentence S which associates it with the meaning so represented. That makes saying S the right thing to do.   (213)

In the gas example, Bob decided to contribute B'_1, "Ann can get gasoline at the station around the corner" to the conversation. But Bob did *not* utter a sentence S meaning B'_1. Bob decided to utter a sentence meaning B_1 "There is a gasoline station around the corner" instead. Lepore and Stone describe just one way a speaker can choose to contribute a content to the conversation: by saying and asserting it. A speaker can equally properly implicate the same thing rather than saying it. That choice is not determined by convention. Both modes of expression are conventional.

4.2 Malapropisms

Malapropisms provide even clearer cases in which what a speaker means is not conventional.

(16)   Yogi: Texas has a lot of electrical votes.
   (a)   Yogi meant that Texas has a lot of electoral votes. (True)
   (b)   Yogi did not say that Texas has a lot of electoral votes. (True)
   (c)   'Texas has a lot of electrical votes' does not mean that Texas has a lot of electoral votes. (True)

Yogi's utterance was a malapropism because (16)(b) and (c) are true as well as (a). Here is Lepore and Stone's response, reworded to fit this example.

In cases such as (16), the Gricean view has difficulty distinguishing among the various commitments the speaker has made. The speaker of (16) intends to contribute that Texas has a lot of electoral votes, and he also intends to contribute the conventional meaning of what he said, which is in fact that Texas has a lot of electrical votes. We seem to be equally justified in reporting the situation with either perspective. Of course, following Kripke [1977] among others, we can appeal to the fact that one meaning, but not another, is conventionally encoded: we can talk about what the sentence means as opposed to what the speaker meant...But what we cannot do is privilege convention in attributing meaning to the speaker...Direct intentionalism lets us characterize a speaker as meaning something that she didn't think she intended.

(After Lepore & Stone 2015, 218–19)

Lepore and Stone appear to be implying, uncharitably, that what Yogi actually meant is that Texas has a lot of electrical votes. If Yogi had meant that, then his utterance would not have been a malapropism. He would have properly expressed the belief that Texas has a lot of electrical votes, something only an idiot would believe. Yogi often said the wrong thing, but he was no idiot. It would be very bad form to criticize Yogi on the grounds that votes cannot be electrical. He was not lying or joking either. Yogi's mistake was to say what he did not mean. Malapropisms and slips of the tongue are only possible if something can be meant unconventionally.[6]

Lepore and Stone say that the Gricean has no basis for saying whether (17)(a) or (b) is true.

(17)   (a)   Yogi contributed that Texas has a lot of electrical votes. (?)
       (b)   Yogi contributed that Texas has a lot of electoral votes. (?)

There is no reason to think the Gricean should be able to say. For 'contribute that p' is not a meaningful or even grammatical form in English. We need to distinguish two questions.

(18)   (a)   What proposition did Yogi contribute to the conversation?
       (b)   What was Yogi's contribution to the conversation?
             (i)   Yogi said that Texas has a lot of electrical votes. (True)
             (ii)   Yogi meant that Texas has a lot of electoral votes. (True)

Sentence (18)(b) has a clear enough meaning in standard English. To answer it, we need to say *both* (i) and (ii). We cannot give a complete description of what Yogi did without saying both. Sentence (18)(a) does not have a meaning in standard English. To answer it, we need to know what it is to contribute a proposition. Following Lewis (1979) and Thomason (1990), Lepore and Stone (248) stipulate that 'conversational record' denotes "an abstraction that tracks the interlocutor's contributions to the conversation," and that "the conversational record must track the COMMITMENTS of the interlocutors to the information that characterizes what they are doing in the conversation." Yogi was surely not committed to the proposition that Texas has electrical votes. The belief he expressed was that Texas has electoral votes. If we are committed only to what we *assert*, then Yogi is committed to *neither* proposition. Asserting that p requires both saying and meaning that p. Note that neither the proposition that Texas

---

[6] Not all malapropisms are slips of the tongue, in which the speaker does not say what he intended to say. Yogi's mistake would not have been a verbal slip if he never noticed the difference between *electoral* and *electrical*, or thought *electrical* means "electoral."

has electrical votes nor the proposition that Texas has electoral votes "characterizes what Yogi was doing in the conversation." (18)(i) and (ii) are the propositions that do that.

Consider now a different question Lepore and Stone pose:

(19)   What did Yogi's utterance mean?
    (a)   Yogi's utterance meant that Texas has a lot of electrical votes. (?)
    (b)   Yogi's utterance meant that Texas has a lot of electoral votes. (?)

In everyday English we regularly talk about what speakers and sentences mean, but we do not often talk about what utterances mean. 'Utterance' typically means the act of uttering words, but can also mean the words uttered. When 'utterance' has its act meaning, the only sense that 'Utterance u means that p' has in English is what Grice (1989: 213–14) called the *natural* sense, on which 'means' is closely related to 'indicates' and 'makes it likely', but is factive. In this sense, (19)(a) and (b) are incompatible and both false. Yogi's utterance meant naturally that he once again misused English: we can infer that Yogi again misused English from the fact that his utterance occurred. If his utterance were not a verbal slip, it might have meant that he had a self-deprecating sense of humor. *Bob's utterance in (1) means that there is gas at the station around the corner* would tell us that we can infer that there is gas at the station from the fact that Bob's utterance occurred. This is clearly not the sense Lepore and Stone have in mind, so presumably by 'utterance' in sentences like (19) they mean a word, phrase, or sentence uttered. In that sense, (19)(a) is true and (b) is false. But if we only know what utterances mean in this sense, we cannot know that Yogi's utterance was a malapropism, or an assertion. We also have to know what Yogi meant. Understanding the words uttered is not sufficient for the more important purpose of understanding speakers. And it is often unnecessary. We often don't even notice typos, for example, and focus entirely on what the writer meant.

4.3 Word Meaning on an Occasion

In the second passage from page 199 quoted above, Lepore and Stone say that "listeners normally recover the meanings of utterances by recognizing the conventions involved, not by reasoning about the speaker in any deeper sense." Recall dialogue (1). *Gas* has at least two meanings in English, "gasoline" and "natural gas." So (1) needs to be expanded to (20):

(20)   Ann: I'm out of gas.
        A_1:   I'm out of gasoline.
        A_2:   I'm out of natural gas.
    Bob: There's a gas station around the corner.
        B_1:   There's a gasoline station around the corner.
        B'_1:   Ann can get gasoline at the station around the corner.
        B_2:   There's a natural gas station around the corner.
        B'_2:   Ann can get natural gas at the station around the corner.

Knowledge of the conventions of English does not tell us what the word *gas* meant when Ann made her statement in (20) (the same context as (1)) or when Bob responded. To know that, we have to know what Ann and Bob each meant by gas on this particular occasion. That is a fact about the speakers that cannot be inferred from the conventions that give *gas* its meanings in English. Without knowing what Bob meant by the word, we cannot know what Bob said by uttering what he did, or whether he meant that there is a gasoline station rather than a natural gas station around the corner. We also cannot know what the word means in this context, or on this occasion.[7]

Lepore and Stone (215–16) later acknowledge "a fundamental way in which meaning depends on what the speaker has in mind" since "conventional meaning can be derived only once various ambiguities are settled."

[W]hat ultimately determines the correct resolution of these ambiguities is the way in which the speaker thinks of the utterance.   (Lepore & Stone 2015: 216)

When Bob uttered his sentence, he surely thought that it means "There is a gasoline station around the corner" in English. But his thinking that does not suffice to tell us what Bob meant in (20). For he surely knew and may have thought that it also means "There is a natural gas station around the corner." The conventions of English connect English speakers to both meanings. Bob has to connect one of the meanings to the word on any given occasion. We have to know which of the two propositions he meant by the sentence, and that is determined by what he intends. To know that, we have to reason about the speaker.[8]

Lepore and Stone's conclusion that the resolution of lexical and syntactic ambiguities depends on the speaker's thought conflicts with a claim they made earlier:

So it is not as though the content of the speaker's thought is prior to or independent of the way the speaker has chosen to express that thought in words, the way (195) [Grice's rough definition of speaker meaning] suggests.   (Lepore & Stone 2015: 212)

This claim occurs in a section in which Lepore and Stone are endorsing a Kripkean account of word reference and belief content. Even if it is granted that Ann and Bob have beliefs and intentions about gasoline (or natural gas) only if they are connected to gasoline (natural gas) by a chain of utterances of the word 'gas,' it remains true that whether they meant "gasoline" or "natural gas" by the word 'gas' on this occasion is dependent on a thought the having of which is completely independent of how they chose to express it on this occasion. They could have used *petrol* or spoken French.

4.4 Generalized Conversational Implicatures

Even though linguistic conventions attach generalized implicatures to sentences, they do not determine the interpretation of an utterance either. The fact that sentences

---

[7] I discuss the notion of word meaning on an occasion in Davis (2003: §7.9).

[8] I agree with Lepore and Stone (§5.1) on the importance of abductive reasoning for this purpose, although it is not the only form of inductive reasoning that can be used (see Davis 1998: §4.6).

containing *some* are conventionally used with a *not all* implicature does not determine what Bob meant in (20) any more than the fact that *gas* is conventionally used to mean "gasoline" determines what Ann or Bob mean in (20). To know whether Dan implicated in (2) that Mickey did not eat all of the cookies (scalar implicature), or that Mickey ate all the cookies (understatement), or that he does not know whether Mickey ate all of the cookies (ignorance implicature), or some particularized implicature, depends on Dan's intentions.

5. Are Conventions Constituted by Mutual Expectations?

Like Lepore and Stone, my characterization of a convention as a common practice that, despite being arbitrary, perpetuates itself in part by precedent and its success in serving common purposes, was inspired by Lewis (1969). They, however, take different elements of Lewis' analysis to be constitutive of conventions.

Conventions are simply the mutual expectations that let some group of agents successfully coordinate... People in conversation are rarely complete strangers. They have normally enjoyed a substantial history of interactions with one another. Accordingly, they will likely share a complex tapestry of precedents and mutual expectations that can inform their understandings of one another.   (155)

COORDINATION PROBLEMS name a subset of those strategic situations where agents must choose actions that agree with one another in order to achieve mutually acceptable outcomes. In coordination problems, agents have to make matching choices from among multiple candidate strategies, but there's no intrinsic reason to prefer one over the other. So agents must act solely based on their expectations about one another.   (234)

To coordinate by convention entails recognizing the intentions of other agents.   (241)

Whenever agents aim to use signals to exchange information, they have to coordinate. They have to agree on an arbitrary choice of strategies for producing and interpreting signals.   (254)

Conventions can be viewed abstractly as solutions to coordination problems. In the case of language, there is a common goal: communication. To achieve that goal when using language, speakers have to mean what hearers will take them to mean, and hearers must take speakers to mean what they do mean. It does not follow, however, and it is not true, that coordination in language use requires speakers and hearers to cooperate with each other, agree on anything, or share expectations. Coordination does not have to be intentional. Speakers and hearers can and do communicate by independently following practices they picked up independently from others—practices that perpetuate themselves by precedent, social acceptance, habit and association, traditional transmission from one generation of speakers to another, and their success in serving a number of purposes, including, but not limited to, communication. What is primarily responsible for the coordination required for successful communication is the way conventional practices spread from person to person and generation to generation, and become more ingrained in each individual with each use. Communication is somewhat special because it requires hearers to recognize, or at least correctly guess, what speakers mean, which requires recognizing or guessing their intentions. But speakers need not expect their hearers to understand them. In other cases, it is easier to see that agreements and mutual expectations are inessential to conventional coordination. Just imagine a large interstate highway with many drivers far enough apart so that they cannot see each other. As long as each driver habitually drives on the right, there will be no collisions.

Conventional language use is much more general than conversations among interlocutors who know each other and are cooperating to advance an inquiry or achieve any other shared goal. Much of our daily commerce involves brief exchanges with total strangers (at least for us city-dwellers). Moreover, speakers and hearers are often in situations of competition rather than cooperation, and use language to promote their conflicting goals (see especially Pinker 2007). Speakers may use language to spread *dis*-information. The fact that speakers and hearers may be competing rather than cooperating is yet another reason why conversational implicatures cannot be derived from conversational principles like Grice's presupposing cooperation (section 1).

There are also a wide variety of cases in which speakers are neither cooperating with hearers nor competing with them. People often use language when they do not have an audience that understands their language, or any audience at all. And it is very common for speakers and hearers, and especially writers and readers, to have no interaction with each other. As I write this essay, for example, I am not having a conversation or interacting with anyone. I do not know who will read my work or how carefully anyone will read it. Nevertheless, I am generally following the conventions of English, using sentences to mean, say, and implicate things they mean, say, and implicate in English. I expect, or at least hope, that readers who know English well enough will understand me. The shared knowledge that enables me, and any readers, to communicate is the knowledge of English and the knowledge that I am using it. My readers will have no independent knowledge of me, and my non-linguistic context, as I am writing these words. And I have no independent knowledge of them as they are reading them. My readers and I do not agree on any strategies.[9] I cannot choose my words based on my expectations of what any reader will do except insofar as I expect they will know English, and my readers cannot interpret my words based on their expectations of what I am doing except insofar as they expect me to know English.

Knowledge of what words mean in English cannot be what establishes the pairings of words and meanings that constitute English. The knowledge that *plane* means "airplane" and "carpentry plane" but not "automobile," for example, cannot be that in virtue of which *plane* means "airplane" and "carpentry plane" but not "automobile."

---

[9] There is another sense of 'convention' in which it means "an agreement, compact, or contract," and applies to the Geneva Conventions. Linguistic and driving conventions are not conventions in this sense.

Beliefs are not knowledge unless they are true, and beliefs about word meanings in English are not true simply because people have them. Nor does it suffice to say that *plane* has the meaning "airplane" because speakers commonly use it to mean "airplane" and hearers commonly understand them to mean "airplane" by it. That conjunction could be a mere coincidence or the result of a common error. Linguistic conventions are not mere coincidences or statistical norms. Characterizing conventions as mutual expectations does not capture their dynamic nature: conventions tend to persist, spread, and evolve. To describe a practice as conventional today is in part to explain how that practice came to be common today: it resulted from prior practice in certain ways. The factors that led it to be common today can be expected to persist unless they are counteracted.

Lepore and Stone's characterization of conventions as constituted by mutual expectations is also incompatible with another claim they make:

> A word, in virtue of the conventions, gives us a connection to its meaning.   (212)

On their view, *Aristotle* means the philosopher Aristotle because speakers and hearers have certain mutual expectations. What English speakers mutually expect is that *Aristotle* will commonly be used to mean and refer to Aristotle. A particular speaker S's having the belief that *Aristotle* will commonly be used to mean and refer to Aristotle may connect S to Aristotle. But the fact that the expectation is mutual does not: the fact that T has a belief relating *Aristotle* to Aristotle does not connect S to Aristotle. Lepore and Stone want to say, with Kripke, that the use of *Aristotle* to mean Aristotle originated with Aristotle's "baptism" and spread from user to user through the centuries (and languages). But it is not possible for English speakers to learn the meaning of *Aristotle* from other English speakers if the meaning of *Aristotle* depends on expectations that are shared by all speakers of English. Conventions are causal processes that spread usage expectations from prior speakers of the language to new speakers.

6. Does Any Figurative Speech Involve Conversational Implicature?

Lepore and Stone turn in their Part III to cases in which interpretations are unconventional. In these cases, they appear to draw the radical conclusion that there is no meaning at all.

> Meaning as we understand it—public content that underwrites interlocutors' joint inquiry into how things are—doesn't seem to capture what metaphor is doing most of the time. The insights of metaphor crucially involve perspective taking, seeing things in certain ways, which is a fundamentally different enterprise.   (Lepore & Stone 2015: 170)

> In fact, we think there's surprisingly little evidence to suggest that metaphor EVER contributes information—if we understand information in the semantic sense we have emphasized in Parts I and II of publicly accessible content that supports inquiry.   (Lepore & Stone 2015: 170)

In section 4 we discussed two cases in which speakers mean that something is the case without using sentences that conventionally mean or implicate that it is the case: malapropisms like (16) and particularized implicatures like (1). They illustrated the importance of distinguishing speaker meaning and implicature from sentence meaning and implicature.

6.1 Live Metaphor

The distinction between speakers and sentences is also critical to understanding every-day uses of figurative speech. Consider (21):

> (21) Liz: Can Malia come out tonight?
> Obama: Malia is in the penalty box.
> O: Malia Obama is in the penalty box of a hockey game.
> O': Malia Obama is confined to the house as punishment.

In (21), Obama uses a metaphor to explain why his daughter Malia cannot come out tonight. He therefore means something and expresses a belief by uttering *Malia is in the penalty box*. But the object of the belief he expresses is not the proposition expressed by the sentence he utters. The belief he expresses is, at least roughly, that Malia is confined to the house as punishment, not the belief that she is in the penalty box, where referees send players for violating the rules of hockey. As a result, what Obama *says* is not what he *means*: he says but does not mean that Malia is in the penalty box. He means but does not say that Malia is confined to the house as punishment. (21) is another good example of a particularized conversational implicature. (21) differs from (1), however, in that Obama does not *assert* what he says.

Example (21) seems to be a clear case in which metaphor is used to support inquiry. Malia's father realizes that Liz will want to know why Malia cannot come out tonight, and provides the reason. Assuming that Liz knows hockey and recognizes that Malia's dad is speaking metaphorically, she will readily understand what he means. He will have misled Liz if the real reason were that Malia is sick, or playing with another friend. (21) is representative of an extremely large class of cases in which speakers use metaphor to convey information to hearers.

Why would Lepore and Stone think that Malia's dad is not conveying any information in this case? They were not focusing on everyday uses of metaphor like this one, but on examples of metaphor in literature, to which we will turn in the next section. But let us see if what they say about the literary cases applies to (21).

In each of these cases, the interpretation of the utterance may specify that the utterance requires a particular kind of imaginative engagement. That invites the audience to respond appropriately. But none of these imaginative processes involves anything like grasping some indirect or ulterior proposition that the speaker and the audience coordinate on, again in the technical sense at issue here. (Lepore & Stone 2015: 262)

Recall, for us, the conversational record captures those regimented distinctions that describe the process of meaning-making…In conversation,…the record serves to track the work that interlocutors do to make their perspectives public, by identifying questions that matter to them and working to reach agreement on the answers. This work does not seem to be implicated in the interpretation of figurative or evocative speech.   (Lepore & Stone 2015: 262).

Liz and Malia's father are having a conversation, but they are not working to reach agreement on anything. Obama is simply answering the question why Malia cannot come out. Whether or not Liz and Malia's father are coordinating on anything in Lepore and Stone's technical sense, Obama is answering a question Malia is likely to have. Hence there is a proposition Liz must grasp to understand Malia's father—the proposition that Malia is confined to the house as punishment. This proposition is not expressed by the sentence Obama uttered. It is a proposition he expressed indirectly, by expressing the proposition that Malia is in the penalty box.

Another observation Lepore and Stone would make is that what Malia's dad meant (J') is not conventional in any sense (see 155). It is not something that the sentence he used means or implicates. But as we saw in section 4 with example (1), it does not follow that Malia's dad did not mean anything. Another consideration is that metaphors "are not easily characterized in terms of propositional content" (161). Following Black (1955), Lepore and Stone doubt that a metaphor can be given a "precise literal paraphrase." In particular, what Malia's dad meant in (21) is not the proposition expressed by the sentence *Malia Obama is in a situation similar to being in a penalty box.*[10] Malia's father meant something more specific. That similarity statement would be true if Malia were sitting on a hard bench next to a hockey rink watching the game, or if Malia were in jail. What Malia's father meant is not compatible with either of those situations. But while I think a good paraphrase of what Malia's dad meant can be provided in this case, we cannot expect that everything a speaker might mean can be expressed literally. The speaker's language may not yet have the words to do that. This is a common reason for using metaphor.

6.2 Common and Dead Metaphors

Recall what happened when the use of computers became widespread in the 1970s and self-replicating programs were developed. Some were designed to cause damage and spread from one computer to another. Since this phenomenon was new in human experience, English and other natural languages had no word for it. English speakers began calling them "viruses" metaphorically, meaning that they had certain attributes of biological viruses. This usage caught on and is now fully conventional. The metaphor is dead, and the term *virus* is ambiguous. The conventionalization of metaphors is one of the most common ways in which words acquire new meanings.

---

[10] Lepore and Stone (165) infer from Aristotle's remarks on the relation of metaphor to simile that he endorsed the view that in metaphor, a speaker is expressing belief in a similarity statement. I take Aristotle to have meant only that similes are only slightly more literal than metaphors. Whether the speaker says *Love is like a snowmobile* (simile) or *Love is a snowmobile* (metaphor), the speaker means the same thing, which is not what either sentence means.

The lexicalization process has an intermediate stage in which the word carries a generalized implicature. I believe the term *ground-zero* is at this stage. It is a common metaphor for the point from which major damage of some sort spreads. So a sentence like *The Lehman collapse was ground-zero in the 2008 recession* implicates but does not mean that the collapse of Lehman was the source from which the economic damage of the 2008 recession spread. Given how often this metaphor is used nowadays, I would not be surprised to find it dead in a few years.

Lepore and Stone (163) acknowledge that dead metaphors are a special kind of polysemy, but set them aside because they are interested in live and creative metaphors. The point I wish to make here is that dead metaphors were once live, as we observed with *virus*. The proposition English speakers now express conventionally when uttering *The computer has a virus* was formerly expressed unconventionally using metaphor. If metaphorical uses of *virus* never conveyed information and expressed propositions, the term would not now have a sense denoting a specific condition affecting computers. Lexicalization gives words new meanings, but it does not create new thoughts. Note that we still cannot say that *The computer has a virus* "literally means" that the computer has a computer virus. For only the original biological sense of *virus* is its literal meaning, even though the word *virus* now means "computer virus" in English just as truly as it means "biological virus."

6.3 Metaphor as a Conventional Mode of Expression

One of Lepore and Stone's most important conclusions remains, however. Obama was not *simply* conveying the information that Malia is confined to the house as punishment in (21). He was conveying it in a particular *way*. For one thing, he was implicating rather than asserting it. Lepore and Stone's point is that:

Metaphor invites us to organize our thinking about something through an analogical correspondence with something it is not.   (162)

[T]his imagery, this perspective…is as important to the effect and the point of the metaphor as any propositional information it may convey.   (168)

Even if we can say exactly what we mean using language literally, we often prefer to convey it metaphorically. By engaging our imagination, a metaphor can be much more interesting and insightful. Other figures of speech are defined by the fact that speakers are doing more than implicating rather than asserting something. The goal of overstatement, for example, is to emphasize how great something is in a certain respect, while the goal of understatement is to de-emphasize it.

Lepore and Stone make a second important point in connection with (8), the landmark example. If figurative meanings are not conventional, they ask, how can we understand them so readily?

We give examples where a single utterance is understood in its context to introduce an ambiguity between qualitatively different interpretations, derived according to different interpretive practices by qualitatively different kinds of imaginative engagement. Thus, it must be the practices themselves—rather than the contextual background or general interpretive principles—that enable speakers to use these utterances to get their points across.   (161)

In (8), when Fay said "That building is a landmark," Fay may have been speaking sarcastically (meaning F'_2), or metaphorically (meaning F'_2), or ironically (meaning F'_3). It is true in such cases that what the speaker meant is not what the sentence means or implicates. Nothing in the conventional meaning of the sentence carries her meaning. In this respect, the examples are like (1) rather than (2) or (9) or implicatures that are conventional in Grice's sense. What then could it mean to say that "the practices themselves" enable the speakers to get their point across? It means that hearers are readily able to understand Fay in these different ways because they have learned the practices of metaphor, irony, sarcasm, and so on. Putting it paradoxically, these are *conventional ways of using language unconventionally*.[11] Using language metaphorically is a common way of using language. It perpetuates itself by precedent, social acceptance, habit and association, traditional transmission from one generation of speakers to another, and its success in serving at least two purposes: communicating and engaging our imaginations. The practice is arbitrary, in that we could achieve the same purposes by speaking literally, or by using simile, and so on. So there are alternatives. We learn to use and understand language metaphorically early in life. As with lexical meaning and syntax, this practice is taught to some extent in school, but mainly it is picked up from other speakers. Common metaphors like *ground-zero* carry generalized implicatures, but original metaphors like O′ are particularized. *Malia is in the penalty box* neither means nor implicates that Malia is confined to the house as punishment.

6.4 Two Kinds of Speaker Meaning

Figurative speech is also important in showing that there are two distinct types of speaker meaning, a point first noted by Ziff (1967: 446) and developed by Schiffer (1972: 2–3).

(22) (a)   By the words 'Malia is in the penalty box,' Obama meant "Malia Obama is in the penalty box." He did not mean "Malia Obama is confined to the house as punishment" by them. (True)

(b)   By uttering those words, Obama did not mean that Malia Obama is in the penalty box. He meant that Malia Obama is confined to the house as punishment by uttering them. (True)

Subordinate clauses formed with *that* or quotation marks are typically equivalent, but not always. If (21) is the example of metaphor we intended, then (22)(a) and (b) are both true. So *meaning "p"* is distinct from *meaning that p* for speakers. The latter involves expressing the *belief* that p, directly or indirectly. The former involves directly expressing the *thought* or *proposition* that p, but not necessarily as the object of belief.

---

[11]   I develop this point in Davis (1998: 148–51, 171–2; 2016: §3). In both, I identify many different conventional ways of using language unconventionally.

I therefore call the former type of speaker meaning "cognitive" and the latter "cogitative" (Davis 2003: §2.2). We can think thoughts we do not believe (e.g., "There are three eyed frogs on Mars"), and we believe many things we are not thinking at the moment (countless arithmetic truths I cannot identify without thinking them). In example (1), Bob expressed the belief that Ann could get gasoline at the station around the corner indirectly, by expressing the belief that there is a station around the corner. So Bob *implied* as well as implicated, that Ann could get gas there. Obama expressed the belief that Malia is confined to the house by expressing the thought but not the belief that Malia is in the penalty box. So Obama implicated but did not imply that Malia is confined to the house. Because Obama did not express the thought "Malia Obama is in the penalty box" by expressing any other thought or mental state, he expressed it directly.

One of the other distinctive features of cogitative speaker meaning is that it occurs with subsentential units too. By *Malia*, Obama meant "Malia Obama." If he had meant "Malia Jones," the model, he would have meant "Malia Jones is in the penalty box" by the sentence. Cogitative meaning in this case is the direct expression of a thought part, the idea "Malia Obama." By uttering *Malia* in (21), Obama did not mean *that* anything is the case. This can be confusing, but figures of speech involve meaning by words what the words mean and thereby meaning that something else is the case. When a metaphor is dead, this kind of indirection is gone. When we use *The computer has a virus* today, meaning "The computer has a computer virus" by those words, and meaning that the computer has a computer virus by uttering them, we are not speaking metaphorically. The biological meaning of *virus* plays no role, so there is no indirection. When we use a sentence metaphorically, we do not give the sentence new meanings, and do not mean by it anything it does not mean in our language.

7. Does All Figurative Speech Involve Conversational Implicature?

7.1 Fiction and Poetry

Clear cases in which metaphor and other figures of speech are not used to "contribute information" occur in fiction and poetry. For these genres involve the use of language to express thoughts but not beliefs. Speakers mean things cogitatively but not cognitively. Consequently there is no implicature.[12] Here are representative examples from Ernest Hemingway and Robert Frost.

> (23) He felt the earth move.[13]

---

[12] Authors sometimes hope their fiction will change peoples' beliefs and attitudes, the way *Uncle Tom's Cabin* did. But in their fictional writings, they do not express the beliefs they hope readers will adopt.

[13] Ernest Hemingway, *For Whom the Bell Tolls* (Scribner's 1940), 159. This is actually one clause in an extremely long and un-Hemingwayan conjunction, but the abbreviation does not affect anything.

(24)   The whir of sober birds
       Is sadder than any words.[14]

(23) is a line from Hemingway's *For Whom the Bell Tolls*, which occurs after Robert Jordan and Maria make love for the first time. By (23), Hemingway meant "He felt Earth move." He did not mean "He felt the soil move." Hemingway used the sentence with one of its regular English meanings. But Hemingway did not mean that Robert Jordan felt the earth move. He was expressing a thought, but not a belief. (23) is like (21) in that Hemingway used a metaphor. By expressing the thought "He felt the earth move," Hemingway was expressing another thought, roughly, "He was profoundly moved." Since he expressed this second thought indirectly, it is something he meant by uttering the words, not by the words themselves. (23) is unlike (21), however, in that Hemingway was not expressing a belief metaphorically. He was not trying to advance any inquiry by providing relevant information. Hemingway was just telling a story, and wanted us to use our imagination. Since he was not expressing a belief, he was not implicating anything. This case fits what Lepore and Stone say about figurative speech very well, except for their suggestion that the speaker is not expressing thoughts or propositions in any way.

Similar things can be said about the lines from Frost, although it is difficult to iden-tify the thought he was expressing metaphorically. While Frost clearly expressed the thought that the whir of sober birds is sadder than any words, and surely wanted to be interpreted as engaging in metaphor, it is not implausible that there was no particular thought Frost was expressing about birds other than the thought expressed by the sentence he wrote. Frost may simply have wanted us to imagine what he might have meant.[15] So this case fits what Lepore and Stone say even better.

7.2 Subordinate Clauses

There is another important case in which speakers use sentences to express thoughts figuratively without expressing the corresponding beliefs. Imagine that sentences (25) and (26) occur shortly after (23).

(25)   Either he felt the earth move, or he did not.
(26)   If he felt the earth move, he must be in love.

In these cases, Hemingway would also be using *He felt the earth move* metaphorically, to express the thought but not the belief that Robert Jordan was deeply moved. Whereas we say and implicate that something is the case only by uttering independent clauses, we can still use subordinate clauses figuratively.

---

[14] Robert Frost, "A Late Walk," in E. C. Lathem, *The Poetry of Robert Frost* (New York: Holt, Rinehart and Winston, 1969), 8. I have again abbreviated the stanza.

[15] Another way in which (24) differs from (23) is that the sound and rhythm of the words is at least as important as the ideas they express.

7.3 Additional Arguments Against Calculability

(23) and (24) represent an incredibly voluminous class of cases in which Grice's maxim of Quality, "Make your contribution true" is either violated or does not apply. Robert Jordan is a fictional character, so the thought Hemingway expressed is not true. The Cooperative Principle as Grice stated it does not apply because Hemingway was not having a conversation with anyone. Of course, the violation or inapplicability of his principles is not a problem for Grice's theory of conversational implicature, because there is no implicature in these cases at all. But it does raise the following question. Given the similarity between the cases discussed in this section and the cases of implicature presented earlier, why should we expect what speakers mean in the implicature cases to be explained by or derivable from Gricean conversational principles if what speakers mean in fiction and poetry cannot be? I believe Lepore and Stone would agree that we should not.

References

Bach, K. (1994a) Conversational impliciture. *Mind and Language*, 9, 124–62

Bach, K. and Harnish, R. (1979) *Linguistic Communication and Speech Acts*. Cambridge, MA: MIT Press

Black, M. (1955) Metaphor. *Proceedings of the Aristotelian Society*, 55, 273–394

Davis, W. A. (1998) *Implicature: Intention, Convention, and Principle in the Failure of Gricean Theory*. Cambridge: Cambridge University Press

Davis, W. A. (2003) *Meaning, Expression, and Thought*. New York: Cambridge University Press

Davis, W. A. (2007) How normative is implicature? *Journal of Pragmatics*, 39, 1655–72

Davis, W. A. (2014) Implicature. In *The Stanford Encyclopedia of Philosophy (Fall 2014 Edition)*, ed. E. N. Zalta. Palo Alto, CA: Stanford University Press, http://plato.stanford.edu/archives/fall2014/entries/implicature/

Davis, W. A. (2016) Implicature. In *Oxford Handbooks Online in Philosophy*, ed. S. Goldberg. Oxford: Oxford University Press

Gazdar, G. (1979) *Pragmatics: Implicature, Presupposition, and Logical Form*. New York: Academic Press

Green, M. S. (1995) Quality, volubility, and some varieties of discourse. *Linguistics and Philosophy*, 18, 83–112

Grice, H. P. (1989) *Studies in the Way of Words*. Cambridge, MA: Harvard University Press

Harnish, R. (1976) Logical form and implicature. In *An Integrated Theory of Linguistic Ability*, ed. T. G. Bever, J. J. Katz, and T. Langedoen, pp. 313–92. New York: Thomas Y. Crowell. Reprinted in *Pragmatics: A Reader*, ed. S. Davis, pp. 316–64. Oxford: Oxford University Press (1991)

Horn, L. R. (1984) Towards a new taxonomy for pragmatic inference: Q-based and R-based implicature. In *Georgetown University Round Table on Languages and Linguistics*, ed. D. Schiffrin, pp. 11–42. Washington, DC: Georgetown University Press

Horn, L. R. (1989) *A Natural History of Negation*. Chicago, IL: University of Chicago Press

Horn, L. R. (2004) Implicature. In *The Handbook of Pragmatics*, ed. L. R. Horn and G. Ward, pp. 3–28. Oxford: Blackwell Publishing

Kripke, S. (1977) Speaker reference and semantic reference. *Midwest Studies in Philosophy*, 2, 255–78

Leech, G. (1983) *Principles of Pragmatics*. London: Longmans

Lepore, E. and Stone, M. (2015) *Imagination and Convention: Distinguishing Grammar and Inference in Language*. Oxford: Oxford University Press

Levinson, S. C. (1983) *Pragmatics*. Cambridge: Cambridge University Press

Levinson, S. C. (2000) *Presumptive Meanings: The Theory of Generalized Conversational Implicature*. Cambridge, MA: MIT Press

Lewis, D. (1969) *Convention*. Cambridge, MA: Harvard University Press

Lewis, D. (1979) Scorekeeping in a language game. *Journal of Philosophical Logic*, 8, 339–359

Neale, S. (1992) Paul Grice and the philosophy of language. *Linguistics and Philosophy*, 15, 509–59

Pinker, S. (2007) The evolutionary social psychology of off-record indirect speech acts. *Intercultural Pragmatics*, 4, 437–61

Sadock, J. M. (1978) On testing for conversational implicature. In *Syntax and Semantics, 9: Pragmatics*, ed. P. Cole, pp. 281–97. New York: Academic Press. Reprinted in *Pragmatics: A Reader*, ed. S. Davis, pp. 365–76. Oxford: Oxford University Press. (1991)

Saul, J. (2010) Speaker-meaning, conversational implicature and calculability. In *Meaning and Analysis: New Essays on Grice*, ed. K. Petrus, pp. 170–83. Houndmills: Palgrave Macmillan

Schiffer, S. (1972) *Meaning*. Oxford: Clarendon Press

Sperber, D., and D. Wilson (1986) *Relevance: Communication and Cognition*. Cambridge, MA: Harvard University Press

Thomason, R. (1990) Accommodation, meaning, and implicature: Interdisciplinary foundations for pragmatics. In *Intentions in Communication*, ed. P. R. Cohen, J. L. Morgan, and M. Pollack, pp. 325–63. Cambridge, MA: MIT Press

Wilson, D. and Sperber, D. (1981) On Grice's theory of conversation. In *Conversation and Discourse*, ed. P. Werth, pp. 155–78. New York: St. Martins Press

Ziff, P. (1967) On H. P. Grice's account of meaning. *Analysis*, 28: 1–8

4

Presupposition Triggering
and Disambiguation

Adam Sennet

Introduction

Presupposition triggering is among the wide range of phenomena discussed in Imagination and Convention (I&C). This isn't surprising. Presupposition triggering is the locus of much debate between (neo-)Griceans and conventionalists. The former tend to locate the source of (some) presuppositions in general conversational constraints while the latter tend to think of presupposition as triggered by conventions involving linguistic form. What is more surprising is that the topic of conventional triggering receives somewhat short shrift in I&C. A promise made in chapter 2 to return to the topic of factive presuppositions triggering in chapter 7 is left unfulfilled.

A second phenomenon that is left unmentioned in I&C concerns alleged cases of unarticulated constituents. Perry's (1986) introduction of the phrase into the literature has been part of the locus of debate between those who ground contextual contribution to content in linguistic convention and those who think ground some contextual contributions to content in considerations of relevance. Given that I&C is partly devoted to the explanatory power of linguistic convention over Gricean processes of informational enrichment, it's surprising that a search of the book for the term 'unarticulated' yields zero results.

This essay aims to show that orthodoxy about presupposition triggering can help shed light on the notion of disambiguation that plays a key role in I&C. Disambiguation, moreover, helps shed some light on the proper treatment of some purported cases of unarticulated constituents. Section 1 introduces some of the issues concerning presupposition and presupposition triggering. Section 2 examines the viability of some recent neo-Gricean approaches to presupposition triggering. Section 3 introduces the relevant issues regarding unarticulated constituents. Finally, Section 4 will look at how thinking about cases of presupposition triggering in purported cases of unarticulated constituents interacts with Lepore and Stone's conception of disambiguation.

1. Presupposition and Presupposition Triggering

It's not easy to say, in a theoretically neutral manner, what a linguistic presupposition *is*. Generally, a linguistic presupposition is characterized as information that the speaker indicates is to be considered as background to what is asserted/questioned/ordered etc. by the deployment of a sentence (or, in some cases, sentence fragment). Examples abound. Here are a few:

1. John doesn't know that 'taco bell' is an anagram for 'coal belt'. (Presupposition: 'Taco Bell' is an anagram for 'coal belt')

2. John might have started drinking. (Presupposition: John wasn't drinking at an earlier time)

3. The new Prime Minister of Canada is a Trudeau. (Presupposition: Canada has a new Prime Minister)

4. If it was Ernie who left his credit card, he's not going to be able to pay for dinner. (Presupposition: Someone left his credit card)

5. Philosophy professors only READ the New York Times. (Presupposition: Philosophy professors do something with the New York Times)[1]

Not all felicity conditions governing the utterance of a sentence are presuppositions and not all of the entailments of a sentence are presuppositions. What is characteristic about presuppositions is that they maintain their status as backgrounded information in contexts where the content of the putative presupposition is not entailed. In particular, we can test for putative presuppositions of a sentence S by considering a family of linguistic environments: S, the negation of S, S under the scope of a modal, S as the antecedent of a conditional, and the interrogative and imperative versions of S. For example, consider:

6. Sharon is aware that Canada is beautiful.

(6) entails that Canada is beautiful and that Sharon believes it. But notice that under the scope of a negation or a modal, only one of these is presupposed:

7. Sharon isn't aware that Canada is beautiful.
8. Sharon might be aware that Canada is beautiful.

(7) and (8) are only felicitous if Canada is beautiful. But their felicity does not depend on Sharon believing it. Similarly for:

9. If Sharon is aware that Canada is beautiful, she will plan a trip there.
10. Is Sharon aware that Canada is beautiful?
11. Make Sharon aware that Canada is beautiful![2]

---

[1] To be clear, these cases trigger other presuppositions as well.

[2] As noted by Abusch (2002), somewhat surprisingly, 'Sharon is right that Canada is beautiful' has the exact opposite profile despite having common entailments with (6).

The factive presuppositions of (7)–(11) seem to be free of the linguistic context in which they are generated—they 'project'. The presupposition that Canada is beautiful is not 'trapped' by the negation in (7), the modal in (8), the antecedent of (9), or the non-declarative contexts of (10) and (11).

On the other hand, there are linguistic contexts where the presupposition doesn't seem to project out of the context of the entire sentence. For example:

12. Either Canada isn't beautiful or Sharon isn't aware that it is.
13. Alejandro believes that Stanley didn't quit smoking.

(12) doesn't presuppose that Canada is beautiful and (13) doesn't presuppose that Stanley ever smoked.[3] Whether or not we should think of a presupposition as being triggered 'locally' but cancelled or not triggered at all is a matter of some controversy.[4]

To make matters even more confusing, shifting around the (implicit) question under discussion (QUD) can have an effect on whether or not a presupposition is triggered. Following Simons (2001), consider a context in which we know that Mariah quit something but we don't know what it was. We notice that she shows none of the signs of having ever been a smoker and someone claims:

14. Mariah definitely didn't quit smoking!

The implicit QUD is 'what did Mariah quit?' (14), relative to this QUD, lacks the presupposition that Mariah used to smoke. In fact, it is the evidence that she never smoked that leads the speaker to claim (14).

It gets even worse. As Stalnaker (1974) points out, there are other cases in which an expected presupposition doesn't arise:

15. If Mandy finds out that Craige is in Paris, she'll try to find her.
16. If I find out that Craige is in Paris, I'll try to find her.

(15) but not (16) presupposes that Craige is in Paris. It would be surprising that someone who was presupposing that she was would assert (16) at all!

Finally, there are subtleties in how presuppositions interact with contexts where the speaker seems to explicitly cancel or suspend the presupposition. Compare the following:

17. I don't know if the RNC is run by a King but Reince isn't the King of the Republicans.
18. Ted didn't quit being nice to Donald; he never started!
19. ?I don't know if anyone else ate dinner but Hillary didn't eat dinner either.
20. ?I don't know if Bill took money illicitly but he regrets it![5]

---

[3] Though (13) does presuppose that Alejandro believes that Stanley smoked, the presupposition is trapped under the scope of 'belief'.

[4] Stalnaker (1973) and Karttunen (1974) are early discussions of this issue. See Kadmon (2001) and the SEP article on 'Presupposition' for nice overview discussions of modern views of presupposition projection.

[5] These cases are relevant to the 'hard–soft' triggering distinction (see Abusch 2002). We will mostly be concerned with soft triggers since much of the literature agrees on the conventional status of hard triggers.

A trio of questions arise from these considerations:

The Triggering Problem: what explains and grounds the relationship between a presupposition and the sentence/utterance that generates it?

The Projection Problem: In what linguistic environments does a complex sentence/utterance of a sentence inherit or fail to inherit a given presupposition of (at least one of) its parts?[6]

The Failure Problem: When a presupposition of a sentence/assertion is false, what is the semantic/pragmatic effect on the sentence/assertion?

Our concern is solely with the first question and the debate over conventional versus conversational norm accounts of how presuppositions are triggered. We will conveniently ignore important puzzling questions about how presuppositions can be 'cancelled' in cases such as (14)–(18). We will also ignore issues regarding representing presuppositions in various static and dynamic approaches to meaning. We will be focused on whether there are viable approaches to presupposition triggering that do not rely on positing triggering conventions in lexical items.[7] Orthodoxy has been on the side of conventional approaches to triggering, generally locating the locus of presuppositions in the lexical semantics of triggers or in the linguistic form of the sentence.

Part 1: Presupposition Triggering

Presupposition triggering has a fraught history. Frege, worrying about non-referring names, claimed:

If anything is asserted [by an utterance of a sentence with a proper name] there is always an obvious presupposition that the simple or compound proper names used have reference. If one therefore asserts 'Kepler died in misery' there is a presupposition that the name 'Kepler' designates something; but it does not follow that the sense of the sentence 'Kepler died in misery' contains the thought that the name 'Kepler' designates something. If this were the case the negation would have to run not

- Kepler did not die in misery

But

- Kepler did not die in misery or the name 'Kepler' has no reference.

That the name 'Kepler' designates something is just as much a presupposition for the assertion

- Kepler died in misery

as for the contrary assertion.   (Frege 1948, p. 221–2)

---

[6] These three questions are treated as distinct. But see Simons (ms) for an extended argument that they ultimately cannot be separated. She argues that the choice of triggering mechanisms places constraints on how one treats projection and vice versa.

[7] We will also focus solely on purportedly lexical, rather than structurally based presupposition triggers. We will thus have ignored clefts (e.g. as in (4) above) and appositive structures such as:

- Bernie, who debated Hillary, had a large following. (presupposition: Bernie debated Hillary).

Part of the difficulty in discussing presupposition triggering is that triggering phrases form a fairly heterogeneous category.

Frege's account isn't altogether clear—in particular, it's not clear how the presupposition arises from the use of a name or why. But the idea that presuppositions are triggered by certain expressions, such as proper names, is an enduring one. Strawson, writing in a similar vein, offers the following memorable passage:

Now suppose someone were in fact to say to you with a perfectly serious air: "The King of France is wise". Would you say, "That's untrue"? I think it is quite certain that you would not. But suppose that he went on to ask you whether you thought that what he had just said was true, or was false; whether you agreed or disagreed with what he had just said. I think you would be inclined, with some hesitation, to say that you did not do either; that the question of whether his statement was true or false simply did not arise, because there was no such person as the King of France. You might, if he were obviously serious (had a dazed, astray-in-the-centuries look), say something like: "I'm afraid you must be under a misapprehension. France is not a monarchy. There is no King of France." (Strawson 1950, p. 230)

Both of these accounts posit presupposition generation without explaining how the presuppositions are triggered. The conventionalist answer is that names and definite descriptions conventionally trigger background presuppositions regarding their referring. The account can be generalized to other cases of presupposition triggering. The idea is that phrase types such as definite descriptions, change of state verbs, names, factive verbs etc. trigger presuppositions as part of their conventional meaning. As Lepore and Stone put it:

It's natural to expect that this effect [factive presuppositions] is part of what the verb *know* means...For example, if we adopt a framework for sentence meaning like Discourse Representation Theory (Kamp and Reyle 1993), where meanings are thought of as structured, we can capture the effect by treating the verb 'know' as a presupposition trigger: whenever *know* is used, its meaning enriches the interpretation of the utterance with the constraint that the speaker takes the sentential complement to be true. (Lepore and Stone 2015, p. 27)

One way to put the point is that the presence of the word 'know' in a sentence is at least partly responsible for generating presuppositions, rather than merely the asserted content of a sentence with 'know' as a constituent. Similar points hold for 'quit', 'the present King of France' and other presupposition triggers.

Non-conventionalists about triggering have worried that the integration of 'triggering' into semantic theory is both unnecessary and theoretically undermotivated. On these approaches, 'triggering' isn't grounded in conventions concerning meaning but in the interaction of the content of sentences with general conversational principles (such as the Cooperative Principle). Stalnaker (1974) provides the general theoretical basis for this line of thought.[8] As Stalnaker puts it:

It is clear that "x knows that P" entails that P. It is also clear that in most cases when anyone asserts or denies that x knows that P, he presupposes that P. Can this latter fact be explained without building it into the semantics of the word? I think it can. Suppose a speaker were to assert that x

---

[8] See Grice (1975) and (1981) for pragmatic considerations about communication and presupposition.

knows that P in a context where the truth of P is in doubt or dispute. He would be saying in one breath something that could be challenged in two different ways. He would be leaving unclear whether his main point was to make a claim about the truth of P, or to make a claim about the epistemic situation of x (the knower), and thus leaving unclear what direction he intended or expected the conversation to take. Thus, given what "x knows that P" means, and given that people normally want to communicate in an orderly way, and normally have some purpose in mind, it would be unreasonable to assert that *x knows that P* in such a context.   (Stalnaker 1999, p. 55)

Stalnaker's idea is that given certain principles of orderly conversation, the presuppositions of (an utterance of) 'x knows that P' can be worked out without positing triggering conventions. If it was an open question whether or not P, it would be strange to claim that someone knew it. Similarly, it would be an odd way to pursue inquiries regarding the truth of P by claiming that someone didn't know whether P. Thus, on this line of explanation, we need not posit knowledge of triggering conventions or add information to our account of 'know' (and other apparent triggers) as there are no conventionalized triggers to explain the presence of backgrounded information. 'Know' doesn't have factivity built into its meaning, but many utterances containing 'know' will generate factive presuppositions by rational calculation of what they express in a cooperative framework. Put otherwise:

> GA: (Some) Presuppositions, like conversational implicatures, are explained by the application of conversational norms, not conventions about particular words.

Stalnaker offers the following suggestion of a general conversational principle to explain how presuppositions can be triggered by the content of an utterance:

The propositions that P and that Q may be related to each other, and to common beliefs and intentions, in such a way that it is hard to think of a reason that anyone would raise the question whether P, or care about its answer, unless he already believed that Q.   (Stalnaker 1999, p. 55)

Stalnaker's suggestion is clearly a sketch and requires elaboration. Simons (2001) and Abrusán (2011) provide accounts of presupposition triggering that elaborate on Stalnaker's idea that rationality requires treating some information as backgrounded in order to make sense of the speakers' assertion (question or command). This quote has served as a starting point for theories which, in the Gricean mold, try to see presupposition triggering as simply a product of rational cooperation in conversing. In this case, the idea is to appeal to the idea that actual use of language is structured, in part, around asking and answering questions. This idea seems plausible if not obvious. Taking our cue from Roberts (1996) we can call the question(s) being answered that structures a conversation the QUD. Now, some conversational points are structured around explicit QUDs. Often this is done by, not surprisingly, asking a question. Now, consider someone who asks:

21.   Is Rachel still working at the hospital?

There are various conditions under which 'yes' is the right answer to the question and various ones in which 'no' is the right answer to the question. If Rachel never worked at the hospital, the answer to the question seems to be 'no'. But, following Stalnaker, it is very difficult to see why the speaker who raised (21) would care about the possibility of a 'no' answer if she thought it was an open possibility that Rachel had never worked at the hospital. A similar point holds for:

22.   Did Obama close Guantanamo?

The speaker would be doing something rather odd if he thought that Guantanamo had never been open in the first place. Why would he ask about whether or not Obama had closed something that had never been open? So, the thought goes, we can safely infer that the speaker believes that Guantanamo exists and was open when Obama took power. This, of course, is true about a whole host of other propositions as well: that Obama was able to close Guantanamo (why would the speaker ask if Obama did something he thought that it was impossible for Obama to do?), that the speaker thinks 'Obama' is a referring term, that 'Guantanamo' is a referring term, etc.

So far, so good. However, not all questions under discussion are announced explicitly. Nonetheless, it is plausible that, thinking of conversation as a type of inquiry, asserting P is a way of answering or making a question a QUD. Moreover, we use various cues to convey to one another what the implicit QUD might be. Focal stress is well known to have this effect:

23.   OBAMA didn't close Guantanamo.
24.   Obama didn't close GUANTANAMO.

(23) seems to indicate that the QUD is who did or didn't close Guantanamo. The QUD of (24) is what did or didn't Obama close (to see this, suppose that someone asked 'Who didn't close Guantamo' and notice that (23) but not (24) is a felicitous answer.) (23) seems to commit the speaker to a backgrounded belief that someone closed Guantanamo while (24) seems to commit the speaker to the backgrounded belief that Obama closed something.

Putting all of this together, we get the idea that a speaker who asserts (23) can be seen as raising (if it isn't already raised) and answering the question 'who didn't close Guatanamo'? As suggested above, it is hard to see how one would be raising that question (or caring about the answer) if they didn't already presume that Guantanamo was open.

Similar points attend factive constructions. If someone tells you that:

25.   John knows that P.

She seems to answer the question:

26.   Does John know that P?

Now, let's take an off the shelf analysis of questions as sets of sets of worlds (worlds which can be construed as answers). Some of the answers to the question include worlds at which P is false (except for cases in which P is necessary). However, the inquisitor who (implicitly) raises (26) as the QUD is doing something very odd if it isn't taken for granted that P is true. Thus, the speaker indicates that they are taking it for granted that the only set of answers are ones in which P is true. Now, given that:

27.   John doesn't know that P.

raises the same question as (25), we can see that in both cases the truth of P is taken for granted.

Simons (2001) articulates this Stalnakerian line of thinking by proposing the following principle:

Interpretation Principle (tentative)
Suppose that P entails but is not entailed by Q. A speaker who raises the question whether P indicates a belief that Q is true.

The Interpretation Principle attempts to use the QUD plus the entailments of the positive answer to the question to provide the basis for generating presuppositions. We now are in a position to derive the relevant results. Someone who utters either (25) or (27) raises (26) as a QUD. (25) entails that P but neither are entailed by P. Thus, someone who asserts (25) or (27) indicates a belief that P is true and that acceptable answers to the QUD are all worlds in which P is true.

Before we go on to objections, it's worth noticing that this theory is thoroughly Gricean in both letter and spirit. Rather than resorting to triggering conventions governing either lexical items or certain syntactic structures, the theory attempts to predict the creation of presuppositions by a mix of rationality and the general goals of conversation. And the entire enterprise of presupposition generation begins with what is said and the speaker's commitments to what is entailed by what is said, rather than how it is said.

Sadly, the Interpretation Principle fails to achieve empirical adequacy. First, it over-generates presuppositions. For example, 'John killed Bill' shouldn't presuppose that Bill was killed (unless 'John' is focally stressed). Another counterexample is due to Roger Schwartzhild who notes that (28) entails (29) but, as we will see, fails to presuppose it:

28.   Jessica stopped eating at Arby's.
29.   Jessica wasn't eating at Arby's for some interval after the stopping event.

We can quibble about what counts as the time of the event of stopping, but clearly Jessica can't stop eating at Arby's without refraining from eating there for some period of time. But notice that (29) is *not* presupposed by:

30.   Jessica didn't stop eating at Arby's.
31.   Jessica may have stopped eating at Arby's.
32.   If Jessica stopped eating at Arby's, Sam will be relieved.

33.   Jessica, stop eating at Arby's!

34.   Did Jessica stop eating at Arby's?

The problem is easy to generalize. Consider (6) again:

6.   Sharon is aware that Canada is beautiful.

(6) entails that:

35.   Sharon believes that Canada is beautiful.

This is unwelcome in a theory of presupposition generation based on entailment given that (36) doesn't presuppose (35):

36.   Sharon isn't aware that Canada is beautiful.

If anything, (36) suggests that Sharon doesn't believe that Canada is beautiful.

We shouldn't take the failure of the Interpretation Principle as the death knell of the general research program. Perhaps we just need a filter on the entailment set of P in order to rid ourselves of the problematic entailments. This project is exactly what Abrusán (2011) takes up: she attempts to ground presupposition triggering in identifying particular entailments of a sentence (as opposed to all and any entailments of a sentence). Her leading idea is that sentences describe events and have (at least one) main event that they are about. Information not about the 'main event' is presupposed *unless* something in the context makes it the focus of attention. In other words, grammar and context make certain events the focus of attention and what is not made the focus of attention is thereby presupposed. To simplify, Abrusán assumes a mapping of events to event times and it is the grammar of the sentence that specifies which event time is the 'main' event time—generally the time of the matrix predicate. To use one of her examples (numbering mine):

37.   John knows that it was raining.

(37)'s matrix verb is 'knows' and the time of the main event is the time of the John's knowing that it is raining. (37) is then said to be *about* that time. The time of the raining event is (at least potentially) a distinct time. The formal details of the model need not concern us here but the idea is clear. The principle of presupposition triggering is:

Presupposition triggering (3rd, final version)
Entailments of a sentence S that can be expressed by sentences that are neither necessarily about the event time of the matrix predicate of S nor about the event time of the sentence expressing the most direct answer to the (grammatically signaled) background question are presupposed.

The notion of 'can be expressed by sentences' is of some concern but we will put that aside for now; 'grammatically signaled' concerns issues discussed above, such as focal stress which can indicate the QUD. The main idea is clear: where the entailed information concerns the time of the main verb (where attention is focused) the information is not presupposed. Otherwise, it is. This provides a filter on the entailments that form the basis of the presupposed set of propositions. Time, in effect, is being used as a stand-in for relevance. As Abrusán puts it:

The intuition that we want to capture is that presuppositional assertions describe complex states of events, some parts of which are independent from the main events. So what we want to achieve is to tell independent events apart: Select the main event described by the sentence, and decide what other information conveyed by the sentence describe independent events from the main one... The idea of looking at event times instead of events themselves serves the purpose of making independence more tractable: Events that happen at different times are clearly different events.   (Abrusán 2011, p. 502).

The proposal is in some respects far less Gricean than Simons', which employed only rules about raising questions with utterances and asymmetric entailment. But it preserves the Stalnakerian idea that it isn't conventions about words themselves that explain presupposition triggering, it is some relationship between the informational focus and that which isn't in focus that does the relevant explaining of presupposition triggering.

The proposal helps with one of the worries above. (6) asymmetrically entails (35) but doesn't presuppose (35). This was a worry for Simons' proposal but Abrusán's has a fairly clean treatment of the concern. The event time of (35) coincides with the event time of (6). (35) is only a valid entailment if the time of the belief coincides with the time of the awareness. Canada's beauty is in no way forced to be about the time of the awareness.

The grammatical necessity of temporal overlap matters. Consider:

38.   Jerry forgot (at t1) that it was raining (at t1).

In (35) the raining event may well concern the same time as the forgetting event. But the grammar doesn't require the coinciding of the times even if the times happen to coincide. Abrusán writes:

An entailment p is only accidentally about the matrix tense of S if there is a well-formed alternative S' to S such that the corresponding entailment p' of S' can be expressed by a sentence that is not about the event time of the matrix clause of S'.   (Abrusán 2011, p. 512)

The rough idea is that (38) has a well-formed alternative where the relevant times the sentences are about don't coincide, in particular:

39.   Jerry forgot (at t1) that it was raining (at t2).

By contrast, (40) doesn't enjoy a coherent, well-formed alternative:

40.   Jerry managed (at t1) to find the missing child (at t2?)

The managing time and the finding time are forced to coincide. This restriction predicts that 'Jerry found the missing child' is not a presupposition of (39), which is intuitively correct. Moreover, this restriction helps with one of the problems that bedeviled Simons' account. On Abrusán's account (6) no longer is predicted to presuppose (35). The entailment is forced to temporally coincide with the time of the awareness.

Abrusán's account is thus an improvement to the basic story on which the presupposition set of a sentence (in a context, relative to a QUD) is a filtered set of its entailments. While the mechanics are not as obviously Gricean as Simons', what explains the backgrounding effect of non-temporally overlapping information is the interaction of conversational expectations with hearer attention. This justification suggests that speakers of the same language with different attentional needs may well not take utterances of sentences like (6) to presuppose anything at all. This is very unlike a view that takes words like 'quit', 'aware' etc. to trigger, as a convention, presuppositions.

Unfortunately, Abrusán's account is empirically inadequate. The first problem concerns overgeneration. The account fares well in filtering out (35) as a presupposition of (6). However, it does not fare so well in filtering out a host of other cases, including the case of (28) and (29) repeated here with slight modification:

41.   Jessica stopped eating at Arby's.
42.   Jessica wasn't eating at Arby's.

(42) need not coincide temporally with (41). Of course, it is true that, at the temporal interval, that includes the stopping that Jessica wasn't eating at Arby's (assuming one can't stop doing F while doing F). But that doesn't force the times described by the matrix and embedded clauses to coincide.

One might complain, with some justice, that the *relevant* interval in which Jessica wasn't eating at Arby's has to overlap the time of the quitting—intuitively, one can't alter the facts regarding (42) without altering the facts regarding (40). That's true. But this is an artifact of the case. We can illustrate the point with other cases. For example,

43.   John threw the ball towards Sarah.
44.   John didn't have the ball.[9]

(44) is clearly entailed, but clearly not presupposed, by (43) (check the negation) and presumably (44) is mapped to an interval just after (43). (44) is also not the most direct answer to a question under discussion. The account thus overgenerates.

Second, the account struggles with contextual entailments. (45) clearly does not presuppose (46) but does presuppose (47):

45.   Tamar killed Bill at t1.
46.   Bill is dead at t1.
47.   Bill was alive at t2 < t1.

Abrusán explains this as follows:

---

[9]   I'm assuming the throwing has ended by the time the ball leaves the person's hand.

Notice again the contrast between the entailment of (45) that Bill was alive at t2 and the inference that Bill continued to be dead after the event time of the killing. While the first is indeed
a lexical entailment, the second is only a pragmatic inference that follows from our world
knowledge.   (Abrusán 2011, p. 521, numbering mine)

Fair enough. However, a few pages later, Abrusán offers an explanation of how in
context 'announce' may presuppose its complement despite not entailing it. The cases
she considers are as follows:

48. Context: Mary is 30 years old and expected to be reliable in her utterances.
     Sentence: Mary announced that she is pregnant.
49. Context: Mary is 7 years old and not expected to be reliable in her utterances.
     Sentence: Mary announced that she is pregnant.
50. Mary is pregnant.

Abrusán points out that relative to the context described in (48), but not (49) the complement is presupposed. Abrusán explains:

What is needed is to allow contextual entailments to enter the pool of candidate entailments
for presuppositions. Then if the embedded proposition is contextually entailed, it is also
predicted to be presupposed. Otherwise it isn't. Thus (48) is predicted to presuppose its complement, but not (49). So far this is simply an extension of the above mechanism to include
contextual entailments.   (Abrusán 2011, p. 530, numbering mine.)

Something has to give: it is hard to square the 'not strictly an entailment' explanation
with an insistence that contextual entailments are presupposed a few pages later. Surely
in most contexts (45) contextually entails (46)! Notice, moreover, that it can be cancelled in similar manners (i.e. if it is known in context that the person who is killed is
capable of being resurrected).

Finally, it's worth noticing how limited in scope the account is. First, it is applicable only to atomic sentences. That seems like a good starting point so long as there
are at least clues for how to extend the theory to non-atomic cases. One would
expect that similar mechanisms would extend to non-atomic cases but it isn't easy
to see how to do so while keeping the spirit of the view. Simons' (ms) provides the
following case:

51. [Every ballerina in the corps]$_i$ fears that [she$_i$ will regret that [she$_i$ ate a donut
     for breakfast]].

The complement of 'fears' looks like it should be presupposed on Abrusán's view but
there is nothing to presuppose as there is no proposition expressed by:

52. She$_i$ will regret that [she$_i$ ate a donut for breakfast].

(52) expresses a function from variable assignments to truth values, not a presupposable
piece of information. It's thus not the case that we can make sense of how to let the
time of the embedded clause interact with the time of the main clause to generate

presuppositions. As Simons notes, there are two options—revise the proposal, though it's not clear how to keep the main idea alive, given the ubiquity of cases like (52) and the range of presuppositions and entailments there are to deal with. Alternatively, one may simply claim that in cases such as (52), a different mechanism is responsible, at the level of the sentence, not by sentence-internal interactions. Simons worries about this approach:

> In general, it [this approach to subsentential clauses that don't denote propositions] would seem to lead to the view that presuppositions—at least, the kind of verbally triggered presuppositions Abrusán deals with—are properties only of proposition denoting constituents. This seems quite a reasonable move, given Abrusán's proposal that these propositions are derivable from content, rather than associated by convention with particular lexical items.
>
> But, we would then be left with the substantial question of how it is determined what the presuppositions of quantified sentences are.   (Simons ms, p. 17)

These objections don't constitute a knockdown argument to the general Gricean approach, characterized by (GI). But they do suggest that locating the source of presuppositions within conventions attending to particular lexical items and informational structures aren't going away anytime soon. So I will assume that any answer to the triggering question involves assigning by convention to lexical items their triggering potentials. Of course, the content of the presupposition is often determined in part by the semantic value of units that are larger than the triggering word or phrase—(6) presupposes that Canada is beautiful because of the presence of 'is aware' combined with the complement (that Canada is beautiful). But the story requires positing conventional features of the lexical item 'aware'. With that in place, we can turn to the next topic, unarticulated constituents.

Part 2: Unarticulated Constituents

I'll allow the philosopher who coined the phrase 'unarticulated constituent' to explain what they are. The discussion concerns an utterance of:

53.   It's raining.

Perry writes:

> In order to assign a truth-value to my son's statement [of (53)]...I needed a place. But no component of his statement stood for a place...Palo Alto is a constituent of the content of my son's remark, which no component of his statement designated; it is an unarticulated constituent
> (Perry 1986, p. 206, my numbering).

Perry's intention is to call attention to the lack of representation of a location in the sentence even though the communicated information concerns a location. Perry concludes that the location his son was talking about in uttering (53) is part of the information (a constituent) but not represented (unarticulated). Moreover, given that it's not articulated (or represented), but that utterances of (53) frequently do manage to communicate information regarding the rain in a location, it must be part of our general ability to enrich the information expressed by the sentence. Many have noticed that this sort of enrichment can be given a Gricean spin. The plausible line of reasoning isn't hard to supply. Assume that Perry and his son are both in Palo Alto and that his son utters (53). Perry, *qua* hearer, knows that interpreting (53) requires him to work out the location of the raining event. An utterance of (53) that concerned somewhere besides Palo Alto would presumably be irrelevant given the general goals Perry and his son have. Perry has no reason to think that his son is being uncooperative and believes that his son believes that of him, and that his son thinks that Perry is smart enough to realize that treating Palo Alto as the location of the event is the best way to restore conversational cooperativeness. Thus, Perry can work out that his son intends that Palo Alto is part of the information provided.

The phenomenon seems to appear in a range of other cases, including quantifier domain restriction, relational adjectives, relational nouns, verbs with dropped arguments etc. Here are a few examples with the unarticulated constituents represented by phrases in square brackets:

54.   Every student [in this class] failed.
55.   Pauline isn't ready [to run a marathon].
56.   The Capital [of France] is a nice place.
57.   I quit [smoking cigarettes].

Much ink and many pixels have been devoted to a host of questions about these cases: what does 'unarticulated' mean?[10] What is the relevant notion of a 'sentence'? Is the pseudo-Gricean story being told the best way to explain communication? Is 'rain' context sensitive?[11] Can the context sensitivity be traced to grammatical form? And, how can we explain what makes some information 'the best' when it comes to restoring conversational cooperativeness?[12] We will put most of these aside for now.

It's an oddity of I&C that it doesn't spend much time addressing an area in which Gricean-style relevance reasoning, rather than convention, has largely been taken to be orthodoxy.[13] In general, cases such as (53)–(57) have been trotted out to show that the conventions governing linguistic interpretation are too weak to ground communication unless supplemented by a theory that bridges the gap between what the conventional interpretation of (53)–(57) in context delivers and what people actually express in contexts using these sentences. Relevance theory was designed to explain how the

---

[10] See Sennet (2011) for some considerations on how to define 'unarticulated constituent'.

[11] See King and Stanley (2005) for an overview of some of these issues.

[12] Sperber and Wilson's *Relevance* (1995) presents a prime example of a theory meant to address this question.

[13] The oddity is furthered by the fact that Lepore and Stone use (53)—Perry's initial case for positing unarticulated constituents—as an example to motivate some of their views about convention and communication.

reasoning might go, starting with the Gricean notion of relevance and assuming that the conventionally derived meaning was too weak to explain what is said by an utterer.

If orthodoxy about unarticulated constituents is correct, *pace* I&C, linguistic conventions seem to be somewhat limited in providing a theory of interpretation. In some ways Lepore and Stone agree—interpretation requires assumptions about the speakers. But their idea that interpretation is a matter of working out a grammatical analysis in order to work out what an utterance means is at odds with the spirit of those arguing for unarticulated constituents.

So far so good. But what do unarticulated constituents have to do with presupposition triggering?

Part 3: Presuppositions, Unarticulated Constituents and Disambiguation

Lepore and Sennet (2014) aimed to show that accepting the orthodoxy about presupposition triggering, given some apparent data, constrains approaches to explaining cases of putative unarticulated constituents. Repeating the argument will help shed some light on the theory of communication presented in I&C, in particular, their notion of disambiguation.

The data mentioned above concerns cases in which an utterance of a sentence triggers a presupposition but the relevant trigger is left unarticulated. For example, consider a context in which we see someone leaving a meeting for ex-smokers, throwing out a pack of cigarettes and generally missing nicotine. You assert (regarding a mutual friend)

58.   Good for him. It's too bad Tipper isn't ready.

Plausibly in context you will work out that Tipper isn't ready to quit smoking. And moreover, if you knew that Tipper never smoked, you would treat (58) as infelicitous due to presupposition failure. Similar points attend:

59.   If Tipper isn't ready, then she won't show up to the meeting.
60.   Tipper might be ready.

The point is that utterances of (58)–(60) trigger the presupposition that Tipper smokes. Similar points attend to:

61.   Tipper isn't strong enough.
62.   Tipper can't.

The data suggests an interesting point regarding the interaction of the sort of phenomenon that Perry was worried about and presupposition triggering. If presupposition triggering requires presupposition triggers, then (58)–(62) need to contain the requisite triggers, even if they aren't literally said aloud. The argument is as follows:

P1.   (58)–(62) trigger presuppositions. (data)
P2.   Presuppositions are triggered by linguistic form, not merely by assignment of content. (Orthodoxy about triggering)
C.   The linguistic form of (58)–(62) triggers the presuppositions. (P1, P2)
P3.   The triggers of the presuppositions in (58)–(62) are unarticulated.
C2.   The linguistic form of (58)–(62) is unarticulated.

This leaves us with a dilemma. In what sense are the triggers 'present' given that they aren't articulated? How can we make sense of the idea that presuppositions are triggered by linguistic form when the relevant linguistic form has been left unsaid? How can the trigger both be present to provide the relevant triggering and be absent at the same time?

There are a few routes to answering this question. One is to deny (P2) and insist that speakers work out the relevant presuppositions based on the content of what was uttered and reasonable Gricean assumptions about cooperation. However, we have seen how difficult it is to provide a non-lexical triggering story of the relevant presuppositions. Another is to insist that, in some sense, (58)–(62) contain more words and structure that trigger the presuppositions. But in what sense do (58)–(62) contain these items? How can we make sense of the relevant notion of containment? Simply saying that the structure is articulated at a syntactic level such as LF is, in context, insufficient. In virtue of what do (58)–(62) 'have' these LFs? Presumably, any answer will involve speaker intentions and goals. But if this is what determines the relevant LF, couldn't we simply cut out the recovery of the particular triggering LF and claim that hearers simply work out what the speaker is trying to presuppose?

Lepore and Sennet (2014) claimed that (58)–(62), in context, have to bear relevant expressive relations to sentences that have more complete structures, presupposition triggers included. We were, however, a bit skimpy on the details. Lepore and Stone's notion of disambiguation seems at least to be a promising start to an answer. Their notion of disambiguation is in stark contrast to notions of pragmatic disambiguation that enrich meaning. To use an example, consider temporal interpretation of conjunctions. Their example is:

63.   Short sellers aim to buy low and sell high, but not in that order. They sell shares they don't own now (they are short of these shares) in hopes of buying them cheaper later on.

The phrase 'but not in that order' has been taken by Griceans to constitute a *cancellation*, or a way of alerting the hearer that the ordering they might have rationally expected based on conversational rules is not to be inferred as an implicature. This allows one to hold that 'and' is not ambiguous between an interpretation on which the conjuncts are ordered by the times the events they describe occur and one on which they do not. Lepore and Stone offer a competing diagnosis—the 'but' phrase is a standard referential disambiguation concerning the times picked out by 'buy' and 'sell'. And this, moreover, is in part a matter of working out which discourse relation is being expressed. Thus, their notion of disambiguation isn't one that involves working out enrichments to what is expressed by (63) but working out what (63) expresses in context. As they put it:

> In particular, we have come to see disambiguation as a powerful mechanism that inevitably connects utterance interpretation to speakers' goals and points of view in conversation. The idea is that the rules of language fix meanings for sentences in context only under a specific grammatical analysis. When a speaker makes an utterance, there is often ambiguity. If the speaker is cooperative, however, it will be clear how to resolve the ambiguity, and the resulting interpretation will be one that fits the accepted purpose or direction of the conversation.
>
> (Lepore and Stone 2015, p. 148)

In other words, disambiguation for them indicates the intended grammatical structure (here thought of as including discourse relations, information structure and the like) and pairing it with meaning.

The idea is, to my mind, one of the most interesting in the book. Disambiguation requires a grammatical analysis in order to fix utterance meanings and that, moreover, this grammatical analysis includes a whole host of features that are not obvious simply from the vehicle used to express a sentence. For example, if Lepore and Stone are right, part of the grammatical analysis of a sentence involves features such as focal stress. Reading these words, you are currently (if Lepore and Stone are right) imposing an information structure, a grammatical parsing of where the stress in the sentence belongs, a series of discourse relations and the like, in order to interpret me. Moreover, you are using a plethora of conventional clues to guide you, coupled with expectations of my goals in writing these words. The mere orthography doesn't make it clear in all of these cases; and yet we've managed to cooperate and coordinate all the same.

My proposal, in a nutshell, is to think about presupposition triggering along similar lines, even in cases where the triggers aren't explicitly uttered or written. (58) is understood in part by thinking of the speakers' intentions and imposing a grammatical analysis that includes things such as presupposition triggers. This, moreover, suggests that in a host of cases the right approach to interpretation in cases such as (52) doesn't involve positing unarticulated constituents but instead determining a grammatical analysis that includes lexical items (such as, perhaps, 'quit'). Of course, to work out which grammatical analysis to impose will require a great deal of reasoning about the speaker's intentions, goals, the conversational record, and the like. But if the view pursued in *I&C* is on the right track, this reasoning is a means to recovering a grammatical analysis and letting convention do its thing.

The argument for this notion of disambiguation as being the key notion, as opposed to a Gricean notion of implicated meaning or a relevance theoretic notion of meaning enrichment, is an integral part of I&C. I won't rehearse it here, but I will use the considerations to resolve the dilemma from the previous section. Lepore and Stone's notion of disambiguation gives us a purchase on how this might go: hearers work out an utterer's intended meaning by disambiguating a grammatical structure that conventionally triggers the presupposition in question.

This application of their view requires seeing sentences such as (58)–(62) as ambiguous, and that the resolution of this ambiguity isn't a matter of working out the meaning of 'ready' or 'can't' in context but of working out a grammatical form containing lexical items (i.e. 'quit smoking' in the relevant cases). This may seem strange at first. But if Lepore and Stone are right, this process has to be done for a great deal of grammatical structure that is left unarticulated in a similar sense. To my mind, this is a small price to pay once we are playing with a theory in which elements of meaning, such as information structure and discourse relations, are part of the grammatical form to be disambiguated.

In other words, one way of putting Lepore and Stone's result is that worries about unarticulated constituents in cases such as (53) are only one of a very large and heterogeneous group of grammatically and conventionally relevant aspects of meaning that a hearer has to work out to provide a coherent interpretation of an utterance. Given that hearers have to impose potentially complex information structures onto sentences to attain a coherent interpretation, working out a few lexical items as part of the grammatical analysis of the sentence starts to seem like the easiest and potentially most consciously tractable part of disambiguation, not the hardest or most mysterious.

Of course, one could reject orthodoxy and embrace a Gricean–Stalnakerian view of presupposition triggering. To my mind, this would be a large victory for views that take disambiguation to be a process of enrichment or inference from conversational maxims rather than pairing form and meaning as Lepore and Stone would have us think. So the issue is an important one and deserves more study, at least more than it receives in *I&C*. Hopefully this essay has shed some light on how the research may proceed.

References

Abrusán, M. (2011) 'Predicting the Presuppositions of Soft Triggers', *Linguistics and Philosophy*, 34(6): 491–535.

Abusch, D. (2002) 'Lexical Alternatives as a Source of Pragmatic Presupposition', in Brendan Jackson (ed.), *Proceedings of Semantics and Linguistic Theory* 12, CLC Publications, Cornell University, Ithaca, NY, 1–19.

Frege, G. (1948) 'Sense and Reference', *Philosophical Review*, 57(3): 209–30.

Grice, H. Paul (1975) 'Logic and Conversation', in Peter Cole and Jerry Morgan (eds.), *Syntax and Semantics*, New York: Academic Press, volume 3: Speech Acts, 43–58.

Grice, P. (1981) 'Presupposition and Conversational Implicature', in Peter Cole (ed.), *Radical Pragmatics*. New York: Academic Press, 183–98.

Kadmon, N. (2001) *Formal Pragmatics: Semantics, Pragmatics, Presupposition, and Focus*. Oxford: Blackwell Publishers.

Kamp, H. and Reyle, U. (1993) *From Discourse to Logic*. Dordrecht: Kluwer.

Karttunen, L. (1974) 'Presuppositions and Linguistic Context', *Theoretical Linguistics*, 1: 181–94.

King, J. and Stanley, J. (2005) 'Semantics, Pragmatics, and the Role of Semantic Content', in Zoltán Szabó (ed.), *Semantics Versus Pragmatics*. Oxford: Oxford University Press, 111–64.

Lepore, E. and Sennet, A. (2014) 'Presupposition and Context Sensitivity', *Mind and Language*, 29(5): 613–27.

Lepore E., and Stone, M. (2015) *Imagination and Convention: Distinguishing Grammar and Inference in Language*. London: Oxford University Press.

Perry, J. (1986) 'Thought Without Representation', in *Proceedings of the Aristotelian Society* Supplementary Volume 60, 263–83; reprinted in *The Problem of the Essential Indexical and Other Essays*, Oxford: Oxford University Press.

Roberts, C. (1996) 'Information Structure in Discourse: Towards an Integrated Formal Theory of Pragmatics', in *Papers in Semantics*, OSU Working Papers in Linguistics, Vol 49. Department of Linguistics, the Ohio State University, Columbus, 91–136.

Sennet, A. (2011) 'Unarticulated Constituents and Propositional Structure', in *Mind and Language* 26: 412–35.

Simons, M. (2001) 'On the Conversational Basis of some Presuppositions', in R. Hastings, B. Jackson, and S. Zvolenzky (eds.) *Proceedings of SALT* 11, Cornell University, CLC Publications, 431–48.

Simons, M. (ms) On the Non-independence of Triggering and Projection, https://www.semanticscholar.org/paper/On-the-Non-independence-of-Triggering-and-Simons/d572b88363c68b4ddf4505ff05ce7824ddb2863c/pdf

Sperber, D. and Wilson, D. (1995) *Relevance: Communication and Cognition* Oxford/Cambridge: Blackwell Publishers.

Stalnaker, R. (1973) 'Presuppositions', *The Journal of Philosophical Logic*, 2: 447–57.

Stalnaker, R. (1974) 'Pragmatic Presuppositions', in M. Munitz, and P. Unger (eds.) *Semantics and Philosophy*. New York: New York University Press, 197–214.

Stalnaker, R. (1999) *Context and content: Essays on intentionality in speech and thought*. Oxford: Oxford University Press.

Strawson, P. F. (1950) 'On Referring', *Mind* 59: 320–44.

5

Discourse, Context, and Coherence

The Grammar of Prominence

Una Stojnić

Introduction

What we say when we speak depends not solely on the words and expressions we use, but also on the context in which these words and expressions are uttered. If I say "I am hungry" and you also say "I am hungry", we have said two different things. If I say "She is happy," pointing at Ann, and you say "She is happy," pointing at Sue, we have said two different things. This phenomenon has to do (at least in part) with expressions such as 'I' and 'she'.[1] The unifying feature of these expressions is that their interpretation varies with a context of utterance: they are context-sensitive. Context-sensitivity permeates all aspects of our linguistic communication. Yet, we resolve it effortlessly, "on the fly."[2]

How is this achieved? What are the means by which the interpretation of a particular context-sensitive expression is determined on an occasion of use? And what sorts of interpretive resources do interlocutors appeal to when settling on an interpretation of a context-sensitive expression? It is quite common, in the philosophical and linguistic literature, to appeal to context-sensitivity of a particular item, while leaving the question of how context-sensitivity is resolved more or less open. For certain purposes this

---

[1] I say "in part" because the fact that the information conveyed varies with context of utterance is partly tied to considerations concerning other context-sensitive elements, such as tense, etc.

[2] Which expressions are context-sensitive is a matter of great controversy; some believe that the class is rather small, containing only the so-called indexicals and demonstrative pronouns (e.g. 'I' and 'she') (Lepore and Cappelen, 2005), others believe that the class is so large that it comprises virtually all expressions (Travis, 1989). Most, however, believe that the class contains more than just a few, but fewer than (almost) all expressions. But even so, they still disagree about which particular expressions are context-sensitive (and in what way). So, for example, we find debates over context-sensitivity of modals (Egan, Hawthorne, and Weatherson, 2005; von Fintel and Gillies, 2008; Kolodny and MacFarlane, 2010; Yalcin, 2007), predicates of personal taste (Cappelen and Hawthorne, 2009; Egan, 2010), knowledge ascriptions (Cohen, 1998; DeRose, 1995, 2009; Hawthorne, 2004; Schaffer and Szabó, 2013; Stanley, 2005), just to mention a few.

strategy might be warranted. However, ultimately it is important to provide an adequate answer to this question. An adequate theory of linguistic communication has to provide an account of how context-sensitivity is integrated within the semantics–pragmatics interface. Moreover, philosophers often posit context-sensitivity of particular philosophically interesting expressions (e.g. 'know', 'good', 'true'), and then use this context-sensitivity to motivate various philosophical conclusions about the under-lying phenomena (e.g. knowledge, goodness, truth). There has virtually been no area in philosophy where the contextualist move hasn't been exploited in one way or another. It is important, in assessing these arguments, to determine whether context-sensitivity is capable of the kind of patterns of resolution they predict and rely on.

So, how is context-sensitivity resolved?[3] Linguistic communication is obviously constrained by grammar, but it also seems to depend on various features of an utter-ance situation; for example, which gestures accompany my utterance, which contribu-tion the speaker intended to get across, and whether it was intended literally or figuratively. Accordingly, most theorists hold that meaning largely relies on communi-cative situations and intentions, and the interpretation involves general reasoning about these utterance features.[4] This is manifest in the standard assumptions about the resolution of context-sensitivity. To see this, it is useful to recall Kaplan's (1989a) distinction between 'pure indexicals' and 'true demonstratives.' Pure indexicals, in Kaplan's sense, are context-sensitive expressions whose linguistic meaning fully governs their resolution. The standard example is the first person pronoun 'I.' The linguistic meaning of 'I', its *character*, in Kaplan's terminology, is roughly, *the speaker of the context*. This character is sufficient to fully determine, given a context, what the referent of 'I' is; one needn't look into the speaker's mind in order to determine this. 'I' selects the speaker, regardless of whom the speaker intended to refer to, how manifest this inten-tion was, and who or what was salient in the utterance situation. On the other hand, we have true demonstratives, expressions like 'he' or 'that', whose character does not com-pletely determine their meaning given a context. If I say 'That is lovely', it doesn't suffice that you know that the character of 'that' is something like *the salient object in the context*. Some supplementation is needed to tell us how salience is determined. And

---

[3] Sometimes, the theory of how context determines interpretation is called *metasemantics* (Glanzberg, 2007a; Kaplan, 1989a, 1989b; King, 2014a), though one should bear in mind that the term 'metasemantics' has been used in different ways by different authors. For instance, it is sometimes used to denote *pre-semantic* processes that need to take place before the mechanisms of semantic interpretation can even kick in (e.g. disambiguation), and sometimes to denote the theory of how semantic facts get fixed (Kripke, 1980). The present essay is *not* concerned with metasemantics, in the latter two senses. Nor is my project concerned with metasemantics in the sense of Yalcin (2015), who understands it, roughly, as a theory of the grounds of the semantic properties postulated by first-order semantic theorizing.

[4] The idea that interpretation relies on mind reading goes back at least to Locke (1689) and, with important modifications, continues to be the dominant model through Grice (1975) and Kaplan (1989a). However, whereas Locke thought communication is entirely a matter of encoding and decoding content through linguistic forms, currently it is almost universally accepted, as Grice and Kaplan would have it, that meaning is at least partly determined through non-linguistic features of utterances. It is the Gricean/Kaplanean model that has dominated the discussions on context-sensitivity resolution.

this supplementation has traditionally been thought to go beyond the scope of grammar. What 'that' picks out depends on what the speaker intends and what the utterance situation is like; correlatively, the audience exploits whatever epistemic cues a speaker and her situation render available to discern her intentions.

Most context-sensitive expressions have traditionally been thought to pattern as true demonstratives. So, the standard answer to the question of how context-sensitivity is resolved, going back to at least Grice (1975) and Kaplan (1989a), is that the resolution of context-sensitive items depends, largely, on non-linguistic features of utterances. It is ultimately the speaker's (referential and/or communicative) intentions that determine the resolution of context-sensitive items, perhaps aided by certain contextual features that serve as epistemic cues that help make the relevant intention manifest.[5] This model predicts significant flexibility in the effects of context on the interpretation of context-sensitive items.

By contrast with the tradition, I will propose an account according to which context-sensitive expressions quite generally are best thought of as pure indexicals in the sense described above; their character fully determines their content, given a context. The account builds on the approach to demonstrative pronouns I developed in prior work (Stojnić, Stone, and Lepore, 2013, 2017). To illustrate the approach, take the paradigm example of a true demonstrative, a demonstrative pronoun, 'she.' The character of 'she' is, roughly, the most prominent individual in the context, satisfying the number, gender, and person requirements associated with the pronoun. What I suggest is that, given this character, the semantic content of 'she' is determined automatically, as a function of context, much like the semantic value of 'I' is. One does not need to appeal to extra-linguistic features of context (e.g. world-knowledge and speaker's mental states), as determinants of semantic content. This is because, I suggest, the prominence

---

[5] There are many proponents of the view that in some form or other the key meaning-determining role is played by speaker intentions. See, for instance, Cohen (1998), Dowell (2011), King (2014a, 2014b), King and Stanley (2005), Neale (2004, 1990), Reimer (1992), and Schiffer (1981). There are important differences among the proponents of different views in this tradition, but they all in one way or another emphasize the role of speaker intentions. One should note that most authors reject the naïve form of intentionalism, according to which the semantic content of a context-sensitive expression simply is what the speaker intended it to be. To illustrate the problem, suppose that the speaker points at John, and utters 'He is happy', while in fact intending to refer to Tim, her friend, who is neither present nor in any other way salient to the interlocutors. It seems implausible that her utterance expresses that Tim is happy. In response to this problem, some authors have noted the need for additional constraints on the communicative/referential intentions, requiring, for example, that they be appropriately manifest, as well as putting constraints on what can be reasonably intended. See in particular King (2014a, 2014b). Others have argued for what is sometimes labeled 'objective' metasemantics, that does not give a privileged role to speaker intentions, but rather maintains that (at least in certain cases), more objective features of context and general facts about the world fix the resolution of context-sensitive expressions (Glanzberg, 2007b; Lewis, ms., Wettstein, 1984). According to this view, general features of utterance situation do not merely serve as epistemic cues that allow the interpreters to recognize the meaning-determining intention, but rather they themselves can play a meaning-determining role. On such views the presence of an intention is neither necessary nor sufficient for determining semantic content. The view I shall defend differs from all of these types of view, since it maintains that meaning conventions, rather then referential/communicative intentions, or general non-linguistic facts about the world or context, play the content-determining role.

of potential referents in a context is itself maintained through a set of linguistic rules. The content of a pronoun is automatically determined as whatever is the most prominent referent in the context satisfying its character, at the point at which the pronoun occurs. So, it is the linguistic meaning of the term, together with linguistic mechanisms governing prominence, that determine the referent; no extra-linguistic supplementation is required.

In the present essay, I shall advocate this kind of a metasemantic account not only as a metasemantic account of pronoun resolution, but as a general metasemantics of context-sensitivity. In particular, I shall argue that contextual parameters governing the resolution of context-sensitive expressions are set to particular values at particular points in discourse through linguistic mechanisms that govern how these values are made prominent, or demoted, as the discourse evolves. Though my account treats all context-sensitive expressions as pure indexicals, it preserves an important insight behind the original Kaplanean distinction between pure indexicals and true demonstratives. Namely, I suggest that most context-sensitive expressions have been thought of as true demonstratives, because, unlike the character of 'I', their character is sensitive to the *prominence* of a particular value of a contextual parameter determining its meaning. I will call such expressions *prominence-sensitive* expressions.[6] However, by contrast with the tradition, which maintains that prominence is largely a matter of non-linguistic features of utterance, I shall argue that the dynamics of contextual prominence is governed by linguistic mechanisms. These linguistic mechanisms are what sets up contextual parameters to a particular value at any given point in a discourse; given thus antecedently set contextual parameters, the character of an expression fully determines the meaning in the context, much as in the case of 'I'.

Before proceeding I note that, given the programmatic character of the present proposal, the account developed here will remain provisional, as I only consider a circumscribed, if paradigm, set of context-sensitive items. However, the hope is that the

---

[6] This is not to say that the value of a contextual parameter governing the meaning of the first person pronoun is not dynamically changing as the discourse evolves. After all, interlocutors normally take turns speaking. However, the character of a prominence-sensitive expression is directly sensitive to a prominence ranking, having roughly the following form: 'the most prominent value satisfying the property X', where *the property X* is whichever property captures the linguistic constraints on the potential value of the term in question (e.g. phi-features of a pronoun). The character of 'I' does not reference prominence in this way. Another way to get at this distinction is to note that prominence-sensitive expressions typically allow for discourse and operator bound anaphoric readings—that is, their interpretation can co-vary with an expression introduced antecedently in the discourse. Expressions like the English first person pronoun 'I' do not allow for such readings. Their interpretation is sensitive to a parameter that plays a particular contextual role that is not sensitive to prominence (e.g. the character of 'I' is just 'the speaker of the context', not 'the prominent individual speaking'). Note that, interestingly, 'here' and 'now', though they are often classified as pure indexicals, together with 'I', do allow for readings on which they select a prominent value from the context. This explains why they can be bound, or discourse bound (unlike 'I'). While traditionally this has been thought of as a challenge to the claim that these expressions are pure indexicals, we shall see that all such examples demonstrate is that these expressions are prominence-sensitive. As we shall see, this is perfectly compatible with them being pure indexicals. For a detailed development of an account of prominence-sensitivity of 'now' along the lines of the theory I propose here, see Stojnić and Altshuler (2016).

discussion of the limited set of examples, provides substantive enough support for the general account that motivates potential developments of formally precise applications to specific cases, which lie outside of the scope of the present essay.[7]

1. Coherence

Consider the contrast between (1) and (2), from Hobbs (1979):

(1)   John took a train from Paris to Istanbul. He has family there.
(2)   John took a train from Paris to Istanbul. He likes spinach.

While (1) is perfectly fine, (2) sounds bad. Why is this? Crucially, (1) is not a mere sequence of random facts about John. The two bits of discourse are connected in a meaningful way—naturally, (1) is understood as conveying that John took a train from Paris to Istanbul *because* he has family there. A failure to grasp this explanatory connection is a failure to fully understand the speaker's contribution.

And it is precisely such a failure of establishing a connection that results in the badness of (2). The interlocutors are left searching for an explanatory connection. Unable to affirm it, they cannot fully grasp what is conveyed by (2). The same interpretive effort is invoked in interpreting both discourses. Understanding the connection in both cases is a part of understanding the discourse.

Coherence theorists materialize these observations by positing an implicit organization of the discourse that establishes coherence relations—such as the explanatory connection in (1)—among successive utterances, signaling how the speaker is organizing her contributions (Asher and Lascarides, 2003; Hobbs, 1979; Kehler, 2002). These relations signal what the speaker is doing with a given utterance—what kind of a discourse move she is making; she might be providing an explanation, continuing a narrative, elaborating on a previously mentioned event, etc.[8]

---

[7] Elsewhere, I have developed and defended a formally precise application of the present account to the context-sensitivity of demonstrative pronouns (Stojnić, Stone, and Lepore, 2013, 2017), modal expressions (Stojnić, 2017a, 2017b), quantifiers (Stojnić, ms.), and the temporal indexical 'now' (Stojnić and Altshuler, 2016). Insofar as those specific accounts are on the right track, they provide further support for the general view.

[8] What kinds of inferential connections can we expect to find in a discourse? Kehler (2002) suggests that coherence relations cluster in three broad categories. A discourse can be organized around a sequence of unfolding events, or an extended elaboration of a particular event, illustrating the class of what Kehler calls *contiguity* relations, as in (i):

(i) Max spilt a bucket of water. He spilt it all over the rug. (Kehler, 2002)

A discourse can also be organized around the cause–effect (or event–result) relations:

(ii) Max spilt a bucket of water. He tripped over his shoelaces. (Kehler, 2002)

Finally, a discourse could be organized around the so-called *resemblance* relations, comparing and contrasting two events along a certain dimension of (dis)similarity, as in (iii):

(iii) Max spilt a bucket of water. John dropped a jar of cookies.

Each of these three broad classes of coherence relations contains further more fine-grained instances, and the research suggests that interlocutors draw on a wide variety of specific relations (see, e.g. Mann and

Importantly, the tasks of establishing coherence in a discourse, and of pronoun resolution are mutually correlated, not independent tasks. To illustrate, consider the following example from Smyth (1994):

(3)   Phil tickled Stanley, and Liz poked him.

Two alternative ways of interpreting (3) tend to suggest themselves. According to one interpretation, the second clause is describing the result of the event described in the first clause—Phil tickled Stanley, *and consequently* Liz poked him. Alternatively, one can understand (3) as comparing and contrasting two events—Phil tickled Stanley, *and similarly*, Liz poked him. Crucially, when (3) is understood as organized by the Result relation, the referent of 'him' in (3) is Phil, and when the organizing relation is Parallel, the referent is Stanley.[9]

Elsewhere I have argued that these two tasks are more then merely correlated (Stojnić, Stone, and Lepore, 2013, 2017). In particular, I have argued that coherence relations, as a matter of a linguistic convention, make certain referents prominent for anaphora resolution, demoting others. Of course, it might seem that given a particular choice of a coherence relation, only a certain resolution makes sense. For instance, if the pronoun occurs in a narrative flow about a particular person, it is only natural that it refers to that person. However, as I argued, the effects of coherence relations on pronoun resolution are present even when that leads to an overall implausible, and even incoherent reading, and moreover even when a perfectly plausible alternative interpretation is available. The following example from Kehler (2002) illustrates the point:

(4)   Margaret Thatcher admires Ronald Reagan, and George W. Bush absolutely worships her.

English speakers find (4) infelicitous, interpreting it as if the speaker has mistakenly used 'her' to refer to Reagan.[10] While there is a perfectly accessible, suitable antecedent for the pronoun 'her' that is a well-known object of Bush's admiration, namely, Thatcher, the interlocutors do not opt for this interpretation, but rather recover an infelicitous one, that requires attributing an error to the speaker. Why is this? Note that 'admires' in the first sentence is followed by a stronger alternative, 'worships,' thus signaling that the discourse is organized around a comparison of Thatcher's and Bush's respective attitudes toward Reagan. This signals Parallel relation between the two conjuncts, that in turn makes Reagan prominent for subsequent reference resolution. In particular, Parallel requires that the pronoun in the object position is resolved

Thompson, 1988; Knott, 1996; Asher and Lascarides, 2003). Yet the broad classification is illustrative of the kind of dependencies we might expect to find.

[9] That pronoun resolution and the choice of a coherence relation are thusly correlated has been confirmed by a number of empirical studies. See, for example, Kaiser (2009), Kehler et al. (2008), and Wolf, Gibson, and Desmet (2004).

[10] See Kehler (2002, 2004, 2008) for empirical support for this claim.

to an antecedent introduced in the object position, which is Reagan. This effect of Parallel relation cannot be simply overridden by common sense, world-knowledge and plausibility considerations: the infelicitous interpretation is recovered even though there is a perfectly plausible nearby interpretation. This suggests that the effect of Parallel on pronoun resolution is conventionalized.

Moreover, though coherence relations have a certain effect on reference resolution *in English*, these effects differ across languages. Languages with overt markers for shifting attentional prominence, and signaling preference for reference resolution, tend to be much more constrained in what sorts of shifts they allow to happen implicitly, as an effect of discourse coherence. Since common-sense reasoning, and real world and plausibility considerations are presumably the same the world over, such cross-linguistic variations point to conventionality as the mechanism underlying these effects.[11]

I shall argue that discourse structuring mechanisms affect, and indeed, determine, the resolution of context-sensitivity *quite generally*, and do so as a matter of linguistic conventions, not as a matter of general common-sense reasoning in search of the overall most plausible interpretation. In particular, we shall see that the kind of effects of discourse structuring mechanisms we see on pronouns carry over to other types of context-sensitive expressions, and that, as with pronouns, such effects exhibit the hallmark of conventionality.

2. Coherence and Context-Sensitivity

As the examples from the previous section illustrate, mechanisms of discourse coherence make certain referents prominent as antecedents for subsequent pronouns. One way to think about the effects of discourse coherence on pronoun resolution, the one I have argued for elsewhere (Stojnić, Stone, and Lepore, 2013, 2017), builds on the idea that we can rank candidate referents in a discourse according to their relative prominence, those higher in the ranking being preferred resolutions to those lower in the ranking.[12] We can think of coherence relations as affecting prominence by updating the prominence ranking of candidate referents—making certain referents prominent and demoting others. A pronoun is then simply resolved to the highest ranked candidate referent that satisfies its character; for instance, 'she' denotes the top-ranked female, third person, singular referent at that particular point in the discourse. So, insofar as we think of the character of a pronoun as determining its semantic value as a

---

[11] See Stojnić, Stone, and Lepore (2017) for discussion and further examples. In the interest of space, I do not rehearse all the arguments here.

[12] The idea that we can rank candidate referents for anaphora resolution according to relative prominence comes from Centering Theory (Bittner, 2014; Grosz, Joshi, and Weinstein, 1995; Sidner, 1983). Note, however, that while within Centering Theory dynamics of prominence has typically been understood in psychological terms, the present account maintains that it is governed by linguistic conventions.

function of context, we can think of the prominence ranking as a parameter of the context the character is operating on.

In a Kaplanean framework, a context is a tuple comprising the parameters that affect the resolution of context-sensitive expressions (a tuple comprising the speaker, world, time, and location of the utterance). But we can generalize this idea, by envisioning context as a *conversational record*, in the sense of Lewis (1979), an abstract scoreboard that keeps track of the relevant information about the conversation. In particular, the scoreboard keeps track of the standard parameters fixing the meaning of the indexicals, such as who is speaking, at what time, in which world, who is the addressee, and so forth. More importantly, it is also keeping track of the information about how the relevant contextual parameters change as the discourse evolves. It tracks which moves have been made in the conversation, what has been said, which propositions have been mentioned, which individuals have been made prominent. In this way, we can think of the prominence ranking of candidate referents as of one aspect of a conversational scoreboard. Thus, unlike the Kaplanean context, which is static, the conversational scoreboard keeps track of the dynamic change in relevant contextual parameters as the discourse evolves. Given this notion of a context, a character of a demonstrative pronoun determines its semantic value as a function of context—for example, 'she' selects the top-ranked candidate referent, which is singular, third person, female.[13] Coherence relations can then be seen as affecting prominence by promoting certain referents, while demoting others. More precisely, a part of the linguistic contribution of a coherence relation is a prominence re-ranking update.

As I shall argue presently, coherence relations can be seen as changing parameters of the scoreboard that determine the resolution of context-sensitive items more generally: the contextual prominence of values of parameters governing the resolution of prominence-sensitive expressions quite generally is affected by the same mechanisms which affect prominence of candidate referents for pronoun resolution. Consider the case of an obviously prominence-sensitive class of expressions: that of quantifiers. An utterance of 'Everyone had fun today' does not typically mean that *everyone in the universe* had fun on the day of utterance. Typically, it conveys something more restricted, perhaps that everyone who attended some particular event had fun. The restriction on the domain of quantification is normally thought to be contextually determined.[14] Moreover, just as pronouns are prominence-sensitive insofar as they are looking for an antecedent that can be provided either by the non-linguistic context, or by a prior discourse, quantifiers, too, are looking for a prominent restrictor either from the non-linguistic context or from a prior discourse.

---

[13] It is worth pointing out that this type of an account allows for an implementation that captures both referential and bound (including discourse bound, or E-type) readings of pronouns. In particular, the semantics will treat all uses of pronouns as covarying with an antecedent expression, and thus, as bound variables. For formal details, see Stojnić, Stone, and Lepore (2017). For the present purposes, the informal sketch of the view will suffice.

[14] For more on quantifier domain restriction see, for example, von Fintel (1994), and Stanley and Szabó (2000).

For instance, just as one can use (5) to refer to a prominent female in a non-linguistic context, so too one can use (6) to refer to a prominent set of individuals.[15]

(5)   (Referring to a certain significant female) She left me. (Partee, 1984)
(6)   (Looking around the classroom about to start my lecture) Everybody is here, so we can start.

But a restrictor can be provided by the prior discourse, as well:

(7)   Half of the students came to the party. Some brought cookies.

Here the second quantifier is understood to quantify over a subdomain of the first one, thus receiving a more restricted reading—some students *who came to the party* brought cookies. What I shall now argue is that the prominence of potential restrictors on the domain of quantification is governed by mechanisms of discourse coherence, just as the resolution of pronominal anaphora is. We can readily appeal to these mechanisms to predict the intuitively correct interpretation of (7). The first sentence describes a situation about the group of students at a party. The second sentence is naturally understood as elaborating on the first one; the set of students introduced in the first sentence is thus made prominent, and 'Some' is restricted to quantify over that set of students. So, we understand (7) to mean that half of the students came to the party, and some of those students who came to the party brought cookies.

Perhaps a more interesting example is the following one:[16]

(8)   If there is fire, the alarm always rings.
(9)   But the alarm doesn't always ring.

In (8), the consequent of the conditional is understood as elaborating on the information described by the antecedent, and the quantifier, 'always', is understood as restricted by the set situations described in the antecedent, namely the ones that contain a fire event. In (9), however, 'always' in the second sentence is *not* thusly restricted—we cannot, for instance, conclude from (8) and (9) that there is no fire. Assuming that mechanisms of discourse coherence affect the prominence of potential restrictors, we can explain this difference in domain restriction between (8) and (9). The second sentence stands in Contrast relation to the first one. The two sentences are thus understood as contributing contrasting bits of information about some body of information.[17]

---

[15] Whether the domain restriction is captured in terms of sets, or functions from objects to sets, or properties, or perhaps situations, is a matter of debate (Barwise and Etchemendy, 1987; Elbourne, 2008; Kratzer, 1998, 2014; Recanati, 1996; Stanley and Szabó, 2000; von Fintel, 1994). Though specific details are important, we need not worry about them presently. For a more detailed account, see Stojnić (ms.).

[16] The example is based on one from Yalcin (2012).

[17] More precisely, where *p* and *q* stand in Contrast relation, they are required to provide contrasting information about some body of information, regarding some common topic. The relevant topic is typically signaled by the cues in the information structure, the dimension of meaning that signals how information conveyed by an utterance relates to the previous contributions (by dividing it into the topic and comment, or focus and background), how it contrasts with alternative possibilities in the discourse, and which role it plays as a move in the dynamics of conversation. In English, we exploit prosodic accents as signals of a particular information structure (Roberts, 1996a; Rooth, 1992).

Contrast makes the set of situations described by that body of information prominent. As a result, 'always' in the second sentence is understood as quantifying over all those, not just the ones where there is fire.[18] So we understand (8) as conveying that it's not the case that the alarm rings in all of the situations compatible with our overall body of information (regardless of the presence of fire). Compare this case with the following:

(10)   If there is a fire, the alarm always rings.
(11)   The firefighters usually arrive within five minutes.

Superficially, (10) and (11) seem to have exactly the same shape as (8) and (9). However, they are not naturally understood as standing in Contrast relation. Rather, (11) is understood as elaborating on the information described by (10) (where, as before, the consequent of (10) is itself understood as elaborating on the antecedent). As a result of Elaboration, the set situations described by (10)—the ones in which there is fire, and the alarm rings—is made prominent, and the quantifier in (11) is restricted by it. So we get the reading that *in all the situations in which there is a fire*, the alarm always rings, and that in most *of those* the firefighters arrive within five minutes.

Unsurprisingly, a similar kind of behavior is exhibited by modal expressions, which are traditionally understood as quantifiers over a contextually determined set of possibilities.[19] Note first that just like quantifiers (and pronouns), modals too can be restricted by a possibility either made prominent in the non-linguistic context, or mentioned earlier in a discourse.[20] For instance, one can use (12) to describe a hypothetical scenario prominent in the non-linguistic context:

(12)   (Looking at a high-end stereo in an electronics store) My neighbors would kill me. (Stone, 1997)

In turn, in (13), the restriction is provided by the prior discourse:

(13)   A wolf might walk in. It would eat you. (Roberts, 1989)

So, like pronouns and quantifiers, modals are likewise prominence-sensitive, searching for a prominent possibility restricting their domain of quantification. Once again, the prominence of possibilities is governed by mechanisms of discourse coherence. For instance, in (13), we understand the second sentence to elaborate on the first one. Elaboration makes the possibility described by the first sentence prominent.[21] The second sentence is then understood as quantifying over the (epistemically accessible) worlds in which this possibility obtains, and so we get the intuitively correct reading: a wolf would eat you, given that one walks in.

---

[18]   For a formalization of this effect of Contrast, see Stojnić (2017b).
[19]   I have defended this account of modality in detail elsewhere. See Stojnić (2017a, 2017b).
[20]   See Stone (1997, 1999) for a detailed argument in support of the claim that modal expressions exhibit the same range of interpretations as pronouns. Stone's argument parallels Partee's (1973) argument for the parallel between the interpretation of tenses and pronouns.
[21]   For our purposes, a possibility is just a proposition, or a set of worlds.

Again, as before, the effect of coherence on prominence is crucial, as is illustrated by the following example:

(14)   If a wolf walks in, it would eat you. But one probably won't walk in.

The consequent of the first sentence in (14) elaborates on the hypothetical scenario described by the antecedent. Elaboration makes the hypothetical scenario introduced by the antecedent prominent, and as a result, 'would' is understood as restricted by it—a wolf would eat you given that one walks in. Crucially, however, the second sentence does not further elaborate upon a scenario described by the two modals in the first sentence. The two sentences stand in Contrast relation, signaled by the discourse marker 'but', and are understood as contrasting two hypothetical scenarios—one in which a wolf walks in, and one in which one does not. Contrast requires that the first and the second sentence provide contrasting information about some body of information. Which body of information are they about? That depends on which body of information is the most prominent one at the time of utterance of the first sentence. Assuming that it was uttered discourse initially, the first sentence is interpreted as contributing information about the set of epistemically accessible worlds determined by the context discourse initially, describing what might be the case if a wolf walked in, *given this overall body of information.*[22] The second sentence then has to provide a contrasting bit of information, regarding the possibility of a wolf's entrance, about this body of information. Contrast makes this body of information prominent, and as a result, 'would' is understood as quantifying over it. Thus, we get the intuitively correct interpretation that *given this overall body of information,* a wolf probably won't come in.

Similarly, consider (15):

(15)   A wolf might walk in. But, then again one will probably not. It would eat Harvey.

In (15), we cannot understand 'would' in the final sentence as restricted by the proposition describing the epistemic possibility of a wolf walking in. The first two sentences stand in Contrast relation, and the two modals are understood as contributing contrasting bits of information about some body of information, as before (e.g. about the epistemically accessible worlds determined by the context discourse initially). The

---

[22] But how does the context determine a prominent body of information for the interpretation of a modal utterance when that utterance does not follow up on a previous discourse? Won't it be the case that there we need general pragmatic principles to resolve context-sensitivity? This does not follow. As I have argued elsewhere (Stojnić, Stone, and Lepore, 2013; Stojnić, 2017a), how a context-sensitive expression is interpreted discourse initially depends on what type of connection an utterance is understood to bear towards the utterance situation, and the ongoing goals and plans of the interlocutors. In particular it matters what the speaker is doing with her utterance: whether she is summarizing a situation (as well as which situation she is summarizing), assessing it, providing an explanation, addressing a question, etc. These different options will give rise to different interpretive dependences—different coherence relations—which in turn set the value of a contextual parameter in the way described in the main text. The crucial point is that the two tasks are, again, not independent—the choice of the coherence relation still governs the resolution of the context-sensitive item.

third sentence, however, is naturally understood as further elaborating on the second. Elaboration makes the possibility described by the second modal prominent, and that is why the modal in the third sentence, 'would', selects it as its restrictor. But this doesn't allow for the restricted interpretation, where 'it' is understood as the hypothetical wolf described by the first sentence. Note that this interpretation is persistent, despite the intuitive infelicity of (15), and despite the perfectly plausible alternative interpretation, that could have been recovered instead: namely, that a wolf would eat Harvey, if one were to walk in. The latter interpretation is unavailable, even though the possibility of a wolf walking in has been recently explicitly mentioned, and should thus be, intuitively, salient in the given context. Similar behavior is exhibited by other prominence-sensitive expressions. For instance, we see this with the so-called incomplete definite descriptions. To see what is at stake, consider the following example:

(16)   The table is covered with books.

Definite descriptions typically are thought to require some form of uniqueness (so, that 'the F' denotes the unique x satisfying F).[23] But examples like (16) seem to go against this requirement. Even though there are many tables in the world, we can imagine (16) uttered in a room with exactly one table, to successfully convey that the table in the room is covered with books.[24] So, 'the table' in (16) is an incomplete description. It is the context that supplies an extra bit of content that is left implicit. The uniqueness is then merely required within a contextually restricted domain. In other words, definite descriptions, like quantifiers, and modals, require a contextually prominent restriction—they are prominence-sensitive. As before, the restriction can be provided by the non-linguistic context, as in (16), or by the prior discourse, as in (17):

(17)   John has a cat and a dog. He walks the dog twice daily and lets the cat out at night. (Roberts 2011)

Once again, I suggest, prominence is affected by discourse structuring mechanisms. In (17), we understand the second sentence as elaborating on the situation described by the first. Similarly as before, Elaboration makes the situation described prominent. The situation in turn restricts the domain relevant for the interpretation of the definite descriptions in question: the two definite descriptions are understood as denoting the unique dog and cat in the (minimal) situation described by the previous utterance, namely, the one in which John has a cat and a dog[25]

---

[23] This observation goes back to at least Frege (1892) and Russell (1905).

[24] As Roberts (2011) points out, even a weak requirement that the referent be unique merely within the common ground—that is, within the body of information the interlocutors mutually accept for the purposes of the conversation—won't help us get around the problem. A typical common ground will normally entail the existence of many tables.

[25] There is a long-standing tradition of treating domain restriction on incomplete descriptions by exploiting possible situations (Barwise and Etchemendy, 1987; Elbourne, 2008; Kratzer, 1998, 2014; Recanati, 1996). Though this approach is elegant, as noted before, it's not essential for the present account.

A similar, though slightly more complicated, example is the following one from Lewis (1979):

(18) (While Bruce, the cat, is in the room, making itself salient by dashing madly about): The cat is in the carton. The cat will never meet our other cat, because our other cat lives in New Zealand. Our New Zealand cat lives with the Cresswells. And there he'll stay, because Miriam would be sad if the cat went away.

Lewis himself uses this example to illustrate how definite descriptions are sensitive to prominence, arguing that 'the F' denotes the unique F that is most salient in the domain of discourse, although he, of course, was not committed to the specific account of the mechanisms that govern prominence that I propose here. But, assuming that prominence is governed by discourse coherence, we can explain (18) as follows: the first sentence summarizes a perceptually present situation, and as a result, the description is understood as denoting the unique cat within this situation. The first conjunct of the second sentence provides a further elaboration about the cat in the first sentence, making the situation described by the first sentence prominent: the cat in the perceptually present situation will never meet the speaker's other cat; in turn, the situation described by the second conjunct provides an explanation of the first one—it is because the other cat lives in New Zealand that the first cat will never meet it—and, the last two sentences provide further elaboration of this explanation. It is due to this chain of Elaboration relations that the situation described by the second conjunct of the second sentence, and by the third sentence is made prominent, and consequently, we understand 'the cat' in the final sentence to be the unique cat in this situation. Thus, we get the interpretation that the New Zealand cat will stay, because Miriam would be sad if it went away.

Similar kinds of considerations generalize to other kinds of context-sensitive expressions as well. Consider, for instance, a gradable adjective, like 'tall.' Gradable adjectives are typically treated as expressing relations between individuals and degrees, where the individual satisfies the property just in case it possesses the property to at least a contextually specified degree.[26] Thus, gradable adjectives are looking for a contextually prominent degree or threshold. Most accounts assume that what this degree in the context exactly is, is left to pragmatic considerations to determine. However, examples (19) to (20) again suggest that the mechanisms of discourse coherence affect the possible values of this contextual parameter as well, making certain resolutions prominent.

(19) John is tall! His height is 2m.
(20) We should put John on our professional basketball team. He's tall.

For our purposes, we could equally well exploit reference to sets, or properties as mechanisms of domain restriction (von Fintel, 1994; Stanley and Szabó, 2000).

[26] See, for example, Barker (2002), Hamann (1991), Kennedy (2007), and Klein (1991). We need not concern ourselves with specific formal details of the semantics of gradable adjectives for our present purposes.

In (19), the second sentence is related to the first one by Specification, providing more detail about how one should understand the first sentence.[27] In particular, the second sentence makes it clear that being two meters tall suffices to count as tall in the given context. In (20), in turn, Explanation relation ties the two bits of discourse together. This again specifies the relevant degree of height—in particular, John has to be at least as tall as an average basketball player. Resolving the context-sensitivity of 'tall' this way allows the second bit of discourse to provide an explanation of the first one. Hence the awkwardness of (21):

(21)   We should put John on our professional basketball team. He's tall. Of course, he isn't tall enough for a basketball player.

And the same point extends to relational expressions, like 'local', that require a contextually specified 'implicit argument'. Note, first, that an utterance of (22) can convey that John went to a bar local to him, or local to some other, contextually specified person or place. Relational expressions, like 'local', are searching for an implicit argument prominent in the non-linguistic context or in the prior discourse.

(22)   John went to a local bar.

Once again, in the case of relational expressions, the prominence of potential arguments is sensitive to discourse structuring mechanisms. Consider the following example:

(23)   The Maryland Food Bank launched its "Save a Seat at Your Table" campaign in November, a large-scale effort encouraging Marylanders to pledge $1 per day to help feed the 757,000 people who are food insecure in the state. Now, the nonprofit organization is recruiting local restaurants to join the movement.[28]

Here, 'local' occurs within a narrative about Maryland and its Food Bank, and is thus understood as local-to-Maryland. Crucially, 'local' cannot just freely be used to denote a location local to any place or person made salient in the context. Consider the following:

(24)   John was in Paris in May, but on June 1st he arrived in Belgrade. He checked into a hotel, and proceeded to explore the city. He particularly enjoyed a local bar near the Eiffel Tower.

Interestingly, in (24), we naturally interpret the final sentence as conveying information that John enjoyed a local bar in Belgrade, near the Eiffel Tower. Even though the audience may well be aware that there is no Eiffel Tower in Belgrade, and might know perfectly well that the Eiffel Tower is in Paris, and moreover, even though Paris has been explicitly mentioned earlier in the discourse, we do not understand the final

---

[27] For a similar point involving Specification, see Stone and Stojnić (2015). For an account of context-sensitivity resolution of gradable adjectives along these lines, see Stone and Stojnić (ms.).

[28] http://www.baltimoresun.com/entertainment/dining/baltimore-diner-blog/bal-local-restaurants-join-in-maryland-food-bank-s-save-a-seat-campaign-20160311-story.html.

sentence as conveying that John particularly enjoyed a local bar in Paris. Assuming that prominence of a particular resolution of 'local' is dictated by discourse coherence, we can predict this straightforwardly: the final sentence in (24) is introduced in a chain of Elaboration about the Belgrade trip. The Elaboration makes Belgrade prominent, and as a result, 'local' is understood as being local to Belgrade.

What all these examples illustrate is that discourse structuring mechanisms dictate the prominence of potential values of contextual parameters governing the resolution of context-sensitive, prominence-sensitive expressions quite generally. We see similar effects across a range of examples—pronouns, quantifiers, modal expressions, definite descriptions, gradable adjectives and relational expressions. Though of course the set of examples considered here is limited, and thus the discussion provisional, what seems to transpire is that these kinds of effects on prominence are not isolated to a small sample of expressions, but are rather general and pervasive. In all these cases discourse coherence governs contextual prominence in analogous ways.

3. Coherence and Grammar

How does the discussion of the previous section bare on intentionalism and, more generally, on the traditional pragmatic accounts of context-sensitivity resolution? If the impact of coherence on prominence of a particular value for a contextual parameter were merely a byproduct of general pragmatic reasoning—that is, if a particular coherence relation simply served as a cue manifesting (defeasibly) a particular speaker intention, or if it were merely one among many, potentially extra-linguistic, cues that helped fix the supplementation required for the interpretation of a context-sensitive expression given its incomplete character—then the intentionalist, and pragmatic metasemantics would be compatible with the considerations raised in §2. Most context-sensitive expressions would then, indeed, behave like true demonstratives. If, however, the impact of coherence on the prominence of potential values of contextual parameters is a matter of an underlying linguistic convention—a rule of language— then context-sensitive expressions, quite generally, behave like pure indexicals. Given their character, no extra-linguistic information is required to determine their semantic content in a context. More precisely, though the linguistic meaning of a particular context-sensitive expression might require contextual supplementation, if this supplementation is itself determined by linguistic constraints, then it is the rules of language—those governing the use of the expression together with those governing the prominence of potential resolutions—that determine the semantic content of the expression in a context. As foreshadowed in the previous sections, I shall argue that evidence favors the latter view.

We have already seen some evidence that the effects of coherence on pronoun resolution are a matter of underlying linguistic conventions. Recall (4), repeated in (25):

(25)   Margaret Thatcher admires Ronald Reagan, and George W. Bush absolutely worships her.

We have seen that, even if we suppose that the speaker uttered (25) with an intention to refer to Thatcher with the pronoun 'her', (25) is still infelicitous. The choice of a coherence relation—in this case Parallel—requires that the antecedent of the pronoun be introduced in the object position. This is what underwrites the judgment of infelicity. And this is so, even though in this particular case, all the plausibility, relevance and charity considerations would favor a different interpretation: there is an available antecedent that matches the grammatical gender of the pronoun, namely, Thatcher, which is, moreover, a well-known object of Bush's admiration. The interpretation actually recovered, according to which the speaker has mistakenly uttered 'her' to refer to Reagan, is uncharitable. That it is nevertheless the naturally recovered interpretation, despite all these pragmatic considerations, suggests that Parallel dictates a particular interpretation of a pronoun as a matter of an underlying linguistic rule, which is hard to override by such pragmatic considerations.[29]

Evidence suggests that the effects of coherence on prominence more generally exhibit hallmarks of conventionality: these effects seem to be a part of our linguistic repertoire, inert to considerations of common-sense reasoning and plausibility, and variant across different linguistic communities. We have already seen examples that suggest that this is the case with the effects of coherence on domain restriction of modals. For instance, in (15), even though the possibility of a wolf walking in has been explicitly mentioned, and left open in the discourse, the third sentence cannot be understood as restricted by this possibility. It is understood as elaborating on the second sentence, and is thus restricted by the possibility described by the second sentence. This is so despite the fact that this leads to an infelicitous interpretation. So, just as in the case of pronouns, the mechanisms of discourse coherence sometimes force an infelicitous reading of modal utterances, even when the pragmatic account would predict plausible alternative interpretations.[30] Another, perhaps even clearer, example of this is the following one based on Yalcin (2007):

(26)   If it is not raining and it might be raining, then I'm uninformed about the current weather.

As Yalcin notes, (26) is infelicitous. We are left with the impression that we are asked to consider an inconsistent hypothetical scenario. This is puzzling from the standpoint of a contextualist who maintains that modals are simply quantifiers quantifying over contextually provided sets of worlds, where the relevant worlds are determined according to the standard pragmatic metasemantics. The problem is that considerations of charity and plausibility do not predict that (26) should be infelicitous. There are available bodies of information that could serve as a restriction on the domain of quantification for a modal 'might' that would deliver a perfectly consistent interpretation.

---

[29] Note that if the pronoun in (25) is accented, one understands it as referring to Thatcher. However, in that case the discourse is no longer understood as organized by Parallel. Rather, we understand it as explaining how Bush follows Thatcher's opinions. I shall return to this point in §4.

[30] For detailed discussion of this point and further examples, see Stojnić (2017a).

For instance, the modal could be quantifying over the speaker's body of information, thus yielding a perfectly consistent interpretation, namely that, if it is raining, and for all the speaker knows it is not, then the speaker is uninformed about the weather. But the inconsistent reading is predicted if we assume that mechanisms of discourse coherence make certain possibilities prominent as restrictors for modals as a matter of grammar. We naturally understand the second conjunct in the antecedent as elaborating on the first one. Elaboration makes the non-raining scenario described by the first conjunct prominent, and the modal in the second conjunct selects it as its restrictor. Thus, we get the reading that if it is raining and it might not be, *given that it is*, the speaker is uninformed about the weather. Of course, the scenario described by the antecedent, on this reading, is inconsistent, so infelicity is predicted. Again, the fact that this reading is forced even though there are other possible, and vastly more plausible, interpretations, suggests that the effect of Elaboration is a matter of a linguistic convention.[31]

The same kinds of considerations extend to other kinds of examples we have considered so far. For instance, take (24). Clearly, resolving 'local' in such a way so as to mean *local-to-Paris* would make the most sense in (24), especially assuming that all the parties to the conversation know well the relevant facts about Paris and Belgrade. Yet, it's surprisingly difficult to get this reading. In particular, so long as we understand the final sentence in (24) as a part of the chain of elaborations about the Belgrade trip, 'local' is interpreted as *local-to-Belgrade*. This is again surprising if Elaboration merely pragmatically suggests a certain interpretation. And the same point is illustrated by the following example as well:

(27)   Some dogs chased a few cats. Most cats ran away. A few caught one.

Given the available information contributed by the first two sentences in (27), it would clearly make the most sense that 'a few' in the last sentence quantifies over the set of dogs that did the chasing. Yet, this is not the interpretation we find. Rather, we expect that 'a few' quantifies over the set of cats, resulting in an intuitively odd interpretation.

---

[31] Another piece of evidence for thinking that the effects of mechanisms of discourse coherence are a matter of a linguistic convention comes from cross-linguistic variations that these mechanisms and these effects exhibit. To illustrate, while one might expect that understanding the second sentence in (13) as elaborating on the first one, and hence, interpreting (13) as being organized by Elaboration relation, is a matter of common sense reasoning—after all, it only makes sense that the scenario in which the addressee is being eaten provides a further elaboration of the one in which a wolf walks in—Asher and McCready (2007) point out that the Japanese translation of (13) is infelicitous unless it contains an overt discourse marker that signals the appropriate relation. Similarly, in the case of pronouns, languages that use different means of signaling prominence of candidate referents—for instance, word order or topic markers—are often more constrained in the kinds of shifts they associate with coherence. As reasoning about speaker's intentions and general world knowledge is the same the world over, such cross-linguistic variations strongly suggest that these effects are a matter of an underlying convention. For a more detailed discussion of the cross-linguistic data suggesting that the effects of coherence on the interpretation of pronouns and modals are linguistically encoded, see Stojnić, Stone, and Lepore (2017) and Stojnić (2017a), respectively.

The same goes for incomplete definite descriptions. To illustrate, consider the following example:

(28)   I left the living room and walked into the bedroom. The bedroom had no windows. The window was open.

In (28), one cannot understand 'the window' as being the window in the living room, even though the living room has been mentioned, and the bedroom ruled out. This is because we understand both the description of the window being open, and the bedroom being windowless as providing background circumstances to the event of entering the bedroom, and are thus restricted to the situation describing the bedroom. Since the descriptions are incompatible—there can be no window in a windowless room—(28) is infelicitous.

All these examples illustrate the same point—not only do the mechanisms of discourse coherence affect the interpretation of context-sensitive items, but their effect is not reducible to common-sense inference that draws holistically on the epistemic cues reflecting speaker intentions. In particular, these effects seem to draw on the knowledge of linguistic conventions that underscore the dynamics of prominence. These conventions fix interpretations in ways difficult for general world-knowledge or common-sense reasoning about speaker's intentions to override.

4. Discourse Structure, Information Structure, and Grammar

We have seen in the previous sections that mechanisms of discourse coherence affect the resolution of context-sensitive items in a systematic and rule-governed way. Of course, I do not mean to suggest that discourse coherence is the only relevant linguistic factor for context-sensitivity resolution. Other linguistic mechanisms can affect the interpretation in analogous ways. In particular, context-sensitivity resolution is also affected by mechanisms of information structure. Information structure marks the dimension of meaning signaling how the information conveyed with an utterance is related to the prior information, how it is organized with respect to categories such as focus/background, topic/comment, how it contrasts with relevant alternatives, and which move it makes in the dynamics of communication.[32] In English, information structure is typically signaled through intonation.[33]

---

[32] For more on information structure see, for example, Halliday (1967), Vallduví (1992, 1993), Ginzburg (2012), and Roberts (1996a).

[33] This fact is, again, language specific. Many languages use word order, or overt morphology, to signal a particular information structure. This suggests that the signals of information structure, too, are a part of the conventional linguistic repertoire of a given language. See Lepore and Stone (2015) for discussion of this point.

That information structure impacts the interpretation of context-sensitive items has been well noted in the literature (Evans, 1980; Lappin, 1993a, 1993b, 1996). To illustrate, consider the following example, from Evans (1980):

(29)   Everyone has finally realized that Oscar is incompetent. Even HE has finally realized that Oscar is incompetent.[34]

The observation is that, though normally 'he' could not be interpreted as co-referring with Oscar, due to the constraints on binding,[35] when there is contrastive stress on the pronoun 'he', one nevertheless understands 'he' as picking out Oscar. In a similar fashion, (as Kehler himself notes), one can improve (4), by putting contrastive stress on the pronoun her:

(30)   Margaret Thatcher admires Ronald Reagan, and George W. Bush absolutely worships HER.

With this modification, we can understand the pronoun as referring to Thatcher. The focal stress achieves a sort of implicit demonstration, making Thatcher the most prominent referent at this point in a discourse, again. How does this bear on the argument of the previous sections, that coherence relations determine the resolution of pronouns? We have seen in the discussion of (4) that Parallel relation requires that 'her' is resolved to the object of the previous clause—Reagan. Does the effect of focus we see in (30) violate this rule? The answer is negative. It is important to note that, while putting the stress on 'her' improves the overall felicity of the discourse, it also changes its overall interpretation. In particular, one no longer understands the discourse in (30) as comparing Thatcher's and Bush's respective attitudes (toward Reagan), but rather as explaining Bush's respect for Thatcher's opinions. Importantly, there is no reading according to which the discourse is organized by Parallel, yet the pronoun refers to Thatcher.[36]

This observation is further supported by examples like the following one from Kehler (2002):

(31)   The lawyer defended Bill against the accusations, and he did too.

As Kehler notes, even with the contrastive stress on the pronoun, (31) does not have an interpretation according to which 'he' is understood to refer to Bill. The problem is that it is hard to understand (31) as organized by anything other than Parallel, and thus, the pronoun 'he', is expected to co-vary with the NP in the subject position in the first clause. Since, even with the contrastive stress, the Parallel reading is still the only one available, the infelicity of (31) is predicted: Parallel requires that 'he' be the lawyer, whereas the contrastive stress requires that it be someone else—Bill. In effect, it is as

[34] I'm using capitalization to signal focus. See Roberts (1996a). Also, see Rooth (1992) for more on sentential focus.

[35] In particular, this would require a violation of *Principle C* of the Government and Binding Theory (Chomsky, 1981).

[36] See Stojnić, Stone, and Lepore (2017) for further discussion of this point.

though the speaker is pointing in two different directions along with a single use of a pronoun. While both discourse structure and information structure affect prominence, and thereby context-sensitivity resolution, the effects do not override each other; for the interpretation to be felicitous they have to work in tandem.

Another important aspect of information structure has to do with signaling which part of an utterance connects to the prior contributions, and which is the new distinctive contribution that the utterance is making—that is, signaling the distinction between the theme or topic, and rheme or comment. One way to think about this distinction assumes that the theme is signaling which topic, or question at issue, the utterance is answering, while the rheme provides an answer to it (Ginzburg, 2012; Roberts, 1996a). In English, topic/comment signaling also exploits prosodic accents, as illustrated by the following example:

(32)   John likes MARY.
(33)   JOHN likes Mary.

(32) is fine in a context in which we are wondering whom John likes, say, Mary or Sue, but not in a context in which we are wondering who likes Mary, say, Bill or John; the opposite is true of (33).

This dimension of information structure likewise has an impact on the interpretation of context-sensitive items.[37] To illustrate, consider the following:

(34)   John only likes MARY.
(35)   John only LIKES Mary.

Even though *prima facie* (34) and (35) are just one and the same string of words, they convey two different things: (34) is true just in case John likes Mary and nobody else (out of the alternative individuals available in the context), whereas (35) is true just in case John likes Mary, but does not have any other attitude (out of contextually relevant ones) towards her. In other words, the focal stress signals which topic (34) and (35) address: whether the one regarding the possible objects of John's liking, or the one regarding the possible attitudes John might bear towards Mary. In turn, the topic constrains the domain of quantification of 'only', thus affecting the truth-conditions of (34) and (35).[38]

---

[37] See, for instance, Beaver and Clark (2008), Roberts (1996b, 2004, 2011), Rooth (1992), Schaffer and Szabó (2013), and Schoubye and Stokke (2015) for more on this point.

[38] Some authors have suggested that the apparent contextual variability of knowledge ascriptions also seems to be affected by the topic or question under discussion (Dretske, 1981, 1991; Schaffer and Szabó, 2013). They observe the contrast between examples such as (i-a) and (i-b), from Schaffer and Szabó (2013):

(i) Claire has stolen the diamonds. Ann and Ben are wondering what Claire stole, and Ann finds Claire's fingerprints all over the safe. So Ann says to Ben:

(ia) I know that CLAIRE stole the diamonds.

(ib) I know that Claire stole THE DIAMONDS.

Given the scenario described by (i), (i-a) seems true, but (i-b) false. But (i-a) and (i-b) appear to be one and the same string of words; their difference is simply in prosody. In particular, the focal stress in (i-a)

These kinds of examples only illustrate that, though discourse structure affects the resolution of context-sensitive items, it is not the only dimension of grammar that carries this effect. The examples above show that mechanisms of information structure contribute to resolution in similar ways. A natural question then arises about the relation between these two aspects of grammar.[39] Fully addressing this question would take us too far afield. For our purposes, it is important to recognize that while these two aspects of meaning both affect the resolution of context-sensitive items, and while they work in complementary ways, they are nevertheless distinct. In particular, it is often left implicit which question is currently under discussion at a particular point in a discourse, and even when there is an explicit question introduced, the speaker can choose to address it directly or indirectly, by addressing a more specific sub-question. We have seen that in English, prosody is exploited to signal the question that the utterance is addressing, but this is certainly not the only cue used to this effect. In a similar fashion, coherence relations among successive utterances can guide which topic a new utterance is addressing: for instance, cause–effect relations can organize the contribution to address why an event occurred (Explanation), or what resulted from it (Result), occasion relations can be used to address what happened during or after an event (Elaboration, Narration), while resemblance relations can be used to address how events compare to other events (Contrast or Parallel).[40]

Prosody, through signaling the topic, can serve as a cue as to which relation is operative at a particular point in a discourse. However, there are other cues that seem to conventionally signal that a particular relation is operative, and recognizing that a relation is operative can in turn help to recognize which question the speaker will choose to address next with an utterance. To see what is at stake, consider first the following (Stojnić, Stone, and Lepore, forthcoming):

(36)   I knocked the glass off. It broke.
(37)   The glass broke. I knocked it off.

While (36) and (37) are both an instance of a cause–effect relation, and indeed could both be describing the same exact events in the world, the former is understood as organized by Result relation and the latter by Explanation. And while one might think that we understand the second sentence in (37) as explaining the event described in the first because this interpretation "makes the most sense", as argued in Stojnić, Stone, and Lepore (forthcoming), the particular organization seems to involve an element of conventionality. To appreciate this, consider the following example:

(38)   John shot Bill. He was dead.

---

signals that the relevant topic—the question under discussion—is *who stole the diamonds*, whereas in (i-b), it is *what was stolen*.

[39] For some discussion see Roberts (2004).

[40] See Lepore and Stone (2015), Roberts (2004), and van Kuppevelt (1995) for a further discussion of this point.

Though certainly death can result from a shooting event, it is hard to understand the second sentence in (38) as describing the result of the event of shooting. Rather, we understand (38) to convey that Bill was already dead when shot by John. We typically understand stative descriptions as connected by Background relation to descriptions of ongoing events.[41] Clearly, this is not just a matter of common sense or world knowledge—after all, such considerations would favor the reading of (38) according to which the second sentence is reporting a result of the event described by the first one. Thus, which relation is organizing a discourse depends on cues that cross-cut common-sense reasoning about the speaker's intentions and general world knowledge. Recognizing what relation holds in turn leads to a particular understanding of which question the speaker is addressing with her utterance: whether she is describing a result of an event ('What happened as a result?') or background circumstances against which the event took place ('What circumstances were in place when John was shot?'). So, particular cues in the information structure can signal a particular discourse structure, but likewise, a particular organization of the discourse can signal particular information structure. Both of these dimensions of interpretation are dependent on a variety of linguistic cues, and mutually inform each other. They must work in complementary ways to determine an interpretation. Yet both cross-cut general world knowledge, and common-sense and plausibility considerations.

Finally, I close by addressing a possible objection to the metasemantic account I defended. The view I defended maintains that mechanisms of discourse coherence affect the resolution of context-sensitive items by making certain values of contextually relevant parameters prominent as a matter of linguistic convention. However, an intentionalist, or a pragmatist, might then object that, even if coherence relations conventionally promote certain values of contextual parameters, it is ultimately the speaker's intention, and/or general world knowledge, which determines which coherence relation is organizing a discourse, and so we still need to rely on intentions for meaning-determination. In other words, one might argue that even if the metasemantics of, say, a pronoun, is a matter of convention, the metasemantics of coherence relations might still involve speaker intentions, and other contextual cues. To respond to this kind of a worry, it is important to note that, even though discourses may be *ambiguous* with respect to the coherence relation they harbor, I am not suggesting that coherence relations themselves are context-sensitive items that need to be resolved in a context. To see what is at stake recall (3), repeated below as (39):

(39)   Phil tickled Stanley, and Liz poked him.

What I suggest is that discourses like (39), are *ambiguous* between (at least) the logical form harboring Parallel, and the one harboring Result. Thus, determining a coherence relation amounts to choosing between distinct fully specified logical forms of a discourse.[42] And while general reasoning about interlocutors' intentions might

---

[41] See Asher and Lascarides (2003), and Kehler (2002).   [42] See Stojnić, Stone, and Lepore (2017).

well be potentially used as a tool of disambiguation, this does not mean that such reasoning ever contributes content to the logical form. Moreover, speakers often resolve ambiguities by relying on shallow linguistic cues that favor a particular interpretation within a set of alternative interpretations delivered by the grammar, even when such disambiguation is not favored by general pragmatic considerations. This is reflected in examples like (38). The fact that discourse structure can often be ambiguous is hardly a vindication of an intentionalist metasemantics.[43]

5. Conclusion

The often-assumed intentionalist, pragmatic account of the resolution of context-sensitivity is *prima facie* very plausible. After all, speakers typically speak with an intention to convey certain thoughts to their audience, and it is moreover natural to think that in using context-sensitive language, they normally use it with an intention to convey the meaning that would help express their thought. Yet, while all this is true, it does not amount to an intentionalist metasemantics. While speakers typically intend to use context-sensitive language to convey the intended content, this is compatible with the rules of language, rather than an appropriate intention, or a set of general contextual cues, being what ultimately determines the meaning of such expressions.

Indeed, I have argued that context-sensitivity is resolved by appeal to linguistic mechanisms that govern the dynamics of prominence of particular values of contextual parameters associated with context-sensitive expressions. In particular, we have seen that mechanisms of discourse structure and information structure govern the dynamics of prominence in context, and do so as a matter of linguistic convention. The resulting conventionalist metasemantics does not deny that speakers normally have intentions to convey a particular meaning with a particular use of a context-sensitive expression. However, the rules of language constrain the range of contents speakers can convey with the use of a context-sensitive expression.[44] That they should be so constrained is telling: it is because the rules of language determine a particular resolution of a context-sensitive expression, that we cannot use it as flexibly as one would expect on a traditional view.

Acknowledgment

I would like to acknowledge the support of a research fellowship over the summer of 2016 from ANU. Thanks are also due to Jeff King, Ernie Lepore, and Matthew Stone.

---

[43] For a more detailed discussion, see Stojnić, Stone, and Lepore (forthcoming). For a related point about disambiguation see Lepore and Stone (2015).

[44] Of course, the intentionalists do not have to deny this particular point. For instance, King (2014a, 2014b) endorses it, suggesting that speakers are constrained by the conventions of language in what they can reasonably intend to convey by an utterance. But, insofar as we are as thoroughly constrained by linguistic rules with respect to what we can intend, and insofar as the rules are as pervasive as I have suggested they are, it seems that the presence of an appropriate intention will neither be a necessary, nor a sufficient condition for meaning-determination.

References

Altshuler, Daniel and Stojnić, Una. 2016. "The Meaning of 'Now'." Manuscript.

Asher, Nicholas and Lascarides, Alex. 2003. *Logics of Conversation*. Cambridge: Cambridge University Press.

Asher, Nicholas and McCready, Eric. 2007. "Were, Would, Might and a Compositional Account of Counterfactuals." *Journal of Semantics* 24:93–129.

Barker, Chris. 2002. "The Dynamics of Vagueness." *Linguistics and Philosophy* 25:1–36.

Barwise, Jon and Etchemendy, John. 1987. *The Liar: An Essay in Truth and Circularity*. Oxford, New York: Oxford University Press.

Beaver, David and Clark, Brady. 2008. *Sense and Sensitivity: How Focus Determines Meaning*. Oxford: Wiley-Blackwell.

Bittner, Maria. 2014. *Temporality: Universals and Variation*. Oxford: Wiley-Blackwell.

Cappelen, Herman and Hawthorne, John. 2009. *Relativism and Monadic Truth*. Oxford: Oxford University Press.

Chomsky, Noam. 1981. *Lectures on Government and Binding: The Pisa Lectures*. Holland: Foris Publications. (Reprint: 7th Edition. Berlin and New York: Mouton de Gruyter, 1993).

Cohen, Stewart. 1998. "Contextualist Solutions to Epistemological Problems: Scepticism, Gettier, and the Lottery." *Australasian Journal of Philosophy* 76:289–306.

DeRose, Keith. 1995. "Solving the Skeptical Problem." *Philosophical Review* 104:1–52.

DeRose, Keith. 2009. *The Case for Contextualism: Knowledge, Skepticism, and Context*, volume 1. New York: Oxford University Press.

Dowell, Janice L. 2011. "A Flexible Contextualist Account of Epistemic Modals." *Philosophers' Imprint* 11:1–25.

Dretske, Fred. 1981. "The Pragmatic Dimensions of Knowledge." *Philosophical Studies* 40:363–78.

Dretske, Fred. 1991. "Knowledge: Sanford and Cohen." In Brian McLaughlin (ed.), *Dretske and His Critics*, 185–96. New York: Oxford University Press.

Egan, Andy. 2010. "Disputing About Taste." In Richard Feldman and Ted A. Warfield (eds.), *Disagreement*, 247–86. Oxford: Oxford University Press.

Egan, Andy, Hawthorne, John, and Weatherson, Brian. 2005. "Epistemic Modals in Context." In Gerhard Preyer and Peter Georg (eds.), *Contextualism in Philosophy: Knowledge, Meaning, and Truth*, 131–69. Oxford: Oxford University Press.

Elbourne, Paul. 2008. "Implicit Content and the Argument from Binding." In *Proceedings of Semantics and Linguistic Theory XVIII (SALT 18)*, 284–301. Ithaca, NY: CLC Publications.

Evans, Gareth. 1980. "Pronouns." *Linguistics Inquiry* 11:337–62.

Frege, Gotlob. 1892. "Über Sinn und Bedeutung." *Zeitschrift für Philosophie und philosophische Kritik* 100:25–50.

Ginzburg, Jonathan. 2012. *The Interactive Stance: Meaning for Conversation*. Oxford, New York: Oxford University Press.

Glanzberg, Michael. 2007a. "Context and Unrestricted Quantification." In Agustín Rayo and Ganriel Uzquiano (eds.), *Absolute Generality*, 45–74. Oxford, New York: Oxford University Press.

Glanzberg, Michael. 2007b. "Context, Content, and Relativism." *Philosophical Studies* 136:1–29.

Grice, H.P. 1975. "Logic and Conversation." In Peter Cole and Jerry L. Morgan (eds.), *Syntax and Semantics 3: Speech Acts*, 41–58. New York: Academic Press.

Grosz, Barbara J., Joshi, Aravind K., and Weinstein, Scott. 1995. "Centering: A Framework for Modelling the Local Coherence of Discourse." *Computational Linguistics* 21:203–25.

Halliday, M.A.K. 1967. "Notes on Transitivity and Theme in English (Part 2)." *Journal of Linguistics* 3:199–244.

Hamann, Cornelia. 1991. "Adjectival Semantics." In Arnim von Stechow and Dieter Wunderlich (eds.), *Semantics: An International Handbook of Contemporary Research*, 657–73. New York: de Gruyter.

Hawthorne, John. 2004. *Knowledge and Lotteries*. Oxford: Oxford University Press.

Hobbs, Jerry R. 1979. "Coherence and Coreference." *Cognitive Science* 3:67–90.

Kaiser, Elsi. 2009. "Effects of Anaphoric Dependencies and Semantic Representations on Pronoun Interpretation." In *Anaphora Processing and Applications*, 121–30. Heidelberg: Springer.

Kaplan, David. 1989a. "Afterthoughts." In Joseph Almog, John Perry, and Howard Wettstein (eds.), *Themes From Kaplan*, 565–614. New York: Oxford University Press.

Kaplan, David. 1989b. "Demonstratives." In Joseph Almog, John Perry, and Howard Wettstein (eds.), *Themes From Kaplan*, 481–563. New York: Oxford University Press.

Kehler, Andrew. 2002. *Coherence, Reference and the Theory of Grammar*. Stanford, CA: CSLI Publications.

Kehler, Andrew. 2004. "Discourse Coherence." In Laurence R. Horn and Gregory Ward (eds.), *The Handbook of Pragmatics*, 241–65. Oxford: Blackwell Publishing.

Kehler, Andrew. 2008. "Rethinking the SMASH Approach to Pronoun Interpretation." In Jeanette K. Gundel and Nancy Hedberg (eds.), *Reference: Interdisciplinary Perspectives*, 95–122. New York: Oxford University Press.

Kehler, Andrew, Kertz, L, Rohde, Hannah, and Elman, J. 2008. "Coherence and Coreference Revisited." *Journal of Semantics* 25:1–44.

Kennedy, Christopher. 2007. "Vagueness and Grammar: The Semantics of Relative and Absolute Gradable Adjectives." *Linguistics and Philosophy* 30:1–45.

King, Jeffrey C. 2014a. "The Metasemantics of Contextual Sensitivity." In Alexis Burgess and Bret Sherman (eds.), *Metasemantics: New Essays on the Foundations of Meaning*, 97–118. New York: Oxford University Press.

King, Jeffrey C. 2014b. "Speaker Intentions in Context." *Noûs* 48:219–37.

King, Jeffrey C. and Stanley, Jason. 2005. "Semantics, Pragmatics and the Role of Semantic Content." In Zoltán Gendler Szabó (ed.), *Semantics vs. Pragmatics*, 111–64. Oxford: Oxford University Press.

Klein, Ewan. 1991. "Comparatives." In Arnim von Stechow and Dieter Wunderlich (eds.), *Semantics: An International Handbook of Contemporary Research*, 673–91. New York: de Gruyter.

Knott, Alistair. 1996. *A Data Driven Methodology for Motivating a Set of Coherence Relations*. Ph.D. thesis, Department of Artificial Intelligence, University of Edinburgh.

Kolodny, Niko and MacFarlane, John. 2010. "Ifs and Oughts." *Journal of Philosophy* 107:115–43.

Kratzer, Angelika. 1998. "An Investigation of the Lumps of Thought." *Linguistics and Philosophy* 12:607–53.

Kratzer, Angelika. 2014. "Situations in Natural Language Semantics." http://plato.stanford.edu/entries/situations-semantics/.

Kripke, Saul. 1980. *Naming and Necessity*. Cambridge, MA: Harvard University Press.

Lappin, Shalom. 1993a. "Ellipsis Resolution at S-Structure." In *Proceedings of NELS*, volume 23, 255–69. Amherst, MA: University of Massachusetts.

Lappin, Shalom. 1993b. "The Syntactic Basis of Ellipsis Resolution." In Steve Berman Arild Hestvik (ed.), *Proceedings of the Stuttgart Workshop on Ellipsis: Arbeitspapiere des Sounderforschungsbereich*, volume 340, Bericht Nr. 29–1992, SFB 340, 1–47. University of Stuttgart, University of Tuebingen and IBM Germany.

Lappin, Shalom. 1996. "The Interpretation of Ellipsis." In Shalom Lappin (ed.), *Handbook of Contemporary Semantic Theory*, 145–75. Oxford: Blackwell.

Lepore, Ernie and Cappelen, Herman. 2005. *Insensitive Semantics: A Defense of Semantic Minimalism and Speech Act Pluralism*. Oxford: Blackwell Publishing.

Lepore, Ernie and Stone, Matthew. 2015. *Imagination and Convention: Distinguishing Grammar and Inference in Language*. Oxford: Oxford University Press.

Lewis, David K. 1979. "Scorekeeping in a Language Game." *Journal of Philosophical Logic* 8:339–59.

Lewis, Karen. ms. "The Speaker Authority Problem for Context-sensitivity (or: You Can't Always Mean What You Want)." Manuscript.

Locke, John. 1689. *An Essay Concerning Human Understanding*. Peter H. Nidditch (ed.). Oxford: Calderon Press (1975).

Mann, William C. and Thompson, Sandra A. 1988. "Rhetorical Structure Theory: Toward a Functional Theory of Text Organization." *Text* 8:243–81.

Neale, Stephen. 1990. *Descriptions*. Cambridge, MA: MIT Press.

Neale, Stephen. 2004. "This, That and the Other." In Marga Reimer and Anna Bezuidenhout (eds.), *Descriptions and Beyond*, 68–182. New York: Oxford University Press.

Partee, Barbara. 1973. "Some Structural Analogies Between Tenses and Pronouns in English." *Journal of Philosophy* 70(18):601–9.

Partee, Barbara. 1984. "Nominal and Temporal Anaphora." *Linguistics and Philosophy* 7:243–86.

Recanati, François. 1996. "Domains of Discourse." *Linguistics and Philosophy* 19:445–75.

Reimer, Marga. 1992. "Three Views of Demonstrative Reference." *Synthese* 93:373–402.

Roberts, Craige. 1989. "Modal Subordination and Pronominal Anaphora in Discourse." *Linguistics and Philosophy* 12:683–721.

Roberts, Craige. 1996a. "Information Structure: Towards an Integrated Formal Theory of Pragmatics." In Jae Hak Yoon and Andreas Kathol (eds.), *OSUWPL Volume 49: Papers in Semantics*, 91–136. The Ohio State University Department of Linguistics.

Roberts, Craige. 1996b. "Information Structure: Towards an Integrated Formal Theory of Pragmatics." *OSUWPL: Papers in Semantics* 49:91–136.

Roberts, Craige. 2004. "Context in Dynamic Interpretation." In Lawrence R. Horn and Gregory Ward (eds.), *The Handbook of Pragmatics*, 197–220. Oxford: Blackwell.

Roberts, Craige. 2011. "Solving for Interpretation." Manuscript. Ohio State University.

Rooth, Mats. 1992. "A Theory of Focus Interpretation." *Natural Language Semantics* 1:75–116.

Russell, Bertrand. 1905. "On Denoting." *Mind* 14:479–93.

Schaffer, Jonathan and Szabó, Zoltán Gendler. 2013. "Epistemic Comparativism: A Contextualist Semantics for Knowledge Ascriptions." *Philosophical Studies* 2:1–53.

Schiffer, Stephen. 1981. "Indexicals and the Theory of Reference." *Synthese* 49(1):43–100.

Schoubye, Anders J. and Stokke, Andreas. 2015. "What is Said?" *Noûs* 50:759–793.

Sidner, Candice. 1983. "Focusing in the Comprehension of Definite Anaphora." In Michael Brady and Robert C. Berwick (eds.), *Computational Models of Discourse*, 267–330. Cambridge, MA: MIT Press.

Smyth, Ron. 1994. "Grammatical Determinants of Ambiguous Pronoun Resolution." *Journal of Psycholinguistic Research* 23:197–229.

Stanley, Jason. 2005. *Knowledge and Practical Interests*. Oxford: Oxford University Press.

Stanley, Jason and Szabó, Zoltán Gendler. 2000. "On Quantifier Domain Restriction." *Mind and Language* 15:219–61.

Stojnić, Una. 2017a. "Content in a Dynamic Context." *Noûs*. DOI: 10.1111/nous.12220 (first published online, October 2017).

Stojnić, Una. 2017b. "One Man's *Modus Ponens*...: Modality, Coherence and Logic." *Philosophy and Phenomenological Research* 95(1):167–214. DOI: 10.1111/phpr.12307 (first published online: July 2016).

Stojnić, Una. ms. "The Metasemantics of Domain Restriction." Manuscript.

Stojnić, Una and Altshuler, Daniel. 2016. "The Meaning of 'Now.'" Manuscript.

Stojnić, Una, and Stone, Matthew. (ms.) "Vague Utterances in Context." Manuscript.

Stojnić, Una, Stone, Matthew, and Lepore, Ernie. 2013. "Deixis (Even Without Pointing)." *Philosophical Perspectives* 27(1):502–25.

Stojnić, Una, Stone, Matthew, and Lepore, Ernie. 2017. "Discourse and Logical Form." *Linguistics and Philosophy* 40(5):519–47.

Stojnić, Una, Stone, Matthew, and Lepore, Ernie. forthcoming. "Distinguishing Ambiguity from Underspecificity." In Ken Turner and Lawrence Horn (eds.), *An Atlas of Meaning*, volume Current Research in the Semantics/Pragmatics Interface. Leiden: Brill.

Stone, Matthew. 1997. "The Anaphoric Parallel Between Modality and Tense." *IRCS Report* 97–06, University of Pennsylvania.

Stone, Matthew. 1999. "Reference to Possible Worlds." Technical Report 49, Rutgers University, New Brunswick, RuCCS.

Stone, Matthew and Stojnić, Una. 2015. "Meaning and Demonstration." *Review of Philosophy and Psychology* 6:69–97.

Travis, Charles. 1989. *The Uses of Sense: Wittgenstein's Philosophy of Language*. Oxford: Oxford University Press.

Vallduví, Enric. 1992. *The Informational Component*. New York: Garland Press.

Vallduví, Enric. 1993. "Information Packaging: A Survey." Report of the word order, prosody, and information structure initiative, University of Edinburgh.

van Kuppevelt, Jan. 1995. "Discourse Structure, Topicality and Questioning." *Journal of Linguistics* 31:109–47.

von Fintel, Kai. 1994. *Restrictions on Quantifier Domains*. Ph.D. thesis, University of Massachusetts-Amherst.

von Fintel, Kai and Gillies, Anthony S. 2008. "CIA Leaks." *Philosophical Review* 117:77–98.

Wettstein, Howard K. 1984. "How to Bridge the Gap Between Meaning and Reference." *Synthese* 58:63–84.

Wolf, Florian, Gibson, Edward, and Desmet, Timothy. 2004. "Discourse Coherence and Pronoun Resolution." *Language and Cognitive Processes* 19:665–75.

Yalcin, Seth. 2007. "Epistemic Modals." *Mind* 116:983–1026.

Yalcin, Seth. 2012. "A Counterexample to *Modus Tollens.*" *Journal of Philosophical Logic* 41:1001–24.

Yalcin, Seth. 2015. "Semantics and Metasemantics in the Context of Generative Grammar." In Alexis Burgess and Bret Sherman (eds.), *Metasemantics: New Essays on the Foundations of Meaning*, 17–54. New York: Oxford University Press.

6

Socializing Pragmatics

William B. Starr

1. Introduction

Lepore and Stone (2015) focus on two theoretically useful notions of *meaning*. There are interpretive effects generated by linguistic conventions, and there are those generated by the intentions directly supporting the application of those conventions on particular occasions of use. For example, a speaker may refer to a person with the name *Janis*, and the hearer may recognize this because there is a shared expectation between speaker and hearer about what person *Janis* refers to. This is *conventional linguistic meaning*. By contrast, a speaker may refer to a newly discovered stray dog with the name *Luna*, and the hearer may recognize this, because there is a shared expectation that speakers use novel names with a contextually salient referent in mind and other contextual clues make it clear that the speaker intends the stray dog to be this referent. This is an interpretive effect generated by the *intentions* supporting linguistic conventions, and is a species of what Grice called *speaker meaning*.

One ambition of Lepore and Stone (2015) is to significantly simplify the Gricean account of speaker meaning, and to expand the empirical reach of explanations which appeal to linguistic conventions. This point of contest between Lepore and Stone (2015) and those that remain closer to Grice's vision, like Neo-Griceans and Relevance Theorists, will no doubt attract much critical attention. However, another ambition of Lepore and Stone (2015) is to place some interpretive effects like metaphor and imagery in a distinct third class, also contrary to Neo-Griceans who treat it as an implicature, and Relevance Theorists who treat it as the non-conventional, context-specific, loose-use of words that is a routine part of interpreting all utterances (Carston 2002, §5.3). Lepore and Stone (2015) explain these effects in terms of *imaginative engagement*, which is produced by the open-ended psychological processes that hearers creatively recruit when prompted by the speaker's utterance. Lepore and Stone (2015) argue that metaphor and imagery do not involve 'metaphorical meanings' because imaginative engagement does not fit the mold of conventional meaning, or speaker meaning.

This essay[1] argues that besides conventional meaning and speaker meaning, there is a third theoretically important notion of meaning, which I call *significance*. The significance of an utterance is not reducible to the content it makes mutual, because it is partly based on the private commmitments speakers have when they make utterances and the private commmitments hearers form on the basis of utterances. More specifically, significance is the private speaker commitments and hearer effects that explain why utterances of a given type are reproduced in a population of agents (Millikan 2005). Indirectly, this challenges the second ambition of Lepore and Stone (2015). I will not contest their particular account of metaphor. Instead, I will challenge the assumption that any interpretive effect, which does not count as conventional meaning or speaker meaning, does not involve a kind of meaning. I will argue that it often involves significance, and that significance is crucially involved in generating speaker meaning and conventional meaning.

My argument is foreshadowed by considering a question not discussed by Lepore and Stone (2015) or (Lewis 1979): why do the agents in a given population engage in a particular practice of conversational scorekeeping in the first place? Consider the practice of uttering a declarative sentence to update the informational score of a conversation. Suppose it makes the conversationalists mutually aware that this information is being assumed in their conversation. Why is this mutual awareness valuable to those conversationalists? If the conversationalists are going to do more than coordinate their *conversational actions*, this mutual awareness is only instrumentally valuable. It is valuable insofar as it brings about beliefs and actions that influence the world in a beneficial way. So, what makes a given practice of conversational scorekeeping *significant* is its connection to the actual commitments and subsequent actions of the agents involved. Or to put the point less theoretically: language is valuable not for mere conversational coordination, but for coordinating to solve the problems that face us in our actual lives. Without an answer to this more basic question, we have no way of explaining why certain linguistic practices are self-sustaining and how they evolve to meet the practical needs of a linguistic population.

By focusing on the way language affects the conversational record, Lepore and Stone (2015) are able to address two very important issues. First, they address the issue of deception and distrust that plagues previous accounts of speaker meaning and convention, like those of Grice (1957) and Lewis (1969). Since Grice and Lewis focus on the actual effects that a signal has on hearers, one must address uses of that signal that produce deceptive effects (see also Lepore and Stone 2015a, §20.3.3). Second, Lepore and Stone (2015) are able to give a clearer account of which interpretive effects count as semantic by saying that only effects on the conversational record are semantic. I will conclude the essay by discussing how these two issues are addressed in Murray and

---

[1] This essay stemmed from the joint influence of my ongoing collaboration with Sarah Murray on speech acts (Murray and Starr 2018, forthcoming) and my formative experience as a Ph.D. student with Ernie Lepore and Matthew Stone. I am lucky to have had all three as interlocutors on these issues, and their impact on my thinking is too extensive to document in detail.

Starr (2018, forthcoming). I will begin by considering a fictional signaling system, and detailing the explanatory role of conventional meaning and significance.

2. From Signaling to Meaning: Two Paths

I will introduce a hybrid of Wittgenstein's (1953) 'builders' language game, Lewis's (1969) signaling games and Tetris. It will first be used to illustrate the concepts of convention and linguistic meaning articulated by Lewis (1969) and Lepore and Stone (2015). With some sophistications, it will also be used to challenge those accounts in §4.

Agents inhabit a world that naturally furnishes blocks of two precise shapes.

Figure 6.1. Two Basic Shapes of Blocks.

Only some agents—the *builders*—can stack the blocks together into habitable dwellings. Their task is complicated by the fact that only U-and T-shaped blocks fit together. The *collectors* have the exclusive ability to find and transport blocks of any shape (no builders are collectors). All agents need homes, so coordination is necessary. As Lewis (1969 ch.4) spells out, the goal of the coordination is not particular acts—issuing this particular signal now, bringing this particular block now—but of *contingency plans*. A contingency plan informs an agent what to do in each kind of circumstance relevant to their interactions with other agents. The contingency plans for builders and collectors are spelled out as below, and to achieve coordination either the builders must adopt B_{12} and the collectors C_{12} or the builders must adopt B_{21} and the collectors C_{21}.

Blocks Coordination Problem

Builders' Contingency Plans

B_{12}:
- When a builder needs a U-shaped block they produce a signal σ_1
- When a builder needs a T-shaped block they produce a signal σ_2

B_{21}:
- When a builder needs a U-shaped block they produce a signal σ_2
- When a builder needs a T-shaped block they produce a signal σ_1

Collectors' Contingency Plans

C_{12}:
- When a builder produces σ_1, a collector brings a U-shaped block
- When a builder produces σ_2, a collector brings a T-shaped block

C_{21}:
- When a builder produces σ_1, a collector brings a T-shaped block
- When a builder produces σ_2, a collector brings a U-shaped block

Each combination of these strategies can be assigned a utility for each agent. A payoff matrix, like that in Figure 6.2, displays this information—where (n,m) means that the result of combining the two strategies provides utility n for the builder and utility m for the collector.

	C_{12}	C_{21}
B_{12}	(1, 1)	(-9, -9)
B_{21}	(-9, -9)	(1, 1)

Figure 6.2. Payoff Matrix for Basic Blocks Game.

While the selection of numbers is somewhat arbitrary, this particular assignment of utilities indicates that the result of failed coordination is far worse than successful coordination is good. Suppose now that the builders and collectors have somehow solved their coordination problem, routinely adopting the policies of B_{12} and C_{12}. What follows about the conventional meaning of σ_1 and σ_2? Lewis (1969, 143) proposes the following:

Lewis (1969) Theory

1. The builders and collectors acting in accord with B_{12} and C_{12} counts as a convention. because it is an arbitrary, recurrent solution to a coordination problem for all members of that population.

2. The meaning of σ_1 ($[\![\sigma_1]\!]$) can be identified with the ways the world is when B_{12} is followed in accord with the convention, i.e. worlds where the builder needs a U-shaped block—similarly for σ_2.

Lewis (1969, ch.5; 1975) goes on to characterize conventions of the kind outlined in 1 more generally as conventions of truthfulness and trust in a language, as used by a population. The convention of truthfulness governs the speaker's production of a signal in the right situations, and the convention of trust governs the hearer's response to the signal in the right way. Under this description, it is even more clear that the approach has explained how signals get their conventional meanings, at least when conventional meanings are taken to be truth-conditions.[2] In the context of Lewis (1969), the definition of meaning above is a huge success, insofar as it allows one to say how conventional meanings emerge from signaling: "I have been trying to demonstrate that an adequate account of signaling need not mention the meanings of signals—at least, not by name. But of course signals do have meanings" (Lewis 1969, 143).

This is because Lewis (1969) is attempting to give a naturalistic and non-circular definition of meaning. However, in the context of giving an empirically adequate account of natural language, it is less clear that Lewis (1969, 1975) succeeds. Lepore

---

[2] Of course, it's not clear that σ_1 and σ_2 really have truth-conditions—perhaps they are better viewed as imperatives. This issue will come into focus shortly.

and Stone (2015, ch.14) detail two very important limitations on this front, and Lepore and Stone (2015a) add a third:

Empirical Limitations of Lewis (1969) Theory

1.   The difference between imperatives and declaratives is not resolved at the level of conventional meanings or conventional contingency plans.

2.   The difference between semantics and pragmatics, for example, even if σ_1 is always used in situations where a builder is speaking, that does not count as part of its conventional meaning.

3.   Speakers can be deceptive and hearers can be distrustful—so there is no general regularity of most members of the population being truthful and trusting.

These limitations highlight three explanatory goals of a theory of meaning, and how that constrains the concepts we are willing to call meaning.

Explanatory Constraints

1.   A theory of conventional meaning must make certain distinctions that are required by goals internal to semantic theory.

2.   A theory of meaning in general must make certain distinctions that are required by general goals in the explanation of language use.

3.   A theory of meaning must explain how conventions arise despite conflicting interests.

Each of these limitations and constraints deserve further discussion, including an articulation of how the account of conventional meaning in Lepore and Stone (2015) addresses them. The second limitation and constraint are really the central focus of Lepore and Stone (2015) explored thoroughly there. Accordingly, I will focus instead on the first and third.

Lewis (1969) was aware that his theory of conventional meaning did not adequately distinguish declarative and imperative meaning. While Lewis (1969, 144–7) makes a relatively implausible attempt to distinguish them, Lewis (1975, 172) offers an alternative account.[3] In natural languages, imperatives and declaratives are formally distinguished, and so there must actually be two different signals $\sigma_{1.1}$ and $\sigma_{1.2}$, the former declarative and the latter imperative. Lewis (1975, 172) proposes that the two kinds of signals are subject to different conventions of truthfulness and trust. While truthfulness of a declarative signal like $\sigma_{1.1}$ remains the same, the truthfulness of an imperative signal $\sigma_{1.2}$ is identified as taking the action required of the addressee by the convention. Accordingly, $[\![\sigma_{1.2}]\!]$ will be worlds in which the collector brings a U-shaped block,

---

[3] See Zollman (2011) for discussion of the Lewis (1969) idea, and a new proposal based on the idea that imperatives should convey no information about the state of the world but perfect information about the response to an arbitrary receiver, and that declaratives are the reverse. I am ultimately sympathetic to this idea and think it consistent with the position outlined in Murray and Starr (2018, forthcoming). Indeed, its focus on informational dependencies also bears on the points below about mental imagery.

while $[\![\sigma_{1,1}]\!]$ will be worlds where the builder needs a U-shaped block. This approach, however, is not adequate when applied to languages with the compositional complexity of natural language. As discussed and argued in Murray and Starr (2018, forthcoming) and Starr (forthcoming), natural languages allow imperatives and declaratives to embed across connectives, making it impossible to partition sentences of the language into declaratives and imperatives. This means that conventions that assign contents differently depending on the type—like Lewis (1975, 172)—or pragmatic treatments of the difference, fall short.

This limitation is nicely overcome by a theory within the broad approach advocated by Lepore and Stone (2015). On such an approach, the conventional meaning of a sentence is characterized in terms of rules for updating the conversational record. Just as the record can reflect both individuals mentioned, and standards of precision, it can reflect the difference between directive information contributed by imperatives, and representational information contributed by declaratives. Pragmatic theories of this kind already existed with Stalnaker (1978), Roberts (2004), and Portner (2004), but Murray and Starr (2018, forthcoming), Murray (2014), and Starr (forthcoming) show how to translate this into an empirically adequate semantic theory. So by treating semantic conventions as constituted by our rules for updating the conversational record, the broad approach outlined by Lepore and Stone (2015) makes for an empirically superior alternative to Lewis (1975, 172). While their limited discussion of *There is a bug on your back* and *Swat the bug on your back* undersells this point, I think it is fair to say that they have made an important contribution here.

When it comes to deception, Lepore and Stone (2015a) also invoke the framework developed in Lepore and Stone (2015, ch.14). Lewis (1969) requires all speakers to use a signal truthfully and interpret it trustingly to sustain a meaningful language. And yet, we don't. If one adds to the builders/collectors setup that builders occasionally issue σ_1 not when they need a U-shaped block, but when they want collectors to busy themselves while the builder relaxes, then this kind of world will become part of $[\![\sigma_1]\!]$. This highlights that Lewis (1969) has no way of saying which uses of σ_1 are constitutive of its meaning, and which are deviant. This is simply because he identifies the meaning of σ_1 with the way speakers actually use it and hearers actually interpret it.

Lepore and Stone (2015a) propose that this problem can be solved by drawing on Lepore and Stone (2015, ch.14). The conventions of a language coordinate the speaker and hearer, but they do so by providing rules for changing the conversational record. The record is distinct from the speaker and hearer's private beliefs. Even lies are used in accord with this convention: they put a proposition on the scoreboard. So by re-characterizing linguistic conventions in terms of the conversational record, Lepore and Stone (2015a) narrow the scope of what counts as a signal use in a way that sets aside the details of whether the speaker is being sincere or whether the hearer trusts them. This is good, because we live in a world full of insincere speakers and distrustful hearers. So too, we may assume, do the builders and collectors.

3. Why are Linguistic Conventions Self-Sustaining?

The approach of Lepore and Stone (2015) has fared well, so far. But there is a lingering issue that can be brought out by investigating the question of how conventions are self-sustaining on their approach. Lewis (1969) clearly recognized that it was crucial to explain how conventions were self-sustaining. His explanation was individual rationality: each agent has reason to conform if others do, and agents are rational. In short, everyone is rational so they know they want to act so as to end up in a (1,1) cell in Figure 6.1, and think that everyone else is going to do their part to end up in the B_{12}, C_{12} cell. This is why Lewis (1969) must require that all, or almost all, of the agents in the population conform. Lepore and Stone (2015) are able to maintain the universal quantification by narrowly characterizing language use so that even liars and the distrustful conform. But this raises the question of whether they can still adopt Lewis's (1969) explanation of how linguistic conventions are self-perpetuating.

Consider again the builders and collectors, and replace our earlier characterizations of their contingency plans with the new ones entailed by Lepore and Stone (2015):

Blocks Coordination w/Conversational Records

Builders' Contingency Plans

B_{12}^*:

- When a builder wants it to be on the **conversational record** that they need a U-shaped block, they produce a signal σ_1
- When a builder wants it to be on the **conversational record** that they need a T-shaped block, they produce a signal σ_2

B_{21}^*:

- When a builder wants it to be on the **conversational record** that they need a U-shaped block, they produce a signal σ_2
- When a builder wants it to be on the **conversational record** that they need a T-shaped block, they produce a signal σ_1

Collectors' Contingency Plan

C_{12}^*:

- When a builder produces σ_1, it goes on the **record** that the collector is to bring a U-shaped block
- When a builder produces σ_2, it goes on the **record** that the collector is to bring a T-shaped block

C_{21}^*:

- When a builder produces σ_2, it goes on the **record** that the collector is to bring a U-shaped block
- When a builder produces σ_1, it goes on the **record** that the collector is to bring a T-shaped block

Now suppose we offer the analogous payoff matrix:

	C_{12}^*	C_{21}^*
B_{12}^*	(1, 1)	(−9, −9)
B_{21}^*	(−9, −9)	(1, 1)

Figure 6.3. Purported Payoff Matrix for Blocks Game w/Conversational Records.

The real question is if we can justify the payoff (1,1) in Figure 6.3 for these new outcomes. I think it is relatively clear that we cannot, and this poses a serious dilemma for how Lepore and Stone (2015a) propose to handle deception. Merely getting some information and expectations on the record does not guarantee that the builders and collectors will have a home to sleep in—so assigning (1,1) to the outcome of B_{12}^* and C_{12}^* is unjustified. It does not guarantee that the collector brings a U-shaped block, only that it's on the record that they are to do that. At most, keeping score with the conversational record is of instrumental value. It is valuable only insofar as it leads to changes in the actual world. But if that is right, then conventions cannot be sustained by the kind of practical rationality that justifies adopting certain contingency plans on the basis of their valuable consequences. This makes it hard to see how Lepore and Stone (2015a) can adopt both the Lewis (1969) account of how linguistic conventions are self-sustaining and their approach to the problem of deception.

The problem facing Lepore and Stone (2015a) generalizes to many related accounts that attempt to characterize language use primarily in terms of 'conversational scorekeeping'. These accounts all leave open the question of why a scorekeeping practice is self-sustaining in the first place. Leaving this question unasked and unanswered leaves open questions of fundamental interest, such as how the practice can be self-sustaining in the face of conflicting interests.

This issue is related to earlier discussion of force in an interesting way. While it was clear enough how to capture sentence force (declaratives, imperatives, interrogatives) within a scorekeeping approach, it is far less clear how to pull that off for what you might call utterance force. A single imperative *Do community service!* can be used as a command when issued by a judge in court, as advice when issued by a friend, or as an exhortation by a crowd of gathered community members already engaged in community service. While some theorists have proposed to treat this as semantic, and many more theorists have proposed to treat this in terms of speaker meaning, Murray and Starr (2018, forthcoming) argue that these accounts are philosophically and empirically inadequate. Semantic accounts fail to capture generalizations about the relationship between utterance force, context, and linguistic form, while speaker meaning approaches face other challenges. For example, a sign reading *Take off your shoes and have a beer!* at the entryway to an apartment can naturally be read as commanding guests to take off their shoes while merely suggesting that they have a beer. However, speaker meaning only enriches complete sentences at the level of an utterance, and so cannot apply differentially to sub-sentential units.

Murray and Starr (2018, forthcoming) argue that the phenomenon of utterance force can only be captured by talking directly about the appropriate individual (off-the-record) responses to the utterance. However, no account of this is possible without addressing head-on the issue of deception—§4 will present the solution to this problem proposed by Murray and Starr (2018).

Focusing on the self-sustaining nature of conventions raises another difficulty for Lepore and Stone (2015), one which they inherit from Lewis (1969). Some percentage of the population is always deviating from the signaling convention, either to deceive or to explore other solutions. In fact, this is good. This makes individual rationality a poor explanation of how conventions are sustained. This point can be illustrated with yet another twist on the builders/collectors game.

Suppose, like us, builders and collectors are capable of generating private mental imagery while communicating. Suppose further that they, like some of us, greatly enjoy imagining neon-colored squares (the builders) and triangles (the collectors). There may then be two distinguishable conventions in competition for the use of σ_1 and σ_2. B_{12}^+ and C_{12}^+ differ from B_{12} and C_{12} only in that the contingency plans are enriched with mental imagery.

Blocks & Imagery Coordination Problem

Builders' Contingency Plans

B_{12}^+:

- When a builder wants to **imagine a neon pink square** and needs a U-shaped block they produce a signal σ_1
- When a builder wants to **imagine a neon green square** and needs a T-shaped block they produce a signal σ_2

B_{21}:

- When a builder needs a U-shaped block they produce a signal σ_2
- When a builder needs a T-shaped block they produce a signal σ_1

Collectors' Contingency Plans

C_{12}^+:

- When a builder produces σ_1, a collector **imagines a neon blue triangle** and brings a U-shaped block
- When a builder produces σ_2, a collector **imagines a neon yellow triangle** and brings a T-shaped block

C_{21}:

- When a builder produces σ_1, a collector brings a T-shaped block
- When a builder produces σ_2, a collector brings a U-shaped block

Given that the added imagery adds a boost in enjoyment, it makes sense to assign the combination of B_{12}^+ and C_{12}^+ a higher utility than B_{21} and C_{21}, as depicted in Figure 6.4.

	C_{12}^+	C_{21}
B_{12}^+	(3, 3)	(–9, –9)
B_{21}	(–9, –9)	(1, 1)

Figure 6.4. Payoff Matrix for Imagery & Blocks Game.

Since B_{12}^+ and C_{12}^+ might emerge as options only in the presence of B_{21} and C_{21}, it is clear that it would be suboptimal to have a population without defectors. Without some segment of the population to show the rest the benefits of B_{21} and C_{21}, there would be no way for the population to reap the benefits of changing from the equilibrium of B_{21} and C_{21}. But a population without defectors is a population whose conventions are not sustained by individual rationality keeping every single individual acting in accord with a single regularity. This means that both Lepore and Stone (2015) and Lewis (1969) fail to explain a dynamic feature of signaling systems with this structure: why do systems like B_{12}^+ and C_{12}^+ emerge when competing with B_{21} and C_{21}, provided that there are some defectors?

This limitation ramifies in different ways for theories of conventional meaning like Lepore and Stone (2015) and Lewis (1969). Lewis (1969) would say that the mental imagery is part of the meaning of σ_1 in the signaling convention consisting of B_{12}^+ and C_{12}^+—though only the builder's mental imagery. This is some small consolation, since the imagery does end up being relevant to the explanation of how signaling systems like this emerge. But it also seems deeply odd to build it into the *truth-conditions* of σ_1 since it is irrelevant to the action being chosen by the collectors. Lepore and Stone (2015) are in an even more awkward situation, since they would presumably exclude mental imagery from the way σ_1 influences the conversational score. Such a claim about the conversational score seems right. But, is that all that there is to say about the meaning of σ_1? The clear answer seems to be *no*: this does not explain why one convention governing σ_1 wins out in relevant circumstances, and surely this is a fact about σ_1's meaning that needs explaining. After all, B_{12}^+ and C_{12}^+ win out over B_{12} and C_{12} because B_{12}^+ and C_{12}^+ allow σ_1 to do something that B_{12} and C_{12} do not.

This point can be made even more precise by a slight variant on the Imagery & Blocks game. Suppose instead of two competing conventions, there were two competing signals σ_1 and σ_1^+. The former is governed by B_{12} and C_{12} while the latter by B_{12}^+ and C_{12}^+. In such a setting, use of σ_1^+ will proliferate at the expense of σ_1 which will fall into obsolescence. Now the question to be explained is: what difference between σ_1^+ and σ_1 explains why this happened? It's hard to see how any answer could fail to mention the mental imagery associated with σ_1^+ and, in some sense, include this as part of σ_1^+'s meaning.

The relationship of mental imagery and conventional meaning is a central topic of Lepore and Stone (2015). On a first pass, the Imagery & Blocks game beautifully illustrates why they want to exclude imagery from the conventional meaning of a sentence. There is no common feature of the mental imagery that builders have and that collectors generate, which counts as being 'communicated' when σ_1 is issued. Indeed, the builders could just as well have been clueless authors, experiencing no phenomenology themselves, but eliciting mesmeric patterns of neon shapes in the collectors—indeed it is no slight to the great authors of literature to assume that their skill is not in communicating a particular experience, but in generating diverse valuable experiences interactively generated by their audience. Further, the collectors need not have uniform mental imagery: they could all imagine rather different shades of neon blue—or different colors altogether—when builders issue σ_1. And, yet, these effects of σ_1 on mental imagery are still a crucial feature of explaining why this signaling system works. Without referencing them, we would not know why B_{12}^+ and C_{12}^+ proliferate when competing with B_{21} and C_{21}. Similarly with the variant where σ_1^+ and σ_1 are in competition. If we want to explain why σ_1^+ proliferates at the expense of σ_1, one must capture its capacity to generate mental imagery. This presents a clear challenge:

The Challenge of Mental Imagery

The mental imagery that accompanies language use can be an ineliminable part of explaining why a particular signaling system is self-sustaining. If mental imagery is not part of the meaning of signals, one must explain why meanings and psychological effects like mental imagery inhabit distinct explanatory roles.

Nothing so far entails that this challenge cannot be met, but nothing Lepore and Stone (2015) say entails that it can be.

Let me take stock of the issues raised for Lepore and Stone (2015). By divorcing conventions of language from effects on agents' individual psychological states, they undercut Lewis's explanation of how the conventions of language are self-sustaining. Changes to the conversational record are not the intrinsically valuable outcomes that make language self-sustaining. It is changes in the private beliefs and actions that are valuable, that make it impossible to exclude deceptive uses from bearing on a convention by simply limiting the conventional regularity to the conversational record. It also makes it difficult to explain, in a principled way, why mental imagery should be excluded from the meaning of a signal. After all, that imagery can play a crucial role in making a particular practice of signal use, or a particular signal, self-sustaining. But if all of this is right, then we are bereft of some key benefits of the approach articulated by Lepore and Stone (2015). Is there another approach that secures those benefits? If so, where does it differ from Lepore and Stone (2015)?

4. Signaling, Meaning, and Significance: The Middle Way

Millikan (2005, ch.3) offers a very different way than Lewis (1969) of thinking about linguistic conventions and how they relate to theoretically important concepts of meaning. There are really two key ideas in Millikan (2005). One is that Millikan (2005, ch.1) bases her theory of convention on the *reproduction* of signals and the speaker–hearer commitments they invoke. The other is that signals are thereby endowed with a *stabilizing function* (Millikan 2005, ch.3):

Stabilizing Function

The speaker and hearer commitments that a signal generates, which explains why that signal is reproduced (or reproducible) in a population.

Millikan's approach to reproduction is complex and nuanced in ways that I cannot engage with here. The crucial feature of this account, which will be important below, is this: The speaker and hearer commitments that actually result from signal use do, sometimes, have to constitute coordination in the game-theoretic sense. However, there is no need to assume that speakers and hearers always or usually coordinate when they use a signal—just that future uses of the signal are explained by historically successful coordination. Crucially, a convention is self-sustaining not by reasoning about whether others conform, but just by observing cases where signals work to coordinate speaker and hearer, and repeating those behaviors.

Millikan's (2005) approach clearly holds promise for solving the deception problem. It can distinguish all uses of a signal from the convention constituting ones: namely those successful coordinations of speaker–hearer that keep the signal in use. However, Millikan (2005) does not present this account with the level of precision needed to speak directly to the issues raised in §3. Murray and Starr (2018) provides some of the needed tools to do so. It will take a bit of setup to present those tools. The first step is to present the account of communicative acts in Murray and Starr (2018).

Murray and Starr (2018) model communicative acts using *conversational states*. A conversational state is centered on a body of mutual assumptions in a conversational context A_C—this is roughly analogous to the conversational record of Lepore and Stone (2015). But, crucially, it also tracks the private assumptions of speaker A_S and hearer A_H—these are not generally known to other conversationalists. A communicative act is then modeled as a function from one conversational state $c = <A_S, A_C, A_H>$ to another $c' = <A'_S, A'_C, A'_H>$. A speech act type (or *utterance force*) has the stabilizing function of coordinating speaker and hearer. When that function is fulfilled c', is a Nash equilibrium—just as in Lewis (1969). An example helps illustrate this basic idea.

Consider a simple assertion like (1). Its assertive force can be modeled using conversational states, as in (2).

(1)   The bug is on your back. (Asserted by S to H)

(2)   *Assertive Effect on $c = <A_S, A_C, A_H>$*:

- *Effect on A_C*:   information that the bug is on H's back is made mutual.
- *Effect on A_S*: S is privately committed to that mutual information.
- *Effect on A_H*: S is privately committed to that mutual information.

Assigning the utterance of (1) an assertive force is just to say that the utterance type's stabilizing function is to produce the effects in (2a)–(2c). Of course, it can still count as an assertion even if it does not, in fact, produce those effects. When the utterance of (1) does achieve these effects, Millikan (2005, ch.1) would describe it as part of a convention of assertion—after all the utterance and response are reproduced[4] and the fact that this pattern of activity is reproduced is, in part, due to precedent: it's a reproduction of an utterance that coordinated the speaker and hearer. It is important to clarify that this convention concerns the utterance of a sentence, rather than the sentence itself—that is, the sentence being tokened by a speaker, at a time, world, etc. in the presence of a particular hearer. This raises the question, however, of what the convention governing the *sentence* in (1) is. This is a crucial issue if we want to answer the question of how a convention endows a *sentence* with a meaning. In fact, this issue highlights one of the problematic features of many approaches to speech acts like Searle (1969): it does not adequately distinguish the linguistic contribution of the signal from the force of a particular utterance of that sentence (Murray and Starr 2018). Making this distinction is essential for adequately explaining how linguistic and non-linguistic mechanisms interact to produce utterance force (Murray and Starr 2018). Millikan (1984, 2005) does not speak directly to this issue, but Murray and Starr (2018) show how to unify her general approach with a dynamic semantics for sentential mood (declarative, imperative, and interrogative).

Drawing on dynamic semantics, Murray and Starr (2018) propose that the linguistic conventions governing sentences are procedures for updating the mutual assumptions A_C. More concretely, the linguistic meaning of a declarative sentence like (1) is a function mapping one A_C to another that contains the information that the bug is on the hearer's back. This effect is *part of* many different functions the utterance of (1) could serve. For example, making this information mutual might not serve to transmit information from speaker to hearer, as in assertion, but instead to strengthen the social bond between them. Perhaps the speaker once truly told the hearer this and something hilarious happened. This second utterance could initiate a short line of pretense, where the humorous event is reenacted. On such a use, the sentence still serves to update the mutual assumptions—which facilitates the pretense—but utterances like this do not serve the function of transmitting information. Their function is social bonding, a commonly neglected function in research on human communication, but a central idea in work with primates (Tomasello 2008, ch.6). So, on the approach developed in Murray and Starr (2018) the conventional meaning of a sentence constrains the force of an utterance by encoding a procedure for updating the mutual assumptions. But the particular force of an utterance concerns how that utterance type fits into the agents' social lives—more on what this amounts to shortly.

On this approach, linguistic conventions only concern what a sentence makes mutual. This characterizes them more narrowly than Millikan (1984, 2005), who

---

[4] It is important to note that Millikan (1984, 2005) offers a sophisticated theory of reproduction whereby the original does not completely determine the reproduction. This is crucial for language where *A and B* could be a reproduction of *A, B* and *C and D*, and inherit its function from *and, A* and *B*.

characterizes the conventions directly in terms of the speaker and hearer commit-ments they generate.[5] This compels her to posit polysemy via overlapping conventions to capture the diversity of uses to which a sentence type can be put. This is less attractive for the purposes of linguistic analysis than Murray and Starr's (2018) account for two reasons. First, it does not cohere well with linguistic typology, where each of these variants are realized in some language or other with an overt form. Second, it makes it impossible to formulate a general, non-linguistic theory of how mutual contri-butions relate to the private commitments of speakers and hearers. Murray and Starr (2018) propose just such a general theory.

Language provides a way of coordinating mutual assumptions, but each linguistic act also involves a more fundamental form of coordination via three general mechanisms that are not at all specific to language. The first two have been well studied, and some have even attempted to found a complete pragmatic theory on one or both of them.

Mechanisms of Coordination

(Murray and Starr 2018)

1. *Social Conventions* (Austin 1962)
   - An act by an agent with a given social position, with a particular audience, counts as a socially recognized event type.
2. *Communicative Intentions* (Grice 1957)
   - One agent X intends to influence another Y's state of mind, and intends Y's state of mind to change, in part, by recognizing that X intended to change Y's state of mind in that way.
3. *Social Norms* (Bicchieri 2005)
   - Self-fulfilling expectations of what agents like us do in situations like these, enforced by informal sanctions (shame, disgust, exclusion, etc.)

However, neither social conventions nor communicative intentions are generally viable mechanisms for getting things done together. The reason is simple: our social inter-actions are not, under their most fundamental description, coordination games at all. They are 'mixed-motive' games, like the Prisoner's Dilemma. In the Prisoner's Dilemma, two criminals are separately given a choice between informing on the other and getting released, or staying quiet and serving a short sentence. If the two prisoners were allowed to exchange messages neither social conventions, nor communicative intentions would be effective means for enabling communication. Social norms, according to Bicchieri (2005), exist to solve problems like these. If others expect the prisoners to stay quiet, and will sanction defecting heavily enough to outweigh the

---

[5] Millikan (1984) is deeply skeptical of higher-order intentions and mutual knowledge, as it's been used in the Neo-Gricean literature. However, we envision a characterization of the mutual assumptions in a way that avoids these concerns. Following Lewis (1969) instead of Stalnaker (1978), one can think of the mutual assumptions as what each agent is assuming for the purposes of their exchange, what each would be justified in assuming everyone is assuming, and so on. By talking in terms of justification, it is possible to grant that no agent actually needs to maintain higher-order mental states while communicating.

costs of taking a light sentence, then this mixed-motive game is transformed into a coordination game. Similarly, if others expect the prisoners to be truthful in their message exchanges, and will sanction lies heavily enough, then these two prisoners will at least be able to communicate.

Upon reflection, our everyday communication is no different than the Prisoner's Dilemma. It may be better for both of us to communicate than not, but I might want more information than you have time to articulate, and you may not be sure I'll do the same for you when I need it. And, obviously, you might have an interest in my being misinformed. In these cases, there is no Nash equilibrium that allows either of us to end up a bit better off. So, if viewed in terms of narrow self-interest, and in isolation of our social organization, everyday communication seems as unsustainable as it was for the prisoners. One way to resolve this tension is to assume that our everyday communicative interactions are infused with social norms that transform our mixed-motive games into coordination games.

What exactly are social norms, and which particular ones are at play in human communication? Full answers are beyond the scope of this essay, but some simplified ones may make my proposal here more concrete. According to Bicchieri (2005, 11): some social practice is a social norm just in case each agent A prefers to conform to the practice given that conditions (i) and (ii) obtain, and those conditions do obtain (Bicchieri 2005, 11):[6]

i. A expects others to conform and
ii. A either believes that others expect A to conform or that others prefer A to conform and will informally sanction non-conformity (shame, disgust, etc.).

As Bicchieri (2005, 3) clarifies, this is a rational reconstruction of what a social norm is, and is consistent with a psychological implementation that is sub-personal, unconscious and economically approximates the concept defined by the rational reconstruction. This idea can be applied to speech act types. Each speech act type involves a social norm that relates changes to the mutual assumptions and the conversationalists' private commitments. For example, the analysis of assertion from (2) can be understood as involving a norm that says that the speaker is expected to be privately committed to the information they made mutual, and that the hearer is expected to become privately committed to information made mutual by an authority. The relevant forms of sanction exploit humans' impressive social memory and intricate systems of reputation and authority (Scott-Phillips 2011, 2015). As long as these projections of authority and reputation somewhat reliably track a speaker's trustworthiness and competence, trusting their contributions and expecting them to be sincere will keep deception at bay, and facilitate communication. These systems of norms and reputation are an

---

[6] More precisely: a behavioral rule R is a social norm just in case almost everybody knows that R exists and prefers to conform to R on the condition that (a) almost everybody believes that almost everybody conforms to R and either (b) almost everybody believes that almost everybody expects almost everybody to conform to R or (b') almost everybody believes that almost everybody expects almost everybody to conform to R, prefers them to conform to R and may sanction those that don't (Bicchieri 2005, 11).

evolved cultural solution to the problem of living together, and each new generation inherits them when they learn how to live in a society.

I can now return to the issues of §3. Like Lepore and Stone (2015), deceptive uses of a sentence do not bear on the relevant linguistic convention: declaratives update the mutual assumptions appropriately even when they are used to lie. However, unlike Lepore and Stone (2015), there is a clear answer to how this linguistic convention is self-sustaining. It is embedded in behavioral regularities governed by social norms. These norms make it possible to coordinate despite our conflicting interests, and regulate the private commitments conversationalists form. These patterns of coordination are reproduced, and include the relevant linguistic practice of updating our mutual assumptions. This theory of language use relates linguistic conventions to the actual psychological effects certain uses have, even though I am not identifying linguistic conventions with those particular effects. This also offers a principled reason for excluding mental imagery from the linguistic meaning or convention in the Blocks & Imagery Coordination Problem. While those psychological states are essential to explaining how utterances and their interpretations are reproduced, it is not plausible to include them in the distinctively linguistic effect of changing the mutual assumptions. In order to justify including the information that the builder is imagining a neon pink square in the mutual assumptions, something the builder and collector are doing together would have to depend on being able to take that information for granted.[7] Without a far more nuanced signaling system, including perhaps signals about mental states, this is not possible.

Both of these moves seem broadly consistent with the approach in Lepore and Stone (2015). But, the general framework presented above also presents a challenge to a key assumption in Lepore and Stone (2015): that all meaning is either speaker meaning or conventional meaning. Above, we saw a genuine sense of meaning that cannot be reduced to either: the stabilizing function of an utterance. In a homage to Welby (1896a, 1896b) whose central focus seemed to be this sense of *meaning*, I call it *significance*:

Significance

What certain kinds of utterances of σ do which explains why that kind of utterance of σ is reproduced (i.e. the stabilizing function of an utterance).

This is to be contrasted, on my view, with:

Conventional Meaning

What all utterances of σ do to A_C, which explains why σ is reproduced (i.e. the stabilizing function of a signal).

---

[7] This raises a question: is it that the builder's signal doesn't provide the collector with any information at all about the builder's mental imagery, or just that it doesn't make this information *mutual*? The former idea is closely related to the central proposal of Skyrms (2010, ch.3): σ provides information about some state of the world s only if $P(s \mid \sigma) \neq P(s)$. I leave this question for further research.

While significance is clearly a concept of pragmatics, it should also be contrasted with speaker meaning. Some utterances, particularly novel ones, will inherit their significance from the speaker's communicative intentions, but it is perfectly possible for this to not be the case. As a purely theoretical example, a poem that generates some particular imagery or associations in a sizable chunk of the population may justify including that effect in the poem's significance even if the author did not intend it, and it is not part of the information that the poem makes mutual by linguistic conventions. Linda Lovelace's *Ordeal*, a much-discussed example in the feminist literature on pornography (e.g. Langton 1993, 321–2), may best be understood in this way. The book was intended to protest and undermine the pornography industry by providing details and images about the brutality and coercion women in the industry endured. However, it became a sensation among pornography consumers that were aroused by such depictions. It soon came to be sold at adult books stores and widely consumed as pornography. Perhaps it is right to say that its significance was pornographic, even though its conventional and speaker meanings were anything but.

Ordeal is not an isolated example in the feminist literature on language. There, one finds many phenomena that do not fit nicely into the theoretical concepts afforded by the Fregean and Gricean tradition. The particular implementation of utterance significance here suggests that the significant effects of an utterance are often mediated by social norms. As emphasized by Bicchieri (2005), many social norms are deeply oppressive. They transform a mixed-motive game into a coordination game by unjustly endowing a group with the power of sanctions that effectively erases the self-interests of others—foot binding in China is just one such example. Social norms that impact our linguistic practices are not immune from this injustice. The inability of the socially oppressed to have their conversational contributions believed, or even engaged with, is a central issue discussed in work on illocutionary disablement (Langton 1993) and testimonial injustice (Fricker 2007). As proposed in Murray and Starr (2018), these phenomena are easier to understand in terms of social norms and utterance significance. Thinking of significance as drawing on social norms, and emerging from complex interactions in a population of agents amounts to a fundamental shift in the orientation of pragmatics. Socializing pragmatics will require different tools and methodologies, and far more substantive engagement with social philosophy, sociology, and socio-linguistics.

It is no surprise, then, that feminist work on language suggests immediately promising frontiers to explore. Consider McConnell-Ginet (2012, 747):

[C]hildren's books, syntax texts, newspapers, and many other media include many more references to men and boys than to women and girls. Notice that no particular utterer or utterance need have 'meant' that male human beings are more important than female or even more interesting or less problematic to discuss nor does anyone have to embrace such beliefs explicitly. Indeed, many people who themselves contribute to these patterns might be dismayed to realize that they have done so.

This kind of emergent social meaning fits well with the concept of utterance significance defined here. It is a process by which agents' utterances replicate ideology not in virtue of the linguistic conventions, or speaker's intentions, but through the background psychological processes by which we engage with language. Much more work is needed to deliver on this promise, but I hope to have made the case that this kind of pragmatic social meaning can be integrated within a precise formal approach to linguistic meaning. There is no reason to exclude it as Lepore and Stone (2015) do, and, in fact, I have argued that any adequate account of how language is self-sustaining must include it. Perhaps it will also answer the call of philosophers like Hornsby (2000) who have highlighted the limiting individualistic assumptions of the Gricean tradition.

5. Conclusion

Any account of conventional linguistic meaning must explain how particular patterns of use and interpretation are self-sustaining. There are two main tasks in doing so: explain how those practices are valuable to a given population, *and* specify a mechanism by which that value suffices to perpetuate the practice. Lewis and Grice appealed to high-order rationality for the second task, but that proposal is seeming increasingly inadequate. As anticipated by Millikan (1984), there is a wealth of tools from evolutionary biology that can provide more psychologically realistic explanations (Skyrms 2010). Lewis and Grice address the first task by tying use and interpretation to the actual private psychological states of language users. Our linguistic tools are meaningful because they are intertwined with our actual beliefs and desires, intentions and goals. Lepore and Stone (2015) departed from this tradition, instead adopting an account where language is meaningful insofar as it constitutes a rule-governed practice of conversational scorekeeping. However, this does not explain why speaking a language is not a purely recreational game, nor how it is self-sustaining. Filling this gap in Lepore and Stone (2015) requires investigating the *significance* of language. I have said here how the significance of language may be precisely defined and proposed that it opens a new, more social, approach to pragmatics. It may yet provide a way of articulating insights about non-literal language and speech acts that do not fit into the orthodox categories of linguistic meaning or speaker meaning.

References

Austin, John L. 1962. *How to Do Things with Words*. Oxford: Oxford University Press.
Bicchieri, Christina. 2005. *The Grammar of Society: The Nature and Dynamics of Social Norms*. Cambridge: Cambridge University Press.
Carston, Robyn. 2002. *Thoughts and Utterances: The Pragmatics of Explicit Communication*. Malden, MA: Wiley-Blackwell.
Fricker, Miranda. 2007. *Epistemic Injustice: Power and the Ethics of Knowing*. New York: Oxford University Press.

Grice, H. Paul. 1957. "Meaning." *Philosophical Review* 66 (3): 377–88. http://www.jstor.org/stable/2182440.

Hornsby, Jennifer. 2000. "Feminism in Philosophy of Language: Communicative Speech Acts." In *Cambridge Companion to Feminism in Philosophy*, edited by Miranda Fricker and Jennifer Hornsby, 87–106. Cambridge: Cambridge University Press.

Langton, Rae. 1993. "Speech Acts and Unspeakable Acts." *Philosophy & Public Affairs* 22 (4): 293–330. http://www.jstor.org/stable/2265469.

Lepore, Ernie, and Matthew Stone. 2015. *Imagination and Convention: Distinguishing Grammar and Inference in Language*. New York: Oxford University Press.

Lepore, Ernie, and Matthew Stone. 2015a. "David Lewis on Convention." In *A Companion to David Lewis*, edited by Barry Loewer and Jonathan Schaffer, 313–27. Oxford: Wiley. doi:10.1002/9781118398593.ch20.

Lewis, David K. 1969. *Convention: A Philosophical Study*. Cambridge, MA: Harvard University Press.

Lewis, David K. 1975. "Languages and Language." In *Language, Mind, and Knowledge. Minnesota Studies in the Philosophy of Science*, Vol. 7, edited by Keith Gunderson, 3–35. Minneapolis, MN: University of Minnesota Press.

Lewis, David K. 1979. "Scorekeeping in a Language Game." *Journal of Philosophical Logic* 8 (1): 339–59. http://www.jstor.org/stable/30227173.

McConnell-Ginet, Sally. 2012. "Language, Gender and Sexuality." In *Routledge Companion to the Philosophy of Language*, edited by Delia Graff Fara and Gillian Russell, 741–52. New York: Routledge.

Millikan, Ruth Garrett. 1984. *Language, Thought and Other Biological Categories*. Cambridge, MA: MIT Press.

Millikan, Ruth Garrett. 2005. *Language: A Biological Model*. New York: Oxford University Press.

Murray, Sarah E. 2014. "Varieties of Update." *Semantics and Pragmatics* 7 (2): 1–53. http://dx.doi.org/10.3765/sp.7.2.

Murray, Sarah E., and William B. Starr. 2018. "Force and Conversational States." In *New Work on Speech Acts*, edited by Daniel Fogal, Daniel Harris, and Matthew Moss, 202–236. New York: Oxford University Press.

Murray, Sarah E., and William B. Starr forthcoming. "The Structure of Communicative Acts." *Linguistics & Philosophy*.

Portner, Paul. 2004. "The Semantics of Imperatives Within a Theory of Clause Types." In *Proceedings from Semantics and Linguistic Theory* 14, edited by Robert B. Young, 235–52. Ithaca, NY: CLC Publications. http://semanticsarchive.net/Archive/mJlZGQ4N/PortnerSALT04.pdf.

Roberts, Craige. 2004. "Context in Dynamic Interpretation." In *The Handbook of Pragmatics*, edited by Laurence Horn and Gregory Ward, 197–220. Malden, MA: Blackwell. http://www.ling.ohio-state.edu/~croberts/context.pdf.

Scott-Phillips, Thom. 2015. *Speaking Our Minds: Why Human Communication Is Different, and How Language Evolved to Make It Special*. New York: Palgrave Macmillan.

Scott-Phillips, Thomas C. 2011. "Evolutionarily Stable Communication and Pragmatics." In *Language, Games, and Evolution*, edited by Anton Benz, Christian Ebert, Gerhard Jäger, and Robert van Rooij, 6207: 117–33. Lecture Notes in Computer Science. Springer Berlin Heidelberg. doi:10.1007/978-3-642-18006-4_6.

Searle, John R. 1969. *Speech Acts*. Cambridge: Cambridge University Press.

Skyrms, Brian. 2010. *Signals: Evolution, Learning, and Information.* New York: Oxford University Press.

Stalnaker, Robert C. 1978. "Assertion." In *Syntax and Semantics 9: Pragmatics*, edited by Peter Cole, 315–32. New York: Academic Press.

Starr, William B. forthcoming. "A Preference Semantics for Imperatives." *Semantics & Pragmatics.*

Tomasello, Michael. 2008. *Origins of Human Communication.* The Jean Nicod Lectures. Cambridge, MA: MIT Press.

Welby, V. 1896a. "Sense, Meaning and Interpretation I." *Mind*, New series, 5 (17). Oxford University Press on behalf of the Mind Association: 24–37. http://www.jstor.org/stable/2247630.

Welby, V. 1896b. "Sense, Meaning and Interpretation II." *Mind*, New series, 5 (18). Oxford University Press on behalf of the Mind Association: 186–202. http://www.jstor.org/stable/2247581.

Wittgenstein, Ludwig. 1953. *Philosophical Investigations.* Translated by G. E. M. Anscombe. Oxford: Basil Blackwell.

Zollman, Kevin J. S. 2011. "Separating Directives and Assertions Using Simple Signaling Games." *Journal of Philosophy* 108 (3): 158–69.

PART II

Intentions and the Limits of Meaning

7

Varieties of Intentionalism

Jessica Keiser

In *Imagination and Convention: Distinguishing Grammar and Inference in Language*, Ernie Lepore and Matthew Stone offer a multifaceted critique of the widely influential Gricean picture of language use, proposing in its place a novel framework within which to understand the role of convention in linguistic communication. The first few sections of their book are dedicated to the contention that the Gricean conception of the semantics/pragmatics divide is misguided, and that pragmatics plays a much more minimal role in facilitating communication than has been traditionally supposed. The claims made in this part of the book are largely contingent and empirical—the general argument being that paradigmatic cases of conversational implicature are in fact conventionally communicated; we don't reason about each other's mental states in interpretation to the extent supposed by Grice and his followers, but rather draw almost entirely on our shared knowledge of language. Others have defended the Gricean line against these empirical claims—here I will focus instead on the last part of the book, which critiques a general sort of theory of meaning typified by the work of Paul Grice as well as David Lewis.[1,2] Lepore and Stone criticize Lewis' and Grice's commitment to what they call *prospective intentionalism*, according to which the meaning of an utterance is determined by the effects that the speaker intends it to have on the conversation. Instead, they make a case for what they call *direct intentionalism*, according to which the meaning of an utterance is determined by the speaker's intentions to use it under a certain grammatical analysis. I will argue that there is an equivocation behind their critique, both regarding the type of meaning that is at issue, and with respect to the question each theory is attempting to answer; once we prise these issues apart, we find that Lepore and Stone's main contentions are compatible with the broadly Lewisian/Gricean picture.

Lepore and Stone (hereafter L&S) appeal to direct intentions in order to delimit the scope of what they call *utterance meaning*, which they take to be the contents contributed by utterances to conversational inquiry. Their theory presupposes linguistic

---

[1] See Bezuidenhout (2016), Horn (2016), and Szabo (2016).
[2] See Grice (1989), Lewis (1969, 1975).

meaning; it describes a practice that we engage in *using* conventional language, rather than giving a description of the kinds of practices that constitute linguistic meaning. Grice and Lewis, on the other hand, are using prospective intentionalism to define a different kind of meaning, which we can put under the general umbrella term of *speaker meaning*. This is a conception of meaning that does not presuppose linguistic meaning, but is instead used by both Lewis and Grice to provide a reductive account of it. I will argue that prospective intentionalism and direct intentionalism are compatible, and that they can each be used to do a different sort of work in an overall theory of linguistic communication.

1. Varieties of Intentionalism, Varieties of Meaning

L&S identify what they perceive to be competing versions of intentionalism:

Prospective Intentionalism (Grice and Lewis): The meaning of an utterance is determined by the effects that the speaker intends it to have on the conversation.

Direct Intentionalism (Lepore and Stone): The meaning of an utterance is determined by the speaker's intentions to use it under a certain grammatical analysis.[3]

Consider an example: Suppose we are having a conversation and I want to contribute the information that I am sad that Diane Rehm is retiring. It is plausible that I have a range of intentions in performing this utterance. One involves my intentions concerning the effect that my utterance will have on our conversational exchange—roughly, that as a result of my utterance you will come to be informed about my feelings about Diane Rehm's retirement. The fact that I am sad about this event will become shared information between us as conversational participants (supposing for simplicity that we are in a cooperative exchange, you take my sincerity for granted, etc.) We can call this my prospective intention. But you may think that I have another intention, which is more direct in the sense that it functions as a step in helping me to achieve my prospective intention. This is the intention to contribute the standing meaning in English (relative to our context of conversation) of the sentence "I am sad that Diane Rehm is retiring" to our conversation. We can call this my direct intention. So which of these intentions determines the meaning of the utterance? Well, that depends on what you mean by *the meaning of the utterance*. I want to suggest that if we think of utterance meaning in the sense that L&S do, the question becomes one that Lewis and Grice were not apparently concerned to answer in appealing to prospective intentions.

   L&S characterize utterance meaning in terms of a public commitment to a content—a commitment that is made according to rules determined by social agreement. The committed content gets added to what they call the *conversational score*, drawing on Lewis' work on accommodation.[4] The conversational score tracks the commitments made by the conversational participants according to the conventional linguistic rules

---

[3] My formulation, based on Lepore and Stone (2015), pp. 200–20.   [4] See Lewis (1979).

they have (explicitly or implicitly) agreed upon in an effort to coordinate their behavior for the purpose of streamlining communication. In their characterization of utterance meaning and conversational score, L&S have in mind a linguistic practice according to which conversationalists defer to the standing meaning in the community of the expression uttered by the speaker—rather than what the speaker may have had in mind (though this may only make a practical difference when the two come apart)—in order to determine what the speaker has contributed to the conversation.

Our view articulates a clear standard that privileges conventional meaning... We look to the speaker's basic intention to settle which utterance was used and how it is grounded in the causal and informational connections to the environment that constitute meaning. Even when a speaker has false beliefs about the meanings of her words or the identities of objects in her environment, we must still characterize her contribution to the conversation by interpreting her basic intentions against the operative context. When a speaker represents the meaning of a word via deference to some network in a community, then what that word means, for the speaker, is what it means in the community. It doesn't matter if the speaker couldn't articulate what the meaning is or is committed to use some other meaning because of false beliefs she has.[5]

The idea is that the intention determines what you said: What words you used, what syntactic analysis you had in mind, and so forth. You had to represent the utterance to say it, that's all.[6]

On our view, this intention is to use the utterance to contribute its meaning.[7]

L&S's conception of utterance meaning is one that takes for granted the existence of linguistic conventions, rather than functioning as a tool for providing an account of such conventions. According to this conception, the meaning of the speaker's utterance is determined by her direct intention to use it to contribute its conventional meaning within the linguistic community of which she is a participant. Linguistic conventions must already be in place in order for the speaker to have such an intention. The practice of coordinating on the conversational score, which L&S describe, is one which presupposes the existence of linguistic conventions within a community, rather than one that is meant to provide a reductive account of what those conventions *consist in*.

In contrast, Grice and Lewis appeal to prospective intentions to describe something that we can put under the general umbrella term of *speaker meaning*—corresponding to Grice's *uttterer's occasion meaning*, and roughly to Lewis' truthfulness in a language L. Both Lewis and Grice use speaker meaning to provide a reductive account of linguistic meaning; linguistic meaning, for both of them, is ultimately grounded in the prospective intentions of individuals. But this general metasemantic picture is compatible with the existence of a practice like the one described by L&S, according to which conversationalists defer to linguistic rules to settle the contributions of speakers to the scoreboard associated with that particular practice. There are many contexts in which it makes sense to adopt such a practice (for instance, in a

---

[5] Lepore and Stone (2014), p. 219.   [6] Ibid., p. 225.   [7] Ibid., p. 214.

courtroom, or any setting in which speaker meaning and utterance meaning may come apart or be disputed). I will get back to this issue in section 3. The point here is that Grice and Lewis seem to be largely silent on the existence of rules for the kinds of practices that *presuppose* and *utilize* the linguistic conventions that are already in use within a community. Instead, they were focused on much more ground-level questions concerning the nature of communication in general, and how our communicative practices can give rise to linguistic conventions and meaning.

L&S's analogy between coordinating on the conversational scoreboard and playing chess brings out the differences between their project and that of Lewis and Grice:

> If we decide to play chess, what we've decide do in the first instance is that we are deferring to the rules of chess…Whatever the rules of chess turn out to be is what we will play by—generally speaking, of course…But now we can talk separately about what our mental states are—how we're tracking the record—from what the record is. The record itself depends first and foremost on the rules. We think of semantics in much the same way. In conversation, normally, each of us defers to a broad set of background commitments about meaning. These commitments describe how to update the record, but they also describe our responsibilities in using language in accord with the broader community, in introducing and negotiating new meanings in special situations, and in working to make sure that we understand one another as making meaning in established ways. Interlocutors have an interest in understanding one another, but also have broader interests in using their understanding to pursue consistent and public meanings. So while we want to coordinate on the record, we do that by agreeing on a wide range of additional background commitments that cover the full range of conversational dynamics.[8]

The kind of coordination L&S describe in the case of chess is not one that speaks to the question of what the game consists in. Rather, it is taken for granted that the game of chess and its rules exist; the players, who have some knowledge of these rules, coordinate their behavior by choosing to play chess and then subsequently by deferring to the rules of the game. They have reason to thus coordinate, given a shared interest in passing the time with an entertaining, challenging, and organized activity. In the same way, the kind of coordination that L&S describe in the case of language use does not explain what conventional linguistic meaning consists in, but rather takes for granted established linguistic conventions and describes one way in which we can coordinate our behavior after those conventions are already in place. (Again, I will explore some of the reasons we may have for thus coordinating in the next section.)

This way of coordinating by agreement on pre-established rules seems ill-suited to do the kind of work that Lewis and Grice needed it to do—it is unclear how it could be used to provide a reductive account of what it takes for a population to speak a language. Quine gives an explanation of the difficulty in using such a conception of coordination to provide a metasemantic theory in his foreward to Lewis' *Convention*:

> When I was a child I pictured our language as settled and passed down by a board of syndics, seated in a grave convention along a table in the style of Rembrandt. The picture remained

---

[8] Ibid., p. 255.

for a while undisturbed by the question what language the syndics might have used in their deliberations, or by dread of vicious regress.

I suppose this picture has been entertained by many, in uncritical childhood. Many mature thinkers, certainly, have called language conventional. Many have also in other connections been ready with appeals to agreements that were historically never enacted ... In the language case the question of latent content is even more urgent, and more perplexing, in that an original founding of language by overt convention is not merely unhistorical but unthinkable. What is convention when there can be no thought of convening?[9]

A metasemantic theory cannot appeal to *explicit* agreement, since this presupposes a shared language—the thing which we have set out to explain. The notion of *implicit* agreement is much more promising for this job, but also requires an explanation—one which Lewis and Grice both provide by appealing to prospective intentionalism. Lewis was looking for an account of how pre-linguistic beings are able to coordinate on a shared language; this is what prospective intentionalism—and not direct intentionalism— appears suited to do.

Grice and Lewis' commitment to prospective intentionalism is not in conflict with L&S's commitment to direct intentionalism, then, for two reasons: most importantly, Grice and Lewis are committed to prospective intentionalism *as a claim about speaker meaning*, whereas L&S are committed to direct intentionalism *as a claim about utterance meaning*. Second, these claims are being used to answer different theoretical questions about language use; Grice and Lewis—but not L&S—were attempting to answer the foundational question of what makes it the case that a given population speaks a given language. (I will talk about what L&S are up to in the last section.)

2. Diffusing Problems for Prospective Intentionalism

Having established that L&S are using direct intentionalism to address different theoretical questions than were Grice and Lewis, I want to turn to their criticisms of prospective intentionalism and try to diffuse some of the problems they presented for that view. Here is a reminder of the two positions:

Prospective Intentionalism (Grice and Lewis): The meaning of an utterance is determined by the effects that the speaker intends it to have on the conversation.

Direct Intentionalism (Lepore and Stone): The meaning of an utterance is determined by the speaker's intentions to use it in under a certain grammatical analysis.

Their first complaint is that prospective intentionalism assigns utterance meaning based on the speaker's occurrent attitudes, including her goals for the conversation. The more plausible alternative, they claim—which is given by direct intentionalism— would be to base meaning on the standing commitments of interlocutors to rules that govern their communicative practices more broadly. The force of this complaint, however, rides on the equivocation about meaning discussed in the previous section.

---

[9] W.V. Quine, in his foreword to Lewis (1969), p. xi.

The kinds of factors that determine meaning will depend of course on what kind of meaning is at issue. For Grice and Lewis, *speaker meaning* does indeed depend on occurrent attitudes, however *linguistic meaning* will depend on standing commitments as manifested in conventions. It is not clear that either of them ever identified something corresponding to L&S's utterance meaning—it appears compatible with their views to grant that there is a linguistic practice like that described by L&S, according to which utterance meaning, and contributions to the conversational score more generally, are determined by direct intentions. Moreover, while certainly for Grice and Lewis speaker meaning is not *necessarily* determined by a speaker's intention to use it under a certain grammatical analysis, it bears pointing out that it is a possibility—even a likelihood. For Grice, a speaker can mean something without encoding it in a conventional language, and Lewis' interlocutors can solve their communicative coordination problem by non-conventional means. However, they are able to do this with conventional language if they so choose—indeed, if there is a language convention in place, this will in many cases be the most efficient way to transmit speaker meaning or solve the coordination problem. While speaker meaning is necessarily determined by prospective intentions, there is nothing in Grice or Lewis' picture to preclude the idea that on some occasions, part of such an intention may be to use an expression to contribute its standing conventional meaning.[10]

L&S's second complaint is that prospective intentionalism ties meaning too closely to collaboration; they express doubts about there being any particular type of collaboration that is required for meaning in every case. They rule out practical collaboration on the grounds that interlocutors often fail to take up each other's practical goals, illustrating the point with the example of customer service agents; while customer service agents are often not able to help the customers achieve their goals, they nonetheless manage to have meaningful conversations with them. They rule out collaboration at the level of trying to reach agreement about the issues under discussion, citing political debates of examples of how meaning can occur absent this kind of collaboration. However there is nothing in prospective intentionalism—as they have framed it— which involves a commitment to either of these levels of collaboration as a prerequisite for meaning. The more fully fleshed out accounts of Lewis and Grice involve commitment to varying levels of collaboration, which I discuss at length elsewhere.[11] While I agree with L&S that the *particular* accounts of Lewis and Grice commit each of them to too strong a level of collaboration, there is nothing in perspective intentionalism *as such* which would involve either of these levels of commitment. The effect that the speaker intends her utterance to have on the conversation may only be a shared understanding of the meaning, or conversational contribution of that utterance (which could be cashed out in a minimal way). Though this does require some degree of

[10] This can't be the case on every occasion, or the account of linguistic meaning would be circular. But there is room for bootstrapping.

[11] Keiser (2016).

collaboration, it seems as though L&S are also committed to at least this much, insofar as they see interlocutors involved in the project of coordinating on the conversational score. They do, however, go as far as to rule out the necessity of collaborating on achieving mutual understanding, citing uncooperative exchanges in which interlocutors are purposefully obscuring their meaning or refusing to engage in the conversation at all. Such examples do not seem terribly troubling for the prospective intentionalist. For one, it seems as though L&S themselves are committed to interlocutors collaborating in the minimal sense that they want to achieve a shared understanding of the conversational score. Second, it hardly seems like a mark against a theory of meaning that it doesn't capture situations in which people aren't even remotely attempting to understand one another. If not some degree of attempt at mutual understanding, it is hard to see what a theory of meaning is trying to explain.

Finally, L&S are unhappy that prospective intentionalism puts conventionally encoded and improvised meaning on a par, whereas it seems to them as though language use should be considered a special achievement. However, the fact that speaker meaning can be transmitted through conventional as well as unconventional means is a positive feature of Grice's and Lewis' accounts, given the theoretical questions that they were concerned with; it is what provides them with the necessary tools for the reductive metasemantic project of grounding language in speaker's intentions. On this kind of account, language use is still a special social achievement—it is the achievement of implementing a stable and efficient strategy to coordinate on speaker meaning. Moreover, on this account of language use we can appreciate how this achievement is special, while at the same time can recognize how it may have developed from capacities that were present in our ancestors.

3. What Does Direct Intentionalism Delimit?

I have argued that Lewis and Grice were using prospective intentionalism to answer a certain theoretical problem that L&S do not address: the foundational metasemantic question of what grounds linguistic meaning. In contrast, the theoretical problem that L&S address using direct intentionalism is that of delimiting the semantics/pragmatics boundary.

Our goal is to distinguish semantics and pragmatics—to identify the scope of linguistic knowledge in utterance interpretation. We have argued that language requires us to introduce, maintain, and use information with a special abstract status, such as the distinctions of context, attention, information structure, and commitment that we have just outlined. The conversational record captures this distinctively linguistic information.[12]

The conversational record is thus a key construct for clarifying the scope of semantics.[13]

---

[12] Lepore and Stone (2015), p. 250.   [13] Ibid., p. 246.

As they point out, however, this project is one of *characterizing* the semantics/pragmatics boundary rather than *explaining* it:

The chief worry about the conversational record is that it is a theoretical construct. It offers us the freedom to recapitulate distinctions, rather than to explain them. We are committed to the view that figurative and evocative speech fails to update the conversational record to reflect the distinctive insight that it may prompt. It would be good to explain why—or at least make independent sense of the idea. But, we suggest, that's just what our intuitions of the open-endedness of figures of speech amount to. In using figures of speech, we are not coordinating on the information we contribute to conversation. Interlocutors' coordination ends once they undertake to explore the imagery of utterances in some particular way. We don't put the inferences we draw on the record—unless and until later utterances give us explicit instruction to do so. There's clearly more work to do, but we think this development offers an encouraging basis for pursuing it.[14]

The conversational record as characterized by L&S has a relatively limited scope, selecting linguistically encoded information and excluding information that is communicated by—for instance—malapropism or figures of speech. L&S seem to think that we have a practice of coordinating with one another in order to keep track of this kind of information in particular, and that seems correct. The question then becomes why would we need to coordinate on, and keep track of, this information at the exclusion of the broader range of information that was merely speaker meant? I think a promising way to explore this issue is to look at different kinds of conversational contexts, and the different kinds of scoreboards we use depending on our goals and other features of the context. For instance, it does not seem as though L&S's conversational scoreboard plays a predominant role in a casual and agreeable conversation among friends. In this kind of context, one would come across as a bit of a lunatic to insist that the speaker is committed to the literal meaning of her utterance rather than what she *speaker meant*, in the case of malapropism. Similarly, in this kind of context figures of speech seem like perfectly appropriate ways to contribute to the conversation. But there are indeed other kinds of contexts—such as the courtroom or the police interrogation room or an academic exam—where we do defer to linguistic rules rather than the speakers' intentions to determine her commitments and contribution. So what is the difference between the former and the latter settings?

There may not be one single factor at work, but it is notable that deference to utterance meaning (in L&S's sense) rather than speaker meaning can be expected to some degree in any context in which disputes about the message may arise and potentially cause problems. For instance, we defer to utterance meaning in exam settings; one cannot simply complain after receiving a poor grade that one made a typo, and *(speaker) meant* the correct answer. Once the utterance is produced, the message—what gets put on the exam scoreboard, is determined by conventional linguistic rules, regardless of the speaker's communicative intentions, which may have been in conflict with this

---

[14] Ibid., p. 234.

message. So it seems that whether we defer to linguistic rules or speaker's intentions depends on what kind of coordination problem we are trying to solve; the particular coordination problem solved by deference to utterance meaning in this case is not one of communication, broadly speaking, but one of ensuring fairness. Something similar goes on in legal settings; one cannot simply make a confession in a courtroom and then later claim that they were being ironic. (Though there are ways to revoke a confession, they are governed by rules that are, again, solutions to the problem of ensuring fairness rather than the problem of communication.) A landlord cannot claim that she made a typo on the lease in order to get one more month's rent out of tenants that are vacating the apartment. In all of these cases we are using something like L&S's conversational scoreboard to solve coordination problems, but the coordination problem is not that of communication.

So L&S are right on target to suggest that we have a practice of deferring to the conversational scoreboard, which is determined by direct intentions, and that we do this in order to solve a coordination problem. But the problem we are coordinating to solve is not the one that Lewis and Grice were concerned with and used prospective intentionalism to explain—which is that of communication, broadly speaking. Their insight was that, when we develop a stable and regular strategy to solve this problem, we have linguistic meaning within a community. But there are other coordination problems that arise after conventions of language have been established, which we may solve by agreeing to defer to conventionally encoded contributions. It seems as though these are often uncooperative contexts, but there is no reason to suppose that that will always be the case. L&S's insights into the semantics/pragmatics divide will provide a useful framework with which to explore—building on the work of Camp, McKinney, and Pinker, among others—the kinds of situations and reasons we have for coordinating on a record consisting of specifically linguistically encoded information rather than on a record consisting of speaker meaning.[15]

In conclusion, there is space—and need for—both prospective intentionalism and direct intentionalism in an overall theory of meaning and communication. Prospective intentionalism seems to be the best tool for addressing foundational questions about what grounds linguistic meaning. And as L&S have shown, direct intentionalism will help us to understand and explicate important linguistic practices that rest on top of pre-existing linguistic conventions.

Acknowledgments

Thanks to Ernie Lepore and Matthew Stone for rousing a challenging and exciting new conversation on this topic, and thanks to Zoltán Szabó, Jason Stanley, Liz Camp, Daniel Stoljar, Rob Stainton, and the Philosophy of Mind Reading Group at the Australian National University for helpful feedback.

---

[15] See Camp (forthcoming), McKinney (manuscript), and Pinker, Nowak, and Lee (2008).

Bibliography

Bezuidenhout, Anne (2016). What Properly Belongs to Grammar? A Response to Lepore and Stone. *Inquiry* 59 (2): 175–94.

Camp, Elisabeth (2018). Insinuation, Common Ground, and the Conversational Record. In Daniel Fogal, Daniel W. Harris, and Matt Moss (eds.), *New Work on Speech Acts*. New York: Oxford University Press. 40–66.

Grice, H. P. (1989). *Studies in the Way of Words*. Cambridge, MA: Harvard University Press.

Horn, Larry (2016). Conventional Wisdom Reconsidered. *Inquiry* 59 (2): 145–62.

Keiser, Jessica (2016). Coordinating with Language. *Croatian Journal of Philosophy* 16 (2): 229–45.

Lepore, Ernie and Stone, Matthew (2015). *Imagination and Convention: Distinguishing Grammar and Inference in Language*. Oxford: Oxford University Press.

Lewis, David (1969). *Convention: A Philosophical Study*. Cambridge, MA: Harvard University Press.

Lewis, David (1975). Languages and Language. In Keith Gunderson (ed.), *Minnesota Studies in the Philosophy of Science*. Minneapolis, MN: University of Minnesota Press, 3–35.

Lewis, David (1979). Scorekeeping in a Language Game. *Journal of Philosophical Logic* 8 (1): 339–59.

McKinney, Rachel (manuscript). Discursive Antagonism and the Value of Conversation.

Pinker, Stephen, Nowak, Martin, and Lee, James (2008). The Logic of Indirect Speech. *PNAS* 105 (3): 833–8.

Szabó, Zoltán Gendler (2016). In Defense of Indirect Communication. *Inquiry* 59 (2): 163–74.

8

Showing, Expressing, and Figuratively Meaning

Mitchell Green

1. Speaker and Linguistic Meaning

I here first lay out what I take to be some central and well-established points about Grice's work on meaning, including both speaker and linguistic meaning. I do so because at a number of places in *Imagination & Convention* (2015), Lepore and Stone (hereafter L&S) characterize the position inaccurately. It will thus be important for us to guard against being misled by their discussion into rejecting Grice's position on the basis of a misconstrual.

Grice undertook to answer the question whether we can account for linguistic meaning without taking as primitive such notions as convention, reference, or others that are either perplexing in themselves or that presuppose semantic notions. His answer began with the observation that it is possible to mean something without drawing upon linguistic conventions; one can mean something in the relevant sense if one has appropriate intentions to produce effects on the psychological states of others.[1] One who has such intentions might mean something without yet communicating, since her intentions may not be fulfilled. So, as L&S (2015, p. 21) acknowledge, meaning (what is now called 'speaker meaning') does not guarantee communication. Further, as the phenomenon of meaning something without being understood is a familiar one, Grice's approach here is grounded in everyday experience.[2]

Grice also suggests, and others such as Schiffer (1982) and Bennett (1976) have developed in more detail, the idea that an appropriate pattern of one-off cases of speaker meaning can coalesce into a practice, and then a convention, to use a sound,

---

[1] The notion of meaning I am invoking here is what Grice calls non-natural meaning, and which has come to be termed 'speaker meaning' in recent literature. We will return in a moment to its proper characterization.

[2] L&S also claim (2015, p. 21, n. 2), that although it is possible to speaker mean something without communicating, it is not possible conversationally to imply something without its being understood. This seems to me untrue: one may readily think of cases in which we imply things to which our addressees do not cotton on. Fortunately, nothing in what follows will depend on correcting this error in L&S's position.

gesture, or inscription to mean that so-and-so. (In this way a vocalization that resembles the sound of a bee might come with time to be a conventional way of referring to bees, for instance.[3]) What came to be known as Intention-Based Semantics (IBS) offers a way of responding to the ancient charge of circularity that has been leveled against attempts to explain linguistic meaning in terms of conventions. (How can we institute a convention without already possessing a conventional means of communication for doing so?) It also provides a conceptually coherent template for understanding both the acquisition of meaning in ontogeny and the evolution of meaning in phylogeny.[4]

Once a word has been imbued with a conventional meaning according to the IBS story, we would expect speakers using it to defer to that meaning unless they have reasons for acting otherwise. One reason for so deferring is that conventional meanings facilitate the manifestation of our communicative intentions. Thus, to refer to Socrates, I could formulate, verbally or iconically, a set of properties that he alone possesses and then try to get you to identify those properties, infer that Socrates is their unique bearer, and discern that he is the one I have in mind. Instead I could more expediently use a conventional term whose history is the beneficiary of millennia of successful references to that man. Accordingly, one who accepts Grice's conception of speaker meaning and the account of linguistic meaning that it inspires, can also respect what Davidson calls the Autonomy of Linguistic Meaning, according to which once a word or phrase has been endowed with a conventional meaning, that meaning is independent of any particular use to which a speaker may put it in an utterance.[5]

The crucial features of the Gricean approach to meaning are, then, as follows:

1. Speaker meaning is defined in terms of communicative intentions.
2. Since intentions are not always fulfilled, one can speaker mean something without communicating.
3. Speaker meaning is distinct from linguistic meaning. The latter depends on conventions while the former does not.

---

[3] I here assume that a convention is a solution to a coordination problem that (a) is a regularity in behavior, (b) is arbitrary in the sense that at least one other such behavioral regularity could also have solved that coordination problem, and (c) is normative in the sense that it is rational for agents participating in the regularity to do so. (This last condition is just the game-theoretic notion of an equilibrium.) L&S employ a more permissive conception of convention, writing for instance, "our arguments depend only on the idea that conventions are solutions to coordination problems." (2015, p. 96) This magnanimous gesture is actually a proffer of a wooden nickel, for by setting the threshold so low for convention, this conception will make it easy for L&S to argue that conventions of language are vastly more pervasive than much literature acknowledges. Further, this conception is implausible on its face, as it implies that when two perfect strangers who know nothing about the other's culture, solve a coordination problem enabling them to safely pass one another on a narrow, precipitous path, they have instituted a convention.

[4] Whether it is empirically our most promising approach is another question. See Bar-On (2013), and Green (2017 a), for reasons to doubt that it is. Also, IBS does not imply that communicative intentions are logically prior to linguistic meanings. One may remain neutral on this priority question while agreeing that intention and meaning are conceptually connected along the lines of IBS. For this reason it is possible to remain agnostic on the question whether IBS should be understood reductively.

[5] See Green (1997, 2000) for references, and for a qualification of the Autonomy Thesis.

4. Speaker meaning is distinct from what is said. It is possible to say one thing and mean something different (as in irony), as well as say one thing and mean something in addition (as in implicature).

5. Speaker meaning, as commonly formulated, requires a theory of mind, that is, an appreciation of the fact that other individuals besides oneself possess mental states that might differ from one's own.

6. IBS in effect reduces linguistic meaning to patterns of one-off speaker meanings that coalesce over time into conventions of usage, and these conventions are perpetuated by the rational behavior of speakers.[6]

By way of clarifying (1), let us observe that the intentions that speaker meaning requires need not be consciously entertained by the speaker. Grice (1957) is clear that what he calls "explicitly formulated linguistic or quasilinguistic intentions," are comparatively rare in communication, but does not take this fact to undermine his claim that speaker meaning is ubiquitous. Assuming a modicum of consistency, it follows that Grice does not hold that such explicitly formulated intentions are necessary for speaker meaning. Instead, his view is that such intentions could be elucidated if the speaker were asked to do so under appropriate conditions.

Also, to clarify (6), reduction is not elimination. As Rorty (1965) pointed out a half-century ago, some reductions justify elimination of what is being reduced. The finding that what some took to be unicorn horns are just narwhal tusks supports denying that there are such things as unicorn horns. Other reductions do not justify elimination: learning that lightning is an electrical discharge does not justify denying the existence of lightning! Assuming that linguistic meaning does not challenge our scientific worldview in the way that unicorns so, we do best to construe any reduction of it to speaker meaning as preserving rather than eliminating it.

The Gricean approach to meaning is vulnerable to many criticisms, one of which concerns the question whether speaker meaning requires an intention to produce effects on the psychological states of others. Davis (1992) observes that we talk to infants, portraits of the deceased, and people on the freeway from inside the soundproofed safety of our vehicles. In none of these cases is it plausible that we intend to produce psychological effects on addressees. Green (2007) proposes a view of speaker meaning that centers on overtly making one's commitment manifest: one who asserts that P, for instance, makes overt her commitment to be right or wrong depending on whether P is true, and to stand behind P in a way distinctive of assertions as opposed to similar acts such as conjectures or guesses. On such a view of speaker meaning, one who speaker means that P assertorically need not intend to produce psychological effects on others.[7]

---

[6] It is possible to construe IBS non-reductively, and instead as more modestly elucidating conceptual connections between the notions of convention and linguistic meaning on the one hand, and intentions and belief on the other. Avramides (1989) adopts this approach, but in so doing, she seems to renounce the aspiration to explain linguistic meaning in intentionalistic terms.

[7] Davis (2003) offers a different conception of speaker meaning that also does not depend on intentions to influence the psychological states of the audience or addressee. Green (2007) criticizes this conception.

2. Some Challenges to the Gricean Approach

We are now prepared to ask whether L&S's discussion provides any new reasons to reject Grice's approach to speaker and linguistic meaning, as outlined in tenets 1–6 above, beyond those already familiar in the literature. As they warm up to their criticisms of Grice, L&S describe his conception of speaker meaning as *prospective intentionalism* (PI), the idea being that what a speaker means depends on what she intends to achieve by her utterance. That by itself is unobjectionable, though we should bear in mind that what a speaker means might diverge from what her words mean. L&S oppose PI to what they term *direct intentionalism* (DI). We will return presently to PI, DI, and their relative merits. For now, let's consider the L&S criticism of PI. These authors write: "We argue that [this view] carries unavoidable and difficult consequences in linking semantics and pragmatics to intentions and collaboration" (2015, pp. 204–5).

Their criticism depends, so far as I can see, on four challenges concerning occurrent attitudes, unintended meanings, uncooperative conversations, and the causal theory of names.[8] I discuss each of these in turn.

2.1 Occurrent Attitudes

L&S's first objection is that on the Gricean approach, meaning depends on the speaker's occurrent attitudes:

on the Gricean account, meaning depends on the speaker's occurrent attitudes: the specific goals, beliefs, and expectations that eventuate in the speaker's choice of some particular utterance on some particular occasion. The alternative would be to attribute meaning based on *standing commitments* among interlocutors governing the communicative enterprise as a whole.   (2015, p. 205)

Both of the above claims should come as a surprise in light of what we have established thus far. Speaker meaning depends on a speaker's attitudes, but not on her occurrent attitudes. Furthermore, nothing in IBS prevents the Gricean from agreeing with L&S's second claim so long it is referring to linguistic meaning rather than speaker meaning. Linguistic meaning quite plausibly depends on standing commitments among interlocutors.

Indeed, the alternative to PI, L&S say, is DI, which "attributes meaning to standing commitments" (2015, p. 205). These authors also write that, "...the language faculty endows speakers with the affordance not only of performing an utterance of a specified linguistic structure, but of contributing its grammatically specified meaning

---

[8] L&S also devote a section (13.3.4) to the issue of creative uses of language. However, by the end of that section, they concede that the Gricean view is equipped to handle such uses. Instead, L&S tell us that, "...the work that interlocutors do to support creative meanings is real and important, and that it's ultimately a virtue of direct intentionalism that it requires us to give this work a distinctive place front-and-center in theories of meaning" (pp. 224–5). Nothing L&S say here counts as an objection to the Gricean position, and so I shall not pause over creative language uses as a potential objection to Grice.

to an ongoing conversation. We call this view Direct Intentionalism" (2015, p. 208). One who follows Grice, at least insofar as accepting tenets 1–6 above, would have no reason whatsoever for denying this claim: she may accept the existence of a language faculty,[9] of the Gibsonian notion of affordances, and of grammatically specified meanings contributing to conversations, consistent with all six tenets.

What is the frog at the bottom of this mug? Why do these authors think of DI as something against which the Gricean must set her face? It will take a bit to sort matters out, but for now we might begin to suspect that L&S are eliding the familiar distinction within the Gricean tradition between speaker meaning and linguistic meaning. The latter is reducible to the former according to the reductive construal of IBS, but that does not mean that one has to deny the Autonomy of Linguistic Meaning thesis, or at least a properly qualified version of it such as that advocated in Green (1997) and Green (2000). So it is quite within the rights of the Gricean to say, for instance, that in a given case, a speaker intended to say one thing but did not succeed in doing so because she used the wrong words. This observation prepares us to respond to L&S's next criticism, to which we now turn.

2.2 Unintended Meanings

L&S argue that Grice and followers have trouble making sense of cases in which someone mis-speaks, as in:

199: I jeopardize you to handle my duties.

L&S claim that the Gricean view has difficulty distinguishing among the various commitments the speaker has made. Their reason seems to be that in uttering (199), the speaker both commits himself to jeopardizing his addressee, and to deputizing that addressee:

> The speaker of 199 intends to contribute that the hearer is empowered to act in his place, and he also intends to contribute the conventional meaning of what he said, which is in fact that the hearer is at risk. We seem to be equally justified in reporting the situation with either perspective... The speaker has really made several incompatible commitments in [this case].
>
> (2015, p. 18)[10]

It is only in unusual circumstances that we undertake commitments inadvertently.[11] Drinking from a pewter tankard into which an agent of the Crown has surreptitiously

---

[9] If our species is biologically hard-wired to conform to Universal Grammar, then that will constrain the shape of solutions to the coordination problem that is communicating in the absence of a convention for doing so. So long as it does not uniquely specify that solution, however, there will still be ample work for the IBS approach to do in explaining the institution of linguistic meaning.

[10] L&S elsewhere write of case 199: "We say that the speaker has inadvertently contributed to the record that he's committed to putting his audience at risk" (2015, p. 253).

[11] It often happens that in undertaking one commitment we inadvertently undertake another. This is typically how we get committed to contradictory or otherwise absurd views as philosophers. It is much less common to undertake a commitment that itself is absurd, and our first reaction to someone who has seemed to do so is to reinterpret their words to maintain coherence. It is for this reason that we first try to

slipped a shilling, was once sufficient for my being enlisted in the Royal Navy. And jewelers talk about "committing the stone", where one cut of a diamond, even inadvertent, can virtually oblige the jeweler to shaping it in a certain way. In this and in the King's shilling case, we see how a person may inadvertently undertake a commitment. However, language use is not usually so exacting. Just as my inadvertently grabbing a Phillips rather than a Pentalobe screwdriver does not commit me to using the former even when I am planning to work with Pentalobe screws, so, too, inadvertently using one word does not commit me to a course of action corresponding to that word's meaning. Accordingly, while it is true that the speaker in (199) intended to contribute the conventional meaning of the words he uttered to the ongoing conversation, that intention is not unconditional. Rather, the intention is conditional on 'jeopardize' being an appropriate way of expressing his thought. To make the point even more vivid, we may lampoon L&S's passage quoted above with an analogous line of reasoning about screwdrivers:

The person reaching for the screwdriver intends to acquire a Pentalobe, and he also intends to acquire a tool designed to do what *this* one does, which is in fact to turn Philips screws. So he has made several incompatible commitments!

The displayed premise would be true in the situation imagined, but nothing in it should justify concluding that the agent has undertaken incompatible commitments. As we have seen, commitment is a momentous notion and, except in unusual cases, we do not consider speakers to have undertaken commitments unless we can be confident that their actions would withstand their careful reflection. (This does not mean that we cannot be surprised by our commitments, such as when we assert a set of propositions that, taken together, yield a contradiction that we did not foresee. However, non-derivative commitments are harder to come by.)

In (199), then, the speaker presumably intended to say words that meant, 'I deputize you to handle my duties.' However, he either had a slip of the tongue, or he misunderstands the meaning of 'jeopardize' and thinks that 'jeopardize' means 'deputize'. (L&S do not provide enough information about the case for us to tell which of these two it is.) But it is beyond doubt that the speaker speaker-meant that the addressee was deputized to handle his duties. There is simply a divergence between what he speaker-meant and what he said, and he in no way committed himself to the claim that he was jeopardizing his addressee. It is an occupational hazard of speaking that there can be a divergence between what we mean and what our words mean, but that fact is no objection to the Gricean approach, which instead has the resources for understanding it.

---

reinterpret a seemingly Moore-paradoxical utterance (such as 'It is raining, but I don't believe it') as either a mid-utterance change of mind, or as containing an exclamation of surprise. See Green and Williams (2007) for further discussion.

2.3 Uncooperative Conversations

Here we get an example that the authors call attested because they came across it in a Dilbert comic strip. In the example, an IT technician named Alice is giving instructions to an office worker for fixing a computer problem, but does so with no intention of being understood, as made clear by the jargon used in her utterance with no attempt to explain it:

(200a) Alice: "Just disable the local cache mode to fix the MAPI settings and delete the duplicate messaging subsystem registry key."   (2015, p. 221)

Let us suppose that Alice means what she says in (200a). However, she knows the person she is speaking to will not understand her, and so she most likely does not intend her utterance to produce in her audience a belief corresponding to the content expressed by the sentence quoted in (200a). That is, Alice does not appear to meet the conditions of Grice's initial (1957) analysis of speaker meaning, in spite of meaning what she says.

   In this case, unlike the specious problems of occurrent attitudes and unintended meanings, we have a genuine objection to Grice's (1957) analysis of speaker meaning and to many of those that followed it. However, as we have seen above, problems of these kinds have been appreciated for some time, with authors such as Davis (1992) observing that a person can speaker mean something without intending to produce a cognitive effect on an audience. More than one improvement on Grice's analysis of speaker meaning has been proposed to accommodate such cases, and although L&S choose to ignore the refinements that the notion of speaker meaning has undergone in the nearly six decades since its introduction (2015, p. 204), had they not done so they might have noticed some that are relevant. For instance, Green (2007) proposes a view of speaker meaning that centers around overtly making one's commitment manifest: one who asserts that P, for instance, makes overt her commitment to be right or wrong depending on whether P is true, and to stand behind P in a way distinctive of assertions as opposed to other similar acts such as conjectures or guesses. Davis (2003) offers a different conception of speaker meaning that also does not depend on intentions to influence the psychological states of the audience or addressee.

   We need not here adjudicate between these two competing analyses. Rather, what matters is that unless L&S are prepared to argue that neither such analysis can succeed, and further that no other analysis in a similar spirit can possibly succeed either, they are in no position to reject the PI approach to speaker meaning on the basis of an example like (200a). After formulating the objection to the original Gricean analysis that flows from example (200a), L&S write, "So surely practical collaboration is not required for meaning" (p. 220). This is true, but (a) it is not news, and (b) is no objection to the Gricean approach as properly formulated.

2.4 The Causal Theory of Names

We guard against confusion in the Philosophy of Language by distinguishing between the question, in virtue of what do words (phrases, sentences) come to have the meanings that they do, and the question, how shall we characterize such meanings as words (phrases, sentences) have? The former "in-virtue-of-what-question" looks for answers in terms of ideas, conventions, concepts, icons, reliable causal relationships between mental states and the world, and so on. The latter, "characterization question" looks for answers in terms of truth conditions, possible worlds, intensions, characters, and other denizens of semantic theory. Nothing in principle rules out the possibility that a single answer could answer both questions. This would be nice work if we could get it, but it would be rash to assume that a single answer will always do for both questions. Thus, for instance, one could hold that proper names get their meanings in virtue of baptisms à la Kripke, while also holding that their meaning is to be characterized entirely in Millian terms, so that two co-referential proper names must have identical semantic value even if they were introduced in the course of distinct baptisms.

The causal theory of proper names (hereafter CTN) offers an answer to the in-virtue-of-what question by providing an account of how proper names acquire their meanings, and of how those meanings are disseminated in a linguistic community. On its own, CTN offers no guidance on the characterization question.[12] Yet L&S claim that CTN is incompatible with the Gricean view of speaker meaning. Their argument for this claim is by no means limpid, but seems to be that since the Gricean view is a form of PI, it holds that meaning depends on what a speaker intends the future consequences of her utterance to be. However, CTN is backward-looking in that what a proper name refers to depends on what its history is (2015, p. 211).

If this is L&S's reason why the Gricean view is undermined by CTN, then it is an unpersuasive one. Bearing in mind a distinction between speaker meaning and linguistic meaning, the Gricean can agree that a speaker, in meaning something in her use of a word, intends to defer to its standard usage. Nothing in the Gricean approach requires denying that a word's meaning can be given by an initial baptism; nor need the Gricean have any quibble with the idea that such a baptism could instigate a chain of uses leading up to a contemporary speaker. So just as the Gricean view is compatible with Direct Reference as a semantic thesis about proper names, so too is it compatible with CTN as an answer to the question how proper names come to have the meanings that they do.

---

[12] Confusingly, L&S refer to CTN as the theory of Direct Reference, but that is out of step with the more common usage of the latter phrase to refer to the semantic thesis that the meaning of a proper name is given entirely by its bearer. To avoid perpetuating a confusing usage, I will use 'CTN' to refer to the causal theory of names, and 'Direct Reference' to the view that the meaning of a proper name is given entirely by its bearer.

Again, L&S remark in discussing the reference of names such as Gödel and Aristotle, "…it's not as though the content of the speaker's thought is prior to or independent of the way the speaker has chosen to express that thought in words" (212). This is a controversial claim, but we need only point out here that even if it were true, it would at most challenge a simple-minded reductive version of IBS. Such a view would hold that conceptually sophisticated, structured thought is possible in the absence of all linguistic conventions, and it would indeed be challenged by the remark just quoted. However, even a reductive version of IBS could quite reasonably agree that many types of thought are possible only with the conceptual sophistication that conventional language affords. Instead, such a view would envision a bootstrapping operation in which rudimentary thought enables the establishment of rudimentary semantic conventions, which in turn make possible more sophisticated forms of thought, and so on. Accordingly, if the sentence quoted is the gravamen of L&S's criticism of PI, it is attacking a straw version of Grice.

Once we have laid bare the confusions in the L&S criticism of the Gricean approach to meaning, it emerges even more vividly that this approach has no need to set its face against DI. L&S write,

On prospective intentionalism, meaning is a function of the specific expectations that inter-locutors have about one another, their ongoing activity, and the results of a particular utterance. On direct intentionalism, meaning is a function of the background commitments and relation-ships that govern the communicative enterprise generally.   (2015, p. 214)

It should now be clear that L&S's characterization of prospective intentionalism here applies at most to speaker meaning, but not to linguistic meaning. Linguistic meaning is not a function of the "specific expectations that interlocutors have about one another", if that is understood as the view that in a given case, what a speaker's words mean depend entirely on what she intends them to mean. Grice would be at pains to deny such an implausible claim, and could do so in a way entirely consistent with his other commitments. On the other hand, so long as we keep in view the distinction between linguistic meaning and speaker meaning, we may understand direct intentionalism as being concerned with the former rather than the latter. And as a description of linguistic meaning, Grice would have no reason to abjure DI.

Here, at last, is the frog we have been seeking: L&S write, "A crucial advantage of the Gricean picture is that it eliminates the social by reducing it to the psychological" (2015, p. 211). In so saying, these authors make clear that they are assuming that the Gricean is committed to an eliminative version of reduction rather than a "preservative" one. That, in turn, helps to explain why these authors write as if the Gricean cannot help herself to a notion of linguistic meaning as distinct from speaker meaning. However, a careful Gricean should strenuously disclaim any aspiration to eliminate the social even if she does construe IBS reductively. What is more, the realization that L&S are assuming that the Gricean is committed to an eliminative rather than a "preservative" version of reduction helps account for why these authors take the

Gricean as needing to set its face against DI, as needing to deny CTN, and as having trouble accounting even for such a banal phenomenon as mis-speaking. Once the frog has been fished out of the mug, all that remains of L&S's criticism of the Gricean position on meaning is their un-newsworthy and tractable observation about uncooperative conversations.

3. Speaker Meaning Liberalized

I mentioned above that a view of speaker meaning as requiring intentions to produce an effect on an addressee by means of their recognition of one's intention to do so is not mandatory. That is to the good, because as Davis has argued, it is possible to say, and mean, "You're a knucklehead!" directed at a driver who has cut you off in traffic, even when one is quite aware that the driver cannot hear or otherwise be affected by your utterance. So, too, for talking to pre-verbal babies and portraits of dead relatives.

A more satisfactory conception of speaker meaning starts with the observation that Grice's argument for the reflexive component contains a hidden and questionable premise. Observing that Herod's presentation to Salome of St. John's severed head is not a case of Herod's telling Salome that St. John is dead, Grice infers that it cannot also be a case of his (speaker-) meaning that he is dead. The premise is true: Herod is not telling Salome anything. It does not yet follow that Herod does not also mean that St. John is dead. To reach that conclusion, Grice must assume that the only way of meaning something (at least for the case of things meant that can be expressed in propositional as opposed to imperatival or interrogative terms) is by telling.[13] But this may be challenged: I argue elsewhere (Green 2007, 2010) that showing a state of affairs is compatible with meaning that that state of affairs obtains. (Example: we've been searching for the famed ivory-billed woodpecker for years, and now we enter a clearing in which I spot the very thing: I silently, and with eyes wide, point to it. Here it seems plausible *both* that I'm showing you the thing we've been searching for, *and* that I mean that this is the thing we've been searching for.)

Speaker meaning and showing are, that is, compatible, in that not only can one speaker mean and show something simultaneously, but a single act can be a speaker meaning and a showing of one and the same thing. Further, what is crucial about speaker meaning is not an intention to produce an effect on someone (to say nothing of an effect on them by means of their recognition of your intention to produce such an effect), but rather an overt intention to make an aspect of one's commitment and/or psychological state manifest, that is, to show it (Green 2007, pp. 67–75).[14]

If my account of speaker meaning is correct, then examples such as L&S's (200a) are also no challenge to a proper account of speaker meaning. For when Alice says, "Just

---

[13]   L&S (2015, p. 203) also accept this assumption.

[14]   This is a simplification of the view offered in Green (2007), which also discusses cases of speaker meaning in which one makes facts and publicly observable objects manifest.

disable the local cache mode to fix the MAPI settings and delete the duplicate messaging subsystem registry key," she may not be intending that her addressee understands her; but she may yet (for all we know about this cartoon character) be intending overtly to manifest her belief that the thing to do is disable the local cache mode etc. So, too, to speaker mean what I say to the portrait of my deceased uncle, I need only intend overtly to manifest my belief that he should have left more for me in his will than his antique golf clubs.

So far I have defended the core tenets of the Gricean view on meaning from the criticisms of L&S, and have argued that their one cogent criticism of that view may be met with a well-motivated modification of his view of speaker meaning that has been available in the literature for some time. I will not here discuss their criticisms of Grice's account of conversational implicature; though see Szabó (2016) for an effective reply. Instead, I now turn to L&S's treatment of figurative language, particularly metaphor. I will not pause over their criticisms of either Grice's account of metaphor as a species of conversational implicature or of the account of metaphor offered by Relevance theory. Instead I will focus on their treatment of the role of perspective taking in the appreciation of verbal metaphor.

4. Expression and Empathy

Even with a liberalized notion of speaker meaning in hand, we have not exhausted the space of communicative forms of meaning. It is widely agreed that what Grice called natural meaning is non-communicative. (The fact that the 37 rings in the trunk of the just-felled tree mean that it has survived that many years, does not seem particularly germane to communication.) However, there is a large gap between natural and speaker (née non-natural) meaning. One occupant of that space is expressive behavior. A scowl, even when produced inadvertently, looks to be communicative insofar as it is a behavior whose job is to convey information about its possessor's affective state. It is a plausible empirical hypothesis that some human facial expressions function to convey information about affect (Green 2016, and references therein) just as it is a plausible hypothesis that a function of human skin is to aid in thermoregulation and protection against pathogens (Jablonski 2006). Neither of these claims can be settled a priori, but it is clear that a facial expression can telegraph my emotion even when I do not intend for it to do so. Further, even those facial expressions that are under my control might convey information about my affect without being vehicles of speaker meaning: a scowl might be intentional without being overt.

Intuitively, in expressing ourselves, we manifest an aspect of our psychological state even if we do so inadvertently (say by an involuntary scowl) or on purpose (say by a spontaneous smile). Overtness is permissible but not mandatory here. But not just any manifestation of a psychological state will be an expression of that state: my increased galvanic skin response manifests my anxiety (say), but is not an expression of that anxiety. Instead, that manifestation must be designed to convey information about that state. The design in question might be the result of natural selection, artificial selection, cultural evolution, or conscious intention. A scowl, even when inadvertent, strikes us as a better candidate for expressive behavior than does a galvanic skin response because we think of it as designed (if only by natural selection) to convey information about its owner's psychological state.

Aside from facial expressions, we can also use language for expressive purposes. Speech acts characteristically (though not universally) express psychological states (Green 2009, 2014), and vocal intonation often expresses affect. But *what* we say may be used for expressive purposes even when we are not performing illocutionary acts. For instance, in describing a situation hyperbolically ("Roddick's serve was supersonic!"), Dakota might express awe at the speed of Andy Roddick's serve. I doubt that we would want to say that Dakota is asserting that Roddick's serve was supersonic; he knows perfectly well that it was 155 mph. Instead, in so speaking, Dakota is inviting her audience to form an image—both visual and sonic—of a tennis ball breaking the sound barrier. If her addressee does that, they will have a sense of how Dakota feels about Roddick's formidable serve.

If these observations are on the right track, then we have reason to think that expression is communicative even if it does not require the psychological underpinnings mandatory for speaker meaning, and even as that notion is construed more liberally in Section II above. It is well established that facial expressions tend to be "contagious", so that one person's such expression is apt to be "caught" by others (Hatfield et al. 2009). This is a rudimentary but genuine form of communication. At a more sophisticated level, the expression of awe involved in the Roddick example enables others to know how the speaker feels about the tennis star's serve. This in turn enables others to empathize with that speaker. I construe empathizing with someone as successfully imagining how that individual feels (Green 2008). Accordingly, when I contemplate the Roddick image, I am in a position to grasp how astonishingly fast the serve seemed to Dakota, and on this basis get a sense of what her awe was like. (This could happen even if Roddick's serve is not particularly fast as pro tennis players' serves go; what matters is that it was fast enough to impress Dakota.) In so doing, Dakota has conveyed, and I have grasped, information even if it is not to be captured within the bounds of a proposition. We will see below that L&S leave it unclear whether they are able to accept this characterization.

5. Figuration and Communication

Luckily, I have never suffered from clinical depression. I believe, however, that I can empathize with some people who have. Some victims of clinical depression have remarked that it is like constantly having a weight on their shoulders and that, as a result, everyday tasks like making a meal or getting dressed seem daunting. On the basis of this description, I might imagine going through my day with thirty-pound shoulder pads. This would be exhausting, and would make me want to economize my activities as well. That is, the imagery used by the victim of depression not only expresses how she feels, but also enables others to empathize with her by imagining themselves into her situation.[15]

Carston (2010), in discussing the role of imagery in the comprehension of metaphor, quotes from a novel by Zoë Heller in which a character's depression is described metaphorically:

Depression, in Karla's experience, was a dull, inert thing—a toad that squatted wetly on your head until it finally gathered the energy to slither off. The unhappiness she had been living with for the last ten days was a quite different creature. It was frantic and aggressive. It had fists and fangs and hobnailed boots. It didn't sit, it assailed. It hurt her. In the mornings, it slapped her so hard in the face that she reeled as she walked to the bathroom.

(Zoë Heller, *The Believers*, 2008, p. 263)

Heller's imagery enables readers to empathize with Karla by imagining what it would be like to have a fat toad on one's head most of the time; and then for it to turn into something frantic and aggressive. Of course, Karla could also be a real person who employs such imagery in order to share with us how she feels. Suppose for instance that in trying to give us a sense of how she feels, she says,

My depression has fists and fangs and hobnailed boots. It doesn't sit, it assails. In the mornings it slaps me so hard in the face that I reel as I walk to the bathroom.

These are utterances of indicative sentences, but it does not follow that these utterances are assertions, any more than Dakota's 'Roddick's serve was supersonic!', said of the tennis star's daunting 150-plus mph serve, is an assertion. Rather, the sentence about Roddick is used to convey an image, and on that basis to convey a sense of how the speaker feels about the tennis star's prowess. Similarly, Karla's utterances as imagined above need not be seen as assertions, but rather may be understood as offering imagery enabling her addressees to get a sense of what her depression is like. If we as addressees can use that imagery to imagine our way into what Karla's experience might be like, we will have empathized with her. Further, if that happens, then Karla has communicated with us, not via a speech act with an illocutionary force and propositional content, but rather via something less cognitive and more visceral.

L&S espouse a broadly Davidsonian view of metaphor. (They exclude cases of dead metaphor, which they rightly take to involve words and phrases becoming idiomatic and thus conventionalized.) On L&S's view, the mataphorist is not attempting to convey either a proposition or other information. Rather, following Camp (2009), they tell us that the mataphorist is inviting his addressee to adopt a perspective. This perspective, in turn, shapes the listener's imaginative engagement (167) but "…we should

---

[15] The point is defended in further detail in Green 2017c.

not think of this perspective taking as being propositional in nature or even as carrying information" (164). Five pages later, L&S tell us that the particular kind of perspective-taking metaphor involves does not convey information, "...in the usual sense" (169). Unfortunately, these authors nowhere tell us what, if any, unusual kind of information might be at play in the perspective taking that we find in metaphor.

Leaving aside dead metaphor, L&S's characterization points in the direction of a satisfying account of metaphor, but does not bring us to such an account. To get closer to such a thing, I will argue, we need to advert to the expressive role that some verbal metaphors play. Consider L&S's showcase example of a metaphor from Matt Groening:

Love is a snowmobile racing across the tundra and then suddenly it flips over, pinning you underneath. At night, the ice-weasels come.   (2015, p. 163)

On L&S's view, such a metaphor invites its listeners to adopt a perspective on which love is like a snowmobile ride in relevant respects. Adopting such a perspective will help listeners organize their thinking about love: for instance, it starts out as exhilarating, but all too often ends in a slow and painful dénouement in which one feels trapped.

This characterization is unexceptionable as far as it goes. However, in following Davidson, and in denying that metaphors provide information "in the usual sense", L&S leave no obvious room for ways in which a metaphor might be appropriate, poignant, clumsy, or offensive. For if perspectives are subject to assessment in any way, L&S do not tell us how they are. But notice that I might reply to Groening's metaphor with,

No, actually it's a roller coaster ride in some Goth amusement park, with stops for electro-convulsive therapy along the way, and at the end of which you get dropped into a vat of boiling oil.

Or, I say that working with Bjorn on the new advertising account is a walk in the park. You reply that, yes, sure, that sounds right so long as the park I have in mind is one in the middle of a war zone, replete with landmines and sniper fire! These kinds of dispute are not without substance, but at the same time they differ from disputes over how many moves your chess opponent made before putting you in check, or about the Mohs hardness of tungsten.

How can we make sense of such rationality as these cases of metaphorical banter may have? My suggestion is that we can do this by noting metaphor's expressive role, while keeping in view the fact that the emotions thus expressed are capable of being more or less apt as responses to worldly, or even imagined, situations. The snowmobile metaphor suggests a sense of bracing exhilaration that ends with a feeling of being trapped with the expectation of a slow, excruciating demise. The Goth amusement park metaphor also suggests exhilaration punctuated by episodes of great pain, and then predicts a culmination in absolute agony. Two speakers can meaningfully dispute which of these two affective responses is a more apt reaction to falling in love and its likely aftermath. If both have experienced breakups that are dramatic and agonizing rather than slow and excruciating, they will likely find the Goth image a better expression of their feelings than is Groening's.

Similarly, the banter over working with Bjorn is over which perspective is the more appropriate one to characterize experience with him in professional matters. If the first metaphorist's perspective is apt, we would expect that working with Bjorn would be stress-free, and not likely to result in any emotional drama. If the second metaphorist's perspective is apt, we would expect an experience a good deal more fraught.

Accordingly, while a characterization of verbal metaphor in terms of perspective-taking is not itself objectionable, on its own it lacks the resources to account for metaphorical banter, and more generally for our ability to evaluate metaphorical utterances as insightful, ham-handed, or mildly hysterical as the case may be. I have argued that a significant swath of verbal metaphors aim to express the speaker's affective state, and that this helps to account for our ability to evaluate them: we evaluate the metaphor with reference to the aptness of the affective state it expresses, as well as with reference to how eloquently it expresses that state.

6. Perspectives and Conversational Score

If the above is correct, then L&S's determination to exclude verbal metaphors and their sequelae from the progress of a conversation is unduly restrictive. In this final section, I shall give my reasons for this claim. L&S develop Lewis' conception of conversational score in such a way as to distinguish it from, for instance, conversational common ground as that notion is propounded in Stalnaker (2014) and in his earlier work. On the common ground approach, the progress of a conversation is tracked by reference to the information that is held in common ground among all interlocutors: a proposition P is common ground between agents A and B just in case both A and B accept p, both accept that both accept P, both accept that both accept that both accept P, and so on (2014, p. 25). Although a proposition can enter common ground by being asserted by A and overtly accepted by B, an item can make its way into common ground without being due to anyone's utterance: a baseball crashes through the window into the room where we are having a meeting, and this fact will likely become common ground among us unless one of us fails to notice. Thus, not all material in common ground on the Stalnakerian approach has an etiology exclusively in illocutionary acts.[16]

By contrast, L&S elect to work with a notion of conversational score (their preferred term is 'conversational record') that is more restrictive. These authors remark that, "...the ingredients of conversational record are diverse and heterogeneous," (2015, p. 249), including as it does information about what entities are at the center of interlocutors' attention (247), standards of precision (247), what counts as "home base" (247), the status of interlocutors as familiar or unfamiliar (247), domains of discourse (247–8), commitments pertaining to what actions are permissible (248), what commitments

---

[16] See Green 2017b for further discussion.

various interlocutors have undertaken (248), which questions are under discussion (248–9), among others. Nevertheless, L&S are also clear that the information that interlocutors draw from figurative and other kinds of evocative speech must stay off the conversational record (262). What is their reason for this? L&S argue that the only items that can go onto the conversational record are ones that result from coordination, itself a form of joint activity that solves a coordination problem. Neither the errant baseball nor the damage it causes is a solution to a coordination problem—or so one hopes. Likewise, they argue, such messages as we might be able to glean from figurative language are too open-ended, indeterminate, and idiosyncratic to be bases for coordination (263).

I will close with a reason to reject this last claim, and thereby provide grounds for thinking that the results of some figurative uses of language can make their way into the conversational score. Imagine a couple whose young children are still asleep one morning, and they are enjoying a rare moment of peace over breakfast. They chuckle as one reads aloud from the newspaper Groening's above-quoted metaphor about love as a snowmobile ride. After further lingering over French toast and coffee, one of them says,

Well, I guess we should go get the ice-weasels.

This utterance could be a jocular way of suggesting that the exhilarating part of the couple's romantic life is over, and that now they are in some respects buried alive, not under an upturned snowmobile, but rather under diapers, strollers, and feeding times. More important for our purposes, the couple need to coordinate on the reference of the phrase 'ice-weasels' so that they can plan their next action. Neither has ever uttered the phrase or seen it used before, and both know enough biology to know that there are no weasels that are so-called. Yet it is easy to imagine that the addressee effortlessly understands that the speaker is referring to their children. I suggest that this is only possible if the two have coordinated their perspectives (*sensu* Camp) in such a way as to share the understanding that their current stage in life stands to their children as does the snowmobile-trapped lovers stand to the ice-weasels. This is reason to think that the perspective on love that Groening offers has as much right to be part of the conversational record as do centers of attention, standards of precision, degrees of familiarity, and home base. More broadly, when figurative language lends itself to banter of the sort exemplified in the previous section, that is reason to think that it is also fodder for the conversational record.

References

Avramides, A. (1989) *Meaning and Mind: An Examination of a Gricean Account of Language* (MIT).
Bar-On, D. (2013) 'Origins of Meaning: Must We "Go Gricean"?' *Mind & Language* **28**: 342–75.
Bennett, J. (1976) *Linguistic Behaviour* (Cambridge).

Camp, L. (2009) 'Two Varieties of Literary Imagination: Metaphor, Fiction, Thought,' in H. Wettstein (ed.) *Midwest Studies in Philosophy* **23** (Wiley-Blackwell), 107–30.

Carston, R. (2010) 'Metaphor: Ad Hoc Concepts, Literal Meaning and Mental Images,' *Proceedings of the Aristotelian Society* **90**: 295–21.

Davis, W. (1992) 'Speaker Meaning,' *Linguistics and Philosophy* **15**: 223–53.

Davis, W. (2003) *Meaning, Expression, and Thought* (Cambridge).

Green, M. (1997) 'On the Autonomy of Linguistic Meaning,' *Mind* **106**: 217–44.

Green, M. (2000) 'Illocutionary Force and Semantic Content,' *Linguistics & Philosophy* **23**: 435–73.

Green, M. (2007) *Self-Expression* (Oxford).

Green, M. (2008) 'Empathy, Expression and What Artworks Have to Teach,' in G. Hagberg (ed.) *Art and Ethical Criticism* (Blackwell), 95–122.

Green, M. (2009) 'Speech Acts, the Handicap Principle, and the Expression of Psychological States,' *Mind & Language* **24**: 139–63.

Green, M. (2010) 'Showing and Meaning: How We Make Our Ideas Clear,' in Klaus Petrus (ed.) *Meaning and Analysis: Themes from H.P. Grice* (Palgrave Macmillan), 202–20.

Green, M. (2014) 'Speech Acts,' in E. Zalta (ed.) *Stanford Encyclopedia of Philosophy* (https://plato.stanford.edu/entries/speech-acts/).

Green, M. (2016) 'Expressing, Showing, and Representing,' in C. Abell and J. Smith (eds.) *Emotional Expression: Philosophical, Psychological, and Legal Perspectives* (Cambridge), 24–45.

Green, M. (2017a) 'How Much Mentality is Needed for Meaning?' in Andrews and Beck (eds.) *Routledge Handbook of the Philosophy of Animal Minds* (Routledge), 313–23.

Green, M. (2017b) 'Conversation and Common Ground,' *Philosophical Studies* **174**: 1587–604.

Green, M. (2017c) 'Imagery, Expression, and Metaphor,' *Philosophical Studies* **174**: 33–46.

Green, M. and J. Williams (2007) 'Editors' Introduction,' in *Moore's Paradox: New Essays in Belief, Rationality and the First Person* (Oxford), 3–36.

Grice, P. (1957) 'Meaning,' repr. in P. Grice, *Studies in the Way of Words* (Harvard, 1989), 213–23.

Hatfield, E. R. Rapson, and Y.-C. Le (2009) 'Emotional Contagion and Empathy,' in J. Decety and W. Ickes (eds.) *The Social Neuroscience of Empathy* (MIT Press), 19–30.

Jablonski, N. (2006) *Skin: A Natural History* (University of California Press).

Lepore, E. and M. Stone (2015) *Imagination and Convention: Distinguishing Grammar and Inference in Language* (Oxford).

Rorty, R. (1965) 'Mind-Body Identity, Privacy, and Categories,' *Review of Metaphysics* **19**: 24–54.

Schiffer, S. (1982) 'Intention-Based Semantics,' *Notre Dame Journal of Formal Logic* **23**: 119–56.

Stalnaker, R. (2014) *Context* (Oxford).

Szabó, Z. (2016) 'In Defense of Indirect Communication,' *Inquiry* **59**: 163–74.

9

Taking Perspective

Madeleine Arseneault

1. Introduction

In *Imagination and Convention*, Lepore & Stone argue that the complexities of actual language use undermine the way in which semantics has traditionally been distinguished from pragmatics. One of the book's aims is to criticize the Gricean program of delimiting a 'bare bones' semantics and of explicating various phenomena as cases of conversational implicature. The criticisms include arguments that:

(1)   the open-ended reasoning employed in interpreting utterances does not privilege recovering the speaker's intentions on the grounds of the Cooperative Principle;

(2)   the various cases treated uniformly as conversational implicatures are in fact not conversational implicatures;

(3)   the role of utterances is not simply to contribute information to the common ground of the conversation, but instead utterances have heterogeneous roles in shaping conversation.

The authors acknowledge that the Gricean program does some philosophical work: in addition to delimiting a semantic/pragmatic boundary, Lepore & Stone note its potential for naturalizing linguistic knowledge by making intention recognition constitutive of communication and meaning. The theory of conversational implicature has been deployed in addressing various issues concerning direct reference and opaque contexts.[1] It is important to keep in mind all of the advantages of the Gricean program in order to both highlight the costs of giving it up and to highlight the significance of Lepore & Stone's conclusions. If Lepore & Stone succeed in showing that there is no such thing as conversational implicature, this is a wake-up call indeed.

Lepore & Stone argue that phenomena purported to be cases of conversational implicature are not in fact cases of conversational implicature, either (as they argue in Part II of their book) because they are instead the result of convention and knowledge

---

[1]   For example, see Salmon (1986) and Saul (1998).

of linguistic rules, or (as they argue in Part III) because despite *not* being the result of convention and knowledge of linguistic rules, these cases are not calculable via appeal to speaker intentions and principles of rationality. Instead, the authors propose that these latter kinds of cases are better understood as performing a very different role than that assumed by the Gricean theory of meaning and communication.

Since, as Lepore & Stone acknowledge, the conventions identified in Part II could be accommodated within the Gricean framework as conventional implicatures (2015: 150), it is the set of arguments in Part III that poses the real threat to the Gricean division of semantics and pragmatics. The critical aim of their book will only be completed, then, if the remaining cases in Part III, cases that cannot be accommodated as conventional implicature, also fail to secure the existence of conversational implicature. Sarcasm, metaphor, irony, hinting, humor are paradigm cases of the pragmatic: whatever special pragmatic meaning they convey is not amenable to explanation in terms of conventions. If Lepore & Stone are correct that even these will not count as conversational implicatures, then we have lost a clear terrain on which to build our semantic/pragmatic boundary. How well do the arguments of Part III fare? The next sections will evaluate their arguments concerning the case of metaphorical expressions.

2. On Metaphor

2.1 Lepore & Stone on the Gricean Account of Metaphor

A typical Gricean account[2] of metaphors treats them as implicatures that arise because what the speaker literally says is either blatantly false or inappropriate and so obviously flouts conversational maxims. On the assumption that the speaker is nevertheless following the Cooperative Principle (to make one's contribution such as is required, at the stage at which it occurs, by the accepted purpose or direction of the conversation), the audience is thus prompted to assume that the utterance is to be taken metaphorically rather than literally. In the example 'Richard is a bulldozer,' the speaker's intention in using the utterance is reconstructed as that of describing Richard in terms of a machine. In a certain context, the metaphor can be used to implicate that Richard pushes his projects forward against all opposition. In the case of the example 'No man is an island,' the speaker's intention is reconstructed as one of describing people in terms of properties of isolation and connectedness that are metaphorically analogous to geographic relationships he or she literally expresses. In a certain context, this metaphor can be taken to implicate that it is always possible to reach someone. These are possible derived interpretations because, in the contexts of their use, these mechanical and geographic properties would be cooperative contributions to a conversation, characterizing human personalities and relationships.

---

[2] Lepore & Stone also discuss Relevance Theory accounts of metaphor as broadly Gricean accounts; however, for simplicity, this discussion will focus on the central Gricean approach.

What is at issue for Lepore & Stone is the question of which principles and processes are involved in the interpretation of the metaphor. According to Lepore & Stone, Gricean accounts rely on only general background knowledge and general pragmatic principles: a shared background knowledge of associated properties is used to reinterpret the utterance as a better, more cooperative contribution (2015: 158–9), and interpretive effects "should be captured—primarily or entirely—through the action of general pragmatic principles" (2015: 158). It is worth taking a closer look at how Lepore & Stone describe the Gricean approach in order to see how their criticisms of the Gricean approach depend on it.

Lepore & Stone describe Grice's proposal as one centered on communicative intention:

The heart of his proposal is that interpreting an utterance is nothing more than identifying the speaker's communicative intention. Communicative intentions are special in that they must be overtly expressed and are fulfilled only by being recognized (…) In all cases, understanding a particular utterance is accomplished by inferring what the speaker means from whatever evidence the speaker provides.   (2015: 13)

What Lepore & Stone then contest is the claim that, in order to calculate and derive the specific communicative effect, all that is required is the recovery of the speaker's communicative intention, by considering simply the meaning of what was uttered, general background knowledge, and overarching pragmatic principles (2015: 160). Grice's account, they say, uses undifferentiated mechanisms: for Gricean accounts of metaphor,

even though metaphors are creative, there's nothing special about interpreting them. The audience disambiguates the metaphorical speaker's meaning through the same general psychological principles that are involved in all the cases of communication. The audience discovers the import of the metaphor through an undifferentiated process of inference or association that is not interestingly distinguished from any other appeal to background knowledge in understanding.   (2015: 170)

Instead, the authors argue, highly specific strategies are needed (2015: 161). Lepore & Stone conclude that Gricean treatments of metaphor are not able to account for what is distinctive about interpreting metaphors because such treatments must, they think, describe the interpretation of metaphors just as they would for any case of speaker meaning by appeal to the Cooperative Principle.

Lepore & Stone also challenge the view that the purpose of metaphor is to contribute a proposition to the common ground, a view that they think is presupposed by the Gricean treatment of metaphor. According to Lepore & Stone, it is presumed on some accounts that the purpose of communication is to contribute propositions to the common ground, and it is presumed to be characteristic of Grice's account of implicature that it is formulated in terms of *propositions* implicated.[3] Grice's own definition of

---

[3] See, for example, how Lepore & Stone characterize Grice's position at (2015: 61).

implicature ("the speaker S has implicated that *P*") encourages this characterization. On Gricean accounts, the recovery of the implicature is described as the result of an inferential calculation, and inference is commonly understood as a relation among propositions. In the examples above, "Richard is a bulldozer" is said to implicate *that Richard pushes his projects forward against all opposition* and "No man is an island" is said to implicate *that it is always possible to reach someone*. The issues of whether and which propositions are the implied metaphorical meaning for any particular metaphor arise in most discussions of metaphor, and we will turn to Lepore & Stone's stance on these issues; for now, we should note that Lepore & Stone characterize the Gricean account of metaphor as one that presupposes that the use of metaphors implicates propositions.

2.2 Lepore & Stone on Metaphor

One of the main points that Lepore & Stone make in Parts II and III of their book is that the Gricean approach paints with the same brush various cases that have distinct and distinctive interpretive processes. They argue that, instead, each case must have its own process: the same contextual background and general interpretive principles can yield different interpretations—so it must be the specific practices themselves that help us get the point across (2015: 161). In the summary of Part III, Lepore & Stone use the example "that building is a landmark" uttered humorously, metaphorically, sarcastically in order to argue that interpreting these utterances cannot just be a matter of considering the speaker's communicative intentions and the Cooperative Principle—that each utterance has different instructions for drawing different inferences, special to each case, even though the interpretations are exploring the same imagery. The different interpretations "don't follow just from knowing that the speaker and the audience are being cooperative, or from knowing that the audience is trying to extract information as efficiently as possible from what the speaker has said" (2015: 193). And because these latter considerations are, think Lepore & Stone, the only elements in a Gricean approach, these different interpretations are not calculable in Grice's sense.

What is the Gricean approach thus apparently missing? What are the specific practices and interpretive processes that are distinctive of metaphor? Lepore & Stone's characterization of metaphor and metaphorical interpretation is especially influenced by Davidson (1978) and Camp (2009). "Davidson suggests that the point of metaphor involves a special kind of perspective taking" (2015: 164). Any account of metaphor needs to explain the specific interpretive strategy of taking one thing as another.

Metaphor invites us to organize our thinking about something through an analogical correspondence with something it is not. Any explanation of the import of metaphorical utterances will need to appeal to this distinctive perspective-taking operation. General interpretive principles will not explain metaphor on their own.   (2015: 162)

Audiences reason about metaphors like 'No man is an island' by exploring real world analogies in a distinctive way peculiar to metaphorical speech, employing a distinctive cognitive process of imagining something as something else entirely. Metaphorical interpretation is not merely noticing similarities, as this is something that can be done without thinking of people *as* islands (2015: 165). "Metaphorical thinking often requires us to find many analogical correspondences simultaneously. It maps collections of objects, properties, and relationships in a source domain systematically onto corresponding ones in a target domain" (2015: 166). We do not analyze the insights of a metaphor by assigning specific metaphorical meanings to the components of the metaphorical expression: in exploring analogies, our interpretation "proceeds not constituent-by-constituent, but holistically, across extended discourses" (2015: 164). This interpretive strategy of perspective taking is unique to the interpretations of metaphors, and is not, say Lepore & Stone, characteristic of the process of intention recognition that is central to the Gricean account of meaning:

> They [the differences in interpretive processes] don't follow just from knowing that the speaker and the audience are being cooperative, or from knowing that the audience is trying to extract information as efficiently as possible from what the speaker has said. They are not just a side-effect of general mechanisms for resolving ambiguity, drawing conclusions, or reaching understanding. There is, in particular, no hope of substantiating the general explanations of the Gricean program.   (2015: 193)

Lepore & Stone's bottom line criticism is that for anyone who derives pragmatic content from uniform inferential mechanisms, it is impossible to have contingent interpretive practices over and above what rationality provides. Such accounts offer no place to describe the specific strategies an audience exploits in distinguishing among these different cases of metaphor, humor, and sarcasm.

But why is there no place to describe those interpretive processes that distinguish among various cases? How is the Gricean account unable to explain how metaphorical interpretations are calculable? We can extract three different reasons suggested:

(1) the interpretations are not calculable by knowing only the meaning of what was uttered and general constraints of rational behavior; that is, knowing the meaning of what was uttered and the principles of rationality are *not sufficient*. We need, in addition, the interpretive rules and strategies that are particular to that figure of speech (in the case of metaphor, that we employ analogical reasoning in an effort to see one thing as another);

(2) recovering the speaker's communicative intentions guided by general constraints of rationality is *not necessary*: Lepore & Stone say we do not reason about the speaker and what she intends in our engagement with the metaphor (2015: 176). Perhaps their 2010 article can provide helpful elucidation here: during a passage on jokes and humor that Lepore & Stone take to be parallel with metaphor, they note that while we may depend on recognizing speaker intention to recognize that it is a metaphor "from then on, the humor in the utterance is determined by the imaginative possibilities it portrays, not by [the speaker's]

intentions, (...) mutual expectation or the rules of language" (2010: 171). While they do concede that it figures in language use, Lepore & Stone reject the general application of reasoning about the speaker and what she intends (2015: 153);

(3) metaphorical interpretations are not calculable as Gricean accounts would want it because there's nothing to calculate: there is *no metaphorical meaning or proposition* to be recovered. On their Davidsonian approach of perspective taking, Lepore & Stone say "we shouldn't think of this perspective taking as being propositional in nature or even as carrying information" (2015: 164). Lepore & Stone find important discontinuity between metaphor and the Gricean framework of speaker meaning and implicature, given the latter's understanding of the implicature as a belief or proposition that the speaker is trying to communicate to her audience. Metaphor does not fit this understanding of implicature since there is no proposition or metaphorical meaning that is intended to be communicated. The metaphor invites us to imagine something as something else, to take a perspective, one that allows us to draw inferences, conclusions:

we know metaphor is not just general interpretive reasoning—we know that it is a distinctive and creative kind of interpretive engagement—because the insights it brings are often not propositional in nature and so cannot be characterized in the inferential framework of all traditional pragmatic theories.   (2015: 170)

Even if there is information that an audience is supposed to take away from a metaphor, and even if we could specify this information in a proposition, this is not generally the case and so cannot be a requirement for an adequate account of metaphor.

Much of these criticisms are all to the good. Adequate accounts of metaphor need to explain the open-ended and collaborative nature of metaphor interpretation. It is a strength of Lepore & Stone's 2010 and current project that they endorse the Davidsonian claim that what is special about metaphor and the results of metaphorical interpretation is not necessarily propositional. Also, Lepore & Stone's positive characterization of metaphor and its interpretation helps explain why metaphors would be used at all (if the principle function of metaphor was merely to convey propositional information, why not just say that information literally?). But what is not clear is why these criticisms require rejecting the Gricean framework. In the next section, I propose a way to accommodate much of Lepore & Stone's criticism within the theory of implicature and the general Gricean framework.

2.3 Towards Rescuing Implicature Accounts of Metaphor

Lepore & Stone have critically characterized the Gricean approach:

The audience disambiguates the metaphorical speaker's meaning through the same psychological principles that are involved in all cases of communication. The audience discovers the import of the metaphor through an undifferentiated process of inference or association that is not interestingly distinguished from any other appeal to background knowledge in understanding. *Thus, it's a mistake to try to theorize about metaphors in more fine-grained ways, by systematizing and abstracting pervasive metaphors,* as in Lakoff and Johnson (1980), or by explicating the mechanisms of analogical thinking, as in Bowdle and Gentner (2005) or Camp (2008, 2009). *There are no real distinctions to support such projects.*   (2015: 170, italics mine)

Additionally, they dismiss the Gricean approach for not recognizing the non-propositional character of metaphors. However, Lepore & Stone's characterization of metaphor and metaphorical interpretation does not necessitate rejecting the Gricean program. In order to see this, let us return to the three criticisms that Lepore & Stone use to argue that metaphors are not cases of conversational implicature. I address these reasons in reverse order, and in doing so, I suggest a way to rescue a Gricean framework that either explains away or accounts for the points raised by Lepore & Stone:

Regarding reason #3, the *no proposition* reason, Lepore & Stone argue that the effects of metaphor cannot be characterized in terms of an audience's recovery of a single specific proposition (or even of several propositions) that the speaker intends to communicate. They think the interpretive practices that govern non-literal uses of language are collaborative activities: it is characteristic of non-literal language use that a speaker invites the hearer to share in whatever insights either one of them can discover in exploring some particular imaginative world in some particular novel way. There is nothing, think Lepore & Stone, that requires that the exploration and its results contribute propositional content, and there is nothing that privileges just those effects (if any) that the speaker alone intended. Instead of a focus on the proposition implicated, that is, instead of *what* one thinks, Lepore & Stone argue that *how* one thinks is what is important for engaging our imaginations (2015: 161). I agree that there need not be a specific proposition intended by the speaker and that the effects of metaphor need not be propositional, but I argue that this need not be fatal to the Gricean program. Grice (1989), after all, made room for non-'informative' cases of (non-natural) meaning, so we are not restricted to considering only cases in which a proposition is intended by the speaker to be believed by the hearer. The speaker can intend various kinds of effects. For example, the speaker can intend that audiences undertake certain actions in response to her questions and commands. And so the speaker can intend that audiences undertake a process of perspective taking in response to the metaphor uttered. The Gricean framework allows a speaker to implicate something other than beliefs and propositions. A Gricean account, therefore, can accommodate the observation that the goal and effects of the use of metaphors need not be propositional.

Even if there is no specific proposition meant by the speaker, there is still a point to the use of a metaphor, and its point (e.g. for 'no man is an island') is in its invitation for us to explore the perspective of people as territory. An implicature account of metaphor can be adapted as follows: rather than require that a proposition be at the heart of the implicature, it may be the perspective itself that is implicated. I will elaborate this suggestion below.

Reason #2 was the *not necessary* reason, Lepore & Stone's criticism that it is not necessary to recover the speaker's intention when exploring the metaphorical perspective. In responding to whether it is necessary, we need to clarify the role of reasoning about the speaker's intentions when we are interpreting metaphors. One sense in which it is not necessary to reason about the speaker's intentions is that while John Donne is a person, there may be nothing about Donne himself or his intentions that needs to figure into our exploration of the metaphor of people as territory. We might also think that it is not necessary to reason about the speaker's intentions if we agree with Lepore & Stone's previous point that the speaker of the metaphor need not have a particular proposition (or set of propositions) that she is intending to communicate. In that case, we need not reason about the speaker's intentions in order to recover any intended proposition. However, Gricean accounts are not committed to requiring these types of intention recognition. What Gricean accounts are committed to is the requirement that the speaker's intention to engage in conversation be recognized, otherwise, the utterance risks being dismissed as nonsense, as meaningless, or as not addressed to the hearer. The speaker invites the audience to explore the metaphor's imagery and the invitation must be recognized, otherwise the point of the utterance and its metaphorical possibilities are missed. Lepore & Stone acknowledge that "Explicit reasoning about what the speaker might have wanted or believed comes in, if at all, only when something goes wrong" (2015: 13). And in the case of metaphor, it is precisely because of the utterance's incongruity in the conversational context that we recognize the invitation to explore a perspective. This recognition of speaker intentions is necessary, even if, once embarked on exploring the perspective intended by the speaker, the particular interpretive strategies we use need not reference the speaker's intentions.

The remaining reason raised by Lepore & Stone for why the Gricean approach fails is that knowing the meaning of what was uttered and the principles of rationality are *not sufficient* for interpreting metaphors. It is not at all clear that Grice is (or that Griceans are) committed to the claim that knowing the meaning of the words and principles of rationality are sufficient for interpreting metaphors. What the Gricean framework is committed to is that the implicature be something that can be worked out and calculated, that an argument from what was said to what was implicated be constructable. The special, distinctive strategies involved in interpreting metaphors can be incorporated within the Gricean framework by being employed in this working out and calculation. The implicature is to be worked out by the audience recognizing that the speaker must be intending a metaphorical perspective to be taken in order for her utterance of the metaphor to be cooperative; however, none of this rules out that the perspective taking itself will involve those processes of seeing-as that are distinctive of metaphor. If we take a view of the purpose of communication that is broader than merely the efficient exchange of information, communication of beliefs and contribution of propositions to the common ground, then one of the relevant intentions a speaker can have (and thus, that an audience can recognize) is the intention to prompt the insights derived from the experience of perspective taking that the metaphor invites. That an interpretation occurs at all as the audience's uptake is only because of the assumption of the Cooperative Principle and the recognition of the utterance as rational and intentional. The interpretation of the metaphor (e.g., no man is an island) goes through the recognition that the speaker must intend the utterance metaphorically because what is said violates the Maxim of Relevance. That the speaker intends us to take the perspective of people as territory is recognized on the basis that those are the words chosen by the speaker in her metaphorical utterance. The perspective taking itself then follows the interpretive strategy that is distinctive to metaphor.

The current proposal is that we can revise the Gricean analysis of the conversational implicature that arises, e.g., in the case of the metaphor 'no man is an island,' as follows:

A speaker who, by (in, when) saying (or making as if to say) that 'no man is an island' has implicated the perspective of people as territories, may be said to have conversationally implicated the *perspective* of people as territories, provided that (1) she is to be presumed to be observing the conversational maxims, or at least the Cooperative Principle; (2) the supposition that she is aware that, or thinks that, adopting the perspective of people as territories is required in order to make her saying or making as if to say 'no man is an island' (or doing so in those terms) consistent with this presumption; and (3) the speaker thinks (and would expect the hearer to think that the speaker thinks) that it is within the competence of the hearer to work out, or grasp intuitively, that the supposition mentioned in 2 is required.

On this suggestion, the implicature is not any proposition purporting to be the meaning of the metaphor. The implicature is not any particular interpretation of the metaphor. Instead, it is the perspective that is implicated. This proposal makes sense of the truisms about metaphor and metaphorical interpretation: that it is open-ended, that there is no specific proposition that counts as *the* meaning of the metaphor, that there is no literal paraphrase that expresses all that a metaphor conveys. The perspective is open-ended, does not express a singular or privileged proposition, and so does not present something that can simply be literally re-stated.

3. On Idiom

3.1 Convention or Imagination?

Lepore & Stone's discussion of convention and imagination does not address the case of idiomatic phrases; however, in the remaining sections, I want to explore how their discussion can help us understand some of the features of idioms. Idiomatic meaning is usually accounted for as the phrase's conventional meaning, but recent work on idiom has drawn our attention to how idioms support imaginative and figurative elaborations and variations. Lepore & Stone's account of convention and imagination helps to shed light on this.

Because idioms are traditionally characterized as depending on arbitrary links between forms and interpretation, insofar as the content of idiomatic phrases is resolved conventionally, idioms may be folded into the 'convention' and 'knowledge of language' side of Lepore & Stone's division between convention and imagination. However, some features of idioms support imaginative interpretations and hence there is also reason to place idioms on the 'imagination' side of the divide.

Idioms are phrases like 'kick the bucket' and 'drive [someone] up a wall', character-ized by semantic non-compositionality and syntactic inflexibility. The idiomatic meaning of 'drive [someone] up a wall' is not predicted by simply considering the ordinary meanings of the words of the phrase and their organization. Idioms are fixed and inflexible: some transformations which should be syntactically permissible are unacceptable. For example, transforming 'Tim kicked the bucket' to its pseudo-cleft construction, 'What Tim did to the bucket was kick it' loses its idiomatic sense. Traditionally, these features of non-compositionality and inflexibility have been accounted for by treating idiomatic phrases as words, as lexical items to which we con-ventionally assign their idiomatic meaning: 'kick the bucket' is said to just mean 'die.'

However, our use of idiomatic phrases can also exhibit the coordination and imaginative perspective that characterizes metaphor and other cases described in Lepore & Stone's book. Consider the figurative extension and modification of idioms, identified by Andy Egan (2008). In some idiomatic contexts, we figuratively modify and extend idiomatic phrases in a way that depends on the ordinary literal meaning of the words of the idiomatic phrase. The idiom 'to pull strings', for example, can be modi-fied to figuratively characterize the influence being exercised in 'the strings we've been pulling to get you out of prison are fraying badly'. The idiom 'let the cat out of the bag' can be extended to suggest a perspective on the consequences of divulging certain information, as in 'If you let this cat out of the bag, a lot of people are going to get scratched'. And consider two more examples involving the idiomatic phrases 'bought the farm': 'the offer's been accepted and the loan's been approved, but he's taking his time closing on it'; and the idiom 'kicked the bucket' and 'he almost connected yester-day; today he really put the boot on it' (2008: 393).[4]

Lepore & Stone's reasons for excluding sarcasm from semantics can also be used for excluding idiom from semantics. Of sarcasm, Lepore & Stone point out that the possibility of amplifying and extending a sarcastic perspective shows the open-ended nature of sarcastic imagery, and that the more we appreciate the open-endedness in interpreting sarcasm, the more qualms we should have with any characterization of sarcasm that is couched in terms of a simple rule of reversal of meaning (2015: 176). The examples that Egan provides allow us to run the same reasoning for idioms: the possibility of amplifying and extending an idiomatic perspective shows the

---

[4] Egan recognizes that there is a felt difference between the typical use of idiomatic phrases and their figurative extensions (2008: 401). We are self-consciously playing with the words in the case of figurative extensions, but our typical use of the core idiomatic phrase passes for quite standard language use. I have argued elsewhere (Arseneault 2014) that this difference can be explained by treating the use of the core idiomatic phrase as a generalized conversational implicature and the figurative extension of the idiomatic phrase as a particularized conversational implicature.

open-ended nature of idiomatic imagery, and that the more we appreciate the open-endedness in interpreting idiom, the more qualms we should have with any characterization of idiom that is couched in terms of a simple linguistic convention.

3.2 The Case for Idioms as Imaginative

While the use of the core idiomatic phrase may be associated with a specific meaning, one that we can recognize the speaker as intending, the figurative extensions of idioms are much more like metaphors. It is difficult to specify what proposition is being communicated by 'the strings are fraying badly', 'people are going to get scratched', and 'the offer's been accepted and the loan's been approved, but he's taking his time closing on it'. Like in the use of metaphors, the speaker may have a point, and we may even be able to come close to extracting a proposition communicated; however, the extensions may be better understood as invitations to further explore the imagery provided by the core idiomatic phrase, to develop the perspective suggested by the idiom. Insofar as idiomatic phrases are properly understood as invitations to explore the perspectives suggested by their imagery, rather than as a matter of communicated propositions, this approach would help meet various desiderata for theories of idiom. First, if we exclude idiom from semantics we can avoid positing rampant semantic polysemy. Traditional accounts of idiomatic phrases are already committed to extending the lexicon for each idiomatic phrase in its core use. Since 'fraying', 'scratched', 'offer', 'loan', 'closing', 'connected', and 'boot' cannot, on the traditional lexical account, be contributing their ordinary meaning in the figuratively extended contexts, these accounts would need to assign idiomatic meanings to them, or to the whole extended idioms, as well. And the lexicon will need to be similarly increased for each instance of modification and extension. If idiomatic phrases and their figuratively extended uses are not in the business of communicating propositions (that is, if they are invitations to explore imagery), this bloating of the lexicon is not required.

Additionally, a good theory of idioms should illuminate why we use them. If idioms just had their idiomatic meaning as their conventional meaning, why not simply utter a paraphrase of that conventional meaning? The use of idioms appears related to poetical, discursive, and rhetorical purposes, and a good theory of idioms should enhance our understanding of how the use of idioms achieves these purposes. Ritchie & Dyhouse (2008) discuss the humoristic element of some idioms and the use of idioms as a form of word play. According to their example, Speaker A: 'How are you doing?' Speaker B: 'I'm fine as frog's hair', speaker B demonstrates her linguistic skills, and both can derive pleasure in creating and in interpreting word play. The humor and word play exhibited by idioms are difficult to explain, if the traditional lexical view is correct and the words in the idiomatic phrases just conventionally mean their idiomatic content. Insofar as the humor is generated by the ordinary meanings of the words 'frog' and 'hair', the humor should not arise if the ordinary meaning of those words is not contributed by 'fine as frog's hair'. If 'Chuck is driving me up a wall' is just another way of saying 'Chuck is really annoying me', and the constituent words simply contribute what 'Chuck is really annoying me' contributes, there's no explanation of the sense of play carried by the use of the idiom. If, instead, the idiom is employing the semantic resources of the ordinary semantic content of the words to invite the audience to explore imagery, we have the possibility of an account for how idioms can give rise to humor and word play.

4. Conclusion

Imagination and Convention asks us to reconsider the Gricean program as we perhaps have not yet done, and this is significant given the degree to which that program is entrenched and presupposed in linguistics, and philosophy of language and communication. Lepore & Stone raise a serious challenge to the fundamental distinction between semantics and pragmatics through their rejection of the concept of conversational implicature. I have tried to respond to their challenge by addressing their arguments against metaphor as a paradigm case of conversational implicature. I have sketched out a way in which a Gricean might respond, a way that attempts to hold on to the basics of the Gricean program. If something like my suggestion works for metaphor, and if (similar?) ways of accommodating the particular interpretive strategies for humor, sarcasm, hinting, and irony within the larger Gricean framework can be developed, then we need not reject conversational implicature. If we can defend conversational implicature, then we can hold onto our traditional semantic-pragmatic distinction.

The question is, I think, whether the kind of Gricean framework proposed here can accommodate different interpretive strategies, different ways of working out what effects the speaker intends her audience to take up, and whether if, in doing so, it remains sufficiently Gricean to still achieve the other philosophical work that the approach has been credited with. On this proposal, the Cooperative Principle is not carrying all the explanatory weight, and insofar as the actual work and not merely the elegance of the theory depends on having only the one principle apply across all cases, perhaps the revised account is not sufficient to count as a Gricean vindication of the semantic-pragmatic distinction. But agreeing with Lepore & Stone that the Cooperative Principle is not the only tool in the box seems to be putting the complexity and specificity exactly in the right place, at the level of the actual interpretive process for particular cases.

I have also suggested that Lepore & Stone's discussion of imagination may be helpful in explaining some features of some uses of idioms. Idioms, in their figuratively extended uses, appear to be cases of imagination, invitations to explore the imagery expressed by the idiomatic phrase. Some uses of the un-extended core idiomatic phrase do not appear to extend an invitation to explore, yet even their rhetorical effects may depend on not simply relegating idiomatic phrases on the side of linguistic convention. There remain questions about which particular strategies are being employed in our interpretation of idioms, how these are to be distinguished from those strategies described for metaphor, humor, hinting, and irony, and whether the strategies are different for idioms in their core or extended uses. My discussion above suggests that the figurative extension of idioms is to be interpreted through the strategy of metaphorically *seeing A as B*: the loss of influence *as* fraying strings, the delay in dying *as* the drawn-out process of buying a farm. This suggests that the interpretation of metaphor and of extended idioms involves the same interpretive strategies: if so, how are metaphors and extended idioms to be distinguished? Idioms in their extended and core uses may not follow the same interpretive strategies, since the idiom in its core use does not appear to issue any invitation to explore its imagery. There is more work to be done in order to defend a theory of implicature that responds to the requirement of explaining various pragmatic phenomena in a way that both respects the various interpretive strategies that underlie our understanding of them and supports a Gricean semantic-pragmatic distinction.

Works Cited

Arseneault, Madeleine. 2014. "An Implicature Account of Idioms." *International Review of Pragmatics* 6: 59–77.

Camp, Elisabeth. 2009. "Two Varieties of Literary Imagination: Metaphor, Fiction, and Thought Experiments." *Midwest Studies in Philosophy* 33: 107–30.

Davidson, Donald. 1978. "What Metaphors Mean." *Critical Inquiry* 5: 31–47.

Egan, Andy. 2008. "Pretense for the Complete Idiom." *Noûs* 42: 381–409.

Grice, H.P. 1989. *Studies in the Way of Words*. Cambridge, MA: Harvard University Press.

Lepore, Ernie, and Matthew Stone. 2010. "Against Metaphorical Meaning." *Topoi* 29: 165–80.

Lepore, Ernie, and Matthew Stone. 2015. *Imagination and Convention: Distinguishing Grammar and Inference in Language*. Oxford: Oxford University Press.

Ritchie, L. David, and Valrie Dyhouse. 2008. "Hair of the Frog and other Empty Metaphors: The Play Element in Figurative Language." *Metaphor and Symbol* 23: 85–107.

Salmon, Nathan U. 1986. *Frege's Puzzle*. Cambridge, MA: MIT Press.

Saul, Jennifer M. 1998. "The Pragmatics of Attitude Ascription." *Philosophical Studies* 92: 363–89.

10

Perspectives and Slurs

Claudia Bianchi

[handwritten margin note: Camp says that metaphors are an invitation to see the world under the perspective (or that conditions) of the speaker (or the speaker's truth)]

1. Introduction

[handwritten margin note: Camp does too]

In *Imagination and Convention*, Ernie Lepore and Matthew Stone argue that metaphorical interpretation involves a distinctive process of *perspective taking*: metaphor invites us to organize our thinking about something through an analogical correspondence with something it is not. According to them, the same applies to slurs: some words come with an invitation to take a certain perspective, and uses of slurs are associated with ways of thinking about their targets that can harm people. The aim of this essay is to critically evaluate Lepore and Stone's *perspectival proposal*. To this end, I will adopt a speech-acts framework, and focus on what speakers *do* by uttering a slur. In the recent literature on hate speech, acts performed by means of slurs are usually conceived as speech acts in two distinct senses:

i) as perlocutionary acts that *cause* harm and discrimination, and produce changes in attitudes and behaviors, including oppression and violence;

ii) as illocutionary acts that *constitute* harm and discrimination, legitimate beliefs, attitudes and behaviors of discrimination, and advocate oppression and violence.

[handwritten margin mark: A]

I will claim that Lepore and Stone's proposal can be understood both in perlocutionary and illocutionary terms and argue in favor of an illocutionary approach.

The essay is structured as follows: in section 2, I give an overview of Lepore and Stone's take on metaphor and slurs in terms of perspectives. In section 3, I give an account of slurs in terms of speech acts (3.1). I suggest two possible interpretations of the perspectival account: the perlocutionary approach (3.2) and the illocutionary approach (3.3). In section 4, I argue in favor of the illocutionary approach, and show that it actually fares better than the perlocutionary one on a number of adequacy conditions.

2. Perspective Taking: Metaphors and Slurs

In discussing figurative speech, Lepore and Stone argue for two related points: (i) metaphorical interpretation involves a distinctive process of *perspective taking*: metaphor invites us to organize our thinking about something through analogies and correspondences with another domain, in order to deepen and enrich our understanding of the target;[1] (ii) moreover, they claim that not every aspect of the perspective that interlocutors take towards the topic under discussion can be part of meaning. The point a speaker is making when she uses language figuratively is *open-ended*, in the sense that there is no obvious limit to the degree to which a listener can amplify the point of a metaphor. Conversely, meaning as traditionally understood—semantic or pragmatic— cannot be open-ended: the content communicated with a given discourse must be specific, closed, and determinate.[2]

According to Lepore and Stone, both points apply to slurs, namely terms such as 'Boche' and 'wop', which target individuals and groups of individuals on the basis of race, nationality, religion, gender, or sexual orientation.[3] Their view is that (i) slurs come with an invitation to take a certain perspective, and that uses of slurs are associated with ways of thinking about their targets that can cause harm, and (ii) that, moreover, many slurs are conventionally associated with negative stereotypes, but that this is not a matter of content. Perspectives, then, are not meanings: the stereotypical qualities associated with uses of slurs, rather than describing members of the target group, create a lens through which a witness to the slur is supposed to be provoked to see the members of the group. Slurring shapes our responses and guides our thinking, because of the particular kind of perspective taking it provokes without conveying information in the usual sense.

The perspectival account of slurs is promising, and provides an innovative insight both on figurative speech and derogatory speech. But how exactly should we interpret perspectives?

Lepore and Stone argue at length that perspectives cannot be conceived as *meanings*, and criticize Elisabeth Camp on this point: while Camp reifies an open-ended set of relevant, associated stereotypes into meanings or senses,[4] Lepore and Stone view senses as closed, definite and determinate—and take the two notions of open-endedness and communicated content to be incompatible. What is more, meanings should be calculable, and the communicative intentions of the speaker should be specific, determinate, and definite, whereas "an open-ended set of propositions, by definition, cannot be calculable".[5] Assessing this criticism against Camp is beyond the scope of this essay. However, let me note in passing that this claim is disputable, at least as far as implicatures are concerned. At the very end of "Logic and Conversation", Grice contends that conversational implicatures may not be completely determined: "Since, to calculate a conversational implicature is to calculate what has to be supposed in order to preserve the supposition that the Cooperative Principle is being observed, and since there may be various possible specific explanations, a list of which may

---

[1] Lepore and Stone (2015: 167).   [2] Lepore and Stone (2015: 170–1); cf. Lepore and Stone (2014).
[3] See Dummett (1973/1981: 454), Kaplan (1999), Hornsby (2001), Hom (2008), Potts (2007, 2008), Richard (2008), Williamson (2009), Croom (2011, 2013), Jeshion (2013), Anderson and Lepore (2013a, 2013b).
[4] See Camp (2013, 2015).   [5] Lepore and Stone (forthcoming, p. 7).

be open, the conversational *implicatum* in such cases will be disjunction of such specific explications."[6]

Lepore and Stone reject the interpretation of perspectives in terms of meanings, and favor the Fregean notion of "tone" or "coloring". As is well known, Frege distinguishes between sense and tone: two expressions—like "dog" and "cur", or "horse" and "nag"—may have the same sense, but differ in tone or coloring. Those differences in connotation are a non-truth-conditional component of language, but may act on the feelings and the mood of the audience. The distinction may be applied to slurs and their neutral counterparts. In this perspective "Italian" and "wop" share the same sense but differ in tone: the negative tone associated with the slur "wop" accounts for its derogatory import. Again, most scholars disagree with this view: the notion of tone, as applied to slurs, seems too weak and subjective to account for their derogatory force. As Hom puts it, "linguistic coloring or shading cannot account for how competent speakers uniformly and objectively understand the derogatory force associated with epithets...to associate neutral or positive tone with 'nigger' is fundamentally to misunderstand the word".[7] More generally, the Fregean distinction is ill-defined: Frege defines tone as "subjective" but his examples are generally perceived as strongly conventional. Dummett and Williamson criticize Frege on this point: Dummett argues that, being a component of meaning, tone cannot be private and subjective[8] and Williamson maintains that the notion of tone is too "miscellaneous" to give us a satisfactory account of slurs.[9]

It appears that the notion of perspective as applied to slurs may benefit from further, more thorough investigation. In particular, it may be worthwhile to examine the issue from a different point of view and not focus on slurs' content (expressed or conveyed) or their tone, but on what speakers *do* with the slurs they utter. Lepore and Stone themselves—with their picture of what perspectives do ("invite", "provoke", "guide")—seem to suggest that slurs have some sort of *performative* potential. Speech-act theory could then be a stimulating standpoint for the evaluation of their perspectival proposal.

---

[6] Grice 1975/1989: 39–40. Grice doesn't suggest how the indeterminacy and open-endedness of implicatures might be compatible with their calculability. Relevance theorists pursue the idea, and argue that indeterminacy is pervasive at both explicit and implicit levels. In an RT framework, implicatures may be stronger or weaker. When the hearer's expectations of relevance can be satisfied by deriving any one of a range of roughly similar conclusions, at roughly comparable cost, from a range of roughly similar premises, the hearer has to take some responsibility for the particular premises he supplies and the conclusions he derives from them: "The greater the range of alternatives, the weaker the implicatures, and the more responsibility the hearer has to take for the particular choices he makes. Much of human communication is weak in this sense" (Sperber and Wilson 2006: §4). According to Sperber and Wilson, indeterminacy extends to *explicatures*. Explicatures may be stronger or weaker, depending on the degree of indeterminacy introduced by the inferential aspect of comprehension:

> The weaker the explicature, the harder it is to paraphrase what the speaker was saying except by transposing it into an indirect quotation...which is always possible but does not really help to specify the content of what was communicated.   (Sperber and Wilson 2006: §4)

[7] Hom (2008: 421).   [8] Dummett (1973/1981: 85–6).   [9] Williamson (2009: 149).

3. Perspectives as Speech Acts

3.1 An Account of Slurs in Terms of Speech Acts

I said earlier that Lepore and Stone seem to suggest that slurs have a performative dimension. Indeed, they spell out their proposal in the following terms:

> it is our view that some words come with an invitation to take a certain perspective. This is obviously a matter of some nuance on our account... Perhaps: a speaker, in using a word, commits that her audience has a relevant, affectively laden perspective associated with the word's referent, and indicates that she expects her audience to deploy that perspective in understanding what she says.[10]

Let's examine the precise nature of this performative dimension.

Consider an utterance containing a slur, like

(1)   Claudia is a wop

or

(2)   Wop!

The speech-act theory distinction between illocutionary and perlocutionary acts offers a way to set speech that *constitutes* harm apart from speech that merely *causes* harm. As a matter of fact, Austin distinguishes three different acts within the same total speech act, such as the uttering of

(3)   Shoot her!

The *locutionary* act is the act of saying something, the act of uttering certain expressions that are well-formed from a syntactic point of view and meaningful. The *illocutionary* act corresponds to the act carried out in performing a locutionary act, to the particular force that an utterance like (3) has in a particular context: order, request, entreaty, challenge, and so on. By uttering a sentence the speaker can bring about new facts, "as distinguished from producing consequences in the sense of bringing about states of affairs in the 'normal' way, i.e. changes in the natural course of events":[11] she may undertake obligations and legitimate attitudes and behaviors, institute new conventions and modify the social reality. The *perlocutionary* act corresponds to the effects brought about by performing an illocutionary act, to its consequences (intentional or non-intentional) on the feelings, thoughts or actions of the participants.

Drawing on speech-act theory, many scholars (notably Catharine McKinnon, Rae Langton, Lynne Tirrell, Mark Lance, and Rebecca Kukla) focus not on what slurs express or convey, but on what speakers *do* with slurs: slurs are expressions used to

---

[10] Lepore and Stone (forthcoming: 8).   [11] Austin (1975: 117).

perform certain speech acts.[12] More particularly, utterances containing slurs like (1) or (2) may be conceived as speech acts in two distinct senses:

(i) as *perlocutionary* acts that *cause* harm, and produce changes in attitudes and behaviors, including oppression and violence;

(ii) as *illocutionary* acts that *constitute* harm; legitimate beliefs, attitudes, and behaviors of discrimination; advocate oppression; authorize violence.[13]

Let's examine the two approaches, as applied to the perspectival account.

3.2 The Perlocutionary Approach

According to Lepore and Stone, "slurring shapes our responses and guides our thinking, because of the particular kind of perspective-taking it *provokes*". This suggests a causal, or *perlocutionary* interpretation: a speaker who utters (1) or (2), by performing an illocutionary act (say, an assertion) brings about harmful effects and consequences (intentional or non-intentional) on the feelings, thoughts, or actions of her targets and bystanders. The perlocutionary claim is well supported on theoretical and empirical grounds. Slurs may *cause* harm—either physical or psychological—to the targeted individuals and the groups they belong to, *provoke* the formation of unfair beliefs in targets and bystanders, and possibly trigger discriminating actions and even violence.

Critical race studies show that racial insults and slurs cause physical or psychological damage to targets, ranging from nightmares and post-traumatic stress, to hypertension, psychosis, and suicide.[14] Mari Matsuda adds that the use of derogatory language increases the gap between targets and dominant groups, even as far as non-racist members are concerned: on the one hand, even non-racist members of the dominant group feel relieved not to have to endure such abuse; on the other, members of the target group treat with hostility and suspicion even non-racist members of the dominant group.[15] Moreover, empirical studies by Greenberg and Pyszczynski show that slurs have a detrimental impact on not only targets but also bystanders: ethnic slurs prompt negative evaluations of the target group by those who overheard the slur.[16] More recent findings go even further: experimental studies by Carnaghi and collaborators investigate the effects of homophobic labels on the self-perception of heterosexual males, showing that when exposed to homophobic epithets they are motivated to underline their masculinity and claim a distinctly heterosexual identity by taking distance from homosexuals: "derogatory language not only activates prevalently negative images

---

[12] MacKinnon (1987), Langton (1993, 2012, 2014), Hornsby and Langton (1998), Langton and West (1999), Langton, Haslanger, and Anderson (2012), Tirrell (2012), Kukla and Lance (2009), Lance and Kukla (2013), Kukla (2014). A similar approach is suggested by Mark Richard (a supporter of the expressivist view of slurs); cf. Richard (2008: 1): "what makes a word a slur is that it is used to do certain things, that it has . . . a certain illocutionary potential".

[13] Cf. Langton, Haslanger, and Anderson (2012: 758).

[14] Cf. Delgado (1993) and the papers in Matsuda (1993).   [15] Matsuda (1993).

[16] Greenberg and Pyszczynski (1985), Kirkland, Greenberg, and Pyszczynski (1987).

about gays but also triggers identity-protective strategies in heterosexual males, thereby creating an even stronger gap between heterosexuals and homosexuals".[17]

3.3 The Illocutionary Approach

As anticipated, the perspectival proposal may be understood not only in causal, but also in constitutive terms: according to the *illocutionary* approach, the very act of uttering a slur constitutes, rather than causes, harm. Lepore and Stone seem to go in this direction when they claim that slurs "come with an *invitation* to take a certain perspective": slurs are expressions endowed with an illocutionary dimension.

More precisely, scholars working on hate speech draw a distinction between three classes of illocutions that a speaker can perform by uttering a slur.[18] The first class focuses on the harm perpetrated on the targeted individuals and groups. A speaker may use slurs as "weapons of verbal abuse",[19] and perform *assault-like speech acts* such as persecuting and degrading her targets. By uttering (2), the speaker isn't merely *asserting* something, but performing an illocutionary act of attacking, degrading or threatening—an act directed towards an individual, and all Italians.

The second class focuses on the addressees and bystanders (especially when members of the dominant group). By uttering (1), a racist speaker may perform an act of *propaganda*, an act that incites and promotes racism and discrimination, hate and violence. This class includes so-called "self-identifying uses", where the slur, rather than being an instrument of abuse, has the role of expressing the social identity of the speaker.[20]

The third class includes so-called "authoritative subordinating speech acts" like *enacting* or reinforcing unfair hierarchies and systems of social oppression: slurs may be used to classify people as inferior; to legitimate racial oppression, religious or gender discrimination; to deprive minorities of powers and rights.

In the next section, I argue in favor of the illocutionary approach, showing its advantages over the perlocutionary one. For the purposes of this essay, I focus primarily on assault (i) and propaganda acts (ii), for two main reasons. First, Lepore and Stone seem to explicitly reject the very idea of authoritative subordinating speech acts (iii), where racist speakers seem to have the power to *impose* upon their audiences a way of thinking about their targets: "it's in the nature of a perspective, on our view, that a speaker is in no position to access or to dictate the addressee's perspective. Any statement of what's happening must be quite indirect."[21] Second, many potentially destructive objections have been raised against the third class of illocutionary acts, concerning mainly the issue of the *authority* of the speaker. Indeed, authority seems a crucial *felicity condition* for subordinating speech acts. On the contrary, in ordinary instances of hate speech, like (1) or (2) uttered during casual conversations, the speaker

---

[17] Carnaghi, Maass, and Fasoli (2011: 1663); cf. Carnaghi and Maass (2007, 2008).
[18] Langton (2012), Langton, Haslanger, and Anderson (2012).   [19] Richard (2008).
[20] Nunberg (2017: 21, 49).   [21] Lepore and Stone (forthcoming: 8).

seems to lack any kind of standing or authority. Apparently, since they are uttered by ordinary speakers, neither (1) nor (2) can succeed as acts of subordination: in other words, they cannot *constitute* subordination (an illocutionary effect), even if they may *cause* subordination (a perlocutionary effect). The Authority objection, if well founded, would represent a knock-down argument for the class of authoritative subordinating speech acts: I leave its assessment for another occasion.[22]

4. The Explanatory Power of the Illocutionary Approach

In the recent literature concerning hate speech there is a general consensus about a cluster of traits characterizing slurs.[23] My claim is that the illocutionary approach offers a comprehensive account of a number of crucial features of slurs, namely their derogatory autonomy, the feeling of complicity of addressees and bystanders, the phenomenon of appropriation of slurs, the generality of derogatory speech, and the harm inflicted not only on the targets of slurs, but also on bystanders. Let's examine each phenomenon and its explanation in illocutionary terms.

4.1 Derogatory Autonomy

Most scholars take the derogatory potential of slurs as independent of the beliefs and mental states of the speaker.[24] According to the illocutionary approach, by uttering sentences containing slurs, a speaker may perform a variety of harmful speech acts: (i) attacking her targets, (ii) promoting racial oppression, or (iii) legitimizing behaviors of discrimination. In this sense the *mere presence* of a slur makes (2) an act of, say, assault: the slur counts as a sort of illocutionary force indicating device (IFID). Such a claim would actually fit well within Austin's conventionalist framework. Austin characterizes the illocutionary act as the *conventional* aspect of language (to be contrasted with the perlocutionay act). For any speech act "there must exist an accepted conventional procedure having a certain conventional effect, that procedure to include the uttering of certain words by certain persons in certain circumstances":[25] if the conventional procedure is executed according to further conditions, the act is successfully performed. Illocutionary acts are—*inter alia*—performed via conventional devices (like linguistic conventions). In an Austinian framework then, slurs may be regarded as conventional devices apt for performing acts of persecution or propaganda, regardless of the beliefs, attitudes, and intentions of individual speakers. In this sense, slurs

---

[22] For an extensive analysis of "authoritative subordinating speech acts" and of the Authority Problem, see Bianchi (2017).

[23] See Hom (2008), Croom (2011), Tirrell (2012) and Bolinger (2015) for a variety of conditions any satisfactory theory of slurs should satisfy.

[24] Hom (2008) calls this feature "derogatory autonomy", while Bolinger (2015) prefers the label "offensive autonomy".

[25] Condition A.1, Austin (1975: 14).

conventionally signal the attitude of the speaker: a racist speaker decides to use a slur rather than its neutral counterpart and as a result her choice signals that she endorses the perspective typically associated with the slur.[26]

4.2 Complicity

Another distinctive feature of slurs is the phenomenon of complicity: "slurs make recalcitrant hearers feel complicit in the speaker's way of thinking".[27] Silence, or more generally, failure to object to uses of slurs, may result in complicity with the speaker. According to the illocutionary approach, the very act of uttering a slur constitutes, rather than causes, harm. Slurs present content from a certain perspective, in a way that makes it difficult to *deny* that perspective: even if addressees and bystanders have reservations about the use of a slur, as long as they fail to express their reservations, the speaker can end up successfully performing an act of assault or propaganda. Acts of propaganda are especially insidious, in that they present their audience as likely to accept and adopt the same perspective, as potentially endorsing the same attitude: as Lepore and Stone put it, "a speaker, in using a word, commits that her audience has a relevant, affectively laden perspective associated with the word's referent, and indicates that she expects her audience to deploy that perspective in understanding what she says".[28]

4.3 Appropriation

Furthermore, any satisfactory theoretical approach of slurs should give an account of appropriated uses, namely uses by targeted members or groups of their own slurs for non-derogatory purposes, in order to demarcate the group, and show a sense of intimacy and solidarity—as in the appropriation of "nigger" by the African-American community, or the appropriation of "gay" and "queer" by the homosexual community. Sometimes slurs are reclaimed as tools of conscious political or social struggle in order to take back from racists and homophobes a powerful instrument of discrimination, and to soothe or neutralize the offensive effect of the slur. The illocutionary approach has a quite straightforward explanation of appropriation as a type of *pretense*. On this approach, an in-group uttering (1) in an appropriated context is not performing an act of assault or propaganda, but merely *pretending* to perform an act of assault or propaganda, while expecting her audience to see through the pretense and recognize the critical or derisive attitude behind it.[29]

---

[26] For similar views, cf. Bolinger (2015) and Nunberg (2017).

[27] Camp (2013: 333). Cf. Croom (2011: 343): "just hearing (…) [the slur 'nigger'] can leave one feeling as if they have been made complicit in a morally atrocious act".

[28] Lepore and Stone (forthcoming: 8). Cf. Nunberg (2017: 48).

[29] For the notion of pretense, see Walton (1990). For an alternative account of appropriation in terms of echo, see Bianchi (2014).

4.4 Generality

Any account of slurs needs to be generalizable to similar language, such as sexist, gender-biasing, religious epithets, and even to approbative terms.[30] More than alternative views, the illocutionary approach provides us with a general framework for hate speech: slurs are conventional devices used to classify people as inferior; to legitimate racial oppression, religious or gender discrimination; to deprive minorities of powers and rights. Additionally, the illocutionary approach offers a natural explanation for such approbative terms as "angel", "blessed", "stud", "goddess": they are conventional devices apt for performing illocutionary acts of *approval, praise,* and *commendation.*

4.5 Pedagogical Contexts

More controversially, Hom claims that slurs may occur in non-derogatory, non-appropriated (NDNA) contexts—often pedagogical contexts about racism like,

(4)   Racists believe that Italians are wops

or

(5)   Institutions that treat Italians as wops are morally depraved:

"The epithet in NDNA contexts carries its racist content while falling short of derogating its target because that is the very point of its use."[31] The illocutionary approach focuses not on what slurs *say*, but on what they *do*. In NDNA contexts the speaker isn't performing acts of assault or propaganda, but completely different speech acts: *objecting* to discriminatory discourse, *pointing out* the racist contents carried by slurs, *denouncing* the racist presuppositions that come with ordinary uses of slurs.

4.6 Harm Inflicted on Targets and Bystanders

Finally, slurs inflict long-lasting harm not only upon their targets (individuals and groups), but also upon addressees and bystanders even when these do not belong to the target group. The illocutionary approach gives a comprehensive account in terms of speech acts of assault (for the harm perpetrated on targets) and propaganda (for the harm perpetrated on audiences). As a matter of fact, assault and propaganda may be conceived as the *same* speech act as perceived by—or directed to—different audiences: its targets (assault), and addressees and bystanders (propaganda). In other words, propaganda acts like (1) may be used as assault acts towards an Italian bystander. Tirrell underlines the phenomenon when she writes

Sometimes, a third-person derogation is used by a member of the dominant group to a hearer who is a member of the subordinate group as a way of labeling the third person with a label that boomerangs from the target back to the hearer.[32]

---

[30] Hom (2008: 439).   [31] Hom (2008: 429).
[32] Tirrell (2012: 192). Cf. Langton (2012: 131): "Propaganda aimed at turning its hearers into racists could also be used as an attack on an individual."

Additionally, assault acts may be taken as propaganda acts: by uttering (2), the speaker is not simply attacking an individual and all Italians, but also promoting racism and discrimination. As Nunberg notes, the two functions are inseparably linked: "The word ['nigger'] turns a bigot from a hapless, inconsequential 'I' into an intimidating, menacing 'we'."[33]

5. Conclusion

The aim of my essay was to evaluate the perspectival account put forward by Lepore and Stone. I have explored the notion of perspective, as applied to slurs, from an unusual point of view, focusing not on slurs' content (expressed or conveyed) but on their performative potential. I have shown that the perspectival proposal can be stated both in perlocutionary and illocutionary terms, and argued in favor of an illocutionary approach. Understood in constitutive terms, the perspectival proposal gives us significant insights into a number of adequacy conditions, ranging from the derogatory autonomy of slurs, the feeling of complicity of addressees and bystanders, the phenomenon of appropriation of slurs, the generality of derogatory speech, and the harm inflicted not only on the targets of slurs, but also on bystanders. Slurs not only *cause* harm to individuals and groups, they also *constitute* harm, they *do* something, they have normative power. The normative power of slurs is twofold. On the one hand, they have an obvious negative power, allowing us to perform acts of *assault*; on the other, they have positive power, allowing us to perform speech acts of *propaganda*. Slurs, in other terms, do come with an invitation to take a negative perspective towards their targets, but at the same time they contribute to shape and strengthen our identity as a dominant group. In Tirrell's words, "Using such terms helps to construct a strengthened 'us' for the speakers and a weakened 'them' for the targets, thus reinforcing or even realigning social relations."[34]

References

Anderson, Luvell and Lepore, Ernie 2013a. Slurring words. *Noûs*, 47(1), 25–48.

Anderson, Luvell and Lepore, Ernie 2013b. What did you call me? Slurs as prohibited words. *Analytic Philosophy*, 54(3), 350–63.

Austin, John L. 1975. *How to Do Things with Words*, J. O. Urmson and M. Sbisà (eds.). Oxford: Oxford University Press, 2nd edition 1975.

Bianchi, Claudia 2014. Slurs and appropriation: an echoic account. *Journal of Pragmatics*, 66, 35–44.

Bianchi, Claudia 2017. Linguaggio d'odio, autorità e ingiustizia discorsiva. *Rivista di Estetica*, 57(64), 18–34.

---

[33] Nunberg (2017: 54).

[34] Tirrell (2012: 174–5). I wish to thank Bianca Cepollaro, Adam Croom, Fabio Fasoli, Ernie Lepore, Robin Jeshion, Mihaela Popa, Stefano Predelli, and Marina Sbisà for extensive discussion on slurs and hate speech.

Bolinger, Renée Jorgensen 2015. The pragmatics of slurs. *Noûs*, 51(3), 439–62.

Camp, Elizabeth 2013. Slurring perspectives. *Analytic Philosophy*, 54(3), 330–49.

Camp, Elisabeth 2015. Metaphors in literature. In N. Carroll and J. Gibson (eds.), *The Routledge Companion to Philosophy of Literature*. London: Routledge.

Carnaghi, Andrea and Maass, Anne 2007. In-group and out-group perspectives in the use of derogatory group label: *Gay* vs. *fag*. *Journal of Language and Social Psychology*, 26, 142–56.

Carnaghi, Andrea and Maass, Anne 2008. Gay or fag? On the consequences of derogatory labels. In Y. Kashima, K. Fielder, and P. Freytag (eds.), *Stereotype Dynamics: Language-based Approaches to Stereotype Formation, Maintenance, and Transformation*. Mahwah, NJ: Erlbaum, 117–34.

Carnaghi, Andrea, Maass, Anne, and Fasoli, Fabio 2011. Enhancing masculinity by slandering homosexuals: The role of homophobic epithets in heterosexual gender identity. *Personality and Social Psychology Bulletin*, 37(12), 1655–65.

Croom, Adam 2011. Slurs. *Language Sciences*, 33, 343–58.

Croom, Adam 2013. How to do things with slurs: Studies in the way of derogatory words. *Language & Communication*, 33, 177–204.

Delgado, Richard 1993. Words that wound: A tort action for racial insults, epithets, and name calling. In M. J. Matsuda, C. R. Lawrence, R. Delgado, and K. W. Crenshaw (eds.), *Words that Wound: Critical Race Theory, Assaultive Speech, and the First Amendment*. San Francisco, CA: Westview Press, 89–110.

Dummett, Michael 1973/1981. *Frege's Philosophy of Language*. Oxford: Clarendon Press, 2nd edition 1981.

Greenberg, Jeff and Pyszczynski, Tom 1985. The effects of an overheard ethnic slur on evaluations of the target: How to spread a social disease. *Journal of Experimental Social Psychology*, 21, 61–72.

Grice, Herbert Paul 1975/1989. Logic and conversation (1967). In P. Cole and J. Morgan (eds.), *Syntax and Semantics 3: Speech Acts*. New York: Academic Press, 41–58. Reprinted in Grice 1989: 22–40.

Grice, Herbert Paul 1989. *Studies in the Way of Words*. Cambridge, MA: Harvard University Press.

Hom, Christopher 2008. The semantics of racial epithets. *Journal of Philosophy*, 105, 416–40.

Hornsby, Jennifer 2001. Meaning and uselessness: How to think about derogatory words. In P. French and H. Wettstein (eds.), *Midwest Studies in Philosophy*. London: Blackwell, 25, 128–41.

Hornsby, Jennifer and Langton, Rae 1998. Free speech and illocution, *Journal of Legal Theory*, 4, 21–37.

Jeshion, Robin 2013. Slurs and stereotypes, *Analytic Philosophy*, 54(3), 314–29.

Kaplan, David 1999. The meaning of ouch and oops: Explorations in the theory of meaning as use, UCLA, ms.

Kirkland, Shari, Greenberg, Jeff, and Pyszczynski, Tom 1987. Further evidence of the deleterious effects of overheard derogatory ethnic labels: Derogation beyond the target. *Personality and Social Psychology Bulletin*, 13, 216–27.

Kukla, Rebecca 2014. Performative force, convention, and discursive injustice. *Hypatia*, 29(2), 440–57.

Kukla, Rebecca and Lance, Mark 2009. *'Yo!' and 'Lo!': The Pragmatic Topography of the Space of Reasons*. Cambridge, MA: Harvard University Press.

Lance, Mark and Kukla, Rebecca 2013. Leave the gun; Take the cannoli! The pragmatic topography of second-person calls. *Ethics*, 123, 456–78.

Langton, Rae 1993. Speech acts and unspeakable acts. *Philosophy and Public Affairs*, 22, 293–330. Now in Langton 2009. *Sexual Solipsism: Philosophical Essays on Pornography and Objectification*. Oxford: Oxford University Press, 25–63.

Langton, Rae 2012. Beyond belief: Pragmatics in hate speech and pornography. In I. Maitra and M. K. McGowan (eds.), *Speech and Harm: Controversies over Free Speech*. Oxford: Oxford University Press, 72–93.

Langton, Rae 2014. The Authority of Hate Speech. Draft for Analytic Legal Philosophy Conference, Oxford, May 2014.

Langton, Rae, Haslinger, Sally and Anderson, Luvall 2012. Language and race. In Gillian Russell and Delia Graff Fara (eds.), *Routledge Companion to the Philosophy of Language*. New York: Routledge, 753–67.

Langton, Rae and West, Carolilne 1999. Scorekeeping in a pornographic language game. *Australasian Journal of Philosophy*, 77(3), 303–19. Now in R. Langton 2009. *Sexual Solipsism: Philosophical Essays on Pornography and Objectification*. Oxford: Oxford University Press, 173–95.

Lepore, Ernie and Stone, Matthew 2014. Philosophical investigations into figurative speech metaphor and irony. In Y. Jiang and E. Lepore (eds.), *Language and Value, ProtoSociology*, vol. 31, 75–87.

Lepore, Ernie and Stone, Matthew 2015. *Imagination and Convention: Distinguishing Grammar and Inference in Language*. Oxford: Oxford University Press.

Lepore, Ernie and Stone, Matthew (forthcoming) On the perspective-taking and open-endedness of slurring, ms.

MacKinnon, Catharine 1987. *Feminism Unmodified: Discourses on Life and Law*. Cambridge, MA: Harvard University Press.

Matsuda, Mari 1993. Public response to racist speech. In M. J. Matsuda, C. R. Lawrence, R. Delgado, and K. W. Crenshaw (eds.), *Words that Wound: Critical Race Theory, Assaultive Speech and the First Amendment*. Boulder, CO: Westview Press.

Nunberg, Geoffrey 2017. The social life of slurs. In D. Fogal, D. Harris and M. Moss (eds.), *New Work on Speech Acts*. Oxford: Oxford University Press, 237–95.

Potts, Christopher 2007. The centrality of expressive indexes. Reply to commentaries. *Theoretical Linguistics*, 33(2), 255–68.

Potts, Christopher 2008. The pragmatics of conventional implicature and expressive content. In C. Maienborn and P. Portner (eds.), *Semantics: An International Handbook of Natural Language Meaning*. Berlin: Mouton de Gruyter.

Richard, Mark 2008. *When Truth Gives Out*. Oxford: Oxford University Press.

Sperber, Dan and Wilson, Deirdre 2006. Pragmatics. In F. Jackson and M. Smith (eds.), *Oxford Handbook of Contemporary Philosophy*. Oxford: Oxford University Press, 468–501.

Tirrell, Lynne 2012. Genocidal language games. In I. Maitra and M. K. McGowan (eds.), *Speech and Harm: Controversies over Free Speech*. Oxford: Oxford University Press, 174–221.

Walton, Kendall 1990. *Mimesis as Make-believe: On the Foundations of the Representational Arts*. Cambridge, MA: Harvard University Press.

Williamson, Timothy 2009. Reference, inference, and the semantics of pejoratives. In J. Almog and P. Leonardi (eds.), *The Philosophy of David Kaplan*. New York: Oxford University Press, 137–58.

PART III

Cognitive Science Connections

11

Composing Meaning and Thinking

Roberto G. de Almeida

"...take the expression *to weigh one's words*. Now how can you weigh words? When I hear the word *weigh* I see a large scale—like the one we had in Rezhitsa in our shop, where they put bread on one side and a weight on the other. The arrow shifts to one side, then stops in the middle...But what do you have here—to *weigh one's words!*" —S., 1934 (In A. R. Luria, *The Mind of a Mnemonist*, 1968, p. 119)

Solomon V. Shereshevsky or simply "S." was a man with an extraordinary memory. He was able to encode long lists of words, addresses, digits, and events in no time. He was then able to recite them perfectly, even backwards. He would recall long and complex (sometimes random) mathematical formulas and tables full of numbers after just one reading. These virtually intact representations would last for many years. Shereshevsky described his memorization abilities as being entirely based on images. He would "see" everything told to him, or everything he read, as a sequence of images. Sometimes he would place them all on a "street" scene and would "walk" back and forth recalling them in any order. Infrequently missed items—he explained— would have been mistakenly left in a dark alley, invisible to his mental walk. His interpretations of what was read or heard were illustrated by vivid images representing words, numbers, and phrases. Often he would use synesthesia—associating words or numbers with colors, yielding a comprehension process that was a constant barrage of Ideas in the form of images and colors. But the cost of doing so was a comprehension impairment of sorts: he could not understand most figurative expressions, nor could he make sense of abstract ideas or simple words used metaphorically and in the context of poems. He would struggle with such occurrences of normal language use to a point of being overwhelmed by them.

I read that 'the work got under way normally.' As for *work*, I see that work is going on...there's a factory. But there's that word *normally*. What I see is a big, ruddy-cheeked woman, a *normal* woman...Then the expression *get under way*. Who? What is all this? You have industry...that is, a factory, and this normal woman—but how does all this fit together? How much I have to get rid of just to get the simple idea of the thing!" –S. (Luria, 1968, p. 128)

Putting aside all methodological caveats that interpreting cognitive "impairments" requires, Shereshevsky's case is illustrative of the task at hand: we seem to know what a sentence means when it is interpreted *literally*, but somehow the criteria for interpreting deviations from literal meaning (or simply "meaning") could potentially lead to havoc. Unlike Shereshevsky, however, it looks as though we make sense of such deviations: the absurdity of a metaphor is supposed to be quickly—and perhaps conventionally—corrected to some default interpretation. Indirect requests lead to efficient actions with little effort on the part of the listener. The apparent vagueness of an indeterminate sentence is filled in with appropriate semantic material. We even make sense of aphorisms and "deep thoughts", often peppered with hard-to-grasp analogies. But how do we do it? How do we successfully achieve our communicative goals by such imperfect ways?

It is now more than an article of faith in cognitive science that compositionality is a key characteristic of human cognitive architecture—that without compositionality there can't be productivity, and that without productivity we would be out to fend for ourselves producing or interpreting novel sentences, decoding objects,[1] or simply having thoughts we never had before. Far from being too dramatic, the picture that emerges of our linguistic and cognitive systems without compositionality is that of Shereshevsky's mind and its struggles with non-literal language, for without compositional meaning we would have just a not-so-vast memory likely incapable of "fitting it all together", even a "simple idea".

Granted these common semantic terms—the likes of "literal", "meaning", "compositionality" and many others—still linger in philosophy and cognitive science with little hope of finding consensus. And, by extension, so does a division of labor between semantics and pragmatics. Of more direct concern in the present essay is where exactly we can draw a line between semantics and pragmatics—or more specifically, between *linguistic-driven* computations and those of other cognitive systems bearing on meaning and utterance interpretation. With this goal in mind, I plan to examine Lepore and Stone's (2015) survey and hypotheses on semantics and pragmatics. They propose, in particular, that the language faculty contains numerous principles that yield linguistically motivated enriched interpretations, dispensing with much of the mind-reading job that is supposed to constitute pragmatic interpretation. Their analytic work provides a very fertile ground for the investigation of the algorithms and heuristics that guide interpretation towards semantic composition and beyond. My discussion of their approach will focus on a few cases that may pose a challenge to an enriched analysis of several types of linguistic expressions—keeping an eye on the intentional fallacy that plagues semantics. I will discuss so-called "bullshit" sentences, the "good-enough" approach to parsing, and in particular metaphors and so-called "indeterminate" sentences. The choice of topics is not merely for their central role in the debate on

---

[1] I assume that object representations rely largely on low-level compositional processes based on volumetric parts—as in models such as Biederman's (1987).

where to draw the line between semantics and pragmatics, but also for convenient proximity, as they have been topics of my own investigation.

To anticipate a bit, my line will be traced close to where Lepore and Stone trace theirs, even if it may seem that their commitment to a variety of linguistic conventions as part of the language faculty appears to render the line blurred. I also take interpretation to be largely determined by information in the linguistic material (plus linguistic-perceptual computations; see below). I agree that linguistic principles are probably richer than we commonly think and that they play a key role in building or at least proposing interpretations. And, finally, I also agree that, to a large extent, "pragmatics merely disambiguates" (p. 94). But I differ from Lepore and Stone's approach in mood, if not in substance: I'm less optimistic about the breadth of linguistic rules that could successfully determine interpretations. Also, I take it that the main role of these rules is to compose meaning, and that, beyond meaning-composition, some heuristics might be applied to interpretation, but that largely holistic processes rule.

In section 1, I discuss some guiding assumptions on cognitive architecture, which constrain the nature of linguistic and cognitive representations and processes—and by implication the conception of the semantics/pragmatics divide I have to offer. The phenomena that I examine in section 2, relying on both linguistic arguments and experimental evidence, suggest that for certain constructions there is an early "literal" process of interpretation followed by a period of uncertainty, indicating that the early linguistic computations produce a "shallow" semantic representation, not a fully enriched one. The cases I discuss, culminating with metaphors and so-called indeterminate sentences, challenge the prowess of linguistic computations for resolving—even suggesting—interpretations. I provide evidence for the availability of true and false propositions computed from the meaning one attains about a sentence. In addition, I propose that "indeterminacy" cannot be resolved linguistically, not at least without appealing to an analytic/synthetic distinction—an appeal that should be avoided. I argue, in summary, that rules for converting linguistic utterances into mental representations bearing on meaning—semantic or pragmatic—are largely rules for disposing higher interpretive mechanisms with a rough compositional meaning, with potential semantic "gaps" being filled by abductive-inferential processes beyond compositionality.

1. Guiding Assumptions

I will start off with several guiding assumptions—some of which will be expanded on in later sections, where I discuss particular empirical cases, and others will simply be taken for granted as guiding my approach to sentence comprehension. A few of these assumptions might be fairly standard while some are certainly the object of numerous controversies in philosophy and cognitive science. I will start with the assumptions that are to be taken for granted throughout. As Napoleon would have said, "On s'engage et puis... on voit."

1.1 Symbols, Computations, and Propositions

I take mental representations to be symbolic, and mental processes to be computations over these symbolic representations. Symbolic representations can be simple or complex, and computations (viz., mental processes) are sensitive to both. A computation can be sensitive to a simple symbol (say, a symbol that stands for a morpheme in natural language) when the symbol can change the course of computations performed on its host symbolic expression. To put in more concrete terms, the difference between (1a) and (1b) might be captured by a system that takes verb types to be coded for their distributional properties—say, that *cut* can enter into both an *inchoative* form as in (1a) or a transitive form as in (1b).

(1) a. This knife cuts easily
     b. This meat cuts easily[2]

If so, the computations performed over these token sentences might be sensitive to the two possibilities, allowing for the parser to be committed either to just one analysis or to both. By contrast, linguistic computations might not be sensitive to distinctions such as those in (2), where both verbs and their arguments have the same distributional properties.

(2) a. The water froze
     b. The ice melted

The difference between sentences in (2) is like the one observed in those in (3).

(3) a. The dress is black
     b. The dress is blue

Even though their differences in content might be relevant in particular situations, they are, as Grimshaw (2005) observed, linguistically inactive. It is the content of these expressions, however, what matters to a pragmatist—say, the state of the weather in (2), and a difference of opinion or optics, as uttered in (3). As this initial assumption implies, the computations that the linguistic system performs are initially sensitive to structure but not the content of the utterances. Indeed, the semantic representation that, by hypothesis, the system outputs to higher cognitive mechanisms is largely dependent not on the content of utterances, but on their structure—a point to which we'll return shortly.

So far, we have seen examples in which computations are sensitive to particular symbols. Computations are also sensitive to complex symbolic expressions in cases where the structure of symbols might be ambiguous (such as in syntactic ambiguity), in cases where there are long-distance dependencies between elements in a structure,

---

[2] Just a reminder that (1b) is *transitive*, not intransitive as the linear surface form might imply. Although *meat* appears in the subject position, it is the object of *cut* (see de Almeida & Manouilidou, 2015, for discussion).

such as between syntactically specified constituents and lexical ones, and in cases of analytic inferences in which, for instance, conjoined expressions entail their parts (e.g., P&Q —> P).

Moreover, I assume that sentences convey propositions and that propositions are complex symbolic expressions that have constituents (simple symbols) and constituent structure (how symbols are arranged to represent a particular token sentence). Sentences in (1) by hypothesis convey propositions that are different in form, while those in (2) convey propositions that are similar in form. Interpretive processes can be, in principle, operations over propositions, computations over form, not content. Many forms of "enrichment" can be seen, thus, as computations over propositions instigated by linguistic principles encoded symbolically.

Another assumption is that understanding linguistic utterances involves a fair amount of symbolic computations and these computations at least at a linguistic level of analysis are hard-wired, based on rough-and-ready algorithms for outputting standard representations of linguistic utterances. But what happens after these algorithms perform their standard job—or in parallel to them—is at the heart of the distinction between semantics and pragmatics: operations over content are supposedly heuristic and contingent on a wide array of information sources, including *co-text*, wider utterance context, the listener's beliefs, background assumptions, and social norms.

Besides establishing a framework for the discussion that ensues, these explicit commitments to a symbolic-computational architecture help to clear the theoretical vocabulary from ill-posed terms such as "association", "activation", and the "strength" of a representation, all involving mental processes. And they also help clear the vocabulary of *representations*, distinguishing them from, say, "images". This terminological pruning also serves to constrain the nature of the products of linguistic computations and their relations to other representations. For instance, "context", "background knowledge", "common ground" and other such notions can be conceived as sets of propositions rather than unstructured units of activation. What a variety of tropes bring to mind— the thoughts that they evoke—are too to be conceived as propositions, and so are the contents of semantic memory about events and states.[3] In summary, operations over token expressions—sentences and the likes of context—can be conceived in terms of algorithms and heuristics computed over propositions.[4]

There is yet another advantage in putting it all in terms of symbols and computations over symbols: the vocabulary of representations and processes can be seen as the same

---

[3] This propositional view of complex mental representations is certainly not new. Similar views have been around at least since Frege (though not explicitly *qua mental* representation) but in particular in works such as Pylyshyn (1973) and Kintsch (1974), in both incarnations of the "language of thought" hypothesis (Fodor, 1975, 2008), and in psychological theories of text interpretation (see, e.g., McKoon & Ratcliff's, 1992, "minimalist hypothesis" of propositional encoding). The differences between these approaches will not be of concern here.

[4] This distinction can be misleading, for heuristic processes are also encoded in terms of algorithms— the difference being that they do not have to have guaranteed end results. I will refer to "algorithmic" and "heuristic" simply to differentiate between fixed and malleable processes.

for different input modalities and different sources of information. To wit, it is because we have a common vocabulary of representations for different cognitive systems that we can "talk about what we see," to use McNamara's (1978) expression. By the same token, we can use both representations from linguistically derived elements (e.g., names, pronouns, demonstratives) and representations of visually "grabbed" elements to *refer*. It is only because they employ a common code that both forms of reference can meet and talk to each other.

And finally, the commitment to a symbolic/computational view of how linguistic and cognitive processes run allows for compositionality, and compositionality is a property that only symbolic architectures instantiate.

1.2 Compositionality

Another assumption guiding the present work is that sentence meaning is obtained compositionally, that is, by the meaning of its constituents and how they are structured together to yield propositions. I take this to be the default, the null hypothesis. Much has been said about cases that are supposed to violate compositionality (see, e.g., Pelletier, 2004, for discussion). But the claim here is that compositionality applies to propositions, not necessarily to sentences. Thus, cases such as linguistic disfluencies (*uh, well, ... I ... perhaps ... you can go!*) can yield unambiguous and complete proposi- tions. Idioms can be taken as lexicalized (thus, fixed) or they can be initially processed as non-idiomatic (*The maid kicked the bucket* is not necessarily parsed as an idiom, not even at the offset of *bucket*).[5] Most cases that are taken to challenge a strict form of compositionality are deep down cases for which linguistic analyses may yield com- positional representations. This is not to suggest that semantics should be bloated with ad hoc analyses so that compositionality is ultimately attained (see below on the perils of intentional fallacy). As I will argue in section 2.3, even copular metaphors (viz., those with a form *x is y*) are compositional.

1.3 Modularity

These architectural commitments are tied to the idea that language is modular—in principle, a cognitively impenetrable faculty of the mind. Here is how these ideas con- nect: the assumption that linguistic processes are computational depends on some of these computations being insensitive to contextual demands, background knowledge, and beliefs. Language processing relies on compositional meaning being obtained autonomously, at most as a relation between a proposition and information within its co-text. Intra-modular computations ought to be the ones that are algorithmic, the ones that are sensitive not to the content of the expressions it computes, but to their

---

[5] Online (i.e., real-time) studies on idiom processing have suggested that idioms are treated as lexical- ized forms (Swinney & Cutler, 1979), but also that idioms vary with respect to the point at which they are recognized as such (i.e., at the point at which the meaning of the expression is perceived not to correspond to the meanings of the parts put together), with some idioms being recognized early, while others being recognized late, only at the last word or after (see Cacciari & Tabossi, 1988).

symbols and how they are structured in expressions. Quite likely, many computations performed by other systems, including higher cognitive ones, are "algorithmic" in that sense (e.g., solving a *modus ponens* problem). And it is also quite possible that some of the computations that the language module performs are heuristic, such as employing parsing strategies. But if language is a module, at least some of its main computations ought to be algorithmic, insensitive to the content of the symbols it computes.

It is an empirical issue as to which representations are computed within the modular system and which ones are not. If we regard many of the computations that are deemed pragmatic to be in fact rule-based syntactic or semantic computations performed by the language faculty, the line that divides modular input analysis from other cognitive systems is traced very high. Lepore and Stone (2015) have indeed assumed that many computations deemed "pragmatic" are products of the language faculty. But their approach also takes the position that this faculty is somewhat penetrable—that it adapts to new conventions over time and that linguistic symbols can affect computations in novel ways, catering to new conventions.

The view of modularity assumed here takes *semantic* computations to be part of the module (see de Almeida & Lepore, 2018, for extensive discussion). This is compatible with Fodor's view of modularity, as he laid out in his monograph:

> [W]hile there could perhaps be an algorithm for parsing, there surely could not be an algorithm for estimating communicative intentions in anything like their full diversity. Arguments about what an author meant are thus able to be interminable in ways in which arguments about what he said are not.   (Fodor, 1983, p. 90)

The sense of semantics that is taken to be part of the module is not a semantics that is concerned with idiosyncrasies of content, but one that is concerned with linguistically active properties of words and sentences, the ones that affect computation and the structure of propositions. As Chomsky puts it,

> [The work often called "natural-language semantics" and "lexical semantics"] can be regarded as part of syntax, but oriented to a different interface and different aspects of language use. Insofar as the relation of rhyme that holds between "chase" and "lace" is based on properties of I-sound, and the relation of entailment that holds between "chase" and "follow" on properties of I-meaning, both fall under syntax, in a traditional sense.
>
> Virtually all work in syntax in the narrower sense has been intimately related to questions of semantic (and of course phonetic) interpretation, and motivated by such questions. The fact has often been misunderstood because many researchers have chosen to call this work "syntax," reserving the term "semantics" for relations of expressions to something extra-linguistic.
>
> (Chomsky, 2000, p. 174)

Along the lines of the constraints above (in 1.1 and 1.2), Chomsky sees semantics also operating over "properties and arrangements of symbolic objects" (p. 174). Of course, the empirical question is exactly which aspects of semantics ("syntax") might constitute part of the module and which ones might constitute "something extra-linguistic".

1.4 Processing Constraint

Finally, the distinction between semantics and pragmatics should be sensitive to the nature of the computations that unfold over time—which we can call a "processing constraint" (PC). Although somewhat trivial, this is rarely taken into account in philosophical discussions regarding sentence interpretation. The PC can be rather informally stated as in (4).

(4)   Processing a sentence (or other unit of linguistic discourse) relies primarily on identifying constituents and building constituents' structural relations over time, with minimal commitments as to the hierarchical structure of the yet-to-come constituents and with as minimal revisions in structure as possible to attain a representation of the input.

There are several assumptions embedded in (4), of which I will highlight three: (i) The first is that obviously parsing and interpretation occur over time—with representations bearing linguistic and non-linguistic information built incrementally, on a millisecond-by-millisecond basis. This seldom needs further clarification in psycholinguistic circles, even if there is neither agreement on what sorts of representations are built, nor on the relative autonomy of linguistic analyses from non-linguistic ones. The time constraint is important because whatever one builds over time might ultimately influence what one takes to be the "meaning" that one attains. Consider a simple local ambiguity, in a typical "garden-path" sentence such as (5a) and its unambiguous pair (5b).

(5)   a. While Beyoncé was singing the song was playing on the radio
      b. The song was playing on the radio while Beyoncé was singing

Taken as a whole, there is no ambiguity in either sentence. But over time, the representation of the syntactic structure at the point where the noun phrase *the song* is processed in (5a) might be committed to a transitive reading of *singing* and thus the structure that is built at that point might require syntactic revision. Alternatively, the parser might be committed to an intransitive reading of *singing* or even allow for both possibilities to be initially entertained.[6] Nonetheless, the partial syntactic analysis may also yield a partial semantic representation, one that might be temporarily at odds with the nature of the event that the whole sentence describes. One may, at any given point, build partial or even full but false propositions compatible with the available (partial) stimulus. For instance, the proposition that *Beyoncé was singing the song* might be available at some point, possibly at the offset of the noun phrase *the song*.[7]

---

[6] Most early evidence gathered from this type of sentence showed processing delays at the disambiguating point, suggesting that the parser is temporarily committed to one structure (see Ferreira & Clifton, 1986). More recent models have considered other factors such as thematic properties (by assumption, a *semantic* information) as well as more fine-grained lexical constraints on parsing (see Townsend & Bever, 2001).

[7] A few observations about this example: First, there is nothing in either (5a) or (5b) that points to what Beyoncé was singing (could have been the national anthem, *Carmen*, or simply a song). Second, I refer to (5b) as being unambiguous, but if ambiguity arises as a function of the structures that the alternating verb

Indeed Christianson et al. (2001) found some evidence for this, not during but after sentences similar to (5a): about 40 percent of the time, subjects report having read sentences that are compatible with the partial input but which are at odds with the full sentence (e.g., *Beyoncé was singing the song*) while also accepting true probes (e.g., *The song was playing on the radio*). And as we will see in section 2, both true and false propositions computed from the incremental analysis of a sentence might be available in memory for quite some time after the sentence offset.

(ii) A second assumption embedded in (4), which only partially overlaps with assumption (i) above, is that what parsing does in real time is to yield—as rapidly and as efficiently as possible—a representation of the input based on linguistic constituents and syntax. Recall that computations are sensitive to both, properties of the symbols and properties of symbolic expressions. While relations between constituents obey primarily the former, higher-order grammatical principles might also affect the course of computations. For instance, parsing commitments may be determined by principles such as the canonical *position* of constituents and, consequently, by the role these constituents play in the event or state described by the sentence.[8] Parsing models may vary with regards to how much structure is built in advance and also how much parsing decisions depend on the nature of each constituent (see Townsend & Bever, 2001, for review). In all those circumstances, parsing computations are taken to be linguistically based—even if structural decisions are based on lexically encoded properties rather than on syntactic projection.

(iii) Another assumption embedded in (4) is that both processes of *building* and *revising* structure during potential misparses may also be linguistically driven. That is, potential misparses may be corrected by principles encoded within the parsing system. However, there is nothing in (4) that rules out other re-analyses being driven by higher cognitive mechanisms. For instance, the real-world plausibility of a particular token sentence is not something that the linguistic system is supposed to be checking. It is quite possible that the parser initially takes *meat* in (1b), *The meat cuts well*, to be the instrument or "logical subject" of *cut*. Revisions in assignment of thematic structure or revisions in the role that a constituent plays in a token sentence might as well be entirely driven by world knowledge (viz., that meats are cut and not used for cutting something else). But, what is perhaps most important, those revisions are not computations over the *sentence* itself but over the *proposition(s)*

---

to sing allows, it is also the case that (5b) is temporarily ambiguous at the offset of *singing*, although this won't have consequences for the parsing of the sentence. Finally, it is also possible that the proposition *Beyoncé was singing the song* is a pragmatic inference from the simpler proposition that *Beyoncé was singing* (see Brewer, 1977). The study by Christianson et al. (2001) also found that probes that are compatible with misparses have greater acceptance if they are pragmatically more plausible.

[8] Alzheimer's patients show more difficulty with non-canonical [*Theme, Experiencer*] structures than with more canonical [*Agent, Theme*] or even [*Experiencer, Theme*] structures, suggesting that syntactic-semantic mapping may be sensitive to a thematic hierarchy, which takes *Agent* to be canonically assigned to the first noun phrase position. See Manouilidou, de Almeida, Schwartz, & Nair (2009).

that the sentence expresses and might be based on inferences that the proposition triggers—way beyond linguistic analyses.

Recovering the linguistic properties of a given utterance relies primarily on computing its input as such, but it also involves computing covert representations. As an analogy, consider object recognition processes. Recognition begins with a viewer-centered representation, that is, a representation from the viewer's perspective. But in order to build an object-centered 3-D model, the viewer needs to rely on both, visible surfaces and encoded canonical representations of objects and parts of objects (see Biederman, 1987, 2013).[9] This 3-D model is determined by visible properties that are assumed to be non-accidental, that is, unlikely to be an accident of viewpoint (e.g., continuity of lines, orientation of edges based on visible vertices, concave creases marking object parts) together with representations that are stored or computed anew. Occluded surfaces are largely determined by the volumetric properties of object parts.[10]

The meaning of a sentence relies to a large extent on what is "visible"—i.e., what is in the acoustic or visual (in case of reading) input, with its "occluded surfaces" emerging from the analysis that the input undergoes: they come in the form of the likes of co-reference assignment between nouns and pronouns, ellipsis of verb phrases, presuppositions, and other rules for building representations of what is heard or read. The processes involved are not that of *construction* but that of decoding plus applying rules and matching incoming constituents with stored representations—in real time.

It should be said that PC does not take compositional and non-compositional processes to be serially arranged; that we build non-compositional interpretations only *after* compositional processes end or halt. It is quite possible that compositional and non-compositional processes (e.g., inferences) work in parallel—that whichever thoughts the first incoming constituents of a sentence evoke go on to trigger other thoughts. But that does not preclude compositional analysis to proceed autonomously. Inferences about what one hears might be computed in real time, but as I will argue, these are not far from what a sentence means—in fact the original *un-enriched* proposition might linger, even if it competes with "enriched" forms of propositional representation.

Adopting PC, as roughly formulated in (4), is important also for designing and evaluating experiments investigating the time-course of events in sentence interpretation. Many studies on metaphors, for instance, rely on off-line experimental techniques such as asking participants to press a button "as soon as they understood each statement" (Bowdle & Gentner, 2005). Clearly, response times to such decisions will be affected not by the moment-by-moment processing but by more general processes of appreciation of the statement, providing little information on the nature of the computations

---

[9] Although this view of object recognition is heavily contested, the alternative, view-based models (see Peissig & Tarr, 2007) have yet to determine how object representations are productive, if not by compositional processes akin to those proposed for language.

[10] I am not claiming that these representations are visual *tout court*. They are, at some level, symbolic such as proposition-like expressions specifying geometrical properties of parts of objects and their relations (see, e.g., Pylyshyn, 2003).

underlying the sentence. As we will see in the discussion of some experiments involving sentence comprehension, what matters is not what happens when, say, a metaphorical sentence has been appreciated in all its beauty or absurdity, but what goes on at the points in which the properties of its constituent symbols might affect the course of its computation.

2. Composing Meaning and Thinking (Fast)

Considerations regarding linguistic and cognitive architecture are important in guiding research on how different representations might enter semantic computations and beyond. In principle, semantic computations are sensitive to local—that is, within the sentence or co-text—properties of its symbols, but insensitive to non-local information such as context and different uses. However, what sort of information semantic computations are sensitive to, it turns out, is an empirical matter. There is no agreement on whether the information that linguistic constituents contribute to their host expressions is fixed, as there is no agreement on the range of possible "occluded" properties of a sentence. For instance, for Pustejovsky (1995), what a word contributes to a sentence is highly sensitive to other constituents as well as to properties of events that its host sentence describes. According to this view, the sense one gets of *window* might change whether one is talking about its *aperture* sense or its *physical object* sense, as in (6a) and (6b), respectively.

(6) a. Mary jumped through the window
   b. The window is rotting

Notice that, for Pustejovsky, lexical items encode a vast array of properties about their referents, including how they come into being, their physical properties, their purposes, etc. And different types of information encoded with the lexical item come to the fore in a variety of uses of the item, and communicate different aspects of its referent in the event or state it partakes. If it turns out that computations are sensitive to that level of specificity, there can't be a line between semantics and pragmatics, for computations would have to be sensitive to token utterances, not types. The idiosyncrasies of content (and intention) would have to play a part in determining the meaning of the message.

While the nuances of particular linguistic utterances play a significant role in linguistic communication and social interactions, this view of the semantics–pragmatics divide (or lack thereof) is hardly amenable to investigation. Quine (1953) had already alerted us to the perils of fiddling around with vague notions of meaning, but in particular, that a commitment to analyticity leads to a dead end for semantics.

In this section, I work through some challenging cases aiming to trace the line between semantics and pragmatics. In particular, I attempt to trace the line between context-insensitive (but *co-text* sensitive) expressions yielding propositions, on the semantics side, and largely abductive-inferential processes, on the pragmatics side.

True to the commitments in section 1, my focus will be on the primacy of symbolic computations that might yield a representation of the proposition that a sentence might convey. I will argue from the perspective of the null hypothesis: that compositionality rules, with the meaning of a sentence being composed from its "visible" and its "occluded" surfaces.[11] But the "occluded" surfaces, I will argue, have to be linguistically determined. I have little to say about what happens on the pragmatic side—and that is also why I differ from Lepore and Stone in mood. The phenomena that I examine suggest that for certain constructions there is an early "literal" process of interpretation—the building of propositions faithful to the input. The process is not optimal, for it often produces misparses (as we briefly saw above in the discussion of (1) and (5)) and thus yields wrong propositions corresponding to parsing commitments made along the way. Also true to the PC informally stated in (4), propositions are built over time and often (veridical or not) remain in memory past full sentence interpretation and pragmatic enrichment.

Separating linguistically determined computations from "extra-linguistic" ones is certainly difficult, requiring multiple methods, from linguistic analysis to experimental investigation. It is, as Lepore and Stone say, an empirical issue. So I will start by discussing a fallacy often committed in semantic analysis, but also one that is committed in other cognitive science areas, and I will work from there into other cases.

2.1 Intentional Fallacy and "Sneaky" Semantics

The processes of understanding people's utterances can be a lot like those involved in understanding a piece of literary work, even a poem or the lyrics of a song, with their inevitable appeals to figurative language. Like in a dialogue, such works may seem to carry information about the author's state of mind, social situation, and beliefs. Often times we know the author much like we know our interlocutors—their biographies or purposes—and this content can be confounded with the meaning of the message. But these confounding factors may not affect exclusively those who simply consume a literary piece. Even literary critics fall for them. In their attempt to draw a line between literary criticism and the task of reading authors' intentions, Wimsatt and Beardsley (1946) coined the term "intentional fallacy". They wanted literary criticism to be free of the critic's attempt to read the author's mind—what she might have intended to tell us with this or that jargon or verse. We are, rather, supposed to fend for ourselves, interpret the work as we wish—and so should the critic, for the work should stand on its own without appealing to what Wimsatt and Beardsley called the "author's psychology". Here are some relevant passages, which serve as an analogy with Lepore and Stone's project as well as with my goals presently:

> Intention is design or plan in the author's mind. Intention has obvious affinities for the author's attitude toward his work, the way he felt, what made him write. (p. 469)

---

[11] See, for instance, Gillon (2008) for many cases of potentially "implicit" arguments, as linguistically motivated constituents.

(…) One must ask how a critic expects to get an answer to the question about intention. How is he to find out what the poet tried to do? (p. 469)

(…) Judging a poem is like judging a pudding or a machine. One demands that it works. A poem can *be* only through its meaning—since its medium is words—yet it *is*, simply *is*, in the sense that we have no excuse for inquiring what part is intended or meant. (p. 469)

[The meaning of a poem] is discovered through the semantics and syntax of a poem, through our habitual knowledge of the language, through grammars, dictionaries, and all the literature which is the source of dictionaries, in general through all that makes a language and culture. (p. 477)

We could replace the role of "critic" with that of the listener, and "poet" with speaker, and we would have a similar formula: ultimately, what counts for meaning determination by the listener is the linguistic statement of the speaker, the "habitual knowledge of the language", its grammar and lexical properties ("dictionaries"). But that does not deny that literary works are forms of language *use*, just like many of our utterances in real-world situations are. One can certainly understand a poem in its literal form, but it's best appreciated beyond that, in whatever thoughts one might entertain that are triggered by the actual words and sentences that constitute the poem—that's the very point of a literary work (*le plaisir du texte*, as Roland Barthes put it).

Wimsatt and Beardsley called the critics who committed the fallacy "intentionalists". Authors (and artists in general) are often intentionalists, too, when they "explain" their own work. Goethe, as Wimsatt and Beardsley pointed out, proposed what he thought would be "constructive criticism", which included of course an evaluation of the author's intention and whether or not he succeeded in implementing it in the work. While we are often "intentionalists" in our linguistic exchanges—asking for clarifications, making (warranted or false) assumptions, reading into gestures, movements of the eyes and eyebrows—what we start off with are the sentences of the speaker: there can't be clarifications on what one hasn't evaluated *linguistically*.

The intentional fallacy also makes its way into cognitive science methods. In psychology, it has been called "stimulus error" (see Pylyshyn, 2003), and works like this:[12] the researcher assumes that a stimulus has particular properties—say, that a particular sentence has some postulated semantic material that is taken to determine its interpretation. The researcher in fact *knows* the (intended) meaning of the sentence; she knows the message that it is normally supposed to convey in the real world. Then, she attributes these properties to mental representations. It's a very common mistake to assume that the properties one knows (or believes) to exist in a stimulus are actually mentally represented as such. The fallacy is so widespread that it affects how experiments are carried out, as Pylyshyn has shown with regards to mental imagery, with many experimental results being determined not by the computations that the

---

[12] Although Pylyshyn (2003) refers to work on vision, I am adapting it to research on language.

participant performs on the stimulus properties, but by the knowledge and beliefs that the participant has about the stimulus. It is here that the intentional fallacy of the researcher meets the cognitive penetrability of the experiment (or analysis) she conducts. Shereshevsky's confusions—and Luria's recount—are typical of this situation: even if what Shereshevsky experienced were "vivid images", we cannot assume that these were the underlying culprits of his confusions with literal language—that images are the ultimate forms of mental representations.

Unfortunately, the intentional fallacy permeates work in semantics and, by extension, plays a key role in discussions on where the semantics–pragmatics line should be traced. In semantics, as we saw, the fallacy plays a similar role as that in psychology and involves the postulation of phonologically or syntactically null semantic constituents or analyses that are the product of the knowledge or intention of the semanticist. This *sneaky* semantic strategy, as Cappelen and Lepore (2004) once called it, can be demonstrated in the proposed analyses for sentences such as (7).[13]

(7)   a.   One more can of beer and I'm leaving
      b.   A little water in the face and he goes indoors
      c.   His fists were clenched. A word, and he would lose his temper
      d.   A few days more of this and I'll go mad

For Culicover (1970), the sentences in (7) carry an implicit conditional, which does not account for the actual content of the events, but impose on them a logical relation. Culicover says that these sentences carry "considerable amount of semantic material which is unspecified" (p. 368). The supposedly missing semantic material has scope over the overt nominal in the "antecedent" clause of the implicit conditionals, as in (8) (other examples being parallel to these).

(8)   a.   [If {somebody throws at me / you give me / I see / you drink / I crush / etc.}
            one more can of beer, {then} I'm leaving]
      b.   [If {somebody throws at him / he gets / etc.}
            a little water in the face, {then} he goes indoors]

While it is tempting to take (7a–b) to communicate the content in (8a–b), there is nothing in any of these sentences forcing us to come up with an implicit conditional interpretation; simply put, the first clause does not necessarily work as a logical antecedent of the second clause. One could as well conceive of countless situations that take, say, (7a) to be simply a case of conjunction with temporal order; to wit, its form is *P&Q*, rather then *Q* as a consequence of *P*. Temporal order of conjoined events does not bring about logical implication, even when it appears to be the case that there is logical consequence. Compare (9a) with (9b).

(9)   a.   Mary fell on the sidewalk and hit her head
      b.   Mary hit her head and fell on the sidewalk

---

[13] Examples (7a)–(7b) are from Culicover (1970) and (7c)–(7d) are from Jespersen (1909).

Observe here, again, that the imposed connection between events is simply that of a temporal order, not necessary a *logical* relation between antecedent and consequent. Consider (10).

(10)   a. Mary had a car accident and burned her house
      b. Mary had a car accident and her house burned

How are we supposed to connect the events in (10a)? Are we supposed to attribute the burning of the house to the car accident? To Mary's rage or frustration? While the story we impose on (10a) is of that kind, in (10b) this story needs to be changed, even if the conjoined events are the same as those in (10a):[14] Should we now make up a story about how incredibly unlucky Mary is? If so, this story serves to account for (9) as well, because Mary may have suffered both incidents, falling on the sidewalk and hitting her head many hours apart on an unlucky day.

One way to conceive of sentences in (7) as carrying an implication, while also accounting for the intuitive differences between sentences in (9) and (10), is to assume that '*and*' is ambiguous. Johnson-Laird (1967, 1969) and others[15] have pointed out that '*and*' could be ambiguous between the simple logical conjunction (and_1), a temporal (and_2; or 'and_1 *subsequently*'), and a causal (and_3; or 'and_1 *consequently*') sense. If so, sentences in (7)–(10) would be interpreted according to different senses—say and_3 for (7), and_2 for (9) and (10). But, as Johnson-Laird observes, '*and*' would still need a "setting" to disambiguate between its different senses. And even in cases such as (11a), where '*and then*' is overtly temporal (thus, equivalent to and_2), the conjoined events can be reversed, as in (11b) (examples from Johnson-Laird, 1969).

(11)   a. The man was throwing the stick and then the dog was retrieving it
      b. The dog was retrieving the stick and then the man was throwing it

But clearly other factors are at play in (11). The aspectual, iterative properties of the conjoined events allow for an interpretation in which both events occur independently but linked. If so, there is no need to postulate an ambiguity for '*and*'. It might be the case that we have a univocal '*and*', with the *content* of the conjoined events determining whether they are in temporal, causal, or simple constituency.

While it is possible to conceive of the semantic computations in sentences such as (7) to carry information about an implicit conditional, it does not seem to be the case that their enrichment is linguistically motivated, for they cannot dispense with an evaluation of their content and context. The "considerable semantic material" they require (such as in (8)), as Culicover put it, is not specified either. More likely, we impose on conjoined events a logical structure upon thinking about their possible

---

[14] Notice that the second clause in both sentences may convey different propositions, even if in (10a) the event is causative and, in (10b), inchoative. In (10a) Mary may have burned her housed unintentionally, just as in (9b), but only in (9b) she may not have anything to do with the burning of her house.

[15] According to Johnson-Laird, similar proposals have been around at least since XIX century lexicographers.

relations. Just as the examples in (10) suggest, the relations between events require a background story—one that is not semantic but pragmatic. If we are supposed to count on pragmatics to disambiguate the sentences, then there is no need to postulate an analysis that enriches sentences semantically.

2.2 "Bullshit" Sentences and "Good Enough" Interpretations

There are numerous cases in which pragmatic enrichment may seem to be required, cases for which there is no clear semantic path to the computation of propositions. Let us assume that the language faculty is truly rich in principles that, for most unmarked cases, determine the course of interpretation. A system this rich should be efficient in interpreting "prophetic" or "mystic" sentences following the same principles it deploys in the analysis of more mundane ones. Strictly speaking, the system that computes syntax and that, by hypothesis, computes the meaning of a sentence, should not be the one to judge whether or not a grammatical sentence is good or bad, conveying superficial ideas or deep thoughts. It shouldn't be able to determine whether or not words are being used metaphorically, except when processes of interpretation halt: as when a transitive verb is used intransitively, a pronoun lacks antecedent, a definite noun phrase suddenly appears in discourse, and many other cases that might derail local computations.

The case of metaphors appears to be one for which we have no way of determining interpretation from lower parsing analyses. It appears—as Lepore and Stone (2015) suggest—that appealing to linguistic conventions won't do. In section 2.3, I discuss cases of simple copular metaphors (*My lawyer is a shark, Juliet is the sun*). But before I do that, let's look at sentences that express a juxtaposition of aphorisms, metaphors, analogies, as well as literal statements: cases of so-called "pseudo-profound bullshit" (henceforth, BS), such as the statements in (12) (Pennycook et al., 2015).

(12)   a. Every material particle is a relationship of probability waves in a field of infinite possibilities. You are that.

b. Matter is the experience in consciousness of a deeper non-material reality.

c. Our minds extend across space and time as waves in the ocean of the one mind.

d. We are non-local beings that localize as a dot then inflate to become non-local again. The universe is mirrored in us.

These statements—from the Twitter account of Deepak Chopra—together with others, randomly generated by sites that use similar vocabulary to produce "Chopra-like" statements, were given by Pennycook et al. to a group of subjects to rate for "profoundness" (defined as "of deep meaning; of great and broadly inclusive significance"). These statements were considered on average 55 percent profound (in their 1 to 5 scale, that's 2.77 or in between "somewhat profound" and "fairly profound"). Perhaps unsurprisingly, participants who showed greater BS acceptance were also more religious, had greater propensity to make ontological confusions (e.g., relations between the material and the immaterial world), and were more susceptible to "epistemically suspect" claims (such as the existence of angels).

Clearly, accepting BS as "deep" is related to having the talent to suspend reality or to endorse an "alternative reality". But what is interesting about these examples is that they further the idea that appreciation of BS—perhaps along the lines of several forms of figurative expressions—is a cognitive exercise. However, this exercise seems to be triggered by a failure to interpret what lower-level linguistic computations deliver to higher-level interpretive systems. Crucially, the failure or success in understanding deep BS must rely on some prior form of linguistic analysis. Although Pennycook et al. did not investigate real-time comprehension of BS statements, one can surmise that participants computed the propositions that the statements initially yielded—that, as in (12d), *We are non-local beings*, that *we localize as a dot*, that *we inflate…* etc. This is necessary to obtain the representations that participants did. It is only by computing those propositions—whatever they mean—that participants are then able to elaborate on possible connections with other propositions to make a "profoundness" judgment. It is only by composing the propositions that the expressions yield that participants are free to think whatever they want about the expressions.

The idea that BS sentences might allow for multiple veridical and false interpretations, however, might be challenged by some pervasive effects in the literature, which suggest that rather than "deep", interpretations are superficial. Consider the questions in (13), discussed below.

(13)   a. How many animals of each kind did Moses take on the ark?
        b. What was the nationality of Thomas Edison, inventor of the telephone?

For a question such as (13a), 81 percent of the participants who had the knowledge that the tale was about Noah responded "two" (Erickson & Mattson, 1981). A question such as (13b) produced a weaker but still significant effect (44 percent). While it is possible that this type of error might be due to a misinformation effect, it is clear that subjects composed the meanings of the questions, perhaps not attending to important points about their content. However, this effect—known as the "Moses illusion"—led many to believe that what is going on is a form of "shallow" processing: subjects are not engaging in full compositional process and thus interpret the questions without actually linking the pieces of meaning and grammar with the knowledge of the events that are presupposed.

A more subtle effect of this general illusion can be obtained with simple cases such as the one in (14a).

(14)   a. The dog was bitten by the man
        b. The man was bitten by the dog
        c. The man bit the dog
        d. The dog bit the man

Ferreira and colleagues (e.g., Ferreira, 2003; Christianson et al., 2001) conducted several studies showing that when people are presented with sentences such as (14a), about 25 percent of the time they respond that the "doer" of the action is the dog—an error rate that is much higher than with other sentences such as (14b) or (14c). The theory that Ferreira has been advancing assumes that, for many cases, there is a form of normalization that has its origins not on a full parsing of the sentence but on a superficial one. Ferreira and colleagues term this sort of processing effect "good enough".

However, a recent study by Riven (2017; see also Riven & de Almeida forthcoming a) found that when the task (identifying the "doer" in a sentence such as (14a)) involves a memory load interference (subjects have to keep in mind a series of digits during sentence presentation and response), native-language (L1) speakers of English do better than second-language (L2) English speakers (native speakers of French) performing the same task. Without the memory load interference, L2 speakers do better than L1 speakers. One hypothesis is that L1s make more errors than L2s in the simple version of the task (as in Ferreira's 2003) because L2s rely on explicit, metalinguistic knowledge of sentence properties. Conversely, L1s do better in the task with the memory load interference because they are able to tap into their native, implicit interpretive mechanisms to make a judgment, while L2s' conscious judgments are disrupted by the memory task. What the original task probes, then, is not low-level compositional processes but metalinguistic judgments, which are more prone to interference and, hence, errors. If this is right, the compositional representation stays intact and is not fooled by the "pragmatic normalization" (Fillenbaum, 1974) that might occur in evaluating what the man did to the dog in (14a).

In summary, it is quite possible that compositional representations are fully processed but that inattention or processing bottlenecks might lead to further interpretation errors. This effect might also help us understand acceptance of BS sentences: underlying compositional mechanisms deliver consistent, grammatical compositions of the sentence, which are disrupted by their odd content. These errors of interpretation are not necessarily foreign to what one attains of a sentence (as per PC). False propositions remain in long-term memory, long after a sentence is processed—and so do *un-enriched* propositions, as we will see in 2.4.

2.3 Minimal Metaphors

BS statements represent the extreme case of figurative expressions, requiring more than analogical reasoning to appreciate the intricacies they appear to convey. But they are not far from copular metaphors such as (15) in expressing blatantly false or absurd relations between constituents.

(15) a. Roads are snakes
      b. My lawyer is a shark.

c. Memory is a heap of broken images where the sun beats and the dead tree gives no shelter[16]

In fact, some BS statements such as (12a) and (12b) have the same *x is y* form as those in (15) and could be treated just as a case of metaphor. In contrast with BS statements, however, the metaphor kind I will discuss here is more conventional in expressing a relation between a "topic" (e.g., *lawyer*) and a "vehicle" (*shark*). The question I am interested in is whether there are *linguistic* principles driving metaphorical interpretation and, beyond that, whether there are particular cognitive principles deployed in metaphor appreciation. This is perhaps where I differ from Lepore and Stone's approach in substance rather than just in mood. For them, "there are no linguistic cues and no linguistic reflexes for the insights that the speaker is offering" (p. 164). I will argue, however, that there is, at a minimum, syntactic clues suggesting how a metaphor ought to be interpreted initially. Moreover, I will suggest that there are further variables that affect how the content of a metaphorical expression is explored. The caveat, however, is that the "clues" are fragile and might not be, after all, true conventions in the sense they adopted.

While there is general agreement that lawyers are not sharks, we are far from any agreement on what one does with an expression like (15) during or after its first parse. Some researchers have postulated that interpretation of metaphors might be "direct" (Gibbs & Colston, 2012; Glucksberg, 2003), but this postulation is based mostly on off-line tasks indicating that metaphors don't differ in acceptance time from similarly structured but literal statements. In addition, there is no agreement on how exactly the metaphor produces its effect. Some have assumed that the process of interpretation itself is a process of "domain mapping" (Bowdle & Gentner, 2005) creating analogies, or that it involves novel categorizations (Glucksberg, 2003), or the creation of *ad hoc* concepts (Carston, 2010).

Lepore and Stone (2015) assume that metaphor interpretation is not determined linguistically, but they also seem to agree with a view such as that of Bowdle and Gentner (2005) for whom metaphor interpretation ultimately relies on processes of building analogies between predicates. As Lepore and Stone propose, "speakers and their audiences explore these analogies in open-ended ways" (p. 163). But the building of analogies must rely on content upon which analogies are formed. One could think of sets of inferences that different entities trigger—like meaning postulates (see de Almeida, 1999). But in Bowdle and Gentner's perspective, metaphor interpretation relies on specific mechanisms involving "alignment" between predicates and the "projection" of elements from the vehicle to the topic. Their mapping processes are based, to a large extent, on semantic decomposition: one decomposes the meaning of both topic and vehicle and compares the properties they yield by aligning these properties

---

[16] See Katz et al. (1988) and Roncero & de Almeida (2015) for corpora of metaphors and their semantic properties.

in terms of corresponding predicates. Thus, an expression such as (16a) would yield an interpretation roughly such as (16b), which could be read as in (16c).

(16)   a. Socrates was a midwife

b. [HELP [Socrates [PRODUCE [Student, Idea]]] and [HELP [Midwife [PRODUCE [Mother, Child]]] & [GRADUALLY [DEVELOP [WITHIN [Child, Mother]]]]]].[17]

c. "Socrates did not simply teach his students new ideas but rather helped them realize ideas that had been developing within them all along." (Bowdle & Gentner, 2005, p. 196)

It seems, however, that this is not the kind of analogy Lepore and Stone would want to be committed to—for one, they would have to handle the heavy analytic baggage that Bowdle and Gentner carry. It is important to distinguish the view that metaphors create analogies (perhaps among many other kinds of propositional content) from the view that the *semantic* representation of a metaphorical expression is something like a simile, as in (16).

(17)   a. Roads are like snakes

b. My lawyer is like a shark

c. Memory is like a heap of broken images where the sun beats and the dead tree gives no shelter

Notably, metaphors are not similes (contra Aristotle), for they convey different meanings. For Bowdle and Gentner, metaphors have a career, starting as similes—and, thus, being interpreted, relying on analogies such as in (16)—but later turning into metaphors as their vehicles become more conventionalized.[18] Thus, the more *shark* is used in different expressions to denote some set of figurative properties, the more conventionalized it becomes and the more it occurs in metaphors. But a recent study of written posts on the Internet, suggests that metaphors and similes with the same topic–vehicle pairs (such as (15a) and (17a)) occur with the same frequency. Moreover, these posts use explanations significantly more with similes than with metaphors (*Time is like money—because only retired executives have a lot*) suggesting that they are used to convey ideas that call for a supporting co-text (see Roncero et al., 2016; Roncero, Kennedy, & Smyth, 2006).

These novel interpretive explorations are triggered before the explanations come into place, before the absurdity of a metaphor is detected. We have put forth a possible linguistic difference between metaphors and similes that lines up with the idea that

---

[17] This is my notation capturing their "parallel connectivity" graphs. For simplicity, I omitted other ontological categories such as "instrument", "action", and "object".

[18] The notion of "convention" used by Bowdle and Gentner (2005) is different from the linguistic conventions of Lepore and Stone (2015).

linguistic conventions might be at work in determining the interpretation of a simile or a metaphor expression containing the same topic–vehicle pairs (de Almeida et al., 2011). One hypothesis is that an expression of the form *x is y* is predicative—simply put, that *y* predicates something of *x*, with a form in which *e* (an *entity*) is taken to be the topic to which the predicative type <*e, t*> applies, as in (18a).

(18)   a. *BE (e (<e,t>))*
       b. *BE (LIKE (e (e)))*

This hypothesis requires committing to an ontology of semantic types, something one might not be willing to do. But at a minimum one does not have to resort to type-shifting operations (Partee, 1986) to account for the difference between the two expressions, for the type of internal argument is determined structurally: the predicate determines the nature of its internal argument. Crucially, if one is committed to exhausting linguistic resources before committing to a pragmatic-level interpretation, this view assumes that the interpretation of copular metaphors is linguistically determined and that their computations might be different than those involved in interpretation of similes.

Besides their linguistic differences—their potentially different semantic types (*entity* v. *predicate*)—similes and metaphors also seem to be processed differently in real time. In an eye-tracking study involving similes and metaphors such as those in (15a–b) and (17a–b) (Ashby et al., 2018), we found that metaphors take longer to read at the vehicle position (see Figure 11.1), and that metaphors trigger twice as many regressive saccades towards the vehicle from their accompanying explanations than similes do.

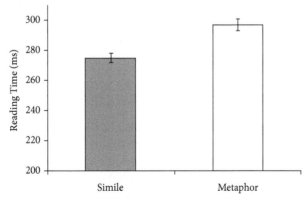

Figure 11.1. Reading times on the vehicles (*shark*) of metaphors (*lawyers are sharks*) and similes (*lawyers are like sharks*) in the study by Ashby et al. (2018, Experiment 1). Bars represent go-past time (total time reading a region before moving to the next one); error bars are standard errors.

These eye-tracking data, together with data from Internet searches and linguistic arguments, seem to indicate that similes are not metaphors. And if they are different linguistic expressions, yielding different types of propositions, interpretive mechanisms that operate on their linguistic outputs might also differ. The key point I am making is that copular metaphor interpretation might be *linguistically determined*—not in all its beauty or absurdity, but minimally in the predicative relation between its arguments, as its form suggests.

In summary, the interpretation of metaphors might rely on an early parsing that promotes the predication of the vehicle to the topic—predicates *sharkness* of lawyers. This is what "syntax" does, allowing for further interpretive mechanisms to elaborate on this predicative relation—perhaps by calling for "properties" (viz., other predicates) that might be related to *shark*. Many of these properties might be driven by what Roncero and colleagues have called "aptness"—how well the predicates computed from a vehicle apply to the topic (see Roncero et al., 2006; Roncero & de Almeida, 2014). The interpretive task might simply rely on that, after the linguistic system has done its job. In the next section, I discuss a case in which semantics produces an unenriched interpretation that lingers, even in strongly biasing utterance contexts.

2.4 Indeterminacy

The final case I would like to discuss is that of sentences such as those in (19).

(19)   a. I finished the chapter
        b. Mary began a book

The phenomenon that these sentences characterize is usually called "coercion", "type-shifting", or "type-coercion" in the semantics literature (see de Swart, 2011, for a review). I will adopt the more neutral term "indeterminacy"[19] because coercion is tied to a particular *hypothesis* on how these sentences might be enriched—namely the hypotheses that complement noun phrases are "coerced" to be interpreted as an event, or "coerced" to provide information about an event that fills-in the sentence interpretation. This is so because, intuitively, these sentences are taken to be interpreted as in (20).

(20)   a. I finished [writing/reading/typing] the chapter
        b. Mary began [writing/reading/reviewing/eating] a book

The phenomenon of interest here is that, even though it is not clear what sort of activity Mary began doing with a book, we seem to assign default enriched semantic representations to this kind of sentence (e.g., reading or writing) amongst several possible—but perhaps less plausible—interpretations (e.g., eating, burning), such as in (20).

This type of sentence has received some attention in the theoretical literature in cognitive science (e.g., Briscoe, Copestake, & Boguraev, 1990; de Almeida & Dwivedi, 2008;

---

[19] Although the label "indeterminate" might be applied, it should be clear that these sentences are fully grammatical and that they allow for a truth judgment (viz., they are true if, say, Mary began doing anything with a book).

de Almeida & Lepore, 2018; Fodor & Lepore, 2002; Pustejovsky, 1995; see also de Swart, 2011, for review). And it has also been the subject of numerous experiments involving a great variety of psycholinguistic techniques and neuroimaging methods (e.g., de Almeida, 2004; de Almeida et al., 2016; Husband, Kelly, & Zhu, 2011; Katsika et al., 2012; McElree et al., 2006; McElree et al., 2001; Pickering, McElree, & Traxler, 2005; Traxler, Pickering, & McElree, 2002; Pylkkänen & McElree, 2007). Given the range of issues involved, I will focus on one particular theoretical issue and limit the discussion of empirical results to one study (see de Almeida et al., 2016, for a recent review).

The key issues under dispute include the nature of semantic composition and the linguistic and cognitive resources involved in resolving (or attempting to resolve) indeterminacy. Perhaps the first to discuss this issue in print was Culicover (1970) who wrote that sentences such as those in (19) contain an "infinite ambiguity" (p. 368) and, similarly to those in (7), require a "considerable amount" of semantic material that is neither overtly expressed in the sentence, nor linguistically (i.e., syntactically) motivated.

In Pustejovsky's (1995) theory, cases such as (19b) typify the context sensitivity of the verb-complement composition: *begin* is supposed to require *book* to provide information about what *begin the book* might be about. This information is supposed to come from what is stored with the lexical entry for the complement noun. As mentioned above, in his theory, nouns carry information such as *roles* or *functions*, how they *come into being*, what they are *made of*, etc.[20] This information enters into the compositional process yielding (20b), given (19b).

While some early experiments have shown processing delays in post-verbal constituents (say, after *began* in (19b)), compared to a "non-coerced" sentence (e.g., *Mary read a book*; see McElree et al., 2001), the nature of this difference has been explained by different theories. Our position—*contra* coercion—is that this type of sentence is indeterminate with regards to the event, and it keeps its "infinite ambiguity" at the linguistic level of analysis. However, its pragmatic enrichment—if any—comes not from lexical decomposition as proposed by Pustejovsky, nor from some form of type-shifting (see Pylkkänen, 2008), but by its own more complex syntactic structure—as in (21) (see de Almeida & Dwivedi, 2008; and de Almeida & Riven, 2012 for linguistic evidence).

(21)   [VP [V⁰ *began* [V⁰ e [OBJ NP]]]]

The proposal is that the syntactically specified "gap" is tagged at logical form (LF) and that it is a "trigger" for pragmatic inferences bearing on the content of the event.

It is the job of the context—or even the *co-text*—to propose information that may help "disambiguate" the sentence. We found evidence for these sentences tapping extra

---

[20] In Pustejovsky's theory these are "quale" structures, which are part of the lexical entry and constitute the basic information about the content of a word and thus how it might vary its contribution to contexts.

processing resources and, crucially, engaging brain areas that are involved in pragmatic processes of conflict resolution (such as the anterior cingulate cortex and temporal structures in the right-hemisphere; see de Almeida et al., 2016).

Finally, there is evidence that these sentences—although possibly enriched past their initial linguistic analysis—yield dual-representations, one proposition that is true to the initial indeterminate token sentence, and one that is enriched over time, with both propositions lingering several seconds after the initial presentation. Evidence for this hypothesis comes from a study in which subjects are presented aurally with long discourse passages such as (22a) preceding a sentence such as (22b) (Riven & de Almeida forthcoming b).

(22) a. Lisa had been looking forward to the new Grisham novel ever since it came out. She had finally managed to set aside some time this weekend and made sure to make her home library nice and cozy. First thing Saturday morning, Lisa curled up on the sofa in her library with a blanket and a fresh cup of coffee. With everything in place,

b. Lisa began the book.

At the offset of the sentence or at about 25 seconds later (with more intervening neutral discourse presented aurally), subjects are presented visually with either the original sentence (22b) or one of two foils, one that is consistent (23a) and another, inconsistent (23b) with the context.

(23) a. Lisa began reading the book
b. Lisa began writing the book

Subjects perform a sentence probe task (responding "yes" if the presented sentence matches the original—in this case, (22b)—or "no" otherwise). Results showed that while at the sentence offset point subjects perform nearly at ceiling, at the delayed probe point (25 seconds later), they reject the inconsistent probe (23b), but accept the consistent probe (23a) at the same rate as they accept the original sentence (22b): that is, both *began the book* and *began reading the book* in context are accepted at the same rate. Moreover, response times show that subjects hesitate much more in accepting the enriched (23a) than they do accepting the original (22b) sentence. We hypothesized that both acceptance rates and longer response times suggest that propositions computed from the original presentation linger and compete with the contextually consistent foil. These results, in fact, are compatible with other studies on memory for sentences (Brewer, 1977; Brewer & Sampaio, 2006), supporting a dual-propositional representation for linguistic material, a true memory and a false one (Reyna et al., 2016).

We take these results further to support the idea that sentences are *not* enriched when they are initially perceived and that they produce propositions that remain encoded, coming to compete in recognition memory with contextually supported but false propositions. It is quite possible that acceptance of the consistent false probe (23a) is warranted by the context and that it is part of what subjects understand of the sentence. But underlying that representation, the true proposition lingers.

3. Coda: Indeterminacy Rules

Just like Shereshevsky's comprehension troubles suggest, when words and sentences deviate from what they actually *mean* it may be difficult to fit them all together. But we don't possess many of Shereshevsky's traits. For one, we always find a way of making sense of what we hear—if not by the workings of the compositional linguistic system alone, by thinking about its products. We make them fit with all the available information at the time of the utterance—a virtually unlimited and unconstrained array of information.

In summary, after all is said and done about linguistic analysis, indeterminacy about what is not resolved early on will rule. It is even possible that there are actual principles—more likely heuristic ones—that take care of what is not clear, or what is considered anomalous, or what is pseudo-profound "BS", "good enough", or indeterminate, because linguistic analyses do not exhaust the thoughts that a sentence might provoke in the listener. What people ponder about utterances draw a lot from context, but no matter how rich or poor the context is, the literal representation lingers.

As the dialogue from *Seinfeld*, in (24), well depicts, reading intentions is not necessarily the only way people interpret utterances: a representation of the literal interpretation is always under consideration, even if all the clues for alternative interpretations suggest otherwise.

(24) George:—She invites me up at 12 o'clock at night for "coffee" ... and I don't go up. "No, thank you, I don't want coffee, it keeps me up. It's too late for me to drink coffee." I said this to her. People this stupid shouldn't be allowed to live. I can't imagine what she must think of me.

Jerry:—She thinks you are a guy that doesn't like coffee.

George:—She invited me up. "Coffee" is not coffee; "coffee" is sex.

Elaine:—Maybe "coffee" was coffee!

George:—"Coffee" is coffee in the morning, not at 12 o'clock at night!

Finally, as we discussed elsewhere (de Almeida & Lepore, 2018) Fodor rightly thought that a semantics committed to lexical decomposition was necessarily holistic—because there is no account of the analytic/synthetic distinction. Alternatively, there is a view of semantics that keeps it tidy within the module: it's a semantics that is atomistic and operates in consonant with lexical-structural properties and syntactic principles. If so, the language faculty is rich indeed, and much of what is deemed pragmatics is already pre-packaged linguistically. Crucially, what it does is to compose meaning—and then there is thinking.[21]

[21] Research for this article was supported by a grant from the National Sciences and Engineering Research Council of Canada (NSERC). I'm grateful to Caitlyn Antal and Linmin Zhang for comments.

References

Ashby, J., Roncero, C., de Almeida, R. G., & Agauas, S. J. (2018). The early processing of metaphors and similes: Evidence from eye-movements. *The Quarterly Journal of Experimental Psychology, 71*(1), 161–8.

Biederman, I. (1987). Recognition-by-components: A theory of human image understanding. *Psychological Review, 94*(2), 115–47.

Biederman, I. (2013). Human object recognition: Appearance vs. shape. In S. J. Dickinson & Z. Pizlo (Eds.), *Shape perception in human and computer vision* (387–97). London: Springer-Verlag.

Bowdle, B. F. & Gentner, D. (2005). The career of metaphor. *Psychological Review, 112*(1), 193–216.

Brewer, W. F. (1977). Memory for the pragmatic implications of sentences. *Memory & Cognition, 5*(6), 673–8.

Brewer, W. F. & Sampaio, C. (2006). Processes leading to confidence and accuracy in sentence recognition: A metamemory approach. *Memory, 14*, 540–52.

Briscoe, T., Copestake, A., & Boguraev, B. (1990). Enjoy the paper: Lexical semantics via lexicology. In *Proceedings of 13th International Conference on Computational Linguistics* (pp. 42–7). Helsinki: Association of Computational Linguistics.

Cacciari, C. & Tabossi, P. (1988). The comprehension of idioms. *Journal of Memory and Language, 27*, 668–83.

Cappelen, H. & Lepore, E. (2004). *Insensitive semantics.* Oxford: Blackwell Publishers.

Carston, R. (2010). Lexical pragmatics, ad hoc concepts and metaphor: A Relevance Theory perspective. *Italian Journal of Linguistics, 22*, 153–80.

Chomsky, N. (2000). *New horizons in the study of language and mind.* Cambridge: Cambridge University Press.

Christianson, K., Hollingworth, A., Halliwell, J. F., & Ferreira, F. (2001). Thematic roles assigned along the garden path linger. *Cognitive Psychology, 42*, 368–407.

Culicover, P. (1970). One more can of beer. *Linguistic Inquiry, 1*(3), 366–9.

de Almeida, R. G. (1999). What do category-specific semantic deficits tells us about the representation of lexical concepts? *Brain and Language, 68*(1), 241–8.

de Almeida, R. G. (2004). The effect of context on the processing of type-shifting verbs. *Brain and Language, 90*, 249–61.

de Almeida, R. G. & Dwivedi, V. (2008). Coercion without lexical decomposition: Type-shifting effects revisited. *Canadian Journal of Linguistics, 53*, 301–26.

de Almeida, R. G. & Lepore, E. (2018). Semantics for a module. In R. G. de Almeida & L. Gleitman (Eds.), *On concepts, modules, and language: Cognitive science at its core* (pp. 113–38). Oxford: Oxford University Press.

de Almeida, R. G. & Manouilidou, C. (2015). The study of verbs in cognitive science. In R. G. de Almeida & C. Manouilidou (Eds.), *Cognitive science perspectives on verb representation and processing* (pp. 3–39). New York: Springer.

de Almeida, R. G. & Riven, L. (2012). Indeterminacy and coercion effects: Minimal representations with pragmatic enrichment. In A. M. DiSciullo (Ed.), *Towards a biolinguistic understanding of grammar* (pp. 277–301). Amsterdam: John Benjamins.

de Almeida, R. G., Manouilidou, C., Roncero, C., & Riven, L. (2011). Three tales of semantic decomposition: Causatives, coercion, and metaphors. In A. I. França & M. Maia (Eds.), *Papers in psycholinguistics* (pp. 172–90). Rio de Janeiro: Imprint.

de Almeida, R. G., Riven, L., Manouilidou, C., Lungu, O., Dwivedi, V., Jarema, G., & Gillon, B. (2016). The neural correlates of indeterminate sentence interpretation: An fMRI study. *Frontiers in Human Neuroscience, 10*, 614. https://doi.org/10.3389/fnhum.2016.00614.

de Swart, H. (2011). Mismatches and coercion. In C. Maienborn, K. von Leusinger, & P. Portner (Eds.), *Semantics: An international handbook of natural language meaning* (pp. 535–74). Berlin: Mouton de Gruyter.

Erickson, T. A. & Mattson, M. E. (1981). From words to meaning: A semantic illusion. *Journal of Verbal Learning and Verbal Behavior, 20*, 540–52.

Ferreira, F. (2003). The misinterpretation of noncanonical sentences. *Cognitive Psychology, 47*, 164–203.

Ferreira, F. & Clifton, C. (1986). The independence of syntactic processing. *Journal of Memory and Language, 25*, 348–68.

Fillenbaum, S. (1974). Pragmatic normalization: Further results for some conjunctive and disjunctive sentences. *Journal of Experimental Psychology, 102*, 574–8.

Fodor, J. A. (1975). *The language of thought*. Cambridge, MA: Harvard University Press.

Fodor, J. A. (1983). *The modularity of mind*. Cambridge, MA: MIT Press.

Fodor, J. A. (2008). *LOT 2: The language of thought revisited*. Oxford: Oxford University Press.

Fodor, J. A. & Lepore, E. (2002). The emptiness of the lexicon: Reflections on Pustejovsky. In J. A. Fodor & E. Lepore, *The compositionality papers* (pp. 89–119). Oxford: Oxford University Press.

Gibbs, R. & Colston, H. (2012). *Interpreting figurative meaning*. New York: Cambridge University Press.

Gillon, B. (2008). On the semantics/pragmatics distinction. *Synthese, 165*, 373–84.

Glucksberg, S. (2003). The psycholinguistics of metaphor. *Trends in Cognitive Science, 7*, 92–6.

Grimshaw, J. B. (2005). *Words and structure*. Stanford, CA: CSLI Publications.

Husband, M. E., Kelly, L. A., & Zhu, D. C. (2011). Using complement coercion to understand the neural basis of semantic composition: Evidence from an fMRI study. *Journal of Cognitive Neuroscience, 23*, 3254–66.

Jespersen, O. (1909). *A modern English grammar on historical principles*. London: Allen and Unwin.

Johnson-Laird, P. N. (1967). Katz on analyticity. *Journal of Linguistics, 3*, 82.

Johnson-Laird, P. N. (1969). '&'. *Journal of Linguistics, 6*, 111–14.

Katsika, A., Braze, D., Deo, A., & Piñango, M. M. (2012). Complement coercion: Distinguishing between type-shifting and pragmatic inferencing. *Mental Lexicon, 7*, 58–76.

Katz, A. N., Paivio, A., Marschark, M., & Clark, J. M. (1988). Norms for 204 literary and 260 nonliterary metaphors on 10 psychological dimensions. *Metaphor and Symbol, 3*, 191–214.

Kintsch, W. (1974). *The representation of meaning in memory*. Hillsdale, NJ: Lawrence Erlbaum Associates.

Lepore, E. & Stone, M. (2015). *Imagination and convention: Distinguishing grammar and inference in language*. Oxford: Oxford University Press.

Luria, A. R. (1968). *The mind of a mnemonist: A little book about a vast memory*. Cambridge, MA: Harvard University Press.

Manouilidou, C., de Almeida, R. G., Schwartz, G., & Nair, N. P. V. (2009). Thematic roles in Alzheimer's disease: Hierarchy violations in psychological predicates. *Journal of Neurolinguistics, 22*, 167–86.

McElree, B., Pylkkänen, L., Pickering, M. J., & Traxler, M. J. (2006). A time course analysis of enriched composition. *Psychonomic Bulletin & Review, 13*(1), 53–9.

McElree, B., Traxler, M. J., Pickering, M. J., Seely, R. E., & Jackendoff, R. (2001). Reading time evidence for enriched composition. *Cognition, 78*, B17–B25.

McKoon, G. & Ratcliff, R. (1992). Inference during reading. *Psychological Review, 99*, 440–66.

McNamara, J. (1978). How can we talk about what we see? Unpublished manuscript. McGill University.

Partee, B. (1986). Noun phrase interpretation and type-shifting principles. Reprinted in B. Partee (2004), *Compositionality in formal semantics* (pp. 203–30). Oxford: Blackwell.

Peissig, J. J. & Tarr, M. J. (2007). Visual object recognition: Do we know more now than we did 20 years ago? *Annual Review of Psychology, 58*, 75–96.

Pelletier, P. H. (2004). The principle of semantic compositionality. In S. Davis & B. Gillon (Eds.), *Semantics: A reader* (pp. 133–56). Oxford: Oxford University Press.

Pennycook, G., Cheyne, J. A., Barr, N., Koehler, D. J., & Fugelsang, J. A. (2015). On the reception and detection of pseudo-profound bullshit. *Judgment and Decision Making, 10*(6), 549–63.

Pickering, M. J., McElree, B., & Traxler, M. J. (2005). The difficulty of coercion: A response to de Almeida. *Brain and Language, 93*, 1–9.

Pustejovsky, J. (1995). *The generative lexicon*. Cambridge, MA: MIT Press.

Pylkkänen, L. (2008). Mismatching meanings in brain and behaviour. *Language and Linguistic Compass, 2*, 712–38.

Pylkkänen, L. & McElree, B. (2007). An MEG study of silent meaning. *Journal of Cognitive Neuroscience, 19*, 1905–21.

Pylyshyn, Z. (2003). *Seeing and visualizing: It's not what you think*. Cambridge, MA: MIT Press.

Pylyshyn, Z. W. (1973). What the mind's eye tells the mind's brain: A critique of mental imagery. *Psychological Bulletin, 80*, 1–24.

Quine, W. V. O. (1953). *From a logical point of view* (2nd ed.). Cambridge, MA: Harvard University Press.

Reyna, V. F., Corbin, J. C., Weldon, R. B., & Brainerd, C. J. (2016). How fuzzy-trace theory predicts true and false memories for words, sentences, and narratives. *Journal of Applied Research in Memory and Cognition, 5*(1), 1–9.

Riven, L. (2017). *The metalinguistic buffer effect: When language comprehension is good but linguistic judgment is only "good enough"*. Unpublished PhD dissertation, Concordia University.

Riven, L. & de Almeida, R. G. (forthcoming a). *Metalinguistic switch-costs drive "good enough" misinterpretations of passives*. Manuscript submitted for publication.

Riven, L. & de Almeida, R. G. (forthcoming b). *Context breeds enriched interpretations of indeterminate sentences*. Manuscript submitted for publication.

Roncero, C. & de Almeida, R. G. (2014). The importance of being apt: Metaphor comprehension in Alzheimer's disease. *Frontiers in Human Neuroscience, 8*. https://doi.org/10.3389/fnhum.2014.00973.

Roncero, C. & de Almeida, R. G. (2015). Semantic properties, aptness, familiarity, conventionality, and interpretive diversity scores for 84 metaphors and similes. *Behavior Research Methods, 47*, 800–12.

Roncero, C., de Almeida, R. G., Martin, D., & de Caro, M. (2016). Aptness predicts metaphor preference in the lab and on the internet. *Metaphor & Symbol, 31*, 31–46.

Roncero, C., Kennedy, J. M., & Smyth, R. (2006). Similes on the Internet have explanations. *Psychonomic Bulletin & Review, 13*(1), 74–7.

Swinney, D., & Cutler, A. (1979). The access and processing of idiomatic expressions. *Journal of Verbal Learning and Verbal Behavior, 18,* 523–34.

Townsend, D. J., & Bever, T. G. (2001). *Sentence comprehension: The integration of habits and rules.* Cambridge, MA: MIT Press.

Traxler, M. J., Pickering, M. H., & McElree, B. (2002). Coercion in sentence processing: Evidence from eye movements and self-paced reading. *Journal of Memory and Language, 47,* 530–47.

Wimsatt, W. K., & Beardsley, M. C. (1946). The intentional fallacy. *The Sewanee Review, 54*(3), 468–88.

12

About Convention and Grammar

Michael Glanzberg

It is commonplace to talk about language in terms of conventions. The rules of grammar that describe each language appear to be conventional, in that it seems to be just convention that the verbs go in one place in English, another in German, and another in Japanese. The meanings of our words, especially, are often called conventional, in that there is nothing intrinsic about the words themselves that makes them mean what they do. Nothing about the sound / 'kæt / itself determines that it picks out cats; rather it appears that the conventions we English speakers use make it do so.

At the same time, a lot of what happens in communication seems not to be conventional at all, but the result of our being rational agents, able to work out what message is being conveyed to us as the conversation proceeds. This is most clear, for instance, in Gricean and neo-Gricean accounts of implicature.

The division of labor between convention and rational inference in language has been much debated over the years. Recently, in an ambitious book, Lepore and Stone (2015) have argued that much more falls on the side of convention than might have been expected, and certainly much more than most pragmatic traditions have supposed.

I largely agree that the scope of linguistic convention is larger than those traditions take it to be. What I am not so sure about is the nature of the conventions at work in language. Though the observations we just made support calling many rules of language 'conventions', I am not so sure they are conventions in the sense that we usually mean in philosophy.

In this essay, I shall explore this issue, following Lepore and Stone's lead. I shall offer a variety of different ways things might appear conventional in language, one of which is in line with their proposal, but two of which are different. Where the common notion of convention, and the one Lepore and Stone prefer, focuses on social aspects of coordination, the other two I shall identify make minimal use of them. I shall then explore in depth one example of a feature of language that has appeared to many not to be conventional at all. Again following Lepore and Stone, the example I shall use is an aspect of information structure, in particular, the notion of topic. I shall review the state of the art in thinking about topic, and argue with Lepore and Stone that the evidence strongly supports a conventional view. But, I shall also argue, it suggests a sort of convention that relies only minimally on social aspects of coordination.

From this example, I shall conclude, with Lepore and Stone, that we can often extend the reach of conventions in language, but that we should be careful about what those conventions are. Not everything that looks conventional in language is the same, and as we expand the scope of convention, we uncover very different sorts of conventions at work in language.

The plan of this essay is as follows. In sections 1 and 2, I shall discuss linguistic conventions, following Lepore and Stone's lead. In section 1, I shall distinguish three different levels of conventionality. In section 2, I shall argue that though Lepore and Stone's arguments for convention can be effective, they do not place phenomena within the levels. The remainder of the essay uses one example to explore how we might place linguistic phenomena within the levels I distinguish. The example, following Lepore and Stone again, is the information-structural notion of topic. I introduce this notion in sections 3 and 4. Section 3 introduces the general notion of information structure and section 4 introduces the particular notion of topic. Sections 5, 6, and 7 make the case for topic being low among the levels of convention. Section 5 reviews the syntax of topic, section 6 reviews the semantics, and section 7 puts the argument together. I return to a specific notion of contrastive topic that is especially relevant to Lepore and Stone's discussion in section 8, and argue that it is at the same level as syntactically distinguished topics. I conclude, briefly, in section 9.

1. Varieties of Convention

I noted above that rules of grammar and associations of sounds with meanings seem conventional. In calling them conventional, we call attention to their arbitrariness. There is nothing intrinsic about the nature of the things in question, phonemic sequences, syntactic items, and so on, that makes the facts turn out the way they do. It thus appears arbitrary that we made / ˈkæt / mean cat and not dog. It looks, in many cases, like we made arbitrary choices about how to speak, and so, we have conventions.

An important line of thinking about convention emphasizes this aspect of arbitrary choice. Of course, not every arbitrary choice is a convention. Which coffee cup I pull out of the cabinet is arbitrary, but not a convention.

What more makes a convention? An influential analysis comes from Lewis (1969). Lewis, as is well known, thinks of conventions as socially determined regularities in behavior that are both arbitrary and self-perpetuating, and offer solutions to recurrent coordination problems (cf. Rescorla 2015). Lewis goes on to offer a game-theoretic analysis of this kind of coordination. For our purposes, the important point, as Lepore and Stone also make clear, is that Lewis's analysis is broadly Gricean in spirit. As they say, it relies on *collaborative intentions*, which involve not only shared intentions, but shared iterated recognition of intentions. This is the hallmark of Grice's (1969) treatment of meaning. As with Grice's notion of meaning, the account of convention focuses on reasoning about what others' intentions are; reasoning which may be implicit, but can in principle be made explicit as ordinary propositional reasoning, and broadly falls under the heading of our rational abilities. Let us call conventions that broadly fit this model *Lewis conventions*.

Lepore and Stone are rightly dissatisfied with the full Lewisian analysis of convention. One point they make is that equilibria in a coordination game—the main payoff of a convention—can arise in other ways. It can be from physical facts or psychological mechanisms. So, if indeed there is a universal grammar that is part of our innate psychological endowment, then many aspects of our coordination in language are determined just by universal grammar, perhaps plus some mechanisms of parameter setting. As I shall discuss more in a moment, this, it is typically argued, requires no input from rationality, propositional knowledge, or anything beyond exposure to an environment that the language faculty is already tuned to automatically extract needed information out of. This is coordination, but no Lewis conventions.

Lepore and Stone make other modifications to the general Lewisian picture. For instance, they focus on the role of the conversational record in semantics. But they retain the core Lewisian idea that conventions are *socially determined* solutions to coordination problems. Semantics is the domain of the special social competence in coordinating on the conversational record (p. 256). Facts of universal grammar may not be socially determined, but they emphasize their role in supporting social conventions. Even with their modifications and revisions, we still have a view that makes socially determined solutions to coordination problems the main focus. Let us call the general family of views that focus on this, *Lewisian conventions*. The family of Lewisian conventions includes those fitting Lewis's own account, and Lepore and Stone's.

Lepore and Stone made the point that something can help to create and sustain a Lewisian convention without being one. Universal grammar provides an example. But here I want to depart from Lepore and Stone's perspective. I think cases like universal grammar have enough important differences to be treated as a separate category.

Let us assume, with Chomsky (1965, 1986, 2000), that we have a distinct language faculty. It provides us with an innate ability to acquire our languages. It is mainly comprised of general principles, which are the principles of *universal grammar* (UG). The obvious variation across the languages we speak results from these principles being parameterized. How those parameters are set determines just what language we speak. It determines where the verbs appear in our sentences, for instance.[1]

There is good reason to think that parameter setting is not like establishing a Lewisian convention. Parameters are often likened to switches, and are simply set to one position or another. With a limited number of parameters and their settings, the child operates in a highly constrained space within which to acquire language. What

---

[1] See Collins (2004) for more on the nature of the language faculty according to Chomskians. I will not try to review the long debate over the status of the language faculty, but see the position statements of Levinson (2003) and Tomasello (2003b) for opposing views.

the child needs to find is simply enough evidence to set the switches one way or another. This is sometimes likened to hypothesis testing.[2]

Though I am not sure we can say this with any great certainty, I doubt parameter setting is much like establishing a Lewisian convention. Perhaps no one claims it is, but I also doubt it is a matter of social competence or coordination in any substantial sense, and so, I doubt it is like a Lewisian convention at all. It is, of course, true that children often wind up speaking a lot like their parents, and a lot like people in their social environments. But they need not. The phenomenon of Creolization makes this vivid. In certain environments, where no language conforming to UG is broadly present, children speak markedly differently than their parents. Though they often partially follow the social environment, they need not, and do not in some cases.[3] Perhaps children want to sound like their parents, and so, perhaps there is a drive to coordinate behind the way they set parameters. Even if there is, the model of limited hypotheses and testing against evidence does not seem to rely on that drive in any substantial way. It only requires that they be disposed to set parameters in response to the facts about language around them.

A further point is that language acquisition starts very early, while the kind of reasoning that, even if implicit, goes into a full Lewisian convention may well emerge later. At least, there is some evidence that Gricean reasoning emerges later. Particularly, children up to around age 5 seem to have trouble with scalar implicatures (Foppolo et al. 2012; Noveck 2001; Papafragou & Musolino 2003). Much of grammar has emerged before that. By 3–4 years, children have a number of parameters set. This makes it at least questionable if anything like Gricean reasoning, which goes into genuine Lewisian conventions, is available for much of parameter setting.

I am not sure how strong a claim can be made here, but let us consider the following. The principles and parameters model of UG opens the possibility that parameter setting is not a matter of establishing social coordination, and not rely on the kinds of abilities we use to do that generally. It may be social in a limited sense of responding to the social world, but may not be a matter of social coordination in any way.[4]

I do not think Lepore and Stone would disagree with any of that. But I want to highlight that it means that placing something about language in the broad category of Lewisian conventions, and noting they can be supported by UG, misses a distinction. It may be that they are the result of substantial Lewisian convention establishment, or a very different process of parameter setting. I shall try to track this difference as we proceed.

Another reason the distinction is important is it engages important questions about the scope of UG itself. Lepore and Stone often describe their project as extending the understood scope of *grammar*. This can sometimes be understood as just another term

---

[2] For an overview of some of these ideas, see Crain and Thornton (1998) or Guasti (2002).

[3] See the nice overview in Pinker (1994).

[4] Again, I shall not try to review the long controversy about how grammar is acquired, but for a very different view than the one I have been discussing here, see Tomasello (2003a).

for convention, but it can mean more. It can mean the results of UG and parameter setting. Where and when we find that is an interesting question in its own right, and should not be overlooked as we explore the conventional aspects of language. Keeping parameter setting and Lewisian conventions separate helps us to do that.

When thinking about UG, we should note that it suggests an austere conception of grammar. It includes, presumably, the facts about syntax, morphology, and phonology. How much more is disputed. Chomsky himself thinks it includes no semantics (beyond logical form), though others disagree (e.g. Chomsky 2000; Pietroski 2005; with dissent from Larson & Segal 1995). The austere view is compatible with minimalist thinking about syntax, and the much-quoted remark that the language faculty is an "abstract linguistic computational system" which provides a "narrow syntax" whose core property is recursion, enabling it to generate an infinite set of expressions from a finite basis (Hauser et al. 2002 p. 1571). Not everyone takes as austere an approach as Chomsky, and the notion of core or narrow syntax is disputed. But finding something to be a matter of syntax proper is a stronger result than finding it to be broadly conventional, as it places the phenomenon nearer to this austere notion.[5]

As I just noted, it is disputed where semantics fits into the UG picture. But we should pause to note that it is a reasonable hypothesis that enjoys substantial support that the meanings of functional elements could be part of UG. These include tense, determiners (quantifiers), aspect, mood, and so on. We find, with these, a limited range of abstract meanings, which form closed classes, and we find some universals pertaining to these classes. Though it is not an area of consensus, we should also keep in mind the possibility that these aspects of meaning arise from the UG plus parameter setting part of language.[6]

So far, I have emphasized a distinction among the sorts of conventions of grammar to which Lepore and Stone draw our attention. There is an important distinction between genuine Lewisian conventions and results of parameter setting (which may indeed support Lewisian conventions). There is a further distinction I think it is also useful to draw. We observed above that word meaning appears to be conventional. In contrast to the way syntax is acquired on the UG model, the lexicon is genuinely learned, and is usually seen as the home of idiosyncrasy and non-parametric variation in language. This seems to be a likely place to find Lewisian conventions. I shall grant that there are some, but I shall also argue that word learning can present another kind of non-Lewisian conventional or learned status.

In particular, I shall suggest that it looks reasonable to suppose that early word learning is not like establishing Lewisian conventions. I put this point cautiously, as it is disputed, and how we learn our first words is an active area of research. But there is enough evidence to make this possibility one we should take seriously.

---

[5] For a nice discussion of how this austere notion bears on the semantics/pragmatics distinction, see Collins (2007).

[6] I have discussed this in Glanzberg (2014). See the references there, but especially von Fintel and Matthewson (2008).

Let me start with a quick overview of some (amazing!) facts about early word learning. Infants begin word learning quite early. They can differentiate words in speech by about 6 months, and by 12 months are distinguishing words by grammatical category. Also around 12 months, they are acquiring word meanings, often words for body parts. They tend to acquire nouns and link them to categories around 14 months. Around 2 years old, they are sensitive to the transitive/intransitive distinction for verbs, and track the causal meaning of transitives. Children are able to learn word meanings very easily, with very few repetitions of information pairing words to meanings. They may be able to do so with just one exposure (one-trial learning). They can pair words with objects even if there are multiple objects to which a word can refer, and in a messy environment with many words being uttered and many objects in view.[7]

There are several ideas to be found in the literature about how such learning happens. One is that children operate using a hypothesis-testing process, as is posited for parameter setting. But, the task is quite different. Learners represent possible word-meaning mappings, and test them against experiential input. The input is 'noisy', including lots of speech, multiple objects and so on. With this information, they need to form hypotheses about what, for instance, a noun picks out in the environment (e.g. Bloom 2000; Carey 1978; Markman 1990; Waxman & Gelman 2009). It has been argued that this is possible because of a range of constraints children bring to the word learning task (e.g. Golinkoff et al. 1994; Waxman & Markow 1995). For instance, it has been argued that there is a mutual exclusivity constraint: if an object has a name, it should not get another one. These principles are often argued to be innate, and domain specific.

Another very different idea is that early word learning is associative (e.g. Frank et al. 2009; McMurray et al. 2012; Smith et al. 2014; Xu & Tenenbaum 2007; Yu & Smith 2012). The idea is that children are able to 'do statistics' (recognize statistical patterns) on co-occurrences of words with objects. They look at this cross-situationally, and so work with many occurrences of words and objects, and statistically infer word–object mappings. Increasing, evidence suggests that even young children have powerful associationist mechanisms that can compute these kinds of statistics.

Is early word learning like either of our two other cases: parameter setting and Lewisian convention? It is almost certainly not like parameter setting. The operation of pairing an arbitrary word with a meaning is just a different task than setting a specific parameter provided by UG. The idiosyncrasy of the lexicon, and lack of lexical universals not traced back to grammar, attests to this. First words and beginnings of grammar do develop together, but I think it is safe to assume parameter setting and early word learning are different.

How much is early word learning like Lewisian convention? Here, I think the situation is not clear, but there is reason to think they are different. Most strikingly, the kinds of statistical models Smith and her colleagues have offered are not at all like

---

[7] For overviews of these and other facts, see Guasti (2002) and Waxman and Lidz (2006).

solving coordination problems. The same, I think, can be said for the hypothesis-testing models, which require only evidence of word-referent correlation, not coordination. Likewise, we already saw that, where we can identify emergence of Gricean reasoning, it appears to emerge much later than early words. It is also a standard view that children up until around age 4 do not pass the false belief task, which is taken to be evidence they lack a theory of mind. This consensus has been changing in recent years, but it remains at least unclear if a theory of mind is present when first words are learned.[8]

At the same time, the situation is complicated. First, we do see some signs of intention recognition at the same time as children start to learn words. Children can follow gaze and gesture around 9–10 months, for instance, and are more likely to name objects people are attending to (cf. Waxman & Lidz 2006). There is evidence that at 12 months, infants are showing some understanding of others as intentional agents (Tomasello & Haberl 2003). We may thus wonder if in some way, the child is trying to guess what the speaker intends the referent of a word to be. But, in contrast, it also appears that fixed features of the infant's visual field are central to determining how they assign referents to words (Pereira et al. 2014), which seems not to involve thinking about other agents. I think the conclusion we should draw is that, if anything like social coordination is involved in first word learning, it is likely of a highly attenuated form, where limited input from still nascent understanding of intentions is all that might be at work. I am doubtful this will look much like the coordination that is involved in forming a Lewisian convention.

We have now seen two distinct phenomena of language acquisition—two ways knowledge of language can be acquired: parameter setting and the mechanisms of first word learning. I have argued that these seem markedly different from establishing Lewisian conventions. In particular, I suggested parameter setting seems radically different from establishing conventions, while early word learning seems at best to rely on intention recognition and social coordination in highly attenuated ways. We certainly have distinct phenomena here, and I think it is likely that they are far from the broadly Gricean picture of Lewisian conventions (though they can support the creation of Lewisian conventions, of course).

I am not claiming there is no room for full Lewisian conventions in our knowledge of language. I think there is. Here is one plausible candidate: technical terms learned by adults. Take, for instance:

(1)   Zorn's Lemma

This is the name of a widely used mathematical result. The name is useful as it allows us to refer to the result easily. It is, in a way, misleading if you take it at face value, as you might think it is referring to the lemma first proved by Zorn. The common wisdom is that this is not true; the lemma was first proved by either Kuratowski or Tukey (if the common wisdom is right). We call it Zorn's Lemma because somehow that got

---

[8] A classic reference is Wimmer and Perner (1983). For more recent developments, see, for example, Onishi and Baillargeon (2005) or Scott et al. (2010).

established, and it serves our needs of coordination. Likely enough, this is just a Lewis convention in a signaling game.

So, as I said, I think we have three distinct ways we can get rules of language in place. I should add that we might expect a lot in between first words, which I have suggested might be learned with at best a limited role for social coordination, and full Lewisian conventions. As speakers' understanding of intentions and their social skills at coordinating develop, we might expect them to use those skills more and more in word learning. Much word leaning happens before we have clear evidence of the scope of those skills, so this is conjecture, but it is a reasonable possibility.

We thus have three phenomena, which indicate three sources of rules of language, which contribute to our general linguistic competence. Though it is fair to call them all 'conventions' in a loose sense, I have argued the first two are (probably) not like Lewisian conventions.

We thus have something like:

(2)   **Level 1:** Parameter setting.

⇓

Level 2: Learning of first words.

⇓

Continuous development?

⇓

Level 3: Lewisian conventions.

Tradition puts grammar proper, especially on austere views of it, at level 1, but levels 1 and 2 are involved in the regular acquisition of language. All three levels can provide knowledge of language, and so contribute to linguistic competence. I have added level labels to the distinct phenomena we have looked at to mark that we might well expect families of phenomena to group around those levels, but I shall continue to focus on the specific phenomena that we have used to distinguish the levels. I shall continue to loosely talk about 'conventionality' to cover all three levels, and use the level numbers when I wish to distinguish among them.

2. Arguments for Conventionality

Lepore and Stone offer an array of arguments for the conventionality of aspects of language that have often been seen as non-conventional matters of inference. As I said, I largely agree. They also often conclude that conventionality indicates some phenomenon is part of grammar, in a broad sense of grammar rather than the austere one we examined above. Again, I agree.

This way of classifying misses the distinctions that our three levels of 'conventional' status provide. As I argued above, there is interest in understanding the sources of conventions these levels distinguish, and consequences from placing something at a particular level.

The strategy of arguing in favor of conventionality Lepore and Stone typically adopt does not help to distinguish the levels, and was not really supposed to. Typically, Lepore and Stone argue for conventionality by way of the following sorts of considerations. Independence from truth conditional content (Gricean detachability) points to conventional status, as it indicates something cannot be derived from the content of an utterance by general principles. Cross-linguistic differences can show the arbitrariness of some phenomenon, and also show that it is not derived by inference. Precision of meaning can also matter, as we would not expect inferred content to be as precise as that conventionally encoded.

These sorts of arguments are good, as far as they go, but it is easy to see that they do not distinguish the various levels. Any of them, from full Lewisian conventions down to parameter setting, can produce all of these effects. With that in mind, I want to explore how we might place a phenomenon more finely within the levels. I shall use as an example one that Lepore and Stone discuss: information structure. I shall illustrate, with this example, how, if we are careful with the data, and take cross-linguistic evidence into account, we can go further than the argument for conventionality, and make some reasonable hypotheses about where in the levels something falls. More specifically, I shall argue that one information-structural phenomenon is not likely at level 3, and is plausibly at level 1.

3. Information Structure

In the following sections, I shall provide this illustration by looking at some of the details of the information-structural notion of *topic*. I shall broadly agree with Lepore and Stone that it is conventional, but as I said, I shall argue a case can be made for its being low on our scale of levels. To show this, I shall review a range of current work on topics—though, I shall not offer any new data here. My claim is that the currently available data and theories make a reasonable case for placing the topic at low levels, and plausibly at level 1.

Let me first introduce the general notion of information structure. Information structure is a good place to study the range of conventions in language, as it stands at the intersection of not just semantics and pragmatics, but syntax and phonology as well. It is an area where virtually all of language comes together.

The label 'information structure' indicates an area broadly concerned with how the information conveyed in an utterance is packaged. Some of it is old information, some is new, some anchors the utterance in the discourse, some indicates where the discourse should go, and so on.[9]

In English, information structure is typically marked by what linguists call *pitch accents* or simply *accents*. Accents are points of intonational prominence, usually local maxima or minima or distinct contours in the pitch level of an uttered sentence. It is sometimes, less formally, called *stress* (though most phonologists see stress as technically

---

[9] The term 'information structure' goes back to Halliday (1967). A related term 'information packaging' is due to Chafe (1976). Related notions were discussed at length by the Prague school. See the overview in Hajičová et al. (1998).

something different). We will need to keep track of different 'tunes' that accent can produce, but for the most part, thinking of it as stress will be harmless. We often mark accents with capital letters. For instance, *Greek* is accented in:

(3)   He spoke GREEK.

The natural reading here is that speaking Greek, as opposed to Latin, is new information.

It is a tempting idea that accent simply accomplishes a kind of phonological 'pointing', that highlights some part of a sentence. This makes information structure pragmatic in a strong sense: it is just what can be inferred from an unconstrained choice of 'pointing' that comes with an utterance. Such a view is suggested by Sperber and Wilson (1986 p. 203), who explicitly call it a "vocal equivalent of pointing." The same idea is echoed in the title of Bolinger (1972), "Accent is predictable (if you're a mind reader)." Bolinger goes on to talk about "emotional highlighting" (p. 644), which seems much like Sperber and Wilson's pointing.[10]

In contrast, Lepore and Stone argue that information structure is determined by linguistic conventions. I have already said that I agree. However natural and appealing the 'pointing' view may be, the accumulated evidence over recent years makes a strong case for Lepore and Stone's conclusion. I shall get to my main example of how we can go further on this matter than the argument for conventionality allows in a moment, but first, let me make a few comments about our general understanding of the marking of information structure in English, and how it supports a Lepore and Stone-style argument for conventionality.

First, I noted that information structure is typically marked in English by accent. This is clear, for instance, in the distinctive accent that goes with the new information that comprises an answer to a question, as in:

(4)   a. What language did Cicero speak?
       b. He spoke GREEK.

(Shakespeare managed to provide a more scintillating version of this dialog.) This is the typical accent that marks what is called *focus*.

Not surprisingly, accent is complicated. Pitch accents are not all there is to intonational tunes. They come together with other elements that make up intonational phrases. Whether it is the whole phrase or just the pitch accent that marks information structure is disputed. And moreover, pitch accent is a strong correlate of perceived prominence, but not the only feature that leads to judgments of intonational prominence. But with all that said, at the level of detail we are working with here, we can usually use pitch accent as a guide to the marking of information structure.[11]

It is a striking fact about English, German, and other languages that they use specific intonation patterns to mark the semantic and pragmatic functions of information

---

[10] Bolinger's work involves the detailed study of pitch accents. His real interest in this paper is to argue that accent placement cannot be predicted by grammatical—syntactic or phonological—rules.

[11] For some surveys of relevant aspects of phonology, see Büring (2016b), Kadmon (2001), Ladd (1996), and Pierrehumbert and Hirschberg (1990).

structure. But it is more striking how restricted these languages are in the ways they use intonation. Languages like English make use of a highly restricted range of pitch accents: six according to Beckman and Pierrehumbert (1986). Standard systems for describing intonational phrases also make places for an additional two boundary tones and two phrase accents, and many systems add a few more elements. But we have a highly limited stock of building blocks for linguistically relevant tunes, leading to something around 22 tunes that are used. Most of these have clearly distinguished meanings, usually pertaining to information structure, as Pierrehumbert and Hirschberg (1990) discuss. Among the many possible tunes we can form (say, if we are singing), just these are recognized and used by our language.

This gives us an immediate argument, in Lepore and Stone style, for the conventional status of intonational meaning. A small range among the vastly many acoustic differences among utterances have been selected and given specific, but arbitrary meanings. That is the mark of convention. Moreover, we can see substantial variation in how information structure is marked cross-linguistically, as I shall explore more in a moment. The arbitrariness of the way topic and other features of information structure are marked again indicates convention. But as we already noted, this kind of argument does not tell us at what level the conventions fall.

One more general point about the marking of information structure in English is relevant to the general argument for conventionality, and will be important to bear in mind as we go forward. It is a standard view in the study of information structure that the intonational marking realizes a syntactic feature (F when focus is in question). These are ordinary syntactic features, on a par with what distinguishes nouns from verbs, plurals from singulars, nominative from accusative case, and so on. They are interpretable (like gender, number, etc.), but still syntactic. Let me mention a few of the many reasons this is the standard assumption. One is that there are clear relations between accent placement and syntax. As Selkirk (1995) observed, there is a preference for a phrase to be marked by an accent on its internal argument, and not its head:

(5)   a. What did John do?
      b. John drank BEER.

This is entirely felicitous. However, the question–answer congruence indicates that the focus is the verb phrase *drank beer*, while the perceived prominence is on *beer*.[12]

There are a number of other reasons. One is the much-discussed phenomenon of 'second occurrence focus', where semantically a focus is present, but no pitch accent is recognized (Beaver & Clark 2008; Beaver et al. 2007; Partee 1991). Also, it is an old observation that focus seems able to affect grammaticality (Jackendoff 1972). And more recently, important connections between focus and ellipsis have been explored (Merchant 2001; Rooth 1992). A number of authors have noted the role of information

---

[12] This is the phenomenon usually called focus projection. Theories have changed since Selkirk's seminal work, due to the influence of Schwarzschild (1999). For overviews, see Beaver and Clark (2008), Büring (2016b), or Kadmon (2001).

structure in the syntax of copular clauses (e.g. Heycock & Kroch 2002). The persistent connections between syntax, focus and other elements of information structure, and accent placement make a general case that there are syntactic features realized by accents serving information-structural functions. Finally, there are big-picture reasons. Many models of how syntax relates to semantics and phonology hold that semantics and phonology cannot see each other, and so there must be features in the syntax, before phonology and semantics split, that can affect both. Altogether, these pieces of evidence, and others, have led to the standard assumption that information structure is marked in syntax and realized in some languages by accent.

Important at this is, it does not by itself give us any reason to place information structure any more finely in the levels. Merely having something in syntax, and some-thing in meaning associated with it, tells us little. It is compatible with full Lewisian convention. After all, our example of a Lewisian convention is associating a meaning with a word. A word certainly has a morphosyntactic reflex, as there is a lexical entry for it, with all its features. That is what is associated with a meaning. Likewise, early word learners already individuate words, so level 2 is also associating meaning with syntax. Level one is mostly about the syntax, but if we count the meanings of functional expressions as level 1 too, then we can just as well see information structure as part of level 1 (I think we should!). Thus, we have an argument for conventionality, and a link to syntax, but that is not enough to place information structure at any particular level.

Even so, the robust role of syntax in information structure is at least a clue that maybe it can be placed at lower levels. To explore this, we must turn to a more detailed examination of one element of information structure.

4. Topics

The element I shall explore is the notion of *topic*, sometimes called *theme*. This notion often pairs with the notion of *focus*, and in English, is typically marked by a distinctive pitch accent.[13]

The clearest instance of topic in English is what is now often called *contrastive topic*. It is illustrated by the following sort of example (Büring 1999, example 15):

(6)   What did the pop stars wear?
      a. [The FEMALE pop stars]$_{CT}$ wore [CAFTANS]$_F$
      b. #[The FEMALE pop stars]$_F$ wore [CAFTANS]$_{CT}$

Notice that to felicitously utter (6a), a specific intonation pattern is required. The initial DP *the female pop stars* requires a distinct kind of 'fall-rise' tune, while the final *caftans* has a high tone, and then falls.

---

[13] The term 'theme' is used by Daneš (1968), Firbas (1964), and Halliday (1967), and is picked up by Steedman (1991). I am not sure who started the use of 'topic'. It appears in Reinhart (1981). The corresponding term 'focus' is discussed by Halliday (1967) as well, and is extensively discussed by Jackendoff (1972) build-ing on Chomsky (1971).

To fill in just a little more detail, the tune on *the female pop stars* is what Jackendoff (1972) following Bolinger (1958) called the B-accent, and the one on *caftans* is the A-accent. These are typically associated with an L + H* and H* pitch accent,[14] respectively. I already mentioned that the associations of pitch accent to information structure are complicated, but nonetheless, there are intonational markings that speakers perceive, and perceive differently, in the A and B patterns.[15] The A or H* marking indicates new information answering the question asked. This typically indicates *focus*. The B or L + H* marking indicates *aboutness*: the claim is about the female pop stars. But contrastive topic marks aboutness in a complex way. It is what the sentence is about, but also further specifying something about the topic the question set. Hence, in the case above, it marks a move from pop stars to female pop stars.

In keeping with observations from section 3, and following Büring (1999, 2003), I assumed that there is a syntactic feature CT on topic phrases. And, as we saw there, there is an immediate argument for conventionality of the meaning of this feature. But, as we also saw there, this argument does not fix at what level the convention falls. There is a weak argument to be made for an effect from level 1. The syntactic marking of topic (and focus) seems to be something we are only implicitly aware of. Hence, it is hard to see how the mechanisms of Lewisian convention, or word learning, could be brought to bear. This is weak, as of course we are aware of the intonational marking of information structure. So, even if the syntax-phonology mapping is driven by level 1 conventions, the status of the meanings attached to intonation remains undecided.

Even so, we have a hint of a level 1 effect, and I believe there is more we can say to make a case for level 1. To do that, we need to examine the notion of topic, and especially its relation to syntax, more closely.

5. The Syntax of Topic

Many languages mark kinds of topics in purely syntactic ways. To think about the status of topic as conventional, we should pause to note some examples of how that happens.

One comment first. The differences between topic generally and contrastive topic in particular are subtle, as are many information-structural phenomena. This is especially so as we look cross-linguistically. I shall try to keep track of these differences as we go. The first subject we will explore is topic in languages that mark it clearly syntactically. We will ask later how closely this relates to contrastive topic marked intonationally in English.

---

[14] This way of representing accents follows Pierrehumbert (1980), Beckman and Pierrehumbert (1986), and others. See Ladd (1996) for an extensive overview. L marks a low tone, and H a high tone, while the * indicates the tone is aligned with a stressed syllable.

[15] See, among many sources, Büring (2003), Kadmon (2001), Pierrehumbert and Hirschberg (1990), Steedman (1991, 2000), and Vallduví and Zacharski (1994).

It has become quite common to see distinct syntactic positions glossed as topic positions. In many languages, these positions play an important role in word order and other overt syntactic phenomena. I shall discuss two influential cases for such positions, in Hungarian and Italian, and I shall briefly review the case for a topic position in English as well. This barely touches upon the range of languages for which topic positions have been proposed, which also includes Gungbe (e.g. Aboh 2004), Japanese (e.g. Watanabe 2003), Korean (e.g. Choe 1995), and Modern Greek (e.g. Tsimpli 1995), among many others. Yet, the cases of Hungarian and Italian are good representatives of the highly developed views in the current literature, and they will lead naturally to a brief discussion of English.

5.1 Hungarian

The idea that there are distinguished syntactic positions for the information-structural elements of topic and focus has been an important idea in Hungarian linguistics. A great deal of work on Hungarian identifies a pre-verbal focus position which, following Brody (1990), is frequently analyzed as a FocP (Focus Phrase) position. For our purposes, the important fact is that Hungarian also displays a fixed pre-verbal topic position, often analyzed as TopP (Topic Phrase). So, the analysis holds, there is a functional projection for topic; or more simply, there is a full syntactic position for topic, obeying the same rules as other syntactic positions. I shall present a few facts about the topic position, and its analysis as TopP. My presentation will follow that of É. Kiss (2002).[16]

Hungarian word order facts distinguish a pre-verbal syntactic position, that is often analyzed as a topic position. It is generally assumed that phrases occupy this position after moving from a position inside the vP. Frequently DPs are topics, but PPs and some APs can also occupy topic positions. Following É. Kiss (2002 ch. 2, example 10), we have:

(7)

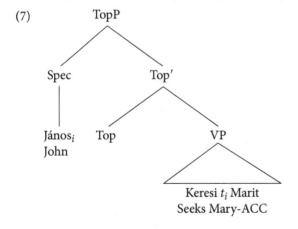

---

[16] Among many other references, see É. Kiss (1998, 2007), Puskás (2000), and Szabolcsi (1981, 1997); but see Surányi (2004) for a dissenting view.

According to É. Kiss (2002), topic movement is an A'-movement, but the exact nature of the movement will not matter to us here. All that we will suppose is that a topicalized phrase originates in the predicate, and moves to topic position somehow. Topic is different from the argument positions assigned by a verb, as subjects and objects can both be topicalized.

We can see the topic position as partitioning a sentence into a topic-predicate structure (also sometimes called a topic–comment structure). The predicate, or more properly, the complement of Top^0, is robustly individuated in Hungarian. The main stress of the sentence falls on the first constituent of the predicate. The topic indicates what the sentence is *about* (hence its being called a topic). The predicate functions to comment on what the sentence is about.

There are a number of important features of the topic position, that is, the specifier of TopP itself. Still following É. Kiss (2002), we can observe that it requires a DP that is both referential and specific (i.e. the position carries features [+referential] and [+specific]). The referential requirement reflects the fact that for the most part, quantifiers cannot be topics (É. Kiss 2002, ch. 2, example 4):

(8)   a. *[$_{Topic}$ Kik][$_{Predicate}$ meg   védték   a várant   a törökök
            who-PL   VM   defended   the fort-ACC   the Turks
         ellen]?
         against
         'Who defended the fort against the Turks?'

      b. *[$_{Topic}$ Kevés várant] [$_{Predicate}$ meg   védtéka   a zsoldosok
            few fort-ACC   VM   defended   the mercenaries
         a törökök   ellen]
         the Turks   against
         'Few forts were defended against the Turks by the mercenaries.'

The specificity requirement reflects the fact that in some cases, indefinites can be topics, if they are given an appropriate specific reading (É. Kiss 2002, ch. 2, example 5c):

(9)   [$_{Topic}$ Egy autó] [$_{Predicate}$ meg állt a házunk előtt]
      'One of the cars has stopped in front of our house.'

The topicalized *egy autó* is understood as specific, in that it picks out a car that is already familiar in the discourse, even if it is an indefinite. É. Kiss (2002) glosses this as specificity in the sense of Enç (1991), which in turn is spelled out generally in terms of the novelty and familiarity conditions of Heim (1982). But the main idea is simple enough: specifics (including specific indefinites) pick out something or things that are already appropriately salient in the discourse, and so, something that is *familiar* in Heim's sense. But unlike definites, specifics need not function as if they were anaphoric on an already identified familiar discourse referent. It is sufficient for specificity that an identifiable familiar referent be available. Hence, specifics are subject to a somewhat modified form of familiarity. In this way, specificity is close to, but not the same as, definiteness. In virtue of moving to a topic position, specific DPs (including specific indefinites) effectively take wide scope (cf. Szabolcsi 1997), but as they are already functioning to pick out some individuals, they are not really functioning as scope-taking operators to begin with.

There are a number of ways in which the requirements of referentiality and specificity need to be treated with care. In addition to issues of specific indefinites, generics can be topicalized when they are understood as referring to kinds. Contrastive topics allow a surprising range of topicalized elements, including some universal quantifiers. According to É. Kiss (2002) following Szabolcsi (1983), when they do so, they function to pick out a set or property, and so basically function as [+referential] and [+specific].

There are a few other properties of the topic position in Hungarian we should note. It is recursive, and so a sentence can have multiple topics (in contrast to the focus position, which is not). Not every sentence in Hungarian needs to have a topic. Among those that do not, again following É. Kiss (2002, ch. 2, examples 13a,b), are those expressing general existence, or creation, or arrival, such as:

(10)   a. Van   elég   pénz.
          is   enough   money
          'There is enough money.'

       b. Született   egy   gyerek.
          was.born   a   child
          'A child was born.'

These constructions reveal something akin to well-known indefiniteness effects; but for our purposes, we can rest with the observation that they do not have topic constituents. Topic-predicate articulation appears to be widespread but optional (in overt syntax) in Hungarian.

I have very briefly reviewed some facts about Hungarian, following work of É. Kiss (2002). I have done so to illustrate the way a notion of topic can appear in syntax. It appears there is a well-defined position in the syntax of Hungarian, which has here been analyzed as the Specifier of TopP. We see this position in the overt syntax of Hungarian, and do not need to appeal to semantic properties of topichood to identify it. Even so, it does have some fairly clear semantic features, which were glossed as [+referential] and [+specific]. The syntactic partition into topic and predicate provides a predication structure, and the topic is understood as the 'logical subject of predication' (É. Kiss 2002, 2007) and as what the sentence is *about*. Aboutness, as we will discuss in a moment, is the key information-structural aspect of topic. Thus, Hungarian shows us that the information-structural notion of topic can be linked not just to a feature, but to a full syntactic projection.

5.2 Italian

Another language that has been argued to reveal a distinguished topic position in overt syntax is Italian, and more generally Romance languages. Following work of Cinque (1990), Rizzi (1997) argues that a topic–comment structure is displayed by the *clitic left dislocation* (CLLD) construction in Italian and other Romance languages. I shall briefly review Rizzi's conclusions, and note that they are strikingly in line with the facts about Hungarian.[17]

In the CLLD construction, Rizzi argues that the left dislocated phrase occupies Spec of TopP, much as we saw in Hungarian (Rizzi 1997, example 3):

(11)

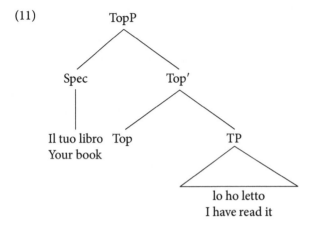

(I have elided some of the peripheral structure Rizzi proposes.) The clitic *lo* helps to distinguish this construction from a related focus-fronting construction. In the focus construction, the fronted constituent bears a pitch accent, and the clitic is not allowed. Left dislocation of topics from object position requires the clitic, while apparently it is optional with topicalized subjects.

So far, we have a specifier of TopP position, which forms a 'high' subject of predication position to which DPs can move, much as we saw with Hungarian. Also as with Hungarian, quantifiers cannot be topicalized in CLLD, except in extraordinary circumstances. Rizzi (1997, example 19b) notes:

(12)   *Tutto, lo ho fatto.
       'Everything, I did it.'

Rizzi also notes the lack of weak crossover effects with CLLD, which is a mark of lack of quantificational force. This is consistent with the observations in Hungarian that though we might have an A′-movement, topic is not quantificational, and rather involves a referential and specific phrase. As Rizzi notes, if we follow the distinction between the quantificational and non-quantificational A′-dependencies of Lasnik and Stowell (1991), this is just what we should expect.

As with Hungarian, CLLD in Italian does allow topicalizing quantifiers in some special cases. According to Rizzi (1997, example 34c), we can have:

(13)   Tutti i tuoi libri, li ho rimessi a posto.
       'All your books, I put them back.'

---

[17] This point is also argued in depth by Puskás (2000).

Rizzi himself offers a syntactic analysis of this phenomenon, effectively putting the restrictor of the quantifier in topic position. But it is tempting to speculate that there may be similar interpretive restrictions to those reported for Hungarian. It is thus tempting to speculate that there may well need to be a salient set of elements, which underlies the interpretation of the restricted quantifier, but also to which the topicalized phrase is understood as in effect referring (cf. Puskás 2000).

Cross-linguistic comparisons of information structure notions can be delicate; but still, the similarities between Italian and Hungarian are striking. Both seem to provide for a high topic position, which produces a topic-predicate articulation well above the vP level. Both require essentially non-quantificational elements to be topics, and only allow quantifiers when they receive marked or specific readings. The gloss as 'logical subject of predication' appears to be apt for both languages. In both cases, the topic position plays a central information-structural role of marking what the sentence is about.[18]

5.3 English

So far, I have reviewed literature indicating there are distinguished topic positions in Hungarian and Italian (or more generally Romance), and I have suggested that they show broadly similar behavior. The case for English is somewhat more delicate, but I shall review reasons to see a topic position in it as well.

There is a widely discussed *topicalization* construction in English, such as:

(14)   This book, you should give *e* to Paul.

The distribution of topicalization in English is somewhat uneven, and there is some variation among speakers, but this sort of construction is widely enough attested to be confident that it is allowed, in at least some forms.

The analysis of English topicalization has been a contentious issue. Even so, it can be brought in line with the analyses of Hungarian and Italian we have seen, as has been argued by Cinque (1990) and Rizzi (1997). Effectively updating Chomsky (1977), they propose that the fronted DP occupies the specifier of TopP, as it does in Hungarian and Italian CLLD. Chomsky crucially argued that there is a null operator mediating between the topic phrase on the left and an empty category in TP. We thus have something like:

(15) $[_{\text{TopP}}$ This book OP$_i$ [you should give e_i to Paul]]

Interestingly, Rizzi suggests that in CLLD, the function of the null operator in the English topic construction is taken up by the resumptive clitic in Italian and that,

---

[18] This conclusion is also reached by Puskás (2000). She takes the stronger position that where Italian CLLD has an overt clitic, Hungarian will rely on a null *pro*, which can be identified via the morphological case system of Hungarian. I do not need this stronger claim about the internal syntactic structure of topicalization, but it does add strength to my conclusion that topic in Hungarian and Italian can be treated as roughly the same.

generally, languages opt for either the null operator or clitic strategy for encoding topic. Either can create an appropriate link between the topic phrase and the open position in the TP.[19]

English imposes semantic constraints on the constituents that occupy the topic position that are, again, strikingly reminiscent of those we saw in Hungarian. The rich data set of Birner and Ward (1998) suggests that topics in English require an element or set of elements they pick out to be identifiable in the discourse (with additional complications for contrastive topics). Indefinites can be topic when they meet this condition (Ward & Prince 1991). These conditions are in line with the [+referential] and [+specific] conditions we saw above, and at least roughly, it appears safe to assume that English shares with Hungarian and with Italian some strong constraints on the interpretation of topic phrases.[20]

I have now reviewed a few details of select syntactic analyses of topic constructions in Hungarian, Italian, and in English. There are a number of details in each analysis, and a number of potentially interesting cross-linguistic variations, which I have only barely touched upon, and have explored only enough to state the basic elements of each analysis. But these elements do indicate that there is plausible reason to take syntax to include a distinguished topic position. It should also be noted that usually, evidence of a syntactic projection in some languages is also (highly partial!) evidence that languages that mark things differently can also contain such a projection. Thus, it is some evidence that languages that mark topics morphologically, or by intonation, might still have a full projection for topic, and not just a morphosyntactic feature.[21]

We have also seen that this position is reasonably called a topic one, as it does relate to what the sentence is about. It provides a 'logical subject of predication', which picks out a given or familiar element. In keeping with this, the position is marked with features requiring something like a specific reading. Identifying a syntactic projection for topic adds some more evidence in favor of topic being a level 1 notion. We already generally supposed there are some syntactic features corresponding to information structure, but in seeing how topic can affect word order, we see that it is clearly part of grammar in the core or austere sense we described above, and so at least the syntax is very likely at level 1. But the case so far is weak, as it leaves open that the semantics

---

[19] There are other sorts of considerations that can be brought to bear to argue for a topic position in English. For instance, Beghelli and Stowell (1997) and Szabolcsi (1997) suggest that the differential scope potentials of quantifiers in English can be accounted for by providing a highly articulated left-peripheral structure, including a position that is effectively a topic position, to which, among other things, specific indefinites move to take wide scope. I have focused on Rizzi's arguments, as they are parallel to those we have examined for Italian. The Chomskian analysis that Rizzi and Cinque essentially follow has been challenged, for instance, by Lasnik and Saito (1992).

[20] Even so, we should be careful in supposing the constraints are exactly alike. English is very permissive in the constituents it allows to be preposed (Birner & Ward 1998), and it is doubtful that every preposing is a TopP-like construction. Indeed, so-called 'Yiddish dialects' of English are extremely permissive in preposing in many ways (Prince 1981a).

[21] For a treatment of topics in a very different framework from the Chomskian one supposed here, see Steedman (2000).

could be fixed by conventions at any level. Our observations so far have been about referentiality and specificity, which square well with the posited information-structural role of topic. It is likely that these are marked in the grammar too, and so could be level 1. But this leaves open whether the interpretations of these features are level 1, 2, or 3. More importantly, it leaves open the possibility that the syntax and minimal semantics of specificity is low level, but that speakers may later form level 3, fully Lewisian, conventions to add the information-structural function of topic marking. Indeed, speakers of languages like Hungarian would have a much more overt grasp of which positions are topic ones, and so could much more easily engage in Gricean reasoning about them.

I think this is likely not so. To see some reasons why, we should turn to the semantics of topichood itself.

6. The Semantics and Pragmatics of Topics

We have noted that the topic position, when visible, is associated with an information-structural content of *aboutness*, which I have roughly glossed as making something given or familiar in a discourse. It is associated with some particular semantically interpretable features, including referentiality and specificity. These are not themselves sufficient to fix the content of topic positions, as clearly specificity, referentiality, and so on appear in non-topic positions as well. In this section, I shall briefly review some ideas about what the distinctive content of topic positions is. I shall be brief, as the theories of topic get very complicated, and what we need for our purposes is only the general idea of what the content of these positions might be like.

6.1 Topics and Aboutness

We will intuitively find that a sentence is 'about' whatever occupies the specifier of TopP. In languages like English, absent other marking, we will often think of the sentence as about its subject or even as about its first DP in linear order.[22] This sense of aboutness for topics is stronger than simply being an argument of a predicate. Though Hungarian and Italian allow multiple topics, the aboutness understanding is not attached to all the arguments of a verb, only the ones that occupy topic positions.

There have been a number of attempts to build such intuitions into a genuine semantics for topichood. Most of these attempts rely on some kind of structured representation of the content of a sentence, which singles out some element as what the sentence is 'about'. This is naturally captured in the apparatus of dynamic semantics, as a distinguished index to a file in the sense of Heim (1982) or a DRS in the sense of Kamp (1984). Such approaches are pursued by a number of authors. Notably Vallduví (1990) uses a DRT-like structure to capture what he views as a

---

[22] It is sometimes suggested that subjects are unmarked topics. More systematically, the tradition of Halliday (1967) identifies topics (more properly *themes*) with sentence-initial elements.

distinguished level of information structure (making the representational properties of DRT essential), while Portner and Yabushita (1998) and Reinhart (1981) pursue non-representational approaches more akin to file change semantics.[23] For our
purposes, the details of these theories will not matter. All we need is to suppose that
semantically, topic distinguishes an individual (or other element), which is the
thing the sentence is about.

6.2   Old and New

The idea that the topic marks what a sentence is about goes together with some ideas
that are, perhaps more clearly, related to information structure. First, it is a common
idea that what a sentence is about should be *old information*, that was already established in a discourse. This is sometimes described as the idea that what the topic is
should be *given*, rather than new. The idea is that what we talk about in discourse is not
typically any random thing, but an established topic. Thus, what the sentence is about
should be given or old in the discourse.

This has been elaborated in different ways by different theories. Some seek to
characterize directly what it is to be given, in terms of either being familiar to the
speaker, or having been evoked or made salient in the discourse.[24] Topics, on this
picture, have a discourse function of linking sentences in contexts to old information
in the discourse.

6.3   Questions Under Discussion

A related idea about the semantics of topic, but one that has been given a much more
extensive formal development, is in terms of questions and answers. The idea is that
sentences are uttered in the presence of a discourse topic. Rather than thinking of a
discourse topic as a thing, think of it as like a question, that sets what we are talking
about. The discourse topic may be set implicitly or explicitly, and when set explicitly, it
is set by asking a question. Following Roberts (1996), we may call this the question
under discussion (QUD). The sentence is supposed to be *about* the QUD, acting as a
discourse topic, and so the topic of the sentence must in the right way be congruent to,
or match, the discourse topic.

This captures a clear notion of aboutness, and it also captures a specific sense in which
topics can be said to be old information, as they must relate to an already established
discourse topic. Hence, we do not need to see this idea as conflicting with the motivations
of either the aboutness or old information approaches. But, it allows for an elegant
formal model of the semantics of topic, and relates closely to work on the semantics of
focus. Topic, especially looking cross-linguistically, is a complicated matter, so I would

[23]   See McNally (1998) for some discussion. The idea of 'aboutness' as a characteristic of topic is quite
common, though it is often put in more pragmatic terms, as a relation between a speaker and the thing they
are talking about (cf. Gundel 1985; Strawson 1964).

[24]   Prince (1981b) gives a good overview of these ideas. See also Birner (1992), Birner and Ward (1998),
Chafe (1976), Prince (1992), Schwarzschild (1999), and Ward (1985).

hardly be surprised if aspects of all these approaches are needed before a theory is completed. But still, to my mind, the question approach holds a lot of promise.

Here is a simple sketch of this approach. Consider a topicalization again:

(16)　a.　i.　What should I do with this book?
　　　　　 ii.　This book, you should give to Paul.
　　　 b.　i.　What should I do with this pen?
　　　　　 ii.　#this book, you should give to Paul

Here the overt question sets up the QUD. Semantically, a question is interpreted as a set of answers (Groenendijk & Stokhof 1984; Hamblin 1973). Very roughly, ⟦What should I do with this book?⟧ looks something like {⟦Give book to Paul⟧, ⟦Take book to library⟧, ⟦Use book as decordation⟧, …}. The topic constituent sets up a requirement that semantic value of the topic-marked sentence has to be in the value of the QUD, i.e. ⟦This book, you should give to Paul⟧ ∈ ⟦What should I do with this book?⟧. This is satisfied in the felicitous case, but it fails in the infelicitous case, as the QUD value is {⟦Give pen to Paul⟧, ⟦Use pen to write⟧, …}. I should note that this illustration is vastly over-simplified, and that in fact, the most interesting QUD-based analyses really address contrastive topic better than the kind of (resumptive) topics we are looking at now. But still, it is an important idea about the semantics and discourse function of topics generally.[25]

We have now seen some ideas about what the semantics of topic might be. I do not think there is yet a full consensus on what the right semantics is, and it may be that ideas from several of the approaches we just reviewed could combine to build a refined analysis. But, we have seen enough to see what the semantics of topic may be like. Not surprisingly, it is much like what we would expect for the semantics of a functional projection. It provides an abstract aspect of meaning, and does not describe things and actions the way nouns and verbs do.

With some ideas about the syntax and semantics in hand, we can now try again to see in what level of conventionality the phenomenon falls.

7.　The Conventional Status of Topic

Above I noted that the presence of a syntactic projection for topic opens the possibility that it is a level 1 phenomenon. It seems to be a robust syntactic phenomenon that could really be part of UG and set parametrically. But I also noted that, even if the syntax of topic is part of UG, that does not establish that the information-structural content is a level 1 convention. It is still open, as we saw, that this could be placed at any level.

---

[25] A real theory in this vein is given by von Fintel (1994), though using the framework of Rooth (1992) rather than the QUD framework. Related ideas about QUD are found in Büring (1999), van Kuppevelt (1995), and of course, Roberts (1996). The most developed theory I know is from Büring (2003), which we will discuss later.

I think there is more we can say in favor of placing topic lower in the scale of conventions. First, the semantics of topic suggests lower-level conventions. As I just mentioned, topic gets just the kind of meaning we should expect for a functional projection. It is a specific, but highly abstract content, encoding in some way the information-structural function of being about. We are not sure just how to characterize that, but it is clear enough that the semantics of topic positions are one of a few abstract information-structural contents that language encodes. This is much like the situation with other functional projections, like tense or determiners. I should also note that it is not clear how much variation there is in the semantics of topics across languages. It might be that with some limits, we have differences between, say, Japanese and Hungarian. But again, we do not see free variation, as best as we can tell. We see simply a small range. This suggests parametric variation, in keeping with level 1 convention.

That raises the possibility that topic really is a level 1 phenomenon. It does not conclusively show it is. It may be that the semantics of topic encoded in UG is quite minimal. As I already mentioned, it might be that it is merely marked as specific, or something along those lines. Then the full semantics would have to be learned, and we would have a level 2 or 3 phenomenon. The abstractness of the content, and similarity to the kinds of contents other functional expressions have, makes me doubt it is level 3. We just do not seem to form full Lewisian conventions about functional meanings. But it could be that the mechanisms that first allow us to learn word meanings, with less than full Lewisian conventional status, are engaged to learn these contents. Topic might thus be a combination of some level 1 content, and some level 2. But the point about functional meanings makes me doubt this too. In general, the kind of learning distinctive of level 2 (and above) pertains to the lexicon, and not to functional categories. Functional category meanings are closed classes, whereas the strategies for word learning, even early word learning, are fitted to open classes. If we associated meanings with the topic position the way we associate meanings with nouns—even our first nouns—we might expect to be able to add more of them as our interests grow. Yet we cannot. There is no information-structural notion of 'being something I read on the internet' associated with any distinguished syntactic position, especially not any topic position. It seems that we cannot even add such a meaning, in keeping with the functional nature of information-structural positions and meanings. This supports the idea that the meaning of topic positions, like other functional category meanings, are not level 2 or higher. That leaves them at level 1.

Topic shows us a full syntactic projection, paired with a functional meaning. That, I have argued, speaks in favor of it falling at level 1. The meaning of topic and other information-structural positions form closed classes. That, I have argued, speaks against their being at level 2 or 3. So, I am inclined to think we see level 1 information structure in the case of topics. Though this cannot be said with certainty, it seems to be the likely result, and there is some substantial evidence to support it.[26]

---

[26] Evidence about the acquisition of topic would be helpful. I am afraid I am not aware of much.

8. Contrastive Topics

With this in mind, let us turn to the original issue, of the kind of contrastive topic that is marked by the B-accent in English. I think the case for topic being level 1 indirectly supports the claim that contrastive topic is also level 1. It is a closely related phenomenon, so it is likely that they fall at the same level.

Even so, contrastive topic raises some specific issues, which we should look at more carefully.

Contrastive topic is called topic, as it signals aboutness. But as its name suggests, it also signals a kind of contrast. This is made vivid in the question–answer congruence of the original example from Büring (1999), repeated here:

(17)   a. What did the pop stars wear?
       b. [The FEMALE pop stars]$_{CT}$ wore [CAFTANS]$_F$.

The topic the sentence is about refines the one set by the QUD. But contrastive topic is compatible with the devices we have to fix topic in English. For instance:

(18)   Well, as for [the FEMALE pop stars]$_{CT}$, they wore [CAFTANS]$_F$.

Intuitively, in the felicitous (18), the utterance is about *the female pop stars*, as signaled by the *as for* construction, and by the question the felicitous utterance is directed towards. The focused constituent *caftans* provides the information answering the question. Contrastive topic intonation is infelicitous with overtly resumptive topics:

(19)   a. What did Max wear?
       b. ??[MAX]$_{CT}$ wore [a CAFTAN]$_F$.

This is generally judged bad (though there is some variation in the judgment). It thus appears that contrastive topic both signals what an utterance 'is about', but also signals some contrast with something already under discussion.

The intonational marking of contrastive topic in English—the occurrence of B-accent or an L + H* accent—is independent of the topicalization construction in English. It can occur, for instance, in both the subject and object position of simple sentences. We find, with the right questions in place, the following are acceptable, as Jackendoff (1972) essentially noted:

(20)   a. We have a bunch of people, and we want to know who ate what?
       b. [FRED]$_{CT}$ ate [the BEANS]$_F$.
(21)   a. We have a bunch of food, and we want to know who ate what?
       b. [FRED]$_F$ ate [the BEANS]$_{CT}$.

But it appears that English topicalization can host contrastive topic accent:

(22)   a. Who should I give these things to?
       b. [This BOOK]$_{CT}$, you should give to Paul.

Similar examples can be found in corpora (see Birner & Ward 1998). Many researchers have concluded that contrastive topic and topic are related information-structural phenomena, but not the same (e.g. Büring 2016a; Roberts 2011).

Semantically, the best developed accounts concentrate on question–answer congruence and QUD, and indeed, those accounts really emerged in studying contrastive topic. Büring (2003) presents the most developed account I know. It works with a richer structure of discourse, involving not just questions and answers, but with whole *strategies* for answering questions. A strategy is a question and a set of sub-questions that address it. A contrastive topic indicates a strategy around the current question under discussion, and answers one of the sub-questions in the strategy. Thus, for instance, if our question under discussion is *Who ate what?*, we find that (20b) indicates a strategy of answering *What did Fred eat? What did Mary eat?...* and answers the question of what Fred ate.[27]

Contrastive topic appears widely cross-linguistically. As in English, Hungarian contrastive topics, bearing what appears to be the same accent, can occur in TopP positions (Molnár 1998). Quantifiers appear easier to topicalize with contrastive topic marking.

I am not sure what the status of contrastive topic marking in Italian CLDD is. It may be incompatible with the L+H* pitch accent, though it seems to host other accents (Bocci 2007). Complicating matters further, it has been suggested that for some language, such as Spanish (Arregi 2003) and perhaps Modern Greek (Alexopoulou & Kolliakou 2002), CLLD constructions act like contrastive topics. Hence, caution is in order, and this illustrates how complicated the cross-linguistic situation can be. We should also mention, finally, the possibility that where we find *in situ* marking of contrastive topic, it might be that we have covert movement to a topic position.

With this brief overview, we can return to the question of what level contrastive topic, marked intonationally, should be placed at. Though it is likely that contrastive topic is a distinct information-structural notion from topic simpliciter, we still have good reason to suspect it is at level 1, as I suggested topic positions might be. The same reasons that supported placing syntactically marked topic at level 1 still support placing contrastive topic there too.

Syntactically, we do not have a full projection overtly visible, and see somewhat limited effects on word order. But we still have good reason to posit a syntactic feature CT, as we discussed above. Does this place contrastive topic within the scope of UG and parameters? Even if the evidence is weaker, as I mentioned, we can argue that if one aspect of information structure is clearly within UG, then it is plausible that closely related ones are too. So, we might conclude, UG knows about topic, focus, and so on. Thus, we still have a case for level 1.

Semantically, the case for level 1 is just as before. The meaning of topic, both contrastive and resumptive, is the kind of meaning we expect for a functional category,

---

[27] Contrastive topic raises some complicated questions for old information accounts, but I shall not explore that issue here.

and not the kind that goes with open-class lexical items. This, plus the closed-class nature of intonational meanings, still suggest a level 1 phenomenon.

In this case, facts about acquisition might add some further support, though the situation is not entirely clear. It is known that children are sensitive to some aspects of prosody very early—as early as 3 or 4 days (cf. Guasti 2002; Speer & Ito 2009)! What children recognize at this stage seems to be more the general tonal structure of an infant's language; but nonetheless, anything that emerges this early seems likely to be part of UG. Thus, lacking overt syntax does not indicate that we have gone outside of austere grammar. As the survey by Speer and Ito (2009) makes clear, studying accent in children has proved challenging, and its development is not fully understood. But they note studies that place sensitivity to accent around 6 or 8 months. When it is that children understand the meaning of accent is less clear. Speer and Ito review studies that suggest that perhaps by age 2, some intonational meaning is acquired. But they also note that children display puzzling asymmetries between comprehension and production of accents, and even 5-year-olds or older showed significant difficulties in comprehending the meanings of some accents. They speculate that the role of context in information structure makes on-line comprehension harder (and certainly makes it harder to design good experiments). So, the limited evidence on acquisition makes it reasonable that accent itself is level 1, but the data leaves open that the meaning of accent could be at any level.

As with syntactically marked topic, I think there is a plausible case to be made for placing contrastive topic at level 1. The case is certainly not conclusive, and as I mentioned before, it remains possible that contrastive topic could be at higher levels (as some of the acquisition data might suggest?). And, we should also leave open the possibility that it is an overlap of level 1 and higher phenomena, as the ways contrastive and syntactic topic can overlap might suggest. But still, I think the evidence pointing to level 1 is substantial.

9. Conclusion

I have followed Lepore and Stone's lead in viewing much of language as conventional, including information structure. But I have also argued that it is useful to distinguish a range of levels with the broad category of the conventional. I then attempted an exercise of placing a phenomenon within those levels. In particular, I argued that the information-structural notion of topic might well be at level 1.

I made this claim in a limited way. I argued that there is evidence that makes the level 1 status of topic plausible, but there is also evidence that suggests other levels, and the result is not conclusive. This is not really surprising. Information structure, as I mentioned, is not only very complicated, but takes in an incredibly wide range of aspects of language, from phonology to syntax to semantics to pragmatics. Our understanding of this has increased over the years, but remains incomplete. Even so, I think the exercise is productive. It illustrates how we can sort evidence from multiple domains, to try to understand the conventional nature of a complex linguistic phenomenon.

With Lepore and Stone, I agree that recognizing the conventional status of aspects of language is a crucial step to understanding them. But I think it is the first step, and there are more to go.

Acknowledgments

Thanks first to Ernie Lepore and Matthew Stone, for their book, and for many conversations. Portions of the material that wound up in this essay were presented at the Non-Canonical Predication Workshop at the University of Western Ontario, 2009, and the Is There Any Such Thing as a Language Conference at the University of South Florida, 2016. Thanks to all the participants at those events, and especially, David Adger, Josh Armstrong, Wolfram Hinzen, and Rob Stainton. Thanks finally to the editor of this volume for support and patience.

References

Aboh, E. O. (2004). 'Left or right? A view from the Kwa periphery'. Adger D., de Cat C., & Tsoulas G. (eds) *Peripheries: Syntactic edges and their effects*, pp. 165–89. Kluwer: Dordrecht.

Alexopoulou, T., & Kolliakou, D. (2002). 'On linkhood, topicalization, and clitic left dislocation', *Journal of Linguistics*, 38: 193–245.

Arregi, K. (2003). 'Clitic left dislocation is contrastive topicalization', *University of Pennsylvania Working Papers in Linguistics*, 9: 31–44.

Beaver, D. I., & Clark, B. Z. (2008). *Sense and sensitivity: How focus determines meaning.* Wiley-Blackwell: Chichester.

Beaver, D. I., Clark, B. Z., Flemming, E., Jaeger, T. F., & Wolters, M. (2007). 'When semantics meets phonetics: Acoustical studies of second-occurrence focus', *Language*, 83: 245–76.

Beckman, M. E., & Pierrehumbert, J. B. (1986). 'Intonational structure in English and Japanese', *Phonology Yearbook*, 3: 255–310.

Beghelli, F., & Stowell, T. (1997). 'Distributivity and negation: The syntax of *each* and *every*'. Szabolcsi A. (ed.) *Ways of scope taking*, pp. 71–107. Kluwer: Dordrecht.

Birner, B. J. (1992). *The discourse function of inversion in English* (Ph.D. Dissertation). Northwestern University.

Birner, B. J., & Ward, G. L. (1998). *Information structure and noncanonical word order in English*. John Benjamins: Amsterdam.

Bloom, P. (2000). *How children learn the meanings of words*. MIT Press: Cambridge, MA.

Bocci, G. (2007). 'Criterial positions and the left periphery in Italian: Evidence for the syntactic encoding of contrastive focus', *Nanzan Linguistics*, 3: 35–70.

Bolinger, D. (1958). 'A theory of pitch accent in English', *Word*, 14: 109–49.

Bolinger, D. (1972). 'Accent is predictable (if you're a mind-reader)', *Language*, 48: 633–44.

Brody, M. (1990). 'Some remarks on the focus field in Hungarian', *UCL Working Papers in Linguistics*, 2: 201–25.

Büring, D. (1999). 'Topic'. Bosch P. & van der Sandt R. (eds) *Focus: Linguistic, cognitive, and computational perspectives*, pp. 142–65. Cambridge University Press: Cambridge.

Büring, D. (2003). 'On D-trees, beans, and B-accents', *Linguistics and Philosophy*, 26: 511–45.

Büring, D. (2016a). '(Contrastive) topic'. Féry C. & Ishihara S. (eds) *Oxford handbook of information structure*, pp. 64–85. Oxford University Press: Oxford.

Büring, D. (2016b). *Intonation and meaning*. Oxford University Press: Oxford.

Carey, S. (1978). 'The child as word learner'. Bresnan J., Miller G., & Halle M. (eds) *Linguistic theory and psychological reality*, pp. 264–93. MIT Press: Cambridge, MA.

Chafe, W. L. (1976). 'Givenness, contrastiveness, definiteness, subjects, topics, and point of view'. Li N. (ed.) *Subject and topic*, pp. 25–55. Academic Press: New York.

Choe, H. S. (1995). 'Focus and topic movement in Korean and licensing'. É. Kiss K. (ed.) *Discourse configurational languages*, pp. 269–334. Oxford University Press: Oxford.

Chomsky, N. (1965). *Aspects of the theory of syntax*. MIT Press: Cambridge, MA.

Chomsky, N. (1971). 'Deep structure, surface structure, and semantic interpretation'. Steinberg D. D. & Jakobovits L. A. (eds) *Semantics*, pp. 183–216. Cambridge University Press: Cambridge.

Chomsky, N. (1977). 'On wh-movement'. Culicover P. W., Wasow T., & Akmajian A. (eds) *Formal syntax*, pp. 71–132. Academic Press: New York.

Chomsky, N. (1986). *Knowledge of language*. New York: Praeger.

Chomsky, N. (2000). *New horizons in the study of language and mind*. Cambridge University Press: Cambridge.

Cinque, G. (1990). *Types of Ā-dependencies*. MIT Press: Cambridge, MA.

Collins, J. (2004). 'Faculty disputes', *Mind and Language*, 19: 503–33.

Collins, J. (2007). 'Syntax, more or less', *Mind*, 116: 805–50.

Crain, S., & Thornton, R. (1998). *Investigations in universal grammar*. MIT Press, Cambridge, MA.

Daneš, F. (1968). 'Some thoughts on the semantic structure of the sentence', *Lingua*, 21: 55–69.

É. Kiss, K. (1998). 'Identificational focus versus information focus', *Language*, 74: 245–73.

É. Kiss, K. (2002). *The syntax of Hungarian*. Cambridge University Press: Cambridge.

É. Kiss, K. (2007). 'Topic and focus: Two structural positions associated with logical functions in the left periphery of the Hungarian sentence', *Interdisciplinary Studies on Information Structure*, 6: 69–81.

Enç, M. (1991). 'The semantics of specificity', *Linguistic Inquiry*, 22: 1–25.

Firbas, J. (1964). 'On defining the theme in functional sentence analysis', *Travaux Linguistiques de Prague*, 1: 267–80.

Foppolo, F., Guasti, M. T., & Chierchia, G. (2012). 'Scalar implicature in child language: Give children a chance', *Language Learning and Development*, 8: 365–94.

Frank, M. C., Goodman, N. D., & Tenenbaum, J. B. (2009). 'Using speakers' referential intentions to model early cross-situational world learning', *Psychological Science*, 20: 578–85.

Glanzberg, M. (2014). 'Explanation and partiality in semantic theory'. Burgess A. & Sherman B. (eds) *Metasemantics: New essays on the foundations of meaning*, pp. 259–92. Oxford University Press: Oxford.

Golinkoff, R. M., Mervis, C. B., & Hirsh-Pasek, K. (1994). 'Early object labels: The case for a developmental lexical principles framework', *Journal of Child Language*, 21: 125–55.

Grice, P. (1969). 'Utterer's meaning and intentions', *Philosophical Review*, 78: 147–77.

Groenendijk, J., & Stokhof, M. (1984). *Studies in the semantics of questions and the pragmatics of answers* (Ph.D. dissertation). University of Amsterdam.

Guasti, M. T. (2002). *Language acquisition: The growth of grammar*. MIT Press: Cambridge, MA.

Gundel, J. K. (1985). 'Shared knowledge and topicality', *Journal of Pragmatics*, 9: 83–107.

Hajičová, E., Partee, B. H., & Sgall, P. (1998). *Topic-focus articulation, tripartite structures, and semantic content*. Kluwer: Dordrecht.

Halliday, M. A. K. (1967). 'Notes on transitivity and theme in English (part 2)', *Journal of Linguistics*, 3: 199–244.

Hamblin, C. L. (1973). 'Questions in Montague English', *Foundations of Language*, 10: 41–53.

Hauser, M. D., Chomsky, N., & Fitch, W. T. (2002). 'The faculty of language: What is it, who has it, and how did it evolve?', *Science*, 298: 1569–79.

Heim, I. (1982). *The semantics of definite and indefinite noun phrases* (Ph.D. dissertation). University of Massachusetts at Amherst.

Heycock, C., & Kroch, A. (2002). 'Topic, focus, and syntactic representation', *Proceedings of the West Coast Conference on Formal Linguistics*, 21: 141–65.

Jackendoff, R. S. (1972). *Semantic interpretation in generative grammar*. MIT Press: Cambridge, MA.

Kadmon, N. (2001). *Formal pragmatics*. Blackwell: Oxford.

Kamp, H. (1984). 'A theory of truth and semantic representation'. Groenendijk J., Janssen T., & Stokhof M. (eds) *Truth, interpretation, and information*, pp. 1–41. Foris: Dordrecht.

Ladd, D. R. (1996). *Intonational phonology*. Cambridge University Press: Cambridge.

Larson, R. K., & Segal, G. (1995). *Knowledge of meaning*. MIT Press: Cambridge, MA.

Lasnik, H., & Saito, M. (1992). *Move α*. MIT Press: Cambridge, MA.

Lasnik, H., & Stowell, T. (1991). 'Weakest crossover', *Linguistic Inquiry*, 22: 687–720.

Lepore, E., & Stone, M. (2015). *Imagination and convention: Distinguishing grammar and inference in language*. Oxford University Press: Oxford.

Levinson, S. C. (2003). 'Language in mind: Let's get the issues straight!' Gentner D. & Goldin-Meadow S. (eds) *Language in mind*, pp. 25–46. MIT Press: Cambridge, MA.

Lewis, D. (1969). *Convention*. Harvard University Press: Cambridge, MA.

Markman, E. M. (1990). 'Constraints children place on word meanings', *Cognitive Science*, 14: 57–77.

McMurray, B., Horst, J. S., & Samuelson, L. K. (2012). 'Word learning emerges from the interaction of online referent selection and slow associative learning', *Psychological Review*, 119: 831–77.

McNally, L. (1998). 'On recent formal analyses of topic'. Ginzburg J., Khasidashvili Z., Vogel C., Lévy J.-J., & Vallduví E. (eds) *The Tbilisi symposium on logic, language and computation*, pp. 147–60. CSLI: Stanford.

Merchant, J. (2001). *The syntax of silence: Sluicing, islands, and the theory of ellipsis*. Oxford University Press: Oxford.

Molnár, V. (1998). 'Topic in focus: The syntax, phonology, semantics, and pragmatics of the so-called "contrastive topic" in Hungarian and German', *Acta Linguistica Hungarica*, 45: 89–166.

Noveck, I. A. (2001). 'When children are more logical than adults: Experimental investigations of scalar implicature', *Cognition*, 78: 165–88.

Onishi, K. H., & Baillargeon, R. (2005). 'Do 15-month-old infants understand false beliefs?', *Science*, 308: 255–8.

Papafragou, A., & Musolino, J. (2003). 'Scalar implicatures: Experiments at the semantics-pragmatics interface', *Cognition*, 86: 253–82.

Partee, B. H. (1991). 'Topic, focus and quantification', *Proceedings of Semantics and Linguistic Theory*, 1: 159–87.

Pereira, A. F., Smith, L. B., & Yu, C. (2014). 'A bottom-up view of toddler word learning', *Psychonomic Bulletin and Review*, 21: 178–85.

Pierrehumbert, J. B. (1980). *The phonology and phonetics of English intonation* (Ph.D. dissertation). MIT.

Pierrehumbert, J. B., & Hirschberg, J. (1990). 'The meaning of intonational contours in the interpretation of discourse'. Cohen P. R., Morgan J., & Pollack M. E. (eds) *Intentions in communication*, pp. 271–311. MIT Press: Cambridge, MA.

Pietroski, P. M. (2005). 'Meaning before truth'. Preyer G. & Peter G. (eds) *Contextualism in philosophy: Knowledge, meaning, and truth*, pp. 253–300. Oxford University Press: Oxford.

Pinker, S. (1994). *The language instinct*. HarperCollins: New York.

Portner, P., & Yabushita, K. (1998). 'The semantics and pragmatics of topic phrases', *Linguistics and Philosophy*, 21: 117–57.

Prince, E. F. (1981a). 'Topicalization, focus-movement, and Yiddish-movement: A pragmatic differentiation', *Proceedings of the Berkeley Linguistics Society*, 7: 249–64.

Prince, E. F. (1981b). 'Toward a taxonomy of given-new information'. Cole P. (ed.) *Radical pragmatics*, pp. 223–55. Academic Press: New York.

Prince, E. F. (1992). 'The ZPG letter: Subjects, definiteness, and information-status'. Thompson S. A. & Mann W. C. (eds) *Discourse description: Diverse analyses of a fundraising letter*, pp. 295–325. John Benjamins: Amsterdam.

Puskás, G. (2000). *Word order in Hungarian*. John Benjamins: Amsterdam.

Reinhart, T. (1981). 'Pragmatics and linguistics: An analysis of sentence topics', *Philosophica*, 27: 53–94.

Rescorla, M. (2015). 'Convention'. Zalta E. N. (ed.) *The Stanford Encyclopedia of Philosophy*, Summer 2015. https://plato.stanford.edu/archives/sum2015/entries/convention/; Metaphysics Research Lab, Stanford University.

Rizzi, L. (1997). 'The fine structure of the left periphery'. Haegeman L. (ed.) *Elements of grammar*, pp. 281–337. Kluwer: Dordrecht.

Roberts, C. (1996). 'Information structure in discourse: Towards an integrated formal theory of pragmatics', *Ohio State University Working Papers in Linguistics*, 49: 91–136.

Roberts, C. (2011). 'Topics'. Maienborn C., Heusinger K. von, & Portner P. (eds) *Semantics: An international handbook of natural language meaning*, Vol. 2, pp. 1908–33. de Gruyter Mouton: Berlin.

Rooth, M. (1992). 'A theory of focus interpretation', *Natural Language Semantics*, 1: 75–116.

Schwarzschild, R. (1999). 'Givenness, avoidF and other constraints on the placement of accent', *Natural Language Semantics*, 7: 141–77.

Scott, R. M., Baillargeon, R., Song, H.-j., & Leslie, A. M. (2010). 'Attributing false beliefs about non-obvious properties at 18 months', *Cognitive Psychology*, 61: 366–95.

Selkirk, E. (1995). 'Sentence prosody: Intonation, stress, and phrasing'. Goldsmith J. A. (ed.) *Handbook of phonological theory*, pp. 550–69. Blackwell: Oxford.

Smith, L. B., Suanda, S. H., & Yu, C. (2014). 'The unrealized promise of infant statistical word-referent learning', *Trends in Cognitive Science*, 18: 251–8.

Speer, S. R., & Ito, K. (2009). 'Prosody in first language acquisition—Acquiring intonation as a tool to organize information in conversation', *Language and Linguistics Compass*, 3: 90–110.

Sperber, D., & Wilson, D. (1986). *Relevance*. Harvard University Press: Cambridge, MA.

Steedman, M. (1991). 'Structure and intonation', *Language*, 67: 260–96.

Steedman, M. (2000). *The syntactic process*. MIT Press: Cambridge, MA.

Strawson, P. F. (1964). 'Identifying reference and truth-values', *Theoria*, 30: 96–118.

Surányi, B. (2004). 'The left periphery and cyclic spellout: The case of Hungarian'. Adger D., de Cat C., & Tsoulas G. (eds) *Peripheries: Syntactic edges and their effects*, pp. 49–73. Kluwer: Dordrecht.

Szabolcsi, A. (1981). 'The semantics of topic-focus articulation'. Groenendijk J., Janssen T., & Stokhof M. (eds) *Formal methods in the study of language* (part 2), pp. 513–40. Mathematisch Centrum: Amsterdam.

Szabolcsi, A. (1983). 'Focusing properties, or the trap of first order', *Theoretical Linguistics*, 10: 125–45.

Szabolcsi, A. (1997). 'Strategies for scope taking'. Szabolcsi A. (ed.) *Ways of scope taking*, pp. 109–54. Kluwer: Dordrecht.

Tomasello, M. (2003a). *Constructing a language: A use-based theory of language acquisition*. Harvard University Press: Cambridge, MA.

Tomasello, M. (2003b). 'The key is social cognition'. Gentner D. & Goldin-Meadow S. (eds) *Language in mind*, pp. 47–57. MIT Press: Cambridge, MA.

Tomasello, M., & Haberl, K. (2003). 'Understanding attention: 12- and 18-month-olds know what is new for other persons', *Developmental Psychology*, 39: 906–12.

Tsimpli, I. M. (1995). 'Focusing in Modern Greek'. É Kiss K. (ed.) *Discourse configurational languages*, pp. 176–206. Oxford University Press: Oxford.

Vallduví, E. (1990). *The informational component* (Ph.D. dissertation). University of Pennsylvania.

Vallduví, E., & Zacharski, R. (1994). 'Accenting phenomena, association with focus, and the recursiveness of focus-ground', *Proceedings of the Amsterdam Colloquium*, 9: 683–702.

van Kuppevelt, J. (1995). 'Discourse structure, topicality and questioning', *Journal of Linguistics*, 31: 109–47.

von Fintel, K. (1994). *Restrictions on quantifier domains* (Ph.D. dissertation). University of Massachusetts at Amherst.

von Fintel, K., & Matthewson, L. (2008). 'Universals in semantics', *Linguistics Review*, 25: 139–201.

Ward, G. L. (1985). *The semantics and pragmatics of preposing* (Ph.D. dissertation). University of Pennsylvania.

Ward, G. L., & Prince, E. F. (1991). 'On the topicalization of indefinite NPs', *Journal of Pragmatics*, 16: 167–77.

Watanabe, A. (2003). 'Wh and operator constructions in Japanese', *Lingua*, 113: 519–58.

Waxman, S. R., & Gelman, S. A. (2009). 'Early word-learning entails reference, not merely association', *Trends in Cognitive Science*, 13: 258–63.

Waxman, S. R., & Lidz, J. L. (2006). 'Early word learning'. Kuhn D. & Siegler R. (eds) *Handbook of child psychology*, Sixth Edn., Vol. 2, pp. 299–335. Wiley: Hoboken.

Waxman, S. R., & Markow, D. B. (1995). 'Words as invitations to form categories: Evidence from 12–13 month-old infants', *Cognitive Psychology*, 29: 257–302.

Wimmer, H., & Perner, J. (1983). 'Beliefs about beliefs: Representation and constraining function of wrong beliefs in young children's understanding of deception', *Cognition*, 13: 103–28.

Xu, F., & Tenenbaum, J. B. (2007). 'Word learning as Bayesian inference', *Psychological Review*, 114: 245–72.

Yu, C., & Smith, L. B. (2012). 'Modeling cross-situational word-referent learning: Prior questions', *Psychological Review*, 119: 21–39.

13

On Convention and Coherence

*Andrew Kehler and Jonathan Cohen**

1. The Controversy

The idea that literal linguistic meaning underdetermines communicated content is central for contemporary theorizing about language. This broad idea is more or less universally accepted, and has proven immensely fruitful for research in semantics, pragmatics, and the interface between the two. However, the broad idea leaves open the hotly disputed question of just how to draw the partition that separates linguistic meaning from the rest of communicated content.

In one of the most influential articulations of the broad idea—and one that kicked off an industry of explanation in semantics and pragmatics, Grice (1975) argues for what, in hindsight, amounts to an extreme position. He proposes that meanings of utterances remain quite close to their explicit linguistic form, differing from the latter only in allowing for resolution of indexicals, tense, and ambiguity. He holds that everything else communicated by utterances falls outside of literal linguistic meaning—that it is supplied by a particular form of pragmatic enrichment ("implicature"), the explanation for which lies in general properties of our cognitive apparatus, such as the rationality of conversational participants and the presumption of cooperativity as they pursue their conversation as a joint collaborative activity. In broad strokes, then, the Gricean program holds that linguistic meaning hews closely to what is specified by overt linguistic form, and that the large residual gap between linguistic meaning and communicated content is filled in by implicature.

Subsequent researchers have offered a range of refinements to the program, often reeling in Grice by pointing out that not all forms of enrichment satisfy the hallmarks of implicature, and that the Gricean schema for working out implicatures does not

* This work is fully collaborative; the authors are listed in anti-alphabetical order.

readily apply to all cases (e.g. Bach 1994; Sperber and Wilson 1986). Still, as far as we can tell, none of these critics have disavowed the central concept of implicature or its role in bridging the gap between linguistic meaning and communicated content.

Lepore and Stone (henceforth, L&S) propose to depart from this consensus in ways that ultimately amount to dismantling the Gricean program almost entirely. Though they nominally agree with Griceans that the meaning of an utterance ("what is said") lies close to what is overtly encoded in its linguistic expression—again, allowing only for the fixing of indexicals and other context-sensitive expressions, tense, and ambiguity resolution—they give a far larger role to ambiguity resolution than Griceans allow. Indeed, L&S argue that nearly everything Griceans characterize as going beyond the recovery of literal meaning is better understood as disambiguation on the way to fixation of literal meaning ("where alternative approaches have postulated pragmatic processes of enrichment, what's really going on is disambiguation: finding the right reading of the utterance, understood as a [conventionally,] grammatically specified pairing of form and meaning" p. 88). Since, on this view, nearly all conveyed content is the product of disambiguation processes, there is little or no role left for any additional processes of extrasemantic enrichment or expansion by Gricean or other tools. This leads L&S to deny a (perhaps *the*) central tenet of pragmatic theory— that speakers construct their utterances to take advantage of their addressees' extralin- guistic cognitive apparatus to communicate more content than they can be said to linguistically express.

Seen from afar, Grice's and L&S's views amount to two opposite but equally extreme positions about the relationship between literal meaning and communicated content. On the one pole, Grice holds that meaning encodes much less than what is communi- cated, and that, consequently, implicature must play a large role in bridging the chasm between the two. On the other, L&S hold that suitably disambiguated, conventionally specified linguistic literal meaning encodes (nearly?) all of what is communicated, and that, consequently, there's very little for implicature or other forms of pragmatic enrichment to do.

In what follows we argue against both extremal positions, and instead contend that the truth lies somewhere in the middle. On the one side, we believe L&S have performed an important service to the field by showing how Grice's program assigns too large a role to implicature—that it "underestimated the scope of linguistic conventions and overestimated the reaches of communicative intentions" (Szabó 2016, p. 169; cf. Horn 2016, p. 151). Indeed, we'll give additional arguments against this sort of Gricean overreach in §2. However, on the other side, in §§3–6, we'll also deny that convention and disambiguation can do all the work that L&S assign to them, and therefore will contend that their ambiguity resolution view fails as well. In §7 we'll argue for a middle ground account that recognizes robust contributions from both convention and pragmatic enrichment (and their interaction), using the interpretation of tense and event structure as a testing ground for theorizing. In §8, we'll conclude.

2. On Gricean Overreach: Coherence-driven Pragmatic Enrichments

L&S object to Gricean explanations by appealing primarily to three phenomena: indirect speech acts, English intonation and its conventional marking of information structure, and enrichments that result from the establishment of discourse coherence. Although we are not prepared to endorse L&S's claim that there is no role for implicature in a theory of language meaning, we agree that these are cases in which Gricean analysts have overplayed their hand.[1] To keep our contribution focused, however, we will concentrate our discussion on the last of these phenomena, which we term COHERENCE-DRIVEN ENRICHMENTS. In this section we'll argue, alongside L&S, that such enrichments are not the result of implicature.

We begin with the oft-made observation that, when confronted with a set of co-occurring utterances in a discourse, comprehenders are not content to merely update their world models with the meanings of each utterance (Asher and Lascarides 2003; Hobbs 1990; Kehler 2002, inter alia). Instead, they seek to establish some sort of semantic relationship—a COHERENCE RELATION—between them. For example, suppose a faculty member (let's call him Andy) uttered (1) to his colleague (let's call him Jonathan) one afternoon:

(1)   We should stay on campus and work this evening. Our paper for the Lepore & Stone volume is overdue.

Andy's utterances are likely to get Jonathan pondering the question of whether he is able to work with Andy on the paper that night, and he would be quite surprised (and perhaps angry) if, after agreeing to rearrange his schedule, it turned out that Andy's only intention was to sink a couple beers at the campus bar. Now, clearly Andy never said that he wanted to work on the paper with Jonathan that evening. It was merely an inference that Jonathan drew.

On the envisaged scenario, Jonathan has a right to be angry nonetheless. For his attempt to bring coherence to (1) will undoubtedly lead him to infer an EXPLANATION relation, whereby the second sentence is understood to describe the cause or reason for the event described in the first. Importantly, the additional inference involved in such examples goes beyond merely assuming that some causal relationship exists. Instead, the relationship needs to be established using the context and the interlocutors' shared knowledge and capacity for inference. A natural assumption to make when

---

[1] There are other cases as well. Levinson (2000, pp. 117–18), for instance, offers a diverse list of phenomena that he argues involve implicature, including noun–noun compound interpretation (*The oil compressor gauge*), possessive interpretation (*Wendy's children*), bridging (*The picnic...the beer*), preferred local coreference (*John came in and he sat down.*), inference to stereotypes (*secretary ⇒ female secretary*), negative strengthening (*I don't like Alice ⇒ I positively dislike Alice*), conditional strengthening (*if ⇒ if and only if*) and conjunction buttressing (*and ⇒ and as a result*). Although of these we will only discuss conjunction buttressing, we are disinclined to view any of these phenomena as involving implicature, and are confident that L&S would agree.

interpreting (1), for instance, is that Andy intends to work on the paper that evening; with this assumption one can see how the late paper could provide a reason for wanting to stay late. Note that if this assumption conflicted with the hearer's knowledge, he would be well within his rights to question it, e.g., with a response such as *I thought your opinion was that our L&S paper is pretty much done.* Our hearer in this case isn't countering anything that is entailed by (1), but instead a pragmatic enrichment that must be drawn to establish its coherence on a natural and salient interpretation.

As L&S note, it has been commonly assumed that such inferences are the result of implicature. Grice himself, for instance, famously argued that implicature explains how the conjunction *and* can be treated as having a single meaning (i.e., that of logical conjunction) even though it has the appearance of being associated with other, more specific meanings (Grice 1981: 186).[2] He considers the minimal pair in (2).

(2)   a. He took off his trousers and went to bed.
     b. He went to bed and took off his trousers.

In typical contexts, the events described in each of examples (2a–b) will be understood to have occurred in the order in which they are presented; hence they receive different construals. Noting the lack of theoretical parsimony associated with multiplying meanings of *and* (here, to include *and then*), he suggests instead that the effect results from compliance with the Maxim of Manner, specifically the submaxim imploring the speaker to "be orderly". Hence, on this analysis, the ordering of events is an extrasemantic enrichment, which for him means an implicature.

However, this analysis runs into immediate problems. To see this, note that (3a) is easily read as conveying nothing about the relative order between the two events.

(3)   a. (For Sue's baby shower,) Mary bought a stroller and Nancy crocheted a baby blanket.

     b. Paul went to the liquor store. He ran out of whiskey.

Likewise, on a natural construal of (3b), the depletion of Paul's whiskey occurs before the trip to the liquor store. The obvious question for the Gricean analysis is why, in light of the fact that it is possible to construe (3a–b) as describing the events in temporal order of occurrence, such enrichments are not drawn.

Luckily, there is a satisfying explanation of these and related facts in terms of coherence and coherence-driven enrichment. Specifically, the idea is that (3a) is an instance of a PARALLEL coherence relation, in which the utterances each instantiate a common, more general theme, or put another way, provide a partial answer to a common question under discussion (Roberts 1998). The fact that no temporal ordering is conveyed results from the fact that the Parallel relation doesn't require one: the two clauses in (3a) can provide answers to the question *Who did what for Sue's baby shower?*

---

[2] Grice's paper appeared in 1981, but an earlier version of it had circulated since 1970.

without providing a temporal order between the events. Similarly, (3b) is a canonical case of an Explanation relation as defined above. Here the hearer will infer that the depletion of whiskey is the reason for, and hence occurred prior to, the trip to the store.[3] Finally, Grice's examples (2a–b) are each most naturally construed to participate in an OCCASION relation, in which the events are understood to be spatio-temporally contiguous. The constraints associated with Occasion thus yield not only a forward sequence of events but other enrichments as well: for instance, in the case of (2b), that the man being referred to took off his trousers *while in bed*.

Subsequent (neo-)Griceans have been similarly quick to treat other cases of coherence-driven enrichment as implicatures. For example, Levinson (2000), who labels cases such as (2) as examples of "conjunction buttressing", advocates a three-way division among Q-, M-, and I-Principles. He classifies these cases as resulting from inferences that arise from his I-Principle, which comes in two parts: a Speaker's maxim of minimization ("Say as little as necessary; that is, produce the minimal linguistic information sufficient to achieve your communicational ends (bearing Q in mind)"), and a Recipient's corollary termed the Enrichment Rule ("Amplify the information content of the speaker's utterance, by finding the most *specific* interpretation, up to what you judge to be the speaker's m-intended point"), the latter which includes a sub-corollary instructing hearers to "Assume the richest temporal, causal and referential connection between described situations or events, consistent with what is taken for granted." On this analysis, the speaker is justified to conjoin the clauses with only *and*, leaving it to the hearer to enrich its meaning to the causal one.

But such Gricean explanations are problematic for several reasons.

A first is that Levinson's phrase "consistent with what is taken for granted" is certainly too narrow to apply to the full range of cases. For example, consider (4), for which a cause–effect reading is not only available, but also natural.

(4)   Fred got bitten by a mosquito, and contracted the Zika virus.

Once again, the availability of this interpretation is captured in terms of coherence: world knowledge that tells us that the fact that mosquito bites *can* cause Zika is enough for (4) to be taken as expressing a Result relation between the clauses. In contrast, we take it that the proposed Gricean account would predict this reading of (4) only if it is presumed to be typical (indeed, taken for granted) that people who get bitten by mosquitoes contract Zika. But the interpretation at issue is easily evoked even for interlocutors who know that an exceedingly small portion of bite victims contract the disease.

---

[3] Of relevance to the Gricean account is the fact that the speaker could have followed the Maxim of Manner by employing a different coherence relation—RESULT—which is like Explanation but in which the cause is described before the effect (*Paul ran out of whiskey and went to the liquor store*). Counter to what we take to be a prediction of the Gricean analysis, the speaker's decision to put the effect before the cause in (3b), and hence be *unorderly*, carries no hint of uncooperativity.

Second, Levinson's picture, as we understand it, predicts that unnecessary prolixity should trigger M(anner)-implicature, in the way that, say, *Mary got the machine to stop* implicates that the stoppage was achieved through atypical means—an inference triggered from the speaker's avoidance of the less prolix *Mary stopped the machine*. However, we find that including a more specific connective in cases like (4)—*Fred got bitten by a mosquito, and as a result, contracted the Zika virus*—does not trigger a similar Gricean inference to atypical or otherwise indirect causation. Indeed, and contrary to the predictions of the Gricean view, here a speaker's inclusion of a more prolix alternative form does not come across as uncooperative, even if she could have conveyed the same meaning without it.

Finally, as Levinson himself (pp. 122–7) and others have noted, the same enrichments we see in (4) regularly occur without the conjunction:

(5)   Fred got bitten by a mosquito. He contracted the Zika virus.

Obviously there cannot be "conjunction buttressing" if there is no conjunction to buttress. Surely we want our story for the operative enrichments in (4) to apply to (5) as well, but to say that in describing the two events in (5) the speaker has somehow *implicated* a causal relationship seems to us to strain credulity. What is true is that *and* serves a function relevant to coherence establishment, in that it is only compatible with certain coherence relations: it disallows Explanation, for instance, as sentence (6a) cannot typically be interpreted to mean what (6b) expresses.[4]

(6)   a. Fred slipped and he stepped on a banana peel.
        b. Fred slipped because he stepped on a banana peel.

But that clearly points to conventional properties of the meaning of *and*. So to speak of drawing a causal relation between clauses as an enrichment of a conjunction meaning gets things back to front: conjunction meanings influence coherence establishment, not the other way around.

3. Interpretation as Ambiguity Resolution

For these reasons (among others) we are extremely sympathetic to L&S's charge that the Gricean program overreaches in its attempt to explain such interpretive phenomena (and many others) in terms of implicature. But why do L&S go on to hold that these and other cases that are standardly understood as extrasemantic enrichment are better understood as disambiguation between conventionally/grammatically specified alternatives?

Their principal support for this claim comes from a single, high-level argument form turning on Grice's criterion of detachability. As an example, they discuss speech

---

[4] The fact that the meaning of (6a) cannot be enriched to that of (6b) is interesting in light of the neo-Gricean account that allows strengthening to stereotypical interpretations. Why can such enrichment not occur here? The relationship seems perfectly stereotypical.

acts such as the use of (7), in response to a waiter's question "what would you like to order?", to make an indirect request:

(7) Can I have the French Toast? (Lepore and Stone 2015, p. 92, ex. 25)

Their case that the capacity to understand (7) as a way of making polite requests must be understood as a consequence of its linguistic form comes from two central claims: (i) that interpreters organize discourses by construing their constituent sentences as standing in relations of coherence (here they cite Asher and Lascarides 2003; Hobbs 1990; Kehler 2002); and (ii) that linguistic competence requires knowing both what coherence relations are available and which of them are associated with which linguistic forms.

We hope it is clear that the combination of (i) and (ii) would indeed license L&S's radically deflationary attitude toward extrasemantic enrichment. Moreover, and as we have discussed above, we agree with L&S's view that much linguistic understanding is mediated by the establishment and recognition of coherence relations, and so are prepared to concede (i) happily. But why should we believe (ii)?

L&S's case for (ii) rests on intra- and inter-linguistic applications of Mill's Methods: they show that coherence and conversational role can vary with shifts in conventions about linguistic form even when rationality and truth-conditional content remain fixed, and so conclude that coherence and conversational role are determined by the former rather than the latter. Thus, on the intralinguistic side, they reason that if the representation of coherence were a result of general, rational processes not specifically and conventionally tied to particular linguistic forms, then replacing an expression with a paraphrase or clause reordering that preserves truth-conditional content but not form should not significantly alter conversational role. But this prediction fails for examples like (8), which, though it is a near content-match with (7), is hard to hear as an indirect request:

(8) Am I able to have the French Toast? (Lepore and Stone 2015, p. 101, ex. 96)

Analogously, on the interlinguistic side, they suggest that if coherence representation were mediated only by language-independent rational considerations, then one should expect coherence to operate in the same way on truth-conditionally-equivalent sentences in different languages (assuming equally rational conversants). Again, they observe that this prediction fails for pairs like (10a–b): where (10a) can be used by speakers of English to offer a beer to a hearer, its Polish translation, (10b), cannot be so used by speakers of Polish (Wierzbicka 1985).[5]

---

[5] This isn't L&S's only argument for (ii). They also argue (100–102) that the indirect speech act of requesting is grammatically licensed by noting (following Horn 1989; Lakoff 1973; Sadock 1974) that (presumably by convention) *please* felicitously combines with marked and unmarked requests (cf. (9a–b)), and that it can be felicitously appended to (7), as in (9c):

(9) a. # I'm thirsty please. (Lepore and Stone 2015, p. 101, ex. 94–6)
    b. I'd like a drink please.
    c. Can I have the French Toast please?

(10) a. Would you like a beer?   (Lepore and Stone 2015, p. 102, ex. 97)

     b. Miałbys ochotę na piwo?   (Lepore and Stone 2015, p. 102, ex. 98)

L&S make the same case for the sort of coherence-driven enrichments described in §2. Specifically, they offer the contrast between (11a), in which the clauses are in the simple past tense, and the variant in (11b), in which the clauses are in the present perfect.

(11) a. Oil prices doubled and demand for consumer goods plunged.

     b. Oil prices have doubled and demand for consumer goods has plunged. (Lepore and Stone 2015, p. 117, ex. 129)

In typical contexts, passage (11a) will be construed to express a Result relation, according to which the doubling caused the plunging.[6] In contrast, however, a Result interpretation is far less inevitable for (11b); indeed the preferred interpretation appears to be one in which a Parallel relation is operative. L&S observe correctly that this pattern of facts is problematic for the Gricean analysis, since the two versions seem to be truth-conditionally equivalent: as long as both events occurred before the speech time, both (11a–b) will be true. That we get different construals thus violates the non-detachability criterion associated with conversational implicature. We find this criticism persuasive, and we take it as another reason to doubt the scope and adequacy of Gricean explanations.

As there is no middle ground between implicature and ambiguity resolution on their view, the arguments against treating such enrichments as the result of implicature entail that coherence establishment is simply an ambiguity resolution problem (see their §6.2), one for which speakers and hearers bring a variety of conventional cues to bear in negotiating discourse construals. Support for that view is provided by the fact that, as dictated by coherence theory, the process of establishing coherence is mandated: hearers have to infer *some* type of relevancy relation between adjacent clauses within a discourse segment as part of discourse comprehension. So as long as the inventory of coherence relations is finite, the process can be justifiably viewed as a problem of disambiguating among the possible relations. Indeed, applying this process iteratively to larger discourse segments yields a mechanism for discourse parsing that is in some ways analogous to sentence parsing, the latter of which is broadly agreed to be a disambiguation process.

4. Conversational Eliciture

Whether or not one finds the ambiguity view of intersentential coherence establishment compelling, we believe that there is a highly related class of cases—ones for which

---

For reasons of space, we'll ignore this apparently subsidiary consideration for L&S in favor of responding to the argument on which they place the most weight.

  [6] L&S actually classify it as a weaker Narrative (i.e., Occasion) relation, according to which the events are related by contingency rather than causality. The boundary between the two relations can be a fine one. Since both impose a requirement for forward movement of time, this difference will not concern us here.

comprehension recruits the same interpretive machinery—that is nonetheless much less naturally cast in this way. These cases, which we have labeled ELICITURES (Cohen and Kehler 2018), are those in which coherence establishment processes apply optionally within clauses, thereby generating pragmatic enrichments that are not linguistically mandated. We can see a simple example of eliciture in (12a), which strongly invites us to infer, but does not entail, that the speaker not only intends to communicate that the company fired the employee *and* the employee was embezzling money, but that the company fired the employee *because* the employee was embezzling money.

(12)   a. The company fired *the manager who was embezzling money*. (Rohde et al. 2011)

      b. The company fired *the manager who was hired in* 2002.

Note that this is merely a defeasible inference: (12a) could be followed with *The reason the manager was fired was because he was rude and always late*. In (12b), on the other hand, being hired in 2002 will normally not be understood to be the cause of the firing; here the relative clause (RC) is merely identificational.

According to the analysis we offer in Cohen and Kehler (2018), elicitures result from the speaker's exploitation, by way of her particular choices of referring expressions, of the same types of cognitive machinery that hearers use to establish discourse coherence between clauses.[7] That is, the relationship inferred for (12a) is unmistakably parallel to that which underlies the establishment of the Explanation relation for the intersentential variant in (13):

(13)   The company fired the manager. He was embezzling money.

Whereas intrasentential cases like (12a) and intersentential ones like (13) differ in that only the latter case mandates that some coherence relation be established between the relevant propositions, we see no reason to think that the inference process itself—including the world knowledge that the hearer brings to bear—is any different.

While we are confident that L&S would agree that implicature is not the source of the causal inference in example (12a), we are likewise confident that they would disagree about what the source is: we still consider it to result from a form of pragmatic enrichment, whereas they are forced to the view that it is a result of ambiguity resolution. How would an ambiguity story go for such cases?

We assume that the ambiguity view would start at the same place as the eliciture view, with the observation that the RCs in (12a–b) each participate in a standard modification relationship with the noun phrase (NP) to which they attach (in these cases, restricting the domain of reference for that NP), as produced straightforwardly by a standard compositional semantics. On the eliciture view, of course, that is all there is to say on the semantics side. For L&S to capture the possibility of additional content

---

[7] And for that matter, the same cognitive machinery they use to understand non-linguistic situations that they encounter in the world (see §5).

resulting from establishing coherence, we suspect that they would follow the approach outlined at the end of §3, specifically by articulating a set of coherence relations that can hold. On this story, in addition to deriving the standard meaning of an RC based on compositional principles, a search would be triggered to find an appropriate coherence relation between two propositions: one expressed by the matrix sentence (*The company fired the manager*), and one derived from the relative clause and the NP to which it attaches (*The manager was embezzling money*). The same world knowledge and inference process that the eliciture view relies on for enrichment is then used to disambiguate the operative coherence relation, which in the case of (12a) would be Explanation.

When we consider a larger set of cases, however, we see this picture grow increasingly complicated and, in our view, completely untenable. Consider first cases like (12b), for which, like the great many sentences containing RCs, there is no eliciture. To account for such examples, the existence of a relation of "No-Relation" would have to be posited, one which just happens to be the overwhelmingly typical case. (Note that this move creates a discontinuity with the theory of intersentential coherence, for which the lack of a No-Relation relation is crucial for accounting for infelicitous discourses.) So at this stage, we have a disambiguation problem for every RC one encounters between two relations, the most common of which is the lack of a relation.

The complexity multiplies when we discover that elicitures are not limited to relationships between the proposition derived from an RC and the one denoted by the matrix. For instance, they can relate a proposition derived from an adjectival and the one denoted by the matrix sentence. Consider (14a–b):

(14)   a. *The drug-addled undergrad* fell off of the Torrey Pines cliffs. (adapted from an example of Webber 1991)

 b. *The well-liked undergrad* fell off of the Torrey Pines cliffs.

Sentences (14a–b) exhibit the same distinction between Explanation and No-Relation that (12a–b) does. Specifically, (14a) sees the inference of a relationship between the proposition denoted by the matrix (*the undergrad fell off of the Torrey Pines cliffs*) and one derived from an adjectival and the nominal that it modifies (*the undergrad was drug-addled*). So if the ambiguity treatment of (12a–b) requires positing a two-way ambiguity for the relationship between RCs and matrix sentences, the same must be done for adjectivals, where again No-Relation will by far be the most common outcome.

Extending this inquiry in the obvious way, it doesn't take long to see that elicitures can relate propositions that are derived from any two constituents, and hence need not even involve the proposition denoted by the matrix. Consider (15a):

(15)   The drunk kid who got into a car accident is home now.

Example (15a) invites the eliciture that the drinking led to the accident. Here the eliciture results from establishing a relation between the content expressed by two modifiers of the subject NP: a proposition derived from an adjectival and the nominal that it modifies (*the kid was drunk*) and a proposition derived from an RC and the NP to which it attaches (*the kid got into a car accident*). The proposition denoted by the matrix (*the kid is home now*) doesn't come into play. Thus, to maintain an ambiguity view of elicitures, one would have to posit a coherence relation between every pair of constituents from which propositions can be derived in any given sentence, triggering a disambiguation process for each, one that will again result in No-Relation in a large majority of cases.

That there would be an explicit search for such relations, with the requisite invocation of machinery for disambiguation on such a broad scale, seems highly implausible to us. But it actually gets worse. Consider (16):

(16)   The drunk pilot was arrested.

Example (16) gives rise to a rich picture of a pilot who was arrested because he was flying (or perhaps preparing to fly) while inebriated. The enrichments that give rise to this picture result despite the fact that (16) could be used to describe a situation in which a pilot, who happened to be drinking a fair bit on his day off, got arrested for cheating on his taxes. On the pragmatic enrichment account, the inferences result from world knowledge that tells us that a pilot—crucially, when flying or preparing to do so—can be arrested for being inebriated; the speaker who utters example (16) therefore takes advantage of this knowledge being in the common ground to convey her message in a particularly efficient way. The ambiguity account, on the other hand, now needs to disambiguate a relation that involves propositions derived from *three* constituents: one derived from the combination of the adjectival and the nominal it modifies (*the pilot was drunk*), one derived from the nominal itself (*the pilot was flying or preparing to*), and one derived from the matrix (*the pilot was arrested*). Examples (17a–c) reveal that variants of (16) which lack any one of these three propositions do not give rise to the same eliciture:

(17)   a. The drunk pilot was hitting on a stewardess at the hotel bar.
        b. The drunk person was arrested.
        c. The tall pilot was arrested.

It is difficult to see how examples like (16) could receive a compelling treatment on a view in which possible interpretations are conventionally prespecified and disambiguated amongst. Not only would (16) require a search for a coherence relation involving three propositions, but one in which these propositions are utilized in a particular configuration to form a two-place relation: here it is the *conjunction* of two propositions (*the pilot was drunk* and *the pilot was flying or preparing to*) that play the role of the cause, with the third proposition (*the pilot was arrested*) providing the effect.[8] Hence,

---

[8] Note that this situation is distinct from one in which multiple constituents give rise to multiple elicitures:

(18)   The drunk kid who got into a car accident is in the hospital.

the ambiguity view must now allow for the conventionally provided possibility of a two-place Explanation relation that combines propositions derived from multiple constituents to fill one of its argument positions.

We could continue to pursue cases of greater complexity, but hope that it has become clear that the ambiguity view is highly implausible as an account of eliciture, and at the same time fails to offer any explanatory advantages over the pragmatic enrichment view. It seems clear to us that such enrichments do not result from a 'search' for an interpretation, but instead are triggered by associations that our cognitive apparatus is built to recognize automatically; ones that are served up linguistically by virtue of the particular expressions that a speaker chooses to employ. That is, the only plausible trigger for these inferences is the machinery that we have that is capable of recognizing such associations; machinery that is already running as we interpret not only language but indeed the world around us.

5. Further Costs of the Ambiguity View

Having offered an initial argument against L&S's ambiguity resolution view based on the properties of eliciture, we now want to argue that there are a number of further theoretical costs that make the view untenable. Specifically, we find that the view gives rise to an unwelcome proliferation of ambiguities, is badly underconstrained, is non-compositional, threatens to make the semantics of natural languages unlearnable, and rests on a surprising coincidence between the content of linguistic conventions and the standard menu of coherence relations. We'll take these points in turn.

To begin, if eliciture-amenable sentences are ambiguous between interpretations in which the relevant elicitures are drawn and interpretations in which they are not, then there will turn out to be *a lot* more ambiguity in natural languages than one might have expected. After all, as Hobbs (1979) points out, it is always possible to build contexts supporting coherence relations between otherwise apparently unrelated discourse elements: even those in a paradigm incoherent discourse like (19) can be brought into coherence, for example, on the supposition that the employee injured himself in an unsuccessful attempt to climb a plum tree with the goal of attaining plums.

(19)   # The employee broke his leg. He likes plums. (variant of example from Knott and Dale 1994)

Similarly, though one might not initially expect a causal eliciture between the event of firing and the RC in the object NP in (20), the eliciture is naturally evoked in a context in which John is a protective parent with a Bieber-fan daughter who also works for his company.

(20)   John fired the employee who looks like Justin Bieber.

Here it is natural to infer both that the drinking led to the accident, and that the accident in turn led to the hospital stay. The situation with (16) is different in that there is only one Explanation relation being established.

The point here is simple: if coherence can be established this freely for more or less arbitrary discourses by manipulating the non-linguistic background, and if, per L&S, elicitures are diagnostic of linguistic ambiguity, then it would seem that more or less every discourse in any natural language will turn out to be (very many ways) ambiguous (cf. Szabó 2016, p. 168).

Additionally, the ambiguity resolution view is seriously underconstrained in its current form. If the view is to avoid the charge of post-hoc storytelling that L&S (appropriately) level at Griceans, we need a detailed account of just which particular elements of linguistic form allow for which ranges of specific disambiguations, and a description of just how disambiguation derives its output from context, world knowledge, and linguistic knowledge. It won't suffice merely to say that linguistic forms turn out to be ambiguous just when, and in just the ways in which, elicitures or other phenomena classically treated as pragmatic enrichment are drawn in light of context and world knowledge. Until the account is provided in far greater detail than L&S have given so far, it's hard to know what the view predicts about cases, and consequently difficult to evaluate that view empirically.

In the case of eliciture, this concern is reinforced by the observation that, in many examples, the enriched content cannot be seen to originate in any single constituent in linguistic form, but only from the combined occurrence of multiple constituents not directly related in the syntax. To see this point, consider (21a–c):

(21)   a. The teacher met with *the student who looks like Harry Potter.*

b. The Hollywood studio representative met with *the student who goes to the local community college.*

c. The Hollywood studio representative met with *the student who looks like Harry Potter.*

We take it that the causal/explanatory eliciture here is much more strongly evoked by (21c) than by either (21a) or (21b): it is (21c), rather than (21a) or (21b), that evokes an image of the representative looking for the next child movie star. Crucially, the eliciture in question cannot be tied to the occurrence of any one constituent: example (21a) fails to evoke the inference even though it features the same RC as (21c), and (21b) fails to evoke the inference even though it features the same subject noun phrase as (21c). The eliciture arises only when both constituents occur together, as in (21c).

It is a consequence of this observation that, at least in many cases, L&S's ambiguities must be choices of whole propositional meanings for complete sentential linguistic forms rather than smaller units. But this means that the information L&S envisage treating as conventionally encoded pairings of form and meaning won't, in general, be compositionally determined from the meanings assigned to subsentential components and syntax. In effect, the conventional pairings at issue will be specifiable only as a look-up table (with the full power of a Turing Machine) connecting whole sentential forms with whole propositional meanings. (This point reinforces our concern that the view will be underconstrained, and therefore open to charges of post-hoccery.)

And, indeed, this point encourages the suspicion that the ambiguity resolution view places severe burdens on language learning. The view requires that linguistic knowledge specify, as possible disambiguations, all the elicitures that could be possibly drawn from sentences/discourses. But, as we have seen, one can nearly always evoke elicitures from a given discourse passage, provided the context is suitable. This suggests that, for L&S, linguistic knowledge will have to predict the full, observed variation in inferential behavior of discourses in an unpredictable range of contexts. Moreover, and as we have also seen, elicitures of sentences are, in general, not compositional: they are not predictable from the interpretations of subsentential constituents and their syntactic configurations. Consequently, linguistic knowledge will have to specify the range of possible effects of each sentence as a separate, unstructured list. If we assume an infinitude of sentences in each natural language, then it becomes difficult to see how finite learners could attain this sort of linguistic knowledge, as required by the ambiguity resolution view.

Finally, the ambiguity resolution view is committed to a surprising coincidence between the content of linguistic convention and the standard coherence relations. We can bring this point into relief by contrasting what the ambiguity resolution theorist will say about linguistic examples like those we have already seen and structurally analogous non-linguistic cases. On the non-linguistic side, consider the following two contrasting situations. In the first, someone sees a chronically tardy employee show up late for work again, and soon thereafter witnesses the employee being fired; in the second, she sees a chronically tardy employee show up late for work again, and soon thereafter witnesses the employee being asked by a customer where the automotive department is located. A reasonable cognitive agent might infer that the firing was due to the lateness in the first situation, but is unlikely to infer any relationship between the customer's question and the employee's lateness in the second. Presumably this is because world knowledge supports the possibility of a causal/explanatory connection in the first situation but not the second. With this pair in mind, we can now consider the interpretation of linguistically expressed reports of the very same situations, such as (22a–b):

(22) a. The boss fired the employee who came in late again.

b. A customer asked the employee who came in late again where the automotive department is.

Just as in the non-linguistic cases, a reasonable agent is likely to draw a causal eliciture in interpreting (22a), but not in interpreting (22b). Considering these cases together, it's hard to avoid the conclusion that the non-linguistic pair and the linguistic pair are related in analogous ways, and that we should aim for a theory that treats both pairs in terms of a common species of cognitive machinery.[9]

---

[9] This is a species of connection that Grice (1975, p. 28) himself famously emphasizes. Perhaps needless to say, it is also a species of connection that comes for free on a theory that treats elicitures as extrasemantic

We presume an ambiguity resolution theorist will agree, and will attempt to capture the apparent structural similarity on display by saying that the very same inferential strategies enlisted in the non-linguistic cases are deployed in the linguistic cases in the service of disambiguation. Specifically, she will claim that linguistic convention dictates that a relative clause such as that in (22a–b) (or adjectival, or what have you) can express a cause or not, and that whatever inferential procedures license or fail to license a causal interpretation in the non-linguistic cases are, in linguistic cases like (22a–b), used to choose between the available disambiguations made available.

But now we should ask: exactly why is it that convention makes available an Explanation-involving disambiguation, in particular, whenever there is a relative clause? Why *this* specific interpretive alternative for *this* specific linguistic form? As L&S correctly emphasize, linguistic and other conventions are deeply contingent: hence, linguistic convention might have paired with RCs either no coherence relation or entirely different coherence relations as potential disambiguations. Why, then, does linguistic convention make the particular pairings it does? The ambiguity resolution theorist cannot answer this question by appeal to the inferential machinery that both sides think are at work, and that she understands as serving disambiguation. After all, her view is that this inferential machinery enters the interpretive process only after convention has already made available the relevant interpretive alternatives. And, of course, the conventions at issue are language-specific, hence, not shared with or explicable in terms of other aspects of our mental processing.

Moreover, the coincidence runs deeper than just this one particular form–content pairing of RCs with the Explanation relation. Indeed, even this single linguistic form is associated with a range of distinct elicitures. Thus, (23a) plausibly invites an interpretation that denies, rather than affirms, a causal relation between the matrix verb *fired* and the RC; (23b) plausibly invites an interpretation involving an Occasion relation, where the subject is understood to have bought the whiskey at the store mentioned in the RC; and, as we have seen, vastly most RCs invite no coherence-driven interpretation (or, if you like, invite interpretation in terms of the No-Relation relation).

(23)   a. The boss fired the employee who had won many corporate rewards.
       b. The employee who went to the liquor store bought a bottle of whiskey.

It would seem, then, that the ambiguity resolution theorist is committed to holding that linguistic convention—which she invokes to explain linguistic but not non-linguistic cases, despite the striking similarities between the two—just happens to make available as possible disambiguations for RCs the same sorts of standard coherence relations (Explanation, Denial, Occasion, No-Relation) that come for free on an enrichment account. That is, to our minds, a surprising coincidence—and one that, as far as we can tell, the ambiguity resolution theorist lacks the resources to explain.

expansions driven by the very inferential mechanisms we use in understanding the non-linguistically presented world.

6. Ambiguity Resolution Reconsidered: Tense and Event Structure

At this point we have offered several arguments against the ambiguity view, resting on a variety of conceptual and empirical grounds. In constructing our arguments, a recurring frustration we have had with L&S's own argumentation is that, while they repeatedly point to a role for convention for the phenomena they address, they typically do not offer detailed linguistic analyses of these phenomena, such that the reader can clearly see how convention and disambiguation combine to cover the same explanatory ground as accounts based on pragmatic enrichment.

Perhaps the treatment for which they paint the clearest picture is in their analysis of how the temporal ordering of events described in a discourse are recovered. Recall from §3 that one of L&S's central arguments against Gricean treatments of such orderings concerns the contrast between (11a) and (11b), repeated below as (24a) and (24b) respectively.

(24)   a. Oil prices doubled and demand for consumer goods plunged.

b. Oil prices have doubled and demand for consumer goods has plunged. (Lepore and Stone 2015, p. 117, ex. 129)

Recall that in typical contexts, passage (24a) will be construed to express a Result relation, according to which the doubling caused (and hence preceded) the plunging, whereas (24b) will be construed as a Parallel relation, in which no such causal (or temporal) relationship is inferred. L&S argue that this difference is problematic for the Gricean analysis, since the two versions appear to have the same truth conditions, violating the non-detachability criterion on implicatures.

L&S take the failure of the Gricean analysis to show that convention and disambiguation, by themselves, account for temporal interpretation: "it's logical form that settles whether a sentence has a narrative reading or another possible interpretation" (p. 116). In this section, we take a closer look at how L&S's appeal to convention can potentially explain the difference witnessed for (24a–b). We ultimately conclude, however, that convention and disambiguation are incapable of doing all the work that L&S assign to them; such an analysis still requires a mechanism for pragmatic enrichment. We then follow in §7 by sketching a middle ground account, one that recognizes robust contributions from both convention and pragmatic enrichment (and their interaction), using the interpretation of tense and event structure as a testing ground for theorizing.

L&S lay out their preferred account (henceforth, 'the anaphoric analysis' of tense) in their §§7.2–7.3, which we briefly summarize here. They list three possible temporal interpretations between events described by successive clauses in the simple past: simultaneity, backward movement, and forward movement. Simply put, they capture these possibilities in terms of a similarly three-way anaphoric ambiguity, whereby the simple tense can refer to "the time of the previous event," a time "immediately leading up to the time of the previously mentioned event," or a time "immediately following some previously mentioned event" (pp. 121–2). On this proposal, the options for temporal relations are specified by the conventions associated with tense; at best, coherence establishment merely plays a role in disambiguating among these options.

An immediate question that arises is what advantages the anaphoric analysis brings to the table, as it seems largely redundant with explanatory tools (such as coherence establishment) that L&S already recognize. If coherence establishment and other reasoning processes they already accept deliver the right interpretive possibilities (as we aim to show below), it's hard to see the point of enlisting convention (and reconstruing coherence establishment as a mechanism for disambiguation) to cover the very same explanatory ground.[10]

The main problem we see, however, is that the anaphoric account cannot cover the same ground that coherence establishment does: pragmatic enrichment will still be required to enrich temporal interpretations beyond those specified by tense on the anaphoric account. To see this, consider (26):

(26) a. Fred was taken to the hospital.
      b. He got bitten by a mosquito and contracted the Zika virus.

On the most accessible understanding of (26), we know three things about the ordering of events: the biting occurred before the hospital trip, the contraction of Zika occurred before the hospital trip, and the contraction of Zika occurred after the biting. These three facts can be plausibly recovered straightforwardly in terms of the establishment of a Result relation between the two events described in (26b), which explains the ordering between the biting and the contraction, and then the inference to an Explanation relation between these events and the trip to the hospital, which explains the other two temporal orderings. Crucially, this explanation does not depend in any way on treating tense as anaphoric.

We don't see that these three temporal relationships can all be recovered by the anaphoric account by itself, however. The fact that the biting occurs before the hospital trip can be recovered by anaphorically resolving the past tense associated with *got bitten* to the interval preceding the hospital trip. The issue is with the other two relationships. Specifically, there seem to be two relevant interpretive possibilities for the

---

[10] This is a slight oversimplification, as there is a difference between the analyses with respect to cases in which a Parallel relation is operative. L&S's treatment of a simultaneity reading as a distinct interpretive possibility is intended to capture examples like (25).

(25) John played the piano. Mary played the kazoo. (Webber 1988)

They note, correctly, that coherence does not deliver this reading; as we've already indicated, Parallel typically does not order events. On the other hand, this ordering can easily be seen as an inference from the assumption that John and Mary are playing together, and even then the inference isn't inevitable (John and Mary could have participated in different songs at the same concert). More to the point, recall that examples like (3a) do not impose an order among the events, and we find this to be true of L&S's own (24a) as well. L&S do not explain how such cases can be captured with the three interpretive possibilities they specify.

simple past associated with *contracted* from which we must pick. On the one hand, if it is anaphorically resolved to the interval preceding the hospital trip, this correctly predicts that the contraction occurred before the trip, but does not capture that the contraction occurred after the biting. On the other hand, if the tense is resolved to the interval immediately following the biting, we can capture that the contraction occurred after the biting, but not that it occurred prior to the hospital trip. Either way, then, the disambiguation of tense only yields one relation, and coherence-driven enrichment will still be required to obtain the other. And, insofar as these enrichments must be understood as going beyond what is specified by convention and disambiguation (for reasons discussed in §3), it follows that the anaphoric analysis is incapable of eliminating the need for pragmatic enrichment in particular.[11]

We therefore conclude that the tools provided by the ambiguity resolution view are both unnecessary and insufficient for accounting for the facts about tense and event structure.

7. Tense and Event Structure Redux

So far we have argued against both Gricean views and L&S's ambiguity resolution view, claiming that neither of these extremal positions adequately accounts for language understanding. In light of these considerations, we strongly suspect that the best way forward will involve a mixed account—one that makes room for substantive contributions from both convention and pragmatic enrichment. In this section, we'll investigate how such an analysis might look for examples like (24a–b).

We can start by first asking what the conventional properties of tense—as they pertain to temporal interpretation and the mental representation of event structure—tell us about cases like (24a–b), and then ask where pragmatic enrichment might take over. We can begin by making an uncontroversial observation: that the semantic properties of the tenses used in a passage constrain the types of coherence relations that can be inferred. For instance, whereas (27a) admits of both Explanation and Result interpretations, (27b) only has the Explanation interpretation.

(27)   a. John slipped. He spilt a bucket of water. (Lascarides and Asher 1993)
        b. John slipped. He had spilt a bucket of water.

L&S, as we have argued, would seek to explain these facts solely by way of the conventional properties of tense. We propose to explain them, on the other hand, with an account that appeals to an interaction between what is conventionally encoded by

---

[11] In making their case, L&S, following Partee and others, point to certain analogies between tense and pronominal reference. There is much to say here, but for now we simply point out that there are significant disanalogies as well. For instance, one might wonder why it's acceptable to begin a discourse with a sentence in the simple past when no antecedent is available, as in (26a). This isn't the case with antecedentless pronouns—replacing *Fred* with *He* in (26a) results in infelicity.

tense and processes of coherence establishment.[12] Specifically, we propose that, on the one hand, the past perfect associated with (27b) is anaphoric: it specifies that the event time is ordered prior to an anaphorically identified reference time, which in this case, will be the event time associated with the slipping. Coherence establishment is then constrained to infer coherence relations consistent with that ordering, which rules out Result. On the other hand, the simple past on our analysis is not anaphoric—instead it merely orders the event time prior to the speech time (cf. Reichenbach 1947). What this means is that the simple pasts in (27a) do not place any constraints on the ordering between two events. Coherence establishment is then free to choose any order, with Result imposing forward movement of time and Explanation backward movement. It would thus seem that the fixing of temporal interpretation follows coherence establishment in this case rather than the other way around. The analysis of these two cases thus instantiates a general picture in which the temporal properties associated with tense may constrain the ordering among events (perhaps only partially), and then coherence establishment, while adhering to those constraints, may further enrich the temporal relationships that are ultimately conveyed.

It is likewise clear that coherence establishment is sensitive not only to tense, but to conventions that pertain to the mental representation of event structure as well. Consider the difference between the perfective and imperfective forms in (28a–b):

(28)   a. Andy handed the corkscrew to Jonathan. Jonathan opened the wine.
       b. ?? Andy was handing the corkscrew to Jonathan. Jonathan opened the wine.

Whereas (28a) is a perfectly coherent Occasion relation, (28b) is odd. The reason is evident: even though the handing event occurred in the past, it is described in (28b) as if it is in process, which is to say the focus is on the ongoing development of the event rather than its consequences. This creates a problem for the inference to Occasion, which requires a salient consequent state for the previous event to serve as the presumed initial state for the subsequent one (Hobbs 1990; Kehler 2002); with no salient consequent state provided by (28b), incoherence results. Note that interpretation could have been such that hearers would simply accommodate the fact that the handing event had successfully completed and hence interpret (28b) much like (28a), but that's not how it works. It matters where the hearer's focus resides within event structure in his mental model of the discourse.

With these observations in hand, let us now return to (24a–b). Whereas (24a–b) may have the same truth conditions, it is well known that the simple past and present perfect are not fully interchangeable. Consider the first clauses of (24a–b), with the possible follow-ons given in (29a–b):

(29)   a. Oil prices doubled (but then promptly retreated soon afterward).
       b. Oil prices have doubled (?? but then promptly retreated soon afterward).

---

[12] This account is spelled out in greater detail in Kehler (2002, ch.7).

Unlike (29a), (29b) sounds odd with a continuation that makes it clear that the state of affairs that resulted from the doubling—that is, prices that are twice as high than at a salient prior time—is no longer true at the speech time. The analysis of Moens and Steedman (1988), which L&S appeal to, captures this through an interaction between times (particularly event, speech, and reference times, per Reichenbach) and event structure. By situating the reference and speech times associated with the present perfect in the consequent state of event structure, they capture the intuition that, in L&S's words, the purpose of the present perfect is to "reference particular consequences of an event located indefinitely in the past, and to present those consequences as still holding in the present".

In light of the effect we saw for (28a–b), it is perhaps not surprising that the component of event structure that a particular choice of tense and aspect places in focus would affect coherence in (24a–b) as well. Here, the meaning of the present perfect—by placing focus on the fact that the result state of the first event continues to hold at the speech time—may disrupt the establishment of a Result relation in cases in which the effect is described as holding before the speech time, since Result orders the relevant times in forward progression. If this is the case, then establishing a Result relation when the first clause is in the present perfect should only be possible if the event described in the second clause not only occurred subsequent to the first event, but also not prior to the speech time.

The predictions associated with this conjecture are easy enough to test; consider (30a–d):

(30)   a. Oil prices doubled and so I'm going to start taking the train to work (next week).

b. Oil prices doubled and so I started taking the train to work (last week).

c. Oil prices have doubled and so I'm going to start taking the train to work (next week).

d. ?? Oil prices have doubled and so I started taking the train to work (last week).

Whereas both (30a–b) are fine in the simple past, the present perfect versions in (30c–d) differ. Specifically, (30d) is odd because the focus on present circumstances that arises from the first clause is incompatible with moving back to the past in the second clause. A continuation that talks about a result that will happen after the speech time, on the other hand, is fine, per (30c).

This explains why the inference to Result in (24b) would be disrupted as well, since the initial event is similarly described with the present perfect, and the second described as having occurred in the past. Indeed, our explanation makes a specific prediction: that the problem with (24b) is due to the first clause being in the present perfect, and not the second. This prediction is confirmed by the status of the following two variants: the version with the first clause in the present perfect and the second in the simple past is odd on a Result interpretation (31a), whereas the version with the first clause in the simple past and the second in the present perfect is fine (31b).

(31) a. ?? Oil prices have doubled and demand for consumer goods plunged.
      b. Oil prices doubled and demand for consumer goods has plunged.

This analysis thus shows how convention can play a greater role in determining construals than Grice envisaged, while at the same time maintaining a role for pragmatic enrichment. Needless to say, there remains much to say about these particular examples and the explanations on offer. Still, we hope we have made the case that L&S's criticisms of Gricean accounts—compelling as they are—do not, by themselves, license the conclusion that there is no important role to be played by pragmatic enrichment. Rather, we take these considerations to show that there exist promising explanations of the phenomena under consideration that give substantive roles to both convention and pragmatic enrichment, but where both of these components and their relationship will have to be understood at a more detailed level than Grice typically pursued.

8. Conclusion

We find L&S's case against the explanatory excesses of the Gricean program persuasive. They have performed an important service for the field in showing the shortcomings of both Griceans' radically minimal conception of what is said, and their oversimplistic characterization of a diverse range of phenomena in terms of a single notion of implicature.

On the other hand, we find that L&S err in the opposite direction by propounding an overunified analysis of their own. While we accept their conclusion that convention plays a greater role than has typically been appreciated, and that it fixes far more at the level of what is said than Griceans allow, we do not believe that all of the interpretive effects L&S hope to explain are adequately accounted for in terms of ambiguity resolution between conventionally specified alternatives.

At the end of the day, we believe that an adequate account of language understanding will have to recognize both extrasemantic expansion (including but not limited to implicature) and a robust role for convention in fixing interpretive alternatives. Indeed, we find it unsurprising that both forces should figure centrally in language use. After all, a language that did not take advantage of context and its users' knowledge stores and capacity for inference would thereby pass up significant opportunities for improved communicative efficiency with respect to the speaker. And at the same time, a language that failed to conventionalize certain common relationships that would otherwise be left to inference would likewise ignore significant opportunities for improved communicative efficiency with respect to the hearer. We expect that the investigation of the precise ways in which these forces are balanced within languages will become a rich source of progress in the field.[13]

References

Asher, Nicholas and Alex Lascarides (2003), *Logics of Conversation*, Cambridge University Press, Cambridge.

Bach, Kent (1994), "Conversational Impliciture," *Mind and Language*, 9 (2), pp. 124–62.

Cohen, Jonathan and Andrew Kehler (2018), "Conversational Eliciture," manuscript, University of California, San Diego.

Grice, H. Paul (1975), "Logic and Conversation," in *Syntax and Semantics*, ed. by Peter Cole and Jerry L. Morgan, Academic Press, New York, vol. 3, pp. 41–58.

Grice, H. Paul (1981), "Presupposition and Conversational Implicature," in *Radical Pragmatics*, ed. by Peter Cole, Academic Press, New York, pp. 183–98.

Hobbs, Jerry R. (1979), "Coherence and Coreference," *Cognitive Science*, 3, pp. 67–90.

Hobbs, Jerry R. (1990), *Literature and Cognition*, CSLI Lecture Notes 21, Stanford, CA.

Horn, Laurence R. (1989), *A Natural History of Negation*, University of Chicago Press, Chicago, IL.

Horn, Laurence R. (2016), "Conventional Wisdom Reconsidered," *Inquiry*, 59 (2), pp. 145–62.

Kehler, Andrew (2002), *Coherence, Reference, and the Theory of Grammar*, CSLI Publications, Stanford, CA.

Knott, Alistair and Robert Dale (1994), "Using Linguistic Phenomena to Motivate a Set of Coherence Relations," *Discourse Processes*, 18 (1), pp. 35–62.

Lakoff, George (1973), "Some Thoughts on Transderivational Constraints," in *Issues in Linguistics: Papers in Honor of Henry and Renee Kahane*, ed. by Braj B. Kachru, Robert B. Lees, Yakov Malkiel, Angelina Pietrangeli, and Sol Sporta, University of Illinois Press, Urbana, IL, pp. 442–52.

Lascarides, Alex and Nicholas Asher (1993), "Temporal Interpretation, Discourse Relations, and Common Sense Entailment," *Linguistics and Philosophy*, 16 (5), pp. 437–93.

Lepore, Ernie and Matthew Stone (2015), *Imagination and Convention: Distinguishing Grammar and Inference in Language*, Oxford University Press, Oxford.

Levinson, Stephen C. (2000), *Presumptive Meanings*, MIT Press, Cambridge, MA.

Moens, Marc and Mark Steedman (1988), "Temporal Ontology and Temporal Reference," *Computational Linguistics*, 14 (2), pp. 15–28.

Reichenbach, Hans (1947), *Elements of Symbolic Logic*, Macmillan, New York.

Roberts, Craige (1998), "Information Structure in Discourse: Towards an Integrated Formal Theory of Pragmatics," in *OSU Working Papers in Linguistics* 49: *Papers in Semantics (1996)*, ed. by J. H. Yoon and Andreas Kathol, Revised version as of September 1998, Ohio State University, pp. 91–136.

Rohde, Hannah, Roger Levy, and Andrew Kehler (2011), "Anticipating Explanations in Relative Clause Processing," *Cognition*, 118, pp. 339–58.

---

[13] We are grateful to participants in the 2017 Philosophy Desert Workshop, and especially to Will Starr, for helpful discussion of an earlier version of this chapter.

Sadock, Jerrold M. (1974), *Towards a Linguistic Theory of Speech Acts*, Academic Press, New York.

Sperber, Dan and Deirdre Wilson (1986), *Relevance: Communication and Cognition*, Harvard University Press, Cambridge, MA.

Szabó, Zoltán Gendler (2016), "In Defense of Indirect Communication," *Inquiry*, 59 (2), pp. 163–74.

Webber, Bonnie Lynn (1988), "Tense as Discourse Anaphor," *Computational Linguistics*, 14 (2), pp. 61–73.

Webber, Bonnie Lynn (1991), "Discourse Modelling: Life at the Bottom," in *AAAI Fall Symposium Series on Dis-course Structure in Natural Language Understanding and Generation*, American Association for Artificial Intelligence, Asilomar, CA, pp. 146–51.

Wierzbicka, Anna (1985), "Different Cultures, Different Languages, Different Speech Acts: Polish vs. English," *Journal of Pragmatics*, 9 (2–3), pp. 145–78.

14

Convention, Intention, and the Conversational Record

Mandy Simons

1. Introduction

This essay concerns one of the central claims made by Lepore and Stone (henceforward, L&S) in their book, *Imagination and Convention*. The claim is this: Aspects of speaker intention identifiable through general inferential processes are not part of the content to which speakers become publicly committed by their linguistic utterances, even though these intentions may be transparently recognized by interlocutors. The argument for this conclusion has two prongs. The first prong of the argument is driven by various empirical arguments. L&S look at a variety of phenomena that have been claimed to involve non-conventionalized elements, and argue against the inferentialist accounts. So, one way to push back against their arguments is to undermine one or more of these arguments. While I think this pushback is invited in various places, I will not take on that project here.

The second prong of their argument is driven by more abstract theoretical considerations. The general idea, as I understand it, is this: The intentions that a speaker has in making an utterance are indeterminately complex. These intentions form a sort of web that radiates out from a basic intention to ever more complex intentions about the ultimate effects of the utterance. L&S argue that the only way to delineate an intention which can count as a truly linguistically relevant intention—an intention whereby we can delineate meaning—is one which makes crucial reference to linguistic convention.

Their picture thus turns the Gricean view on its head. Instead of speaker intentions underlying convention, they propose that convention underlies, and is essential to, speaker intentions.

My main goal in this essay is to present difficulties for their inverted Gricean picture. I will give both conceptual and empirical arguments that intentions are analytically prior to linguistic conventions, and hence giving an analysis of meaning in terms of intentions seems unavoidable. I'll point out, along the way (although this is not one of my major concerns here) that their criticisms of Grice are to some extent misdirected, as they neglect Grice's distinction between speaker meaning and (conventional) expression meaning. I'll then go on to argue that their conception of a conversational scoreboard, which registers only conventionally licensed update, lacks the resources to model certain types of standard conversational events.

2. On Speaker Meaning vs. Sentence Meaning

Can linguistic meaning be analyzed in terms of speaker intention? L&S argue that it cannot. The central argument for this position, developed in chapter 13 of their book, targets what they call *prospective intentionalism*, the view that "meaning directly reports the speaker's commitments and expectations in using an utterance" (p. 216). They attribute this view to Grice, and so take their position to be in opposition to his. Later in this section, I'll argue that this attribution is incorrect. But I begin by reviewing the argument itself.

The central argument is articulated in this paragraph:

We normally undertake our utterances not only with the intention of updating the conversation, but also with further intentions about how these moves will advance our joint problem solving and our other practical interests. This continuity underscores the close link between conversation and practical collaborations. But *it is this very continuity that renders us skeptical — pace Grice — that the distinctive place of meaning in language can be captured with reference to the broad and eclectic network of our intentions in communicative action.*

(pp. 210–11; emphasis added)

To paraphrase: Every linguistic utterance is associated with a complex set of intentions of different types, that "radiate out" from the action. These intentions cannot be straightforwardly separated from each other. If we identify the meaning of an utterance simply with the intentions that the speaker had in uttering it, then we will find ourselves assigning to utterances hopelessly complex meanings that are far removed from what is linguistically determined. Hence, the project of analyzing linguistic meaning in terms of such intentions is hopeless.

L&S, though, fully acknowledge that intention recognition is a vital part of the communicative process. Despite their allusion to the continuity of intentions in the paragraph just quoted, they propose (section 13.2) a very specific taxonomy of intentions, with subtypes of intention distinguishable by various criteria. At the root of this taxonomy is a *basic intention*, which they characterize as follows: The agent uses basic intentions directly in the control of action; basic intentions are concrete and explicit, and must target objects that the agent can interact with directly and to which the agent can envisage changes that align with the agent's fundamental capabilities (p. 208). They go on:

We think of a person picking up an object seen at arm's reach as a prototypical case: The basic intention is to GRASP THAT THING. The actions involved are AFFORDANCES, effects that agents can bring about just in virtue of the kind of being that they are and the kind of engagement they have with the world. (p. 208, emphasis in original)

L&S propose that every utterance is accompanied by a basic intention: the intention to contribute the grammatically specified meaning of the utterance to the ongoing conversation. *Grammar* here should be construed broadly to include any and all linguistic rules or conventions that contribute to the determination of meaning.[1] It's clear from their further arguments that this intention is supposed to be *de dicto*: the speaker's basic intention is to contribute the grammatically specified meaning of her utterance, whatever it might be, whether or not she knows what it is.

Thus, in what appears to be a complete reversal of the Gricean picture, they propose that linguistic convention is analytically prior to the most basic type of linguistically relevant intention. Restating their view somewhat, we might say that for them, the most basic communicative intention an agent can have is to participate in the conventions of the language community whose language they are using. And this, for L&S, is the *only* intention that is relevant in discussion of the meaning of linguistic utterances.

Now that we have outlined L&S's view, let's take a step back to look more carefully at the Gricean view. It's important to remember, as Neale 1992 articulates, that Grice's project has two parts: Neale calls them The Theory of Meaning and The Theory of Conversation. Neal further emphasizes that these are not two *separate* projects, but two halves of *one* integrated project.

The Theory of Meaning aims to provide a reductive analysis of the notion of meaning, and it is within this part of his project that Grice famously attempts to reduce meaning to intentions. He proposes that the analysis of meaning (of any action) requires that we begin with speaker meaning (speaker construed broadly); and speaker meaning is characterized in terms of the intentions of the speaker. But this is crucially *not* an analysis of the *process* of utterance interpretation. Grice's understanding of *this* process is seen in his work on implicature, where of course the notion of *conventional sentence meaning* plays a central role. If it were the case that Grice thought that a speaker's communicative intentions determined the *linguistic* meaning of her utterances then there would be no need for a theory of conversational implicature!

Grice's attempts to formulate a notion of (what we might call) conventional meaning are articulated in his paper "Utterer's Meaning, Sentence-Meaning and Word Meaning," Essay 6 of *Studies in the Way of Words*. The goal of these attempts is precisely to distinguish what a *sentence* (or expression) means from what a particular *utterance* of a sentence/expression means, and in turn to distinguish these from what a *speaker*

---

[1] It might be thought that when the string uttered is syntactically or lexically ambiguous, grammar could not (even on L&S's strong conventionalist view) specify a unique meaning for the utterance. However, L&S *do* allow that speaker intentions determine the structural properties of the utterance, and also determine which of a collection of homophones counts as occurring in the utterance. As they put it, human language users have the capacity to "[perform] an utterance of a specified linguistic structure" (p. 208).

means on a particular occasion of use.[2] The closest Grice gets to a definition of sentence/expression meaning (for a declarative utterance) is this:[3]

"For group G, utterance-type X means that p" $=_{df}$ "At least some (many) members of group G have in their repertoires the procedure of uttering a token of X if, for some A, they want A to believe that p, the retention of this procedure being for them conditional on the assumption that at least some (other) members of G have, or have had, this procedure in their repertoires." (1989: 127)

Grice recognizes that this attempt is incomplete in various ways; how to improve it is not the current issue. The point, rather, is to emphasize that Grice does indeed have a notion of what a sentence or an utterance of a sentence means, which is distinct from what the speaker means on a particular occasion of use of the sentence; and that Grice at least hoped that the notions of sentence meaning and utterance meaning could be spelled out in terms of the linguistic behaviors of groups of agents with particular intentions/desires.

Thus, Grice does not subscribe to the theory of *prospective intentionalism*, which L&S contrast with their own. For on that theory, the meaning of an uttered expression depends on the "occurrent attitudes" (p. 205) of the speaker[4]. But on Grice's theory— or at least, on the theory that he envisaged—the meaning of an uttered expression depends (roughly speaking) on some kind of generalization over the attitudes of members of a community who have used, or have the potential to use, the uttered sentence type. Speaker meaning, indeed, is a matter of the occurrent attitudes of the speaker, but this is a distinct matter, to which we now turn.

Here is the basic picture, no doubt familiar to most readers, of how addressees are expected to identify speaker meaning, given a linguistic utterance. As a first step, addressees identify *what is said*: what we characterized above as utterance meaning (for Grice, applied timeless meaning of the expression type uttered). Then, addressees reason about whether or not what is said could be (the whole of) what the speaker

---

[2] I will use the term *sentence/expression meaning* for Grice's "timeless meaning of an expression type," and the term *utterance meaning* for Grice's "applied timeless meaning for an expression type." The latter terminology is admittedly generous to Grice: the difference between timeless meaning and applied timeless meaning for Grice involves only disambiguation, whereas I take it that utterance meaning involves not only disambiguation but also the resolution of context dependencies, such as the reference of pronouns.

[3] This is modified from the original, which is formulated to generalize over utterances of any force. For simplicity, I use belief inducement as the basic intention associated with declaratives, although this is not Grice's final view on the matter.

[4] L&S do take prospective intentionalism to be Grice's theory. On p. 205, they say:

On the Gricean account, meaning depends on the speaker's occurrent attitudes: The specific goals, beliefs and expectations that eventuate in the speaker's choice of some particular utterance on some particular occasion.

As noted, this is a correct characterization of *speaker meaning* associated with an utterance, but not of sentence or utterance meaning. L&S go on to say: "The alternative would be to attribute meaning based on STANDING commitments among interlocutors." One might plausibly say that Grice's envisioned account of sentence meaning is based on such standing commitments.

meant, given the assumption that the speaker is behaving cooperatively. If not, then further reasoning brings them to a determination of speaker meaning.

Several things should be noted here. First, it is not the case that speaker intentions on a particular occasion determine what the words or sentences they utter mean on that occasion, beyond the power of those intentions to determine a particular disambiguation of the string uttered. Second, the intentions with which a (rational) speaker can use a particular form are constrained by the conventional meaning of that form. Suppose that I say to an interlocutor with whom I have no special history, "I am allergic to cat hair." Suppose that I intend to get that interlocutor to come to believe that I am allergic to *dog* hair. Well (in the absence of any context), too bad. I simply *shouldn't* utter that sentence with that intention. Because (in the absence of special background knowledge), there is no reason for an English speaker who hears me say "I am allergic to cat hair" to form the belief that I intend them to recognize that I intend to convey that I am allergic to dog hair. In other words: the existing norms, within the speech community, for the use of particular expressions heavily constrain which utterances a speaker can reasonably use to carry out her communicative intentions.

With the Gricean picture clarified in this way, I find it difficult to see how the view that L&S advocate is radically different from the Gricean Theory of Conversation. L&S emphatically acknowledge that speakers may use sentences with communicative intentions which go beyond the meanings of the sentences used; so does Grice. L&S propose that we should characterize the meanings of sentences in terms of the conventions that govern their use; so does Grice. One difference is that L&S seem to be driven by an underlying desire to identify one, and only one, thing as meaning. Grice, on the other hand, acknowledges a variety of types of meaning, associated with different things: speaker meanings, utterance meanings, and sentence meanings. In particular, Grice uses the term *speaker meaning* for the contents with respect to which speakers have communicative intentions, and clearly takes it as given that these intentions can be somehow delimited. L&S assign no special status to additional inferences about speaker intentions (although they do not deny that they take place); there is nothing to which they apply the term *speaker meaning*. Their motivation is in part the belief that whatever Grice intends speaker meaning to be cannot be delimited. This contention is the subject of the next section.

3. The Analytical Priority of Intentions

I have just suggested that where the L&S model addresses the same issues as Grice's Theory of Conversation, there is little substantive difference between them (although certainly there is disagreement over where the theory has application). However, there is a major difference between the L&S model and Grice's Theory of Meaning. For L&S, linguistic conventions are (not only practically but also) *analytically* basic. For Grice, although conventional meaning is basic in the practical matter of reconstructing a speaker's intentions, those intentions are analytically basic: the notion of conventional meaning is to be analyzed in terms of the communicative intentions which speakers generally have when they use those expressions. In what follows, I give an argument that communicative intentions indeed are analytically prior to conventions.

3.1 Delimitability of Meaning-determining Intentions: Intentions in Language Learning

When children learn their first language, what they learn is (at least) the conventions governing that language, including the conventional meanings of its expressions. How do children learn the meanings of expressions? Perhaps the most venerable picture of word learning is that children learn the meanings of expressions by observing particulars of the situation in which the expression is used. "A rabbit scurries by, the native [or parent] says 'Gavagai', and the linguist [or language learner] notes down the sentence 'Rabbit' (or 'Lo, a rabbit,') as a tentative translation, subject to testing in further cases" (Quine, 1960: 29). Quine is famously skeptical that this procedure results in a definitive understanding of what 'Gavagai', or any other term, means. The observable stimulus—the world itself—doesn't provide enough constraints to allow the language learner to determine precisely what aspect of the stimulus the linguistic behavior observed corresponds to. Wittgenstein (1953) similarly points out that ostension, as a means of identifying the referent of an expression, is fundamentally ambiguous: "An ostensive definition can be variously interpreted in *every* case" (§28). Unfortunately, there is no getting around the fact that every child acquiring a language is in the same position as Quine's linguist. Yet children do, somehow, learn the language of their speech community.

The question of how children solve the problem of referential indeterminacy is a long-standing concern of research on language acquisition. The consensus is that something more than observation of the state of the world is necessary in order for language learners to identify the meanings of expressions. One widely held view is that children come into the world endowed with various innate constraints on (presumed) word-to-world mapping (Markman 1989, 1994). There are a number of challenges for this view (see Deák 2000; Bloom 2002), but even if it is correct, it is acknowledged to provide only a partial answer to the question. It might tell us why, when the rabbit hops by and the adult says, "Look, a rabbit!" the child takes the word to name the rabbit rather than, say, rabbit fur. But it doesn't tell us why the child takes the word to name something related to the rabbit rather than, say, the patch of grass on which the rabbit is sitting. This aspect of the word learning problem (as well as the more Quinean one) is addressed by a second approach which has been advocated in particular by Paul Bloom and Michael Tomasello (Bloom 2000, 2002; Tomasello 2001, 2003 inter alia). According to this view, children solve the problem by being what Bloom calls "mindreaders." As Tomasello puts it, children utilize their social cognitive skills to "perceive the intentions of the adult as she acts and speaks to the child" (2001: 133).

Putting it crudely, both advocate a view on which children learn conventions by recognizing intentions.

There are now very many experimental results that demonstrate that young children use information about adult speakers' intentions in inferring the meanings of new words. For example, when 18-month-olds are attending to some object (say, playing with a toy for which they do not have a name), and then hear an adult say "Look, a modi!", they will shift their attention to whatever the speaker is looking at, and will associate the new word with that object (Baldwin 1991, 1993). Two-year-olds who hear an adult use a new word while engaging in a previously unnamed action involving a previously unnamed object will differentially associate the word with either the action or the object, depending on to which of them the adult can plausibly be assumed to be referring (Tomasello & Akhtar 1995, study 1). Two-year-olds who hear an adult state an intention to do something using a novel verb (e.g. *I'm going to plunk Big Bird*), and then observe the adult performing one intentional action and one that is marked as unintentional (e.g. accompanied by *whoops*), reliably take the new word to denote the intentional action (Tomasello & Barton 1994, study 3). This involves fairly complex reasoning: the experimenter announces an intention to do something, then does something accidentally. From the perspective of the child, the experimenter could not, at the time of speaking, have known that she would perform that act; therefore, she could not have intended to name it when she announced her future act. The only act the experimenter could have intended to name was the one subsequently performed intentionally; and this is the act that children take the new word to name.

None of the results are terribly surprising. These young children assign meanings in the same way that most adults would. But this is the point: we use our knowledge of normal human behavior to make inferences about what a speaker plausibly intends to refer to, or exclaim about, and we associate the new word with that referent. The results from small children show that this is not just something that adults who are already fully competent language users do; it is what children do—and arguably, need to be able to do—in order to acquire their first language. If Bloom and Tomasello and others of their school are right, then children learn words by identifying the intentions of speakers who use them. If that is right, then L&S's claim that meaning-determining intentions are in principle not delimitable cannot be correct.

L&S might respond in the following way. The intentions that are being recognized are not meaning determining. It is the conventions governing the word that determine its meaning. Language learners indeed do pay attention to speaker intentions, but only with the goal of inferring the conventions that govern the word, given the assumption that speakers generally intend to use words in accord with convention. However, this way of thinking about what language learners are doing seems implausible: language learners acquire conventions, but can hardly be thought to come to the language-learning task equipped with the idea of a convention. More importantly, though, even if this characterization of the process were correct (as in fact it might be for adult learners acquiring the meaning of a new word) it does not undermine the core point, namely, that a speaker intention *can* suffice to delimit meaning. According to the view on which intentions are convention-determining, the story goes like this: When I say "jog," I intend to speak about jogging. I can have this intention because that is what the word conventionally means. By recognizing that this is what I intend when I use the word, a learner learns the convention. But if intention recognition can provide the information needed for this learning task, then it also provides enough information to learn: "When people have this intention, they use this word," that is, enough information to be meaning determining.

In conversation, Matthew Stone has raised a different objection to the argument given here. He points out that according to Grice, meaning-determining intentions are specifically *communicative* intentions (intentions to induce a particular kind of change in the audience's intensional state). The experimental evidence does not show that children (or adults) are using recognition of intentions of this special sort to acquire the meanings of words.

My response to this objection is twofold. First, the argument in L&S is not that Gricean communicative intentions are of the wrong sort to be meaning determining, but rather that it is in principle not possible to delimit a meaning-determining intention. Certainly, there are objections that have been, and can be, raised against the Gricean definition of a meaning-determining intention; but this is not currently our concern. Second, there is a body of experimental work which is argued to show that even very young children distinguish between communicative and non-communicative non-linguistic acts, and respond to them differently (e.g. Behne, Carpenter, & Tomasello 2005; Moore et al. 2015). This experimental literature suggests that children, from a very young age, pay special attention to what they recognize as communicative acts; and that when they understand an act in this way, they attempt to identify the associated intention. This does not yet tell us that learners attempt to identify a specifically communicative intention in the process of identifying expression meaning. But it does tell us that they at least have the capacity to do so.

L&S are clearly correct when they point out that almost every linguistic utterance is produced with a panoply of intentions, many of which cannot be thought to relate to the meaning of the expression produced. But the role of intention recognition in word learning suggests that out of the "blooming, buzzing confusion" of intentions that surround an utterance, learners can indeed identify some core intention that corresponds to the meaning of the word.

3.2 Conventions from Intentions: The Analytical Priority of Intention

The argument so far has been an empirical rejoinder to L&S's theoretical claim that meaning-determining intentions are not delimitable. The response comes from the evidence that intention recognition plays a central role in word learning, which it could not do if L&S's claim were correct. I now expand this response to recapitulate Grice's claim that communicative intention is analytically prior to linguistic convention.

We noted at starting that what children learn when they learn a language are the conventions that govern that language. When children learn a word, they not only learn that *this* speaker used this word on a particular occasion with a particular meaning. They learn that *in general* this word is used with that meaning, and that they themselves can use the word to express that meaning. And they must learn this by observations of the linguistic behavior of others, because that is all that they have to go on.

But the conclusion of the previous section was that the crucial observations about the linguistic behavior of others are observations about the intentions with which they produce particular utterances. What children observe and learn from are not simply word-world correlations, but rather word-intention correlations. When they acquire the convention governing a word, it must be through some generalization over the observations they have made, namely, a generalization about the intentions which speakers have when they use particular expressions.

And this brings us directly back to a Gricean characterization of conventions of meaning. As emphasized in section 2, Grice fully recognized the need for a concept of conventional meaning. In line with his view that the fundamental notion of meaning is speaker meaning, he builds the notion of conventional meaning from this primary notion. For Grice, what it is for a speaker to mean *x* by utterance *U* is for the speaker to produce *U* with a certain special kind of intention involving *x*—what we now call a communicative intention. Conventional meanings for expressions, then, will be generalizations about the communicative intentions that speakers tend to have when producing *U*. And this is just what we should expect if, indeed, the crucial observations that language learners generalize from to develop their conventional language are observations about speaker intentions. The picture is thus one on which intention is analytically (and ontogenetically) prior to convention.

4. Intentions on the Scoreboard

In chapter 14 of their book, L&S lay out the framework that allows them to clearly articulate their conception of semantic content. In this section, I'll begin by recapitulating their proposal, and then move on to challenge one of its fundamental claims.

L&S adopt a Lewisian Conversational Record (Lewis 1979) as the structure for modeling linguistic content. What is novel in their version of the Conversational Record is that the Record reflects *only* what is determined by linguistic convention. As such, it is an *objective* record of what the discourse participants are committed to by virtue of the conventional contents of their linguistic acts—regardless of whether any actual participant knows or believes that they are. The Record is *restricted* to these conventionally incurred commitments. Anything conveyed via nonconventional means—implicatures (if there are any), hints, metaphorically communicated content— lives elsewhere. It may be part of what the interlocutors know or believe about one another; it may be in the common ground of the conversation, which L&S exclude from the Record. But it is not part of the Record.

Let's look at one of L&S's examples in order to get clear on the view. They offer the following invented conversation, where a misunderstanding occurs (their (207), p. 254).

(1) a. A: We're going to the bank after this.
     b. B: Great! Are Kim and Sandy going too?
     c. A: Why would they go?
     d. B: They always like the river...
     e. A: But we're going to the Wells Fargo office!

The crucial issue here is the content of the second utterance, b. The later conversation shows that A, when she says *bank*, intends to refer to a financial institution; B misunderstands, and thinks that A is talking about a river bank. So, which of these gets to be part of the content of B's first utterance? According to L&S, "B inadvertently asks at [(1b.)] whether Kim and Sandy are going along to the financial institution, and B's contribution at [1d.] is an irrelevant one given the true history of the conversation." (p. 254).

Note the crucial role of linguistic rule in this account. B's question involves ellipsis, licensed by identity of the elided element with the PP *to the bank* in A's prior utterance. Plausibly, the rule for ellipsis requires that an elided constituent be semantically identical to its antecedent. By this rule, B's utterance is *required* to be a question about the Wells Fargo office, regardless of B's intention. According to L&S, this linguistic rule determines the meaning of B's utterance, and hence the update to the Conversational Record.

In this section, I will explore this strict conventionalist treatment of the Conversational Record. Let us, for current purposes, grant L&S's position that for every utterance U, there are linguistic rules that fully determine a specific update to the Record. The question I now pose is this: Does a Record limited to being updated only and strictly in accord with these rules have an explanatory role to play in our theory of linguistic meaning or in a theory of communication based on it?

I suggest that the place to look for evidence here is in the dynamics of conversation. The whole point of a Conversational Record is that it is dynamic. It is continuously updated by conversational contributions, but at the same time imposes constraints on possible contributions. If the object that plays this role is as L&S argue, then we should see the effects of its purely conventional nature in constraints that affect allowable conversational moves. I'll argue that in fact these moves suggest that the Record is a far more flexible matter than L&S would like.

4.1 Mis-speaking

My father, like many other fathers, sometimes mistakenly switches the names of his grandchildren. Sometimes he uses my son's name, Isaac, when he means to refer to my nephew Alon, or vice versa. Sometimes he catches himself in his mistake and self-corrects, and sometimes not.

Suppose I am talking to my father on the phone, and he says (2):

(2)   Alon looked very impressive in his kung fu performance.

It's obvious to me that he intends to say that *Isaac* looked very impressive. My father knows the difference between his two grandsons. He knows that Isaac does kung fu, but Alon doesn't, and I have recently sent him video of Isaac in a kung fu performance. There are various responses that are open to me at this point. One option is to point out the error ("You said 'Alon' instead of 'Isaac.'") Another option might be to pick up on the proposition expressed by the sentence actually uttered: I might laugh and say, "Oh, is Alon doing kung fu now?" But another option would be to ignore the error, and proceed *as if* my father had in fact said what he meant to say. In particular, I might say:

(3)   Yes, he's been practicing a lot recently.

And then our conversation might continue with a sequence of utterances containing the pronoun *he*, which both my father and I would take to refer to Isaac.

What would L&S say about this case? According to them, what goes on the Record is the conventional content of my father's utterance. Hence, after my father's utterance of (2), my nephew Alon becomes the highest ranked potential referent for a masculine pronoun. Isaac, who hasn't been mentioned, is not available on the stack at all (or at least would be low ranked). And so *he*, in my utterance of (3), presumably should, by convention, refer to Alon; and Alon should be the subject of our continuing conversation. According to the L&S view, the Conversational Record records this conversation which no one has actually had, but which is the conversation we would have had if I had ignored my father's obvious intention and had paid attention only to the conventional content of his utterance.

One problem with this model is that it doesn't seem like a very good model of what is actually going on in this conversational exchange. An additional and in some sense more severe problem is that the Record now cannot play the role in the theory that it is supposed to play, as we can see by considering what happens as the conversation proceeds.

After this brief conversational glitch, my conversation with my father is still governed by the standard rules of play. This applies even to my use of pronouns. Now that we are using *he* to refer to Isaac, I can't suddenly use *he* to refer to Alon, or anyone else. With the referent of *he* set to Isaac, if I say:

(4)   Yes, and he has a birthday coming up soon

I can only continue to refer to Isaac. It would be natural to explain this constraint in terms of the behavior of the Record—but on L&S's picture, we can't. L&S's Record is busy recording a conversation we are not having about Alon, so can't be invoked to explain why *he* cannot now felicitously be used to refer to Alon.

And of course all the other ordinary constraints governing conversational update apply to my ongoing conversation with my father. All of these constraints are supposed to be characterizable in terms of properties of the Record. But the conversation I'm actually having with my father isn't *on* the Record, on the L&S view. So it's unclear how the Record can function to constrain it.

Here is what L&S say about how cases such as these look from a Gricean perspective. The discussion pertains to Kripke's famous Jones/Smith case (Kripke 1977), where an utterance of *Jones is raking the leaves today* is used to say something about Smith.[5] I quote at some length because I think the passage is important.

> In cases such as [these], the Gricean view has difficulty distinguishing among the various commitments the speaker has made... The speaker of [*Jones is raking the leaves today*] intends to contribute that that person, [the person being observed], is raking the leaves, and she also intends to contribute the conventional meaning of what she said, which is in fact that Jones is raking the leaves... We seem to be equally justified in reporting the situation with either perspective... By contrast, our view articulates a clear standard that privileges conventional meaning in each of these cases.   (pp. 218–19)

L&S clearly take it to be a failing of the model that it allows us to "report the situation with either perspective." But the empirical observations suggest that this is exactly what we want. After the mis-spoken utterance, it is my *choice* as the addressee which intention to utilize in updating the Record. That choice then governs what contributions are appropriate as the conversation continues.

It is worth emphasizing, as this passage from L&S makes clear, that the Gricean view allows us to talk about the conventional meaning of utterances. It is this conventional meaning that constitutes *what is said*. So some of the further criticisms that L&S raise in the continuation of this passage seem misplaced. In favor of their view, they point out (p. 219) that it allows us to characterize a speaker as "meaning something that she didn't think she intended. The meaning we ascribe to her can differ from how she would have described it herself." They go on: "For prospective intentionalism, this is very hard to do."

While for Grice it is indeed incoherent to say that a *speaker* meant something that she did not intend, it is entirely coherent to say that a speaker's *uttered sentence* meant something that she did not intend. We can also say that a speaker's belief that she can accomplish her communicative intention by uttering a particular sentence is mistaken. As far as I can see, this allows us to capture all of the distinctions that we

---

[5] There's an important difference between Kripke's case and mine. In Kripke's case, the speaker has *misidentified* the man. He thinks the man in question *is* Jones. He didn't mis-speak; he used the correct name for the individual he thought was raking leaves. It just so happens that he also meant to be talking about the person he and his interlocutor are currently observing; and the problem is that he has a false belief about that person (i.e. that he is Jones). My father, on the other hand, in the case I constructed, never had any intention to say anything about Alon.

need, without the problematic restriction of the Conversational Record to conventionally contributed content.

4.1.1 AN ASIDE ON BASIC INTENTIONS

On the L&S picture, intentions still have a role to play in the determination of (conventional utterance) meaning. The basic intentions of the speaker have the role of converting an ambiguous string into an unambiguous syntactic structure. For example, if a speaker utters the sentence *Jane hit the man with the baseball bat*, intending *with the baseball bat* as a modifier of *man*, this intention determines that that *is* the sentence she has uttered.

Part of the appeal of these basic intentions for L&S seems to be their transparency. When a speaker says *Jones is raking the leaves today*, we can "read off" the basic intention from the utterance itself: The speaker has uttered *this sentence*, so her basic intention is to contribute one of the grammatically specified meanings of this string to the conversation. This is the source of the conflict in the Jones/Smith case: the speaker's two intentions—the intention to talk about the person she is looking at, and the intention to talk about the person conventionally designated by the name *Jones*—do not coincide, although the speaker thinks that they do.

In the case of mis-speaking that I have been exploring, the situation is different. It seems reasonable to say that my father *never* had the intention of contributing to the conversation the grammatically specified meaning of sentence (2) above. He intended to talk about Isaac, knowing that Isaac's name is *Isaac*, and knowing that the name *Alon* is not a conventional means (or any kind of means) for designating Isaac. The utterance of the name *Alon* seems like a misfire of the basic intention. We certainly have such misfires in the nonlinguistic case. Suppose, for example, I observe a hammer on a table within my reach, and form the basic intention to *grasp that thing*, which sets my motor system into action. But as I reach out, I have a sudden attack of double vision and inadvertently grasp the screwdriver that was on the table next to the hammer. There was never any intention to grasp the screwdriver, but there it is in my hand.

But perhaps this observation provides a solution for the dilemma I raised above. Suppose L&S take me up on this idea. Now they can say this: In this case of a misfire of the basic intention, it is still that intention which should determine the updates to the Conversational Record. There *is* an English sentence—sentence (5) below—with respect to which my father had a basic intention to contribute its grammatically specified meaning to the conversation.

(5)   Isaac looked very impressive in his kung fu performance.

It's the conventional content of *this* sentence that should determine the updates to the Record, and hence we can account for the observations about the constraints that are in play as the conversation continues.

But this strategy just leads us back to the same dilemma. As noted, there are multiple options for how the conversation will continue after the mis-speaking. One of those options is for me to respond to the conventional content of the sentence actually uttered, and then my father and I might indeed continue our conversation talking about Alon, and making him the referent of uses of *he/him*. But if the Record were updated with the conventional content of sentence (5), then this conversation about Alon would be "off the record," putting us back in the problematic situation we discussed above.

4.2 Negotiating the Record

The following is a more-or-less faithful rendition of a conversation between my spouse, T., and another acquaintance, J., which took place in my hearing.

(6)   [Context: Conversation took place outdoors in early February in Pittsburgh. The winter had been exceptionally mild. On the day of the conversation, the temperature had dropped noticeably lower, but was still much warmer than a typical Pittsburgh February. J. and T. have run into each other walking across the campus. Immediately prior to this conversation, T. had been complaining to me about being cold.]

J: How are you?

T: Cold.

J: [laughing], Yes, 40 degrees in February!

T: You're right, it's warm for the time of year. But I've been spoiled.

The conversation involved an interesting misunderstanding. When T. uttered *cold*, he meant the content of his utterance seriously. J., however, took him to be ironic, or humorous, and to be making indirect reference to the mild weather. (This conversation is thus similar to L&S's constructed (1), where the import of an utterance is mistaken by the addressee.) What is particularly interesting is T.'s final move. He first continues (almost) as if J.'s take on his original utterance were correct, acknowledging the mild temperature. But then he goes on to explain his original utterance on its intended, serious, interpretation.

This was a complicated interaction, although compressed into a very brief conversational exchange. It suggests, though, that the Gricean picture where, as L&S put it, neither perspective is privileged, is the right one. Neither conventional content nor literal content nor intended content is guaranteed to be the content that drives the update of the Record.

Similarly, I've been in more than one conversation where I recognize that I've been misunderstood in some mild, non-catastrophic way, and have simply allowed the conversation to shift to a different topic than the one I had actually introduced, or to discussion of a person I wasn't originally talking about. Here is a constructed example:

(7)   [Context: A noisy children's birthday party; lots of kids running around. I am observing a mother of twins dealing with her two four-year-olds at the same

time. The mother's name is Emily, which is also the name of the mother of the child having the birthday party. I address another parent, P.]

Me: I don't know how Emily manages it.

P: Yeah, I know, it's amazing, she always throws these fantastic birthday parties.

Me: Yeah, and she seems to enjoy it, too.

P's response indicates that she has mistaken the reference of my use of *Emily*, (hence also of *it*). But as I am just making conversation, I am just as happy to talk about Emily$_2$ as about Emily$_1$. According to L&S, the Record will reflect the grammatically determined update associated with my original utterance, where the reference of *Emily* is fixed by my basic intention to refer to Emily$_1$. And that should affect which uses of pronouns, and which conversational moves, are subsequently licensed. But any constraints on our continuing conversation seem to come, in fact, from the state of the Record which my interlocutor takes to be correct and which I subsequently adopt, in violation of what convention requires. The posited convention-driven Record is inert in this description of the exchange.

4.3 Conversational Implicature on the Record?

One helpful feature of the L&S approach is that it provides a means of diagnosing what information is required to be on the Record. The Record is supposed to be what governs the appropriateness of conversational moves; a conversational move is licensed if the information on the Record says it is. We can thus make observations about what moves are licensed in particular situations, and use these observations to understand how the Record has evolved.

Here I want to make a simple observation: there are cases where the appropriateness of a conversational move seems to be based on information derived inferentially from a prior utterance or from the utterance that constitutes the move in question. These observations suggest that information derived not from the conventionally determined content of utterances also goes on the Record.

First example:

(8)   a. A: Wanna go get lunch?
       b. B: I have to finish this grading.
       c. A: Oh well. Maybe next time.

A's utterance c. is conversationally coherent only if B's utterance is registered as declining the invitation issued at utterance a. But "I decline" is not part of the conventional content of B's utterance. So, we seem to have two choices: (i) Allow that the declining function of b.'s utterance is registered on the Record; or (ii) Deny that the conversational coherence exhibited here is governed by features of the Conversational Record. But I think that to make move (ii) would be to undermine some of the rationale for the Record model.

The second example involves presupposition:

(9) a. A: What did you think of the movie?
     b. B: I liked the popcorn.
     c. A: I see. Was it the anti-feminist theme that you hated?

On many standard views, A's second utterance, which contains an *it*-cleft, conventionally requires that the Record includes the information that B hated something (about the movie). It is clear how that information would get there; B, by failing to properly answer A's question, implicates this. But again, this required proposition is not the conventional content of any utterance. So if the Record is to govern the felicity of presuppositional utterances, then, it seems, it must reflect content inferentially introduced.

The final case involves the establishment of coherence relations. L&S take coherence relations between discourse units to be part of what is conventionally expressed by utterances. But sometimes, coherence between two discourse segments is due not to the conventional content of the uttered sentences, but to something inferable from that content. Consider the following case, which modifies an actual discourse segment taken from the Santa Barbara corpus:[6]

(10) [Context: Speaker has just been talking about her parents taking trips to various places to go salmon fishing]

     a. They [speaker's parents] were supposed to go up to Oregon…at the end of August

     b. When they [the salmon] usually run,

     c. and,

     d. fish weren't running this year.

     e. They were really bummed.

Consider the relation that holds between the (invented) final segment e., and what precedes it. That utterance serves as a kind of conclusion of the preceding story. In particular, it describes the parents' feelings about a fact that is never actually stated, namely, that they were not able to go fishing. Segment d., in combination with the *supposed to go* of the first segment, allows us to make this inference, and hence allows us to see the final segment as cohering with the rest. If the coherence relation that attaches this utterance to the remainder of the discourse is to be reflected in the update of the Conversational Record, and if that requires a representation of what the utterance coheres *with*, then we seem compelled to have a representation on the record of material derived by inference.

---

[6] Modified from Transcript SBC003. The utterance up to d. is directly from the transcript. Utterance e. is invented.

For the sake of maximizing tendentiousness, I titled this section *Implicature on the Record*. The inferences I point to might be argued to be something other than implicature. But it seems undeniable that they are non-encoded inferences that the speaker invites the addressee to draw, and then utilizes in further conversational moves. Given L&S's strong position that inferences not grounded in linguistic rule have no role to play in update of the Record, the inferential status of the content is all that is necessary to raise a query about the view.

4.4 Nonconventional Forms

Some months ago, I got a voice mail from the school nurse at my son's school. The message started like this:

> (11)   This is the school nurse calling from Minadeo. Not an emergency. I do have Isaac here in the nurse's office, he had fallen at lunch recess and **his elbow, he fell right on a bed of gravel** so umm some of the wounds are superficial... "[detailed description of the injury follows] (May 2015)

I want to focus on the part of the message in boldface: *his elbow, he fell right on a bed of gravel*. This sequence was uttered with normal clausal intonation, with a slight intonational break, such as would follow standard fronting, right after *elbow*. From this part of the utterance, I understood (correctly) that Isaac had fallen on a bed of gravel and scraped up his elbow. I think that the nurse, leaving the message, was taking it that she would thereby communicate that content to me. But there is no conventional rule for deriving that content from the sentence she uttered, which is not even, strictly speaking, grammatical. (Note that the phrase *his elbow* has no grammatical role in the sentence it is attached to.)

I do not think this is a case where we could plausibly say that the nurse was inventing or using an ad hoc convention that she intended me to participate in. This is somewhat like the case of mis-speaking discussed in section 3.1., in that we might say that the speaker *intended* to produce a grammatical sentence, so *intended* to contribute to the conversation the conventional content of a similar sounding sentence. But which sentence that would be I'm not sure. Perhaps what she had in mind was a sequence of sentences: *Isaac fell on the gravel. He scraped up his elbow on the gravel*. But if she'd really had that in mind, it seems unlikely that her basic intention would go so far astray.

It's worth noting that what the nurse actually said was an extremely compact and elegant way to communicate the slightly complex message she had in mind. It was a lovely and nonconventional use of the language to accomplish her communicative goal.

I suspect that a great deal of ordinary language use, which is after all full of false starts and incomplete sentences, is like this. Conventions of grammar and word meaning provide a framework, within which all kinds of creative use happen. But this kind of creative use is not metaphor, nor is it implicature. In this case, the nurse has a very definite message to convey, and that message was straightforwardly retrievable from the form that she used. L&S's strictly conventionalist account seems to rule out updates to the Record that are so derived.

5. Conclusion

One of the goals that L&S set themselves is to distinguish between semantics and pragmatics, which they take to be two substantively distinguishable components involved in linguistic communication. I agree that there is such a substantive distinction, but I think that they are looking to characterize it in the wrong place. To put things in terms of their own picture (which in many ways I endorse): The distinction between semantics and pragmatics is a distinction in *how* speakers bring about changes to the Conversational Record. The semantics of a language is the set of linguistic rules (conventions) that govern the meaning contributions of morphemes and their combinations. Pragmatics is the set of further, non-language specific, procedures and practices that govern how language users map the products of semantics to the rich messages conveyed by speakers. But we don't find the traces of the semantics/pragmatics distinction in the Record that results.

If I may offer a metaphor: Think about a climber climbing up a rock face. To get to the top, she uses a variety of tactics. Sometimes she uses natural hand- and footholds provided by the rock. Sometimes she hammers in her own pegs. Maybe sometimes she uses a peg left by another climber. Often a single step will involve multiple strategies at once. To the person waiting at the top of the rock face, it's all the same: she made it to the top. Now, an expert might examine the details of her climb and observe all the different strategies she used, and when. But if the person at the top was just waiting for the climber to get there, what do they care?

I think communication is rather like that. Most of us are just talking. We want to get our message across; we want to get the messages of others. There is no reason why we should have a special sensitivity to the tools which others have used to convey their messages, any more than the person at the top of the cliff face cares about how their companion got there.

And it is only common sense to think that things would be this way. Language in general, and semantics in particular, does not arise in a vacuum. However language came to be, it came to be as a human artifact. It was created, and is daily re-created, by human beings, with human brains, human cognition, and human dispositions. Humans are creatures who reason, who infer, and who are uniquely sensitive to the intention-driven behaviors of others. So how could language fail to be something that utilizes those particular skills of its designers? Moreover, language and its rules have evolved through use, and use, always, happens in a rich context. By the same reasoning, then, it seems inevitable that human language has evolved so as to take advantage of this always-present resource.

References

Baldwin, D. 1991. Infants' contributions to the achievement of joint reference. *Child Development* 62: 875–90.

Baldwin, D. 1993. Infants' ability to consult the speaker for clues to word reference. *Journal of Child Language* 20: 395–418.

Behne, Tanya, Malinda Carpenter and Michael Tomasello 2005. One-year-olds comprehend the communicative intentions behind gestures in a hiding game. *Developmental Sciences* 8(6): 492–9.

Bloom, P. 2000. *How Children Learn the Meanings of Words*. Cambridge, MA: MIT Press.

Bloom, P. 2002. Mindreading, communication, and the learning of names for things. *Mind and Language* 17(1–2): 37–54.

Deák, G. O. 2000. Hunting the fox of word learning: Why "constraints" fail to capture it. *Developmental Review* 20: 29–80.

Du Bois, John W., Wallace L. Chafe, Charles Meyer, Sandra A. Thompson, Robert Englebretson, and Nii Martey. 2000–2005. *Santa Barbara Corpus of Spoken American English, Parts* 1–4. Philadelphia: Linguistic Data Consortium.

Grice, H. P. 1989. *Studies in the Way of Words*. Cambridge, MA: Harvard University Press.

Kripke, S. 1977. Speaker reference and semantic reference. *Midwest Studies in Philosophy* 2(1): 255–76.

Lepore, E. and M. Stone. 2015. *Imagination and Convention. Distinguishing Grammar and Inference in Language*. New York: Oxford University Press.

Lewis, D. 1979. Scorekeeping in a language game. *Journal of Philosophical Logic* 8(3).

Markman, E. 1989. *Categorization and Naming in Children*. Cambridge, MA: MIT Press.

Markman, E. 1994. Constraints on word meaning in early language acquisition. *Lingua* 92(1–4): 199–227.

Moore, R., B. Mueller, J. Kaminski and M. Tomasello. 2015. Two-year-old children but not domestic dogs understand communicative intentions without language, gestures, or gaze. *Developmental Science* 18(2): 232–42.

Neale, S. 1992. Paul Grice and the philosophy of language. *Linguistics and Philosophy* 15(5): 509–59.

Quine, W. V. O. 1960. *Word and Object*. Cambridge, MA: MIT Press.

Tomasello, M. 2001. Perceiving intentions and learning words in the second year of life. In M. Bowerman and Levinson, S. (eds.), *Language Acquisition and Conceptual Development*. Cambridge: Cambridge University Press: 132–58.

Tomasello, M. 2003. *Constructing a Language*. Cambridge, MA: Harvard University Press.

Tomasello, M. and N. Akhtar. 1995. Two-year-olds use pragmatic cues to differentiate reference to objects and action. *Cognitive Development* 10: 201–24.

Tomasello, M. and M. Barton. 1994. Learning words in non-ostensive contexts. *Developmental Psychology* 30: 639–50.

Wittgenstein, L. 1953. *Philosophical Investigations*. Oxford: Basil Blackwell.

PART IV

New Frontiers in Semantics

15

Issues for Meaning
Conventions, Intentions, and Coherence

Ernie Lepore and Matthew Stone

We think it best to keep our observations general and minimal. The essays in this volume are clear and well argued, but we feel the same about our own book, and so, it would be otiose to dive deeper into the dialectic. Instead, we will briefly highlight a few areas of disagreement where we believe additional research is needed to adjudicate the central issues that the contributions to this volume raise.

Open Issues: Convention

In *Imagination and Convention* (IC; Lepore and Stone 2015), we tried to take a stab at an understanding of convention that fits linguistic meaning. Although our ideas are heavily indebted to David Lewis, we cannot endorse every aspect of his (1969) notion of convention. (See Section 14.3 of IC.) Lewis imposes some requirements that just don't fit language. He requires conventions to have realistically possible alternatives. Language has biological universals. Lewis requires conventions to be deliberatively learned. Language is largely automatic in ways that seem to escape the hierarchies of mutual knowledge that Lewis calls for. Lewis calls for shared interests. People can use language when their interests are not so closely aligned. Lewis also doesn't go far enough. In signaling games, Lewis's conventions underdetermine meaning as philosophers generally conceive it. It seems to be important that we can clarify and contest what utterances mean, even as we inquire or dispute whether those utterances are true, and Lewis's definition doesn't capture this. The uncharitable, but blunt, verdict is that Lewis is simply wrong about convention in language: in this volume, Davis, Glanzberg, Green, and Starr all weigh in on the inadequacies of Lewis's view.

Maybe the right approach to these difficulties is to depart even further from Lewis than we did. Starr—among many others—thinks that Millikan's (1998) notion of linguistic convention is better suited to an approach to language as cognitive science. (Davis and Green are perhaps in this camp; Nicole Wyatt also made this suggestion in a symposium on IC at the Canadian Philosophical Association in 2014.) This seems like a worthwhile direction to explore. We would regard it as a friendly amendment to work up an understanding of the limits of grammar that started from Millikan's approach to convention as a self-perpetuating pattern of behavior. But, as with Lewis, simply recapitulating Millikan's notion of convention won't work to distinguish grammar and inference in language use. For Millikan, implicatures straddle the semantics–pragmatics divide: she suggests that they are calculated, on the usual Gricean grounds, but she still counts them as conventional, because speakers stick with them out of inertia, and that's enough to qualify as a convention on her view. (See Millikan 2005.) Millikan regards it as a positive feature of her definition that it blurs semantics and pragmatics together. We are not so sanguine about this result.

Of course, many of the philosophers and cognitive scientists assembled here—including Bach, Green, Keiser, and Simons—think that the failure of Lewis's account of convention is just another sign that that we are wrong about communicative intentions, and that the traditional account going back to Grice (1957) is the right one. When it comes to meaning, they believe, we should start from a notion of speaker meaning grounded in communicative intentions. "Conventional meaning" is then just a generalization about what speakers tend to mean when they token linguistic items. This is a common view: Many critics have found our resistance to the primacy of speaker meaning problematic, and Bach, Green, Keiser, and Simons develop explicit arguments to this effect here. If experience is any guide, we will not change any minds about this point with what we say here.

Nevertheless, we still think that speaker meaning is not a helpful construct for getting precise on knowledge and reasoning in conversation. For one thing, we remain, following Quine (1951), in sincere doubt that it can even be correctly characterized—if by that is meant providing interesting necessary and sufficient conditions for its application.

For another reason, however one opts to characterize speaker meaning, we think that the main argument of our book survives: that many alleged conversational implicatures must in fact be conventional, and so, are not conversational implicatures at all; and that the rest must be uttered without a Gricean intention to communicate a definite proposition, and so, must not be said, meant, or implicatured after all. Even if you were to give a new definition of speaker meaning, one that escapes all the various counterexamples that have proliferated in the literature, addressing these arguments would remain a separate matter.

Finally, the massive literature on speaker meaning inaugurated a tradition of thinking about the intentions of language users in the highly abstract and theory-laden terms that Grice proposed. This perspective remains a powerful inspiration for some philosophers, as the contributions here from Arseneault, Bach, Green, Keiser, and Simons illustrate. Nevertheless, we believe that the practical rationality of conversation can be captured in much simpler frameworks, and that doing so establishes more straightforward parallels to other kinds of joint activity in other disciplines as well as in philosophy in the acquisition, production and understanding of language. We turn to these issues next.

Open Issues: Intentions

IC offers an extended discussion of the role of intentions and intention recognition in human collaboration (see chapter 13, especially 13.4). We believe that the nuances and open questions here are fraught in ways that research on the semantics–pragmatics divide often glosses over. Even we have found ourselves reading the phrase "communicative intention" essentially as an impressive-sounding synonym for "the interpretation the speaker has in mind." In so doing, we could still understand "communicative intention" in the technical sense of Grice's philosophy and other work in the Gricean tradition (this type of theorizing is defended explicitly in Stone 2004, for example). But, then, guided by common-sense understandings of interpretation, we found we could suddenly tap into unreasonably strong intuitions about elaborate, higher-order commitments that speakers must have undertaken with respect to their audience. Since these abstract commitments do, in some sense, give some insights into how conversation plays out, they seemed unassailable.

But we now think it's important not to move so fast. "Communicative intention" is not a synonym for "the interpretation the speaker has in mind," certainly not if you understand communicative intention in anything like the Gricean sense. Indeed, in the philosophical literature on the effects of utterances as actions, diversity abounds: for instance, Austin (1962), Brandom (1994), Searle (1994), and Williamson (2000) each have their own non-Gricean explication of what rules, effects, and obligations a speaker actuates in offering an assertion. Similarly, semantic theories based on the tacit grammar of a faculty of language—across the different traditions of Chomsky (1980), Davidson (1967), Jackendoff (2002), and Lewis (1975)—all offer specific architectures and representations that let us understand in new and concrete ways what it means for a speaker to have a particular interpretation in mind. In short, it's quite clear that there are countless ways to theorize about such things.

IC attempts to make the gap between common-sense and Gricean theory concrete by fleshing out one particular way of thinking about intentions in communication: a view of "direct intentionalism" that dovetails with the understanding of conventions and linguistic rules we try to articulate in our book. On this view, language users' standing participation in the right kind of background relationships accounts for the meanings of utterances: on our view, simply by making an utterance, speakers can contribute its content to a public record. This is all that our intentions in using language need to envisage—sometimes it's good to just "put things out there"—though, of course, we generally can, and often do, have ulterior motives of various kinds, including ones involving the attitudes and actions of our interlocutors. This is a comparatively thin understanding of how intentions underpin the interpretation a speaker has in mind.

We see a number of advantages in offering a concrete suggestion along these lines. For one thing, it lets us look freshly at questions about the cognitive capacities involved in language understanding and language use. As the contributions from de Almeida, Bach, Glanzberg, and Simons all attest, these are areas where the empirical facts are hard to reconcile with philosophical analyses.

Take young children, for example. On the one hand, as Simons summarizes, they seem to use their understanding of adults' acts of reference—and their successful communicative coordination with adults more generally—to learn the meanings of words. On the other hand, as Glanzberg reminds us, young children seem to be unable to reason about others' mental states the way adults can, especially when it comes to the sophisticated attitudes involved in attributing Gricean communicative intentions.

This apparent conflict requires a resolution. It may be that children's weak mind-reading capacity doesn't hamstring their spontaneous interaction, and so, as Simons suggests, their linguistic behavior does, in fact, reflect a representation of communication in Gricean terms. Alternatively, as Glanzberg suggests, it may be that the mere notion of intention is itself too rich to describe the mind reading that preverbal children engage in as they acquire their native language. Our position in IC is a middle ground. We do suggest that interpretation grounds out in intentions, but we also suggest that these intentions are less expressive and more cognitively constrained than Gricean philosophy might suggest, and are, therefore, simpler to reason about than you might have expected. The debate among us, Glanzberg, and Simons will continue, but, however it gets resolved, we think that it's only by sketching specific new understandings of "the interpretation the speaker has in mind," as IC does, that researchers can frame the issues and adjudicate their resolution.

Another advantage we gain in offering a concrete suggestion along these lines is to provide researchers a framework to articulate in detail what people's intentions are in using language, and thereby, to characterize more precisely the consequences that speakers envision for their words. This stands in sharp contrast to Grice's infamous remark (Grice 1989: 39) that, since the rational explanations for speakers' behavior are so open-ended, it's no surprise that conversational implicatures seem to possess a corresponding indeterminacy. We think such hand waving (unfortunately, still prevalent) not only dodges, but also confuses the philosophical issues.

In fact, computer scientists do try to build agents that calculate whether it's good to perform an utterance using decision theoretic models that take rich, complex, and varied considerations into account. Concretely, such decisions involve taking an executable description of the action (compare the "basic intentions" of IC) and calculating the distribution over outcomes predicted to occur if the action is executed. For Jason Williams's (2008) automated telephone receptionist, for example, a clarification question (e.g., "Bob who?") is a program for a speech synthesizer that can play a prompt to the caller. The program derives its utility from a value-of-information calculation that predicts what might follow (the first thing is probably the caller's answer, though the calculation may anticipate several follow-up rounds of interaction). Suppose this calculation determines that the results will rapidly enable the system to choose more confidently to connect the caller to the right destination (most likely, one or another of the people in its Rolodex named "Robert"). That would make the clarification question a good choice.

As complex and impenetrable as the data-driven models implemented in such systems may be, there is always a specific set of considerations that the program takes into account in its decisions. One can even quantify the extent to which these decisions reflect specific interpretations on the part of the audience (although, perhaps unsurprisingly, in practice it is rare for implemented calculations to play out in such explicitly Gricean terms). So, there is always a specific answer about what the system was aiming for, and whether it achieved it. Ultimately, we suspect that human speakers are no different—this is part and parcel of our acceptance of the Representational Theory of Mind (Fodor 1981). If we were to agree, with Grice (1989), that the uptake speakers intend is indeterminate, we would be forced to say, in effect, that intentions and communication are in the eye of the beholder. This would not be a defense of the idea of conversational implicature. It would, on the contrary, be an advocacy of meaning skepticism.

However, when it comes to spelling out what human speakers' communicative intentions actually are, there is much more to say than we have said so far. In different ways, Arseneault, Bach, Keiser, Simons, and Starr each pick up where we left off. Their proposals are to count a different range of speaker commitments as communicative from ours, and so, to parse the semantics–pragmatics divide in correspondingly contrasting terms. In doing so, they explore different aspects of the broader ramifications of utterances. They look carefully at how speakers plan effects such as ordinary belief, metaphorical insight, practical action, or even acquiescence in the face of misinterpretation. Take metaphor, in particular, as explored by Arseneault or Keiser. Metaphors are certainly used deliberately, effectively, and recognizably by many speakers. The imagery that metaphor prompts can be important and in certain respects anticipated. The analyses that Arseneault and Keiser offer contribute to getting clear on these abilities. In fact, in the broader theory of communication, such detail seems necessary to meet Starr's challenge of understanding how interlocutors get outcomes that they value from talk.

Presenting such intentions, however, leaves open whether to group those intentions in parallel ways to the other intentions speakers have in communication. Arseneault and Keiser argue that they should be, but we remain skeptical. Specific accounts of speakers' intentions in communication are what get this effort underway. However, perhaps surprisingly, we think that once you have such accounts, you find that the theory of joint activity actually places fewer constraints on the theory of meaning than you might have expected.

Collaborative interlocutors get their ideas across deliberately, effectively, and recognizably in all sorts of ways. (We like citing Vi Hart's origami proof of the Pythagorean theorem; see Stone and Stojnic 2015.) The question of the boundary of semantics is, in part, a question about how the effects of utterances hang together, and it involves not only mapping out interlocutors' intentions, but also developing corresponding taxonomies of meanings and assessing their empirical and interpretive coherence. In other words, we have to ask simultaneously what meaning distinctively explains, what properties it has, and what regularities it is governed by.

Any view of intentions in communication establishes a parallel between language use and the practical actions we take in the service of joint activity. This is, of course, precisely the parallel that Grice (1975) draws in motivating his Cooperative Principle. We think it's a good idea to follow Grice, and treat analogous effects of collaborative reasoning on a par. For example, in any collaboration, the evidence of your senses may leave some ambiguity about the contribution an agent is making through her action; expectations about what is reasonable and appropriate can resolve the uncertainty. Ambiguities in language are familiar. You might not know which English word "bat" a speaker has said on the basis of what you hear alone, but if the topic is baseball you can make a pretty good guess. Similarly, in Bach's example, depending on the strategy the speaker is using to make her point, she may have evoked a lizard or its tail with an utterance of "it." But if she's talking about this entity's mental life, it's a good guess it's the lizard. The same ambiguities are just as pervasive in other domains, we think. You might not be able to tell if the white crystals in your host's spoon are sugar or salt, but if she's adding it to your coffee, you can reasonably guess that it's sugar. That's not too different from a lexical ambiguity. You can't see the contents of the brown paper bag, but when your spouse leaves it on the counter for you in the morning, you can guess it's your lunch (and not, as in Monty Python's police raid sketch, "certain substances of an illicit nature to be removed for clinical tests"[1]). That's not too different from the kinds of referential ambiguities we find in pronouns, in our view.

However, while we accept that these cases of collaborative reasoning are analogous, we deny that this fact has anything like the implications for semantics or pragmatics that Grice—or our critics—claim. In particular, the linguistic examples cannot show that meanings are incomplete, or that the speaker's intentions have some privileged place, either in settling her own meanings or in guiding her audience's reasoning. If that were so, then the same arguments would carry over to the practical examples, but they do not. We all know that the physics of cooking describes exactly what will happen in the kitchen; it's not enough just to have culinary intentions. A chef can only make her spoon contain sugar, or make her bag contain sandwiches, if she carries out the right actions in the right real-world circumstances. That means audiences too, in many cases, can understand what's happening just by following the recipe. The commentators on "Iron Chef", as they watch events unfold, may see fit to speculate about how contenders intend to meet each episode's challenge, but, in normal circumstances, the spectators, like the chefs, know in advance what is required.

---

[1] Young Man: (takes paper bag) Well what's in it anyway? (opens it) Sandwiches? Policeman: Sandwiches? Blimey. Whatever did I give the wife?

To be clear, our discussion of intentions is one of the least philosophical and most speculative sections of IC. Making a particular point of view concrete is a long way from offering definitive arguments for one view over another. In the book, we frankly acknowledge problems on all sides—a position that invites further engagement with the empirical literature across cognitive science on the cognitive mechanisms underlying cooperative conversation. Until more evidence comes in, the right response, we think, is to approach Grice's theory with a very deep and pervasive skepticism. Whatever you think of our arguments against it, the arguments in its favor are much weaker than have been generally recognized.

Open Issues: Coherence Relations

Our interest in revisiting received understandings of intention and convention grows out of the data we survey in Parts II and III of IC. This data has convinced us—entirely independently of any broader philosophical considerations—that there can be no enrichment of semantic content by general pragmatic principles. Nevertheless, such pragmatic enrichment remains a central feature, not only of common theoretical analyses in the philosophy of language but also of linguistic explanations of a wide range of empirical data. In this volume, for example, de Almeida, Bach, Kehler and Cohen, Sennet, and Stainton and Viger all present data that, they argue, show the need for pragmatic enrichment in interpretation, and so, undermine our arguments. As a result, a major emphasis of our book is to survey alternative mechanisms for accounting for those specific aspects of utterance interpretation that seem not to be encoded by straightforward truth-conditional semantics.

Here, we want to particularly focus on the role of coherence relations in explaining apparent enrichments of utterance content. The central claim of Coherence Theory is that utterances are generally used in relation to an ongoing discourse. In fact, the specific way the utterance fits into the discourse carries meaning. In our view, this meaning is similar to other sources of linguistic meaning. It is conventional and has to be represented in logical form. It constrains how the audience can sensibly resolve any ambiguities of linguistic structure in the utterance, even as it contributes its own additional information, dovetailing with content presented elsewhere in the utterance to yield a specific overall interpretation. The contributions of coherence are pervasive in our view. One reason that we deny that metaphors and other figurative language carry meaning, in cases where it seems obvious to critics such as Bach and Davis that it does, is that we attribute the meaning in the cases to coherence rather than to the figurative language itself. One reason that we deny that speaker intentions enrich linguistic meanings, in cases where it seems obvious to critics such as de Almeida, Kehler and Cohen, or Keiser that it does, is that we attribute the meaning in the cases in question to established principles of coherence, rather than to improvised collaboration.

In our view, coherence relations need to be understood as diverse and powerful theoretical constructs. What we give in IC is only the tip of the iceberg. In particular, in IC, we summarize an inventory of coherence relations due to Hobbs (1985) and to Kehler (2001) with three broad categories of relations. One category is that of resemblance relations, such as parallelism and contrast, which organize discourse around the points of similarity and difference in the information that the speaker is presenting. Another is that of cause–effect relations, such as reason and result, which organize discourse through implicit explanatory connections. The third is that of occasion relations, such as elaboration and narration, which organize discourse by giving extended descriptions that are tied together because they involve overlapping entities, places, and times. Relations of these three kinds occur frequently in written text and nicely illustrate the importance of coherence for disambiguation and inference.

Hobbs's and Kehler's inventory represents a guide to the kind of contributions that discourse coherence makes to utterance meaning, but it is not a complete account. As Kehler and Cohen note, capturing the full range of language use may involve additional kinds of relations, and, in addition, almost certainly involves addressing a number of open theoretical and empirical challenges. In general, we interpret both the successes that others have in fleshing out our approach, and the challenging examples of indirection, enrichment, and context dependence that our critics here discuss, as setting an agenda for the broader modeling of discourse coherence.

To start, as the chapter by Stojnic (Chapter 5, this volume) indicates, we need to characterize coherence relations in precise, fine-grained ways. In particular, Stojnic suggests that coherence relations have to be characterized not only in terms of inferential connections between linguistic contents, but also in terms of connections between linguistic contexts. By representing discourse coherence in terms of updates to a prominence ranking of candidate referents, Stojnic argues, the resolution of context-dependent items can be given a purely conventional treatment in terms of linguistic rules. If Stojnic's suggestion is on the right track (and we believe it is), then pursuing the program of IC will involve deep new accounts of discourse coherence, even for the comparatively simple cases of context dependence we find with pronouns and tense. (And as Bach, Chapter 2 in this volume, reminds us, those cases aren't all that simple: theorists generally make pervasive appeal to common-sense resolution of ambiguity.) Moreover, as de Almeida and Sennet (Chapters 11 and 4 in this volume) remind us, cases of apparent enrichment include more difficult cases, such as the implicit complements of adjectives like "ready" and verbs like "begin." We don't think such data refute Stojnic's view, but they certainly raise open problems for it.

A different gap in the theory of coherence relations concerns the treatment of utterances in situated, face-to-face interaction—a problem surveyed in Chapter 13 in this volume by Kehler and Cohen. Dialogue motivates a wide range of coherence relations that aren't often found in written text, including meta-talk moves like clarification as well as negotiation moves that advance collaborative problem-solving. (Hobbs 1985 and Asher and Lascarides 2003 present extensive illustrations of such coherence relations.) In addition, when interlocutors talk in dynamic environments, utterances can be summaries of the present situation or reactions to ongoing events. Fully understanding the problem-solving of Grice's gas station example, as Davis challenges us to do, or the contextualized resolutions that both de Almeida and Sennet consider—or even getting clear on the meaning of Stainton and Viger's "God bless you!"—means saying quite a bit more about such coherence relations than anyone has so far.

In fact, in modeling joint activity, we may need to think of practical actions as bringing about conventional updates to the conversational scoreboard that go beyond their natural effects in the physical world. These updates would also be mediated by coherence relations, broadly conceived. (See Stone and Stojnic 2015, or Hunter et al. 2015, for additional motivation for such relations.) Starr's worries about the need to link talk to its practical outcomes point to the need to investigate such connections under the umbrella of discourse coherence.

Finally, there is the problem of coherence of subsentential utterances, a major concern for Kehler and Cohen, and, in certain respects, for Stainton and Viger. As Kehler and Cohen observe, research in discourse has long appreciated the apparent parallels between the inferential connections across sentences and those within sentences. Yet looking within the sentence calls for new coherence relations that are not represented in broader discourse. Schlangen (2003), for example, argues that subsentential fragments in dialogue are interpreted by recognizing that they stand in specific coherence relations to the discourse context (typically, relations of clarification and answerhood that are distinctive to interactive language use). The Penn Discourse Treebank (Prasad et al. 2014), meanwhile, introduces an attribution relation, which typically links the main clause of a sentence to a dependent clause, and is used when one gives the source for the information provided by the other. Their representative example below (example 145 from page 45 of their annotation manual PDTB group 2008), illustrates the need for such relations:

Advocates said the 90-cent-an-hour raise, to $4.25 an hour by April 1991, is too small for the working poor, while opponents argued that the increase will still hurt small business and cost many thousands of jobs.

Here attribution links "advocates said" to its argument, the clause headed "... is too small...."; it also links the clause "opponents argued" to its argument, the clause headed "... will still hurt ... and cost." Such relationships are rarely expressed across sentences, but must be represented within sentences to describe their coherence precisely. Specifically, in this case, the example depends on the informational contrast between the two embedded propositions: what the advocates claim, on the one hand, and what the opponents claim, on the other. Analogously, we suspect that the relative clauses and other modifiers that Kehler and Cohen consider may need to be described in terms of referential specification relations unique to intra-sentential discourse, instead of (or in addition to) such familiar relations as background, elaboration, and explanation, which Kehler and Cohen rightly point out are sometimes entirely lacking.

In sum, our explanation of key empirical data appeals to a theory of coherence relations that is impoverished in terms of its description of specific relations, and in terms of its coverage of the organization of individual sentences, its coverage of multiparty linguistic interaction, and its coverage of situated contributions to practical activity. We are excited about the prospects of filling in these gaps, but we cannot expect everyone to share our optimism. It's natural that others are pursuing other kinds of explanation, such as Davis's conventions of indirect meaning or Starr's analysis of conversational collaboration in terms of Millikan-style self-sustaining patterns. But note that these, too, are explanations that appeal to convention. We still maintain that the interpretive contrasts that occupy us in Parts II and III of IC cannot be explained in terms of the operation of general pragmatic principles.

Open Issues: The Scope of Semantics

The discussion of convention and intention in IC figures in our defense of a distinctive account of the scope of meaning in language. In particular, we suggest that the bulk of what researchers have identified as meaning in language falls together into a natural class: these meanings take the form of conventions (in a suitably broad sense) for updating the conversational scoreboard, as defined by Lewis (1979). Such meanings unify many of the dimensions of content that linguists have identified within and across languages (as surveyed in Part II of IC).

A point we didn't emphasize enough in IC—but have described in several follow-up papers—is that these different dimensions of meaning in fact interact in systematic ways, so a unified account of them will ultimately be necessary. Stojnic's data in Chapter 5 of this volume illustrate these interactions: in her chapter, she shows the benefits of describing truth-conditional content and the dynamics of context dependence within a single compositional formalism. Such interactions demand an understanding of meaning that accounts for these different mechanisms as part of an overarching system. We think it's a mistake to follow the common view in linguistics and philosophy of understanding some of these conventions as properly semantic, while others fall into some distinct realm of linguistic pragmatics or speech-act conventions.

Further, by appealing to an expansive, but precise, notion of meaning, we can make the case that there is no great gulf between utterance meaning and speaker meaning. Our view is that linguistic context is rich enough, and linguistic meanings are powerful enough, that we can generally derive a speaker's meaning on an occasion from the linguistic structure of their utterance through the workings of the grammar of context dependence and context change, the grammar of coherence and information structure, and, of course, the grammar of truth conditions.

In our view, then, speakers know the grammar of their language, and they choose—and ipso facto intend—the utterances that match their thoughts. Their audiences, too, know the grammar, and through this knowledge recover the thoughts the speakers had. This is the picture that underlies the direct intentionalist account of linguistic collaboration we briefly recapped earlier. Szabó (2016) describes ours as a Lockean model of communication, a characterization we accept (with pride).

Many commentators are surprised by the fact that we so seldom problematize the distinction between utterance meaning and speaker meaning. (We see such worries in this volume in chapters by Bach, Green, Keiser, and Simons, at least.) But we see this as a feature of our view, not a bug. Our theory is more transparent and more constrained because of it. Admittedly, it's not always straightforward for us to address the phenomena that seem most naturally parsed by positing a gap between what speakers mean and what their words mean.

By far the trickiest such cases involve apparently improvised speaker meaning, in neologisms and malapropisms for example. These cases represent a key focus of our research since the publication of IC. As we have thought more—and better appreciated the kinds of critiques presented here by Bach, Davis, and Simons (and by others elsewhere)—we have come to realize that we perhaps applied the framework of IC to neologisms and malapropisms only halfheartedly. It now seems to us that there may be better ways to respond to the data, and better counterarguments against the skeptics, than appear in IC.

In the case of malapropisms, in IC, we took for granted the received view that Zwicky's (1979) racing steward says the word "jeopardize" and wants to convey a meaning that that word does not have. A defender of our views could (and as a matter of fact we now do) instead argue that the steward actually says the word "deputize", intentionally evoking its standard meaning, but just utters that word with the wrong pronunciation! When we reflect on the metaphysics of words, the causal determinants of the steward's choice, the nature of convention, and the inference of interpreters, it lends surprising credence to the latter account. In any case, the possibility of such alternative analyses of the data shows that the specific faults that Bach, Davis, and Simons find with the discussion in IC aren't inevitable consequences of our core claims.

Even in the case of neologisms, we suspect, it is a mistake to think that content straightforwardly reflects the speaker's communicative intention—at least if "communicative intention" is understood in the intuitive sense of the speaker's own conceptualization of the information she hopes to present. On an externalist account of content determination, following Kripke (1972) or Putnam (1975), it does not matter how the speaker formulates her ideas to herself or what she plans for her hearers to think. What determines content is the property in the world (if any) that is most directly linked to her baptism of the new word. In short, even when you coin a word, you are transmitting a meaning, not inventing one. This is the sense in which we see Kripkean externalism not as incompatible with Grice, but nevertheless as offering a perspective from which to resist the intuitions and assumptions from which Grice's arguments proceed.

By contrast to these cases, we feel less threatened by arguments that grammar is even more heterogeneous than IC maps out. For example, as Stainton and Viger observe, the rules of language certainly involve distinctions of register that seem conventional, but do not fit into any of the categories of meaning we offer in IC. Perhaps we need to broaden the category of linguistic meaning in response, but perhaps this is the right place to resuscitate the category of linguistic pragmatics that turns out not to be a good fit for presuppositions or information structure. Understanding how register arises and how it interacts with other kinds of meaning seems crucial to settling the issues.

Similarly, as Bianchi notes, slurs are also difficult to characterize. In general, we don't talk much in IC about non-semantic "tone," in Frege's (1897) terminology, that apparently can attach to words. We suspect that what is called tone can recruit diverse kinds of reasoning and bring about its effects through diverse kinds of mechanisms. Some of those may be linguistic in nature, some may perhaps even be semantic, but in our view not all of them will be. Dead metaphors, for example, seem to carry a special kind of tone because a sensitive listener can enrich their established conventional meanings by activating their latent metaphorical perspectives in creative ways. These possibilities make the delimitation of the semantics of individual items—for example, the status of a familiar phrase as an active metaphor or a dead one—a difficult empirical problem. (See Glucksberg 2001.) As with register, broad theoretical and experimental investigations may be necessary to understand how to regiment the contribution of different kinds of tone to interpretation. In this connection, the suggestions Bianchi offers about slurs are intriguing and worthy of further pursuit.

Reacting to Stainton and Viger's or Bianchi's investigations, we see it as no challenge to our view that there may be different, useful ways to delimit meaning in language, as there would be, for example, if compositionality links together one family of rules, while grammar as a whole embraces other possibilities in addition. In fact, we suggest in IC itself that different projects may involve different aspects of semantics. Even if there turns out to be no natural branch of semantics that just involves updating the record, the fact that language does group together rules for updating the record is philosophically important: it still has interesting consequences for the status of context dependence, interaction, and inquiry in conversation. After all, on our view, the phenomena of reference and truth remain philosophically important, even if there's no natural class of linguistic rules that just involve reference and truth.

Acknowledgments

Preparation of this essay was supported in part by NSF grant IIS 1526723.

References

Arseneault, Madeleine. Taking Perspective. This volume.

Asher, Nicholas, and Alex Lascarides. 2003. *Logics of Conversation*. Cambridge: Cambridge University Press.

Austin, John L. 1962. *How to Do Things with Words*, ed. J. O. Urmson and G. J. Warnock. Oxford: Oxford University Press.

Bach, Kent. Exaggeration and Invention. This volume.

Bianchi, Claudia. Perspectives and Slurs. This volume.

Brandom, Robert. 1994. *Making it Explicit.* Cambridge, MA: Harvard University Press.

Chomsky, Noam. 1980. *Rules and Representations.* New York: Columbia University Press.

Davidson, Donald. 1967. Truth and Meaning. *Synthese,* 17: 304–23.

Davis, Wayne A. Calculability, Convention, and Conversational Implicature. This volume.

de Almeida, Roberto G. Composing Meaning and Thinking. This volume.

Fodor, Jerry A. 1981. *Representations: Philosophical Essays on the Foundations of Cognitive Science.* Cambridge, MA: MIT Press.

Frege, Gottlob. 1897. Logic. In H. Hermes, F. Kambartel, and F. Kaulbach (eds), *Posthumous Writings: Gottlob Frege,* tr. P. Long and R. White. Oxford: Blackwell, 1979, 1–8.

Glanzberg, Michael. About Convention and Grammar. This volume.

Glucksberg, Sam. 2001. *Understanding Figurative Language: From Metaphors to Idioms.* Oxford: Oxford University Press.

Green, Mitchell. Showing, Expressing, and Figuratively Meaning. This volume.

Grice, H. Paul. 1957. Meaning. *Philosophical Review,* 66(3): 377–88.

Grice, H. Paul. 1975. Logic and Conversation. In P. Cole and J. Morgan (eds), *Syntax and Semantics III: Speech Acts.* New York: Academic Press, 41–58.

Grice, H. Paul. 1989. *Studies in the Way of Words.* Cambridge, MA: Harvard University Press.

Hobbs, Jerry R. 1985. *On the Coherence and Structure of Discourse.* Tech. Rep. CSLI–85–37. Stanford, CA: Center for the Study of Language and Information, Stanford University.

Hunter, Julie, Nicholas Asher, and Alex Lascarides. 2015. Integrating Non-Linguistic Events into Discourse Structure. In *Proceedings of the 11th International Conference on Computational Semantics (IWCS),* 184–94.

Jackendoff, Ray. 2002. *Foundations of Language: Brain, Meaning, Grammar, Evolution.* Oxford: Oxford University Press.

Kehler, Andrew. 2001. *Coherence, Reference and the Theory of Grammar,* Stanford, CA: CSLI.

Kehler, Andrew and Jonathan Cohen. On Convention and Coherence. This volume.

Keiser, Jessica. Varieties of Intentionalism. This volume.

Kripke, Saul. 1972. Naming and Necessity. In G. Harman and D. Davidson (eds), *Semantics of Natural Language.* Dordrecht: Reidel, 253–355.

Lepore, Ernie and Matthew Stone. 2015. *Imagination and Convention: Distinguishing Grammar and Inference in Language.* Oxford: Oxford University Press.

Lewis, David K. 1969. *Convention: A Philosophical Study.* Cambridge, MA: Harvard University Press.

Lewis, David. 1975. Languages and language. In K. Gunderson (ed.), *Minnesota Studies in the Philosophy of Science.* Minneapolis, MN: University of Minnesota Press, 3–35.

Lewis, David. 1979. Scorekeeping in a Language Game. *Journal of Philosophical Logic,* 8(3): 339–59.

Millikan, Ruth Garrett. 1998. Language Conventions Made Simple. *Journal of Philosophy,* 95(4): 161–80.

Millikan, Ruth Garrett. 2005. Semantics/Pragmatics: (Purposes and Cross-Purposes). In *Language: A Biological Model.* Oxford: Oxford University Press, 187–220.

PDTB Research Group. 2008. The PDTB 2.0. Annotation Manual. Technical Report IRCS-08-01. Institute for Research in Cognitive Science, University of Pennsylvania.

Prasad, Rashmi, Bonnie L. Webber and Aravind K. Joshi. 2014. Reflections on the Penn Discourse TreeBank, Comparable Corpora, and Complementary Annotation. *Computational Linguistics*, 40(4): 921–50.

Putnam, Hilary. 1975. The Meaning of "Meaning." In *Mind, Language and Reality*. Cambridge: Cambridge University Press, 215–71.

Quine, W. V. O. 1951. Two Dogmas of Empiricism. *The Philosophical Review*, 60(1): 20–43.

Schlangen, David. 2003. *A Coherence-Based Approach to the Interpretation of Non-Sentential Utterances in Dialogue*. PhD Dissertation, School of Informatics, University of Edinburgh.

Searle, John. 1994. *Speech Acts*. Cambridge: Cambridge University Press.

Sennet, Adam. Presupposition Triggering and Disambiguation. This volume.

Simons, Mandy. Convention, Intention, and the Conversational Record. This volume.

Stainton, Robert J. and Christopher Viger. Two Questions about Interpretive Effects. This volume.

Starr, William B. Socializing Pragmatics. This volume.

Stojnic, Una. Discourse, Context, and Coherence: The Grammar of Prominence. This volume.

Stone, Matthew. 2004. Intention, Interpretation and the Computational Structure of Language. *Cognitive Science*, 28(5): 781–809.

Stone, Matthew and Una Stojnic. 2015. Meaning and Demonstration. *Review of Philosophy and Psychology*, 6(1): 69–97.

Szabó, Zoltán Gendler. 2016. In Defense of Indirect Communication. *Inquiry*, 59(2): 163–74.

Williams, Jason D. 2008. The Best of Both Worlds: Unifying Conventional Dialog Systems and POMDPs. In *INTERSPEECH*, 1173–6.

Williamson, Timothy. 2000. *Knowledge and its Limits*. Oxford: Oxford University Press.

Zwicky, Arnold M. 1979. Classical Malapropisms. *Language Sciences*, 1(3): 339–48.

Index